Dish of the Day

To Ann, With best wishes on your Birthday
February 1987
from Auntie Ann.

Dish of the Day

Bloomsbury Books

An imprint of Godfrey Cave Associates Limited, London

First published in Great Britain 1984 by
Bloomsbury Books
an imprint of
Godfrey Cave Associates Limited
42 Bloomsbury Street
London WC1B 3QJ

ISBN 0 906223 91 1

Bound in Great Britain by
R. J. Acford

Noodles with tomato sauce

Noodles make an excellent storecupboard standby as they can be quickly and easily transformed into an appealing and filling dish. Often the simplest treatment is all that is required. You can substitute tinned tomatoes for the fresh, the taste is not quite so authentic but add a teaspoon of tomato purée – it helps greatly

LUNCH OR SUPPER Serves 4

Overall timing 30 minutes

Equipment 2 saucepans, blender or sieve

Freezing Not recommended

INGREDIENTS

$1\frac{1}{4}$lb	Tomatoes	600g
1	Onion	1
2oz	Butter	50g
	Salt	
	Freshly-ground black pepper	
	Pinch of sugar	
$\frac{1}{4}$ teasp	Grated nutmeg	1.25ml
12oz	Noodles	350g
2oz	Grated Gruyère *or* cheddar	50g
	Parsley	

METHOD

1 Blanch, peel and chop tomatoes. Peel and finely chop the onion. Heat half the butter in a saucepan. Add onion and fry till transparent.

2 Add the tomatoes, cover and simmer for 10 mins. Add salt, pepper, sugar and nutmeg, simmer for a further 5 mins.

3 Meanwhile, cook the noodles in boiling salted water for about 10 minutes till al dente.

4 Drain the noodles thoroughly and pile into a warmed serving dish. Stir in the remaining butter and the grated cheese and keep hot.

5 Purée the tomato sauce in a blender or push through a sieve and pour over the noodles. Garnish with parsley and serve immediately with a green salad.

VARIATION

Add 1 chopped carrot and 1 chopped stalk of celery to the onion. Fry till the onion is transparent, then add 4oz (125g) diced Parma ham or lean bacon to the pan. When the ham is cooked, complete the recipe as above.

Below: Noodles with tomato sauce – a colourful dish flavoured with Gruyère and nutmeg. Ideal for a vegetarian supper

Above: Chicken livers with Marsala – cooked with wine and fresh sage leaves

Chicken livers with Marsala

Any kind of liver can be used for this method of cooking but chicken liver is especially good because the mildness of the meat is enhanced by the sweetness of the Marsala (cream sherry could be used instead, if necessary)

LIGHT LUNCH OR SUPPER Serves 6

Overall timing 15 minutes

Equipment Frying pan

Freezing Not recommended

INGREDIENTS

2×8oz	Cartons of chicken livers	2×225g
2 tbsp	Oil	2×15ml
1½oz	Butter	40g
4	Sage leaves	4
	Salt and pepper	
4 tbsp	Marsala	4×15ml

METHOD

1 Wash chicken livers and dry on kitchen paper. Heat the oil in a heavy frying pan, add the livers and sage leaves and cook for 5 minutes on a high heat turning the mixture over constantly with a wooden spoon. Season with salt, pepper and cook for 1 minute.

2 Remove liver from pan with a draining spoon and keep warm in a serving dish.

3 Add Marsala to pan juices and cook for a minute, then add the butter. Continue cooking, stirring all the time with a wooden spoon, till the sauce thickens slightly.

TO SERVE

Pour sauce over liver and serve immediately with a green vegetable and sauté potatoes. A little cream may be added to the sauce instead of using butter if you prefer a creamier mixture – use single or double, and cook gently being careful not to let the sauce boil.

Peppered steak rolls

Minute steaks (so called because they take only minutes to cook) are slices of beef very thinly cut, then batted out to make them even thinner and to ensure tenderness. Here they are spread with peppered butter, rolled and chilled (prepare them the evening before) then quickly fried to seal in all the juices and flavour. A concentrated sauce adds extra piquancy

LUNCH OR SUPPER Serves 4

Overall timing 20 minutes plus 1–2 hours chilling

Equipment Small bowl, wooden cocktail sticks, frying pan

Freezing Not recommended

INGREDIENTS

2 tbsp	Brined green peppercorns	2×15ml
5oz	Butter	150g
4	Minute steaks	4
3 tbsp	Plain flour	3×15ml
	Salt	
2 tbsp	Finely chopped mushrooms	2×15ml
1 tbsp	Lemon juice	15ml
2 tbsp	Chopped parsley	2×15ml
	Tomato wedges	
	Watercress	

METHOD

1 Put the drained peppercorns in a small bowl and crush. Add 2oz (50g) of the butter and mix together lightly. Wipe the steaks and put a quarter of the peppered butter across the centre of each. Fold in the sides and roll up, fastening with wooden cocktail sticks. Chill for 2 hours.

2 Mix the flour with a little salt and use to coat the steak rolls. Heat the remaining butter in a frying pan and fry the steak rolls for 2–3 minutes, turning frequently, till browned and tender.

3 Remove from the pan, discard the cocktail sticks and arrange the rolls on a warmed serving dish. Continue cooking the butter gently till deep golden. Add the mushrooms and cook for 2–3 minutes, stirring occasionally.

4 Stir in the lemon juice and parsley, adjust the seasoning and pour over the steaks.

5 Garnish with tomato wedges and watercress. Serve immediately with new potatoes and parsleyed carrots.

Potato and bacon pan fry

Served with eggs, this makes a tasty, nutritious supper or lunch and is easily cooked using storecupboard ingredients. Sliced boiled potatoes are added to onion and bacon, pressed down in the pan and fried, covered, till the edge is slightly crisped

LUNCH OR SUPPER Serves 4

Overall timing 50 minutes

Equipment Saucepan, frying pan with lid

Freezing Not recommended

INGREDIENTS

2lb	Medium-size waxy potatoes	900g
	Salt	
8oz	Smoked streaky bacon rashers	225g
1	Large onion	1
2oz	Butter	50g
	Freshly-ground black pepper	

METHOD

1 Scrub the potatoes, cover with cold salted water, bring to the boil and cook for about 20 minutes till tender.

2 Meanwhile, derind and dice the bacon and peel and thinly slice the onion. Heat the butter in the frying pan and fry the onion and bacon lightly.

3 Drain the potatoes, peel and slice thinly, then halve slices. Add to the pan, season, then fry for 5 minutes, turning carefully. Press the potatoes down into the pan, cover and fry over a moderate heat for a further 10 minutes till the outside is golden.

4 Run a spatula around the edge of the pan to loosen the mixture. Invert on a warmed serving plate and serve immediately with fried eggs.

Below: Potato and bacon pan fry

Celery scramble

Tasty and time-saving, this easy-to-prepare brunch or supper can be made with condensed mushroom or asparagus soup instead of celery

SUPPER OR BRUNCH Serves 3–4

Overall timing 20 minutes

Equipment Saucepan, bowl

Freezing Not recommended

INGREDIENTS

10½oz	Can of condensed celery soup	298g
8	Eggs	8
	Salt and pepper	
1oz	Butter	25g
	Toast	

METHOD

1 Break eggs into a bowl and lightly beat with a fork.

2 Place soup in a saucepan and heat gently, stirring all the time.

3 Pour beaten eggs into warmed soup and cook over low heat, stirring with a wooden spoon, until the eggs are lightly set. Add the butter in tiny pieces and mix well. Serve at once on bread or with buttered fingers of toast.

Mushroom risotto

Add salt if liked, though the stock should make the dish salty enough

LUNCH OR SUPPER Serves 4

Overall timing 35 minutes

Equipment Saucepan, frying pan

Freezing Not recommended

INGREDIENTS

3oz	Butter	75g
1	Onion	1
12oz	Long grain rice	350g
2½ pints	Boiling strong beef stock	1.5 litres
1	Garlic clove	1
8oz	Button mushrooms	225g
	Freshly-ground white pepper	
2oz	Grated Parmesan	50g

METHOD

1 Heat half the butter in a saucepan. Peel and finely chop the onion and fry until lightly browned. Add rice to pan, stirring, then add stock, (made with a double quantity of cubes if necessary) a cupful at a time, adding more as the mixture comes to the boil. Simmer, uncovered, for 20 minutes.

2 Meanwhile, heat remaining butter in a frying pan. Peel and halve garlic and fry till golden. Wipe and trim the mushrooms and add to the frying pan. Cook for 5 minutes, then remove garlic and stir the mushrooms and their cooking liquor into the rice. Cook for a further 10 minutes, stirring occasionally to prevent sticking.

3 Pile rice into a serving dish, sprinkle with white pepper and the grated cheese and mix well.

cook's know-how

Cold scrambled egg can be used in many delicious ways – as a garnish for open sandwiches or appetizers; mixed with finely chopped watercress, gherkins, cucumber, pineapple, mixed pickles, ketchup or other sauce as fillings for sandwiches or hot buttered rolls. Picnic loaves can be made in the same way – cook the egg and leave to go cold, then mix in finely chopped celery and tomato and fill a hollowed-out French loaf. Place on foil and wrap tightly. Cut the loaf into sandwich portions to serve.

Muffins make a splendid base for a scrambled egg supper – toast them on both sides, then split and fill with a mixture of scrambled egg and baked beans. Serve on lettuce. Scrambled eggs can also be used as a topping: place a mixture of cooked leftover meat and canned vegetables such as sweetcorn, mushrooms and carrots in a greased dish, make eggs with added grated cheese and spread it on top of dish. Dot with butter and cook at 400F (200C) Gas 6 for 10–15 minutes till top is golden brown.

Above: Raised chicken and ham pie – chicken in a jellied sauce to be eaten cold either at home or at a picnic

Raised chicken and ham pie

The raised pie, a British contribution to international cooking, is one of the earliest forms of pastry case. The sides are raised up – originally round wooden moulds – to support a lid

LUNCH OR SUPPER Serves 6

Overall timing $2\frac{3}{4}$ hours plus cooling

Equipment Saucepan, 2 bowls, 6 inch (15cm) loose-bottomed cake tin

Freezing When cold and set, wrap pie in foil, seal, label and freeze. Freezer life: 2 months. To use: thaw in wrappings in fridge overnight

INGREDIENTS

	Hot water crust	
4oz	Lard	125g
$\frac{1}{4}$ pint	Water	150ml
12oz	Plain flour	350g
	Pinch of salt	
1	Egg yolk	1
	Filling	
$1\frac{1}{2}$lb	Boneless chicken	700g
1 teasp	Grated lemon rind	5ml
$\frac{1}{4}$ teasp	Dried sage	1.25ml
4oz	Sliced ham	125g
	Salt and pepper	
1 teasp	Powdered gelatine	5ml
6 tbsp	Chicken stock	6×15ml
	To finish	
1	Egg	1

METHOD

1 To make the hot water crust, put lard and water into a saucepan and heat until fat has melted.

2 Sift flour and salt into a bowl and add melted lard and water. Knead lightly and add egg yolk. Keep dough warm or it will harden and become difficult to work.

3 Roll out dough on a lightly-floured surface and cut out 2 circles the same size as the base of the pie tin. Grease tin and put a circle of dough in the bottom. Keep other circle of dough warm.

4 Roll remaining dough into a band to fit round the sides of the tin. Moisten edges of dough base with water and fit sides of pie into tin. Preheat oven to 375F (190C) Gas 5.

5 Finely dice chicken, keeping breast and dark meat separate. Season both well and add lemon rind and sage. Dice ham. Cover dough base with half the breast meat, then with half the dark meat. Spread all the ham on top, then repeat layering of dark and breast meats.

6 Moisten dough edges and place lid in position. Press down firmly to seal. Make a small hole in the centre and decorate top with leaves made from dough trimmings. Crimp edges of dough together and glaze surface with lightly beaten egg.

7 Bake for 1 hour, then reduce oven temperature to 350F (180C) Gas 4 and bake for a further $1–1\frac{1}{4}$ hours. Remove pie from oven, cool for about 30 minutes then remove from tin and leave to get quite cold.

8 Meanwhile, soften the gelatine in the cold stock (made up with half a chicken stock cube if necessary) in a small pan for about 5 minutes. Then heat gently till gelatine dissolves, but do not allow to boil. Leave to cool.

9 When the jelly mixture begins to set, put a funnel or cone of foil or greaseproof paper into the centre hole in the pie. Pour in jelly and leave pie in fridge till set. Serve cold with salad.

Vegetable moussaka

The famous Greek and Turkish dish provided the inspiration for this variation which uses only vegetables. A purée of lentils flavoured with garlic and tomato paste makes an interesting change from the usual custardy cheese topping, and it's layered with aubergines and small artichokes and then baked. Courgettes, halved lengthways, or marrow could also be included

MAIN MEAL Serves 4–6

Overall timing 2 hours

Equipment 2 saucepans, frying pan, ovenproof dish

Freezing Not recommended

INGREDIENTS

4oz	Continental lentils	125g
2	Large onions	2
1	Garlic clove	1
1	Large aubergine	1
	Salt	
2oz	Butter	50g
2 tbsp	Tomato paste	2×15ml
1 pint	Light stock	560ml
4	Small artichokes	4
1 tbsp	Lemon juice	15ml
	Bouquet garni	
4 tbsp	Oil	4×15ml
	Pepper	
	Sprigs of parsley	

METHOD

1 Wash and pick over the lentils. Peel and finely chop the onions and peel the garlic. Wash and slice the aubergine, sprinkle with salt and leave to drain for 15 minutes.

2 Heat the butter in a saucepan, add the onion and crushed garlic and fry till golden. Add the lentils, tomato paste and stock (made with cubes if necessary) and simmer for about 1 hour till tender and a thick purée.

3 While lentils are cooking, wash artichokes, then remove stem and coarse outer leaves. Bring a pan of water to the boil, add the lemon juice, bouquet garni and artichokes and bring back to the boil. Simmer for 20–30 minutes.

4 Rinse the aubergines and dry on kitchen paper. Heat the oil in a frying pan, add the aubergine slices and fry for 5 minutes, turning once, till crisp and golden.

5 Preheat the oven to 350F (180C) Gas 4. Grease the ovenproof dish.

6 Drain the artichokes thoroughly, cut in half and remove the chokes. Arrange cut side up on the base and around the sides of the dish.

7 Taste the lentil purée and adjust the seasoning. Pour half the mixture over the artichokes, then cover with half the fried aubergine slices. Repeat the layers of lentil and aubergine and press down lightly. Bake in the centre of the oven for 30 minutes.

8 Run a knife round the edge of the dish and turn out on to a warmed serving dish. Garnish with parsley and serve immediately with Tuscan bread salad (recipe page 14).

VARIATION

There's lots of scope here for experimenting with different combinations of vegetables. Try this alternative which uses leeks and a parsnip and carrot purée. Line dish with blanched cabbage leaves, leaving plenty overhanging the edge. Purée 1lb (450g) each of cooked carrots and parsnips (thoroughly drained), adding 1oz (25g) butter, 2 beaten eggs, and ½ teasp (2.5ml) nutmeg. Spread half over cabbage leaves, then cover with a layer of sliced leeks, sweated in 1oz (25g) butter till soft. Top with rest of purée. Fold overhanging cabbage leaves into centre, press down lightly, cover with foil and bake in centre of oven at 350F (180C) Gas 4 for 45 minutes.

Lancashire hot-pot

The most famous of all traditional English stews employing lamb

MAIN MEAL Serves 4

Overall timing 2¾ hours

Equipment Ovenproof casserole

Freezing Not recommended

INGREDIENTS

2lb	Middle neck lamb chops	900g
1 tbsp	Plain flour	15ml
	Salt and pepper	
2	Lambs kidneys	2
3	Large onions	3
1lb	Potatoes	450g
½ pint	Stock	300ml
1oz	Butter	25g

METHOD

1 Preheat the oven to 350F (180C) Gas 4. Trim excess fat from chops and coat lightly with seasoned flour. Prepare kidneys, discarding outer membrane and core, and cut into thin slices. Peel and slice onions and potatoes.

2 Arrange meat, kidneys and onions in layers in casserole. Season well and pour in stock (made with cubes if necessary). Arrange potato slices on top. Cover and cook in the centre of the oven for 2 hours.

3 Remove lid, dot potatoes with butter and cook for a further 30 minutes or until potatoes are crisp and brown.

Left: Vegetable moussaka – if you don't want to use dairy products, oil can replace butter when making the lentil purée

Shin of beef soup

Traditionally English, this dish is two courses in one

MAIN MEAL Serves 6–8

Overall timing 4 hours

Equipment 2 saucepans, bowl

Freezing Not recommended

INGREDIENTS

3lb	Shin of beef on the bone	1.4kg
	Plain flour	
	Salt and pepper	
2	Onions	2
4	Stalks of celery	4
1	Leek	1
3	Carrots	3
2	Turnips	2
1lb	Potatoes	450g
1lb	White cabbage	450g
	Sprig of parsley	
	Sprig of thyme	
1 tbsp	Dripping	15ml
1 tbsp	Mushroom ketchup	15ml
2 teasp	Powdered mustard	2×5ml
4	Slices of toast	4

METHOD

1 Wipe beef, slash meat through to bone several times. Make a stiff paste of flour and water and use to seal ends of bone to keep in the marrow. Place in large saucepan with 3 pints (1.7 litres) water, salt and pepper. Bring to the boil, skim off scum, cover. Simmer for 3 hours.

2 Meanwhile, peel and chop 1 onion and prepare other vegetables.

3 Add vegetables to beef with parsley and thyme, cover and cook gently for a further 30 minutes.

4 Peel and chop remaining onion. Heat dripping in a saucepan, add onion and fry till golden brown. Add 1oz (25g) flour and cook for 1 minute, then stir in ½ pint (300ml) stock from beef. Bring to boil, stirring, add mushroom ketchup and seasoning and cook for 5 minutes.

5 Remove meat and vegetable stock from heat. Lift out meat and cut into cubes and slices, reserving the bone. Remove vegetables with a draining spoon and place in serving dish with the meat. Keep hot. Pour stock into a warmed soup tureen and keep hot.

6 Preheat grill. Scoop out marrow from bone. Mix with salt, pepper and mustard and spread on toast. Grill till bubbling, then halve and serve with soup. Pour sauce over meat and vegetables and serve as second course.

Hopping John

Hot Hopping John – black-eyed peas and rice with salted pork and onion – is customary New Year's Day fare in the southern states of America. By tradition, it must be eaten before noon to bring good luck for the year

MAIN MEAL Serves 6

Overall timing 1 hour plus soaking

Equipment Large saucepan or flameproof casserole, frying pan

Freezing Not recommended

INGREDIENTS

12oz	Dried black-eyed peas	350g
1¾ pints	Water	1 litre
1lb	Rashers of salted belly pork	450g
2	Onions	2
12oz	Long grain rice	350g
	Salt	
	Freshly-ground black pepper	

METHOD

1 Wash and pick over the peas, place in a large saucepan or flameproof casserole and pour boiling water over. Leave to soak for 2 hours.

2 Drain the peas, return to the pan and pour the measured water over. Bring to the boil, partially cover with the lid, and simmer gently for 30 minutes.

3 Meanwhile, wipe and trim the pork, removing the rind. Cut into ½ inch (12.5mm) wide strips. Blanch in boiling water for 1 minute, drain thoroughly and pat dry.

4 Put the pork into the frying pan and cook till the fat runs. Stir over high heat till crisp and golden. Remove from pan and drain on kitchen paper.

5 Peel and chop the onions and add to the frying pan. Cook for 5 minutes, stirring occasionally, till transparent but not browned.

6 Meanwhile, rinse the rice under cold running water and stir into the peas with the onions and pork. Bring to the boil, cover tightly and simmer gently for about 20 minutes, till the peas are tender and the rice is fluffy.

7 Taste and adjust seasoning and serve immediately.

old-fashioned peas

From the middle ages dried peas were an important part of the diet, especially for the poorer families. They were cooked in soup stews or "pottage" throughout the winter to eke out scanty supplies of meat and vegetables (there is even a place in England named Pease Pottage!) Their continuous presence in the pot is shown in the nursery rhyme:

Pease pudding hot, pease pudding cold,
Pease pudding in the pot, nine days old!

By the 18th century the popularity of dried peas had waned, although they were still served with pickled pork, salted beef or faggots – literally bundles of minced meats (usually offal) and breadcrumbs bound with pigs caul. Two other dishes remain popular.

Pease pudding The peas were tied in a cloth and boiled at the same time as the meat to make a pudding instead of a pottage. Leftovers were sliced and served the next day fried in bacon fat. Wash and pick over 1lb (450g) yellow split peas and soak overnight in cold water. Drain and put into a saucepan, cover with fresh water and bring to the boil. A ham bone or bouquet garni added to the peas improves the flavour. Simmer for 45 minutes to 1 hour till tender. Drain and mash to make a coarse purée. Beat in 2oz (50g) butter and add salt and freshly-ground black pepper to taste – for a firmer, richer pudding beat in 1 egg. Put into a greased pudding basin or tie in a cloth. Cook in boiling water for 1 hour, turn out on to a serving dish and serve with ham, pickled pork or salt beef.

Mushy peas The traditional accompaniment to faggots, whether Wiltshire, Lancashire or Leicestershire, this dish uses whole dried marrowfat peas which are usually sold with tablets of bicarbonate of soda to help soften them in cooking (there's no vitamin C to remove from dried peas). Wash and pick over 1lb (450g) dried marrowfat peas and soak in cold water overnight. Drain, cover with fresh water, add soda tablets and bring to boil. Simmer for 20 minutes till peas begin to turn mushy. Drain and add 2oz (50g) butter and plenty of salt and pepper. Serve very hot.

Salmon and lemon burgers

A quickly prepared dish for a change, the recipe can easily be adapted to use canned tuna or mackerel, or try serving it with parsley or dill sauce

LUNCH OR SUPPER Serves 4

Overall timing 25 minutes

Equipment 2 bowls, frying pan

Freezing Make as Steps 1–3. Leave to dry, then open freeze till firm. Wrap and label. Freezer life: 1 month. To use: shallow fry straight from frozen

INGREDIENTS

1lb	Boiled potatoes	450g
2 tbsp	Milk	2×15ml
1oz	Butter	25g
7½oz	Can of salmon	212g
2	Lemons	2
	Salt	
	Freshly-ground black pepper	
2	Eggs	2
2 tbsp	Plain flour	2×15ml
4 tbsp	Dried breadcrumbs	4×15ml
¼ pint	Oil	150ml
	Lettuce leaves	

METHOD

1 Mash the boiled potatoes with the milk and butter. Drain canned salmon and discard skin and bones. Mash flesh and add to potatoes.
2 Squeeze juice from 1 of the lemons. Add to salmon with seasoning to taste. Mix well and bind with 1 of the eggs.
3 Lightly beat remaining egg. Spread flour and dried breadcrumbs on separate plates. Divide salmon mixture into 8 and shape into flat patties. Dip first in flour, then egg, then coat lightly with dried breadcrumbs.
4 Heat oil in frying pan. Add patties and fry for 5 minutes each side until crisp and golden.
5 Remove from pan with a draining spoon and arrange on serving plate. Serve immediately, garnished with lettuce leaves and the remaining lemon, cut into wedges.

cook's know-how

DILL SAUCE

Heat 1oz (25g) butter in a saucepan, add 1 tbsp (15ml) finely chopped fresh dill weed and 1oz (25g) plain flour. Cook, stirring, for 1 minute. Pour in 1 pint (560ml) chicken stock and cook for 7 minutes. Season with salt. Lightly beat together 1 egg yolk and 3 tbsp (3×15ml) single cream. Remove pan from heat, stir in cream mixture and 1 tbsp (15ml) chopped dill weed. Serve hot with poached fish, boiled chicken or vegetables.

Below: Salmon and lemon burgers – serve with sauté potatoes or a colourful salad

Chinese prawns and vegetables

Taste, colour, texture and aroma are of major importance in every Chinese dish, and ingredients are chosen to emphasise each of these characteristics. Crunchy vegetables in differing shapes are used to enhance the juicy succulence of fresh tender prawns. Once the preparation is done, the cooking takes little time. Served with rice it makes a good mid-week meal

MAIN MEAL Serves 4

Overall timing 40 minutes

Equipment Bowl, wok or deep frying pan

Freezing Not recommended

INGREDIENTS

1lb	Shelled prawns	450g
2 tbsp	Soy sauce	2×15ml
2 tbsp	Dry sherry	2×15ml
1	Small green capsicum	1
1	Medium-size onion	1
4	Canned water chestnuts	4
8oz	Fresh bean sprouts	225g
1	Stalk of celery	1
3 tbsp	Oil	3×15ml
1 teasp	Cornflour	5ml
¼ pint	Chicken stock	150ml
	Salt	
	Freshly-ground black pepper	

METHOD

1 Put the prawns into a bowl, add the soy sauce and sherry and leave to marinate for 15 minutes.
2 Meanwhile, wash, deseed and slice the capsicum, peel and cut the onion through the stalk into 8 wedges. Slice the water chestnuts, rinse and dry the bean sprouts, wash, trim and diagonally slice the celery.
3 Heat the oil in the wok or frying pan, add the onion, capsicum and celery and stir-fry for 4 minutes. Add the prawns (reserving the marinade), bean sprouts and water chestnuts and stir-fry for a further 3 minutes.
4 Blend the cornflour with the marinade and stock (made with a cube if necessary) and stir into the pan. Bring to the boil, stirring, and cook over a moderate heat for 3 minutes Season to taste. Serve immediately with boiled rice.

Creole haddock

Haddock fillets are covered with a thick tomato sauce, flavoured with lemon juice and baked in the oven

MAIN MEAL Serves 4

Overall timing 1 hour

Equipment Saucepan, ovenproof dish

Freezing Not recommended

INGREDIENTS

1	Onion	1
1	Garlic clove	1
1	Red capsicum	1
1	Green capsicum	1
1oz	Butter	25g
2 tbsp	Oil	2×15ml
14oz	Can of tomatoes	397g
	Salt and pepper	
2lb	Haddock fillets	900g
3 tbsp	Lemon juice	3×15ml
	Chopped parsley	

Above: Creole haddock – a piquant flavoured dish of fish, capsicums and onions cooked in a tomato sauce. Serve with plain boiled potatoes to mop up the juices

METHOD

1 Preheat the oven to 375F (190C) Gas 5.
2 Peel and chop onion and garlic. Wipe, deseed and slice capsicums.
3 Heat the butter and oil in a pan. Add onion, garlic and capsicums and fry gently for 10 minutes.
4 Add tomatoes and mash with a wooden spoon to break them up. Season with salt and pepper. Bring to the boil and simmer gently, uncovered, for 10 minutes.
5 Wash haddock and pat dry on kitchen paper. Place half tomato mixture in ovenproof dish, add haddock and season with salt and pepper. Sprinkle with lemon juice and cover with remaining tomato mixture.
6 Cover with lid or foil and bake towards the top of the oven for about 25 minutes. Sprinkle with chopped parsley before serving with boiled potatoes.

cook's know-how

SHALLOT AND OYSTER STEW

A simple and delicious supper for oyster lovers. Peel and finely chop 2 shallots. Heat 2oz (50g) butter in a frying pan over a low heat, add shallots and fry till transparent. Stir in 1 teasp (5ml) mild curry powder and a pinch of cayenne pepper and cook for 1 minute. Stir in 1oz (25g) flour and cook for further minute. Gradually add $\frac{1}{2}$ pint (300ml) milk and bring to the boil, stirring constantly. Cook for 3 minutes. Remove from heat and add $\frac{1}{4}$ pint (150ml) single cream, 1 tbsp (15ml) chopped parsley and 24 shelled oysters. Heat through gently, taste and adjust seasoning. Serve on thick slices of buttered toast. **Serves 4-6**

Flowering cabbage

Although they don't look alike, the cauliflower is a cultivated variety of cabbage. The name cauliflower actually comes from the Latin *cauliflora* which means flowered cabbage. The white head, consisting of tiny sprigs or "curds" is made up of the immature flowers, just like cauliflower's cousin broccoli.
The cauliflower, believed to have originated in the Mediterranean, was not grown on any large scale until the 18th century. Its scarcity caused it to become a great delicacy. John Murrell, in his book *Delightful Daily Exercise for Ladies and Gentlemen*, published in 1621, describes how "colleflowre" should be cooked in milk, then covered with a sauce of cream, mace, butter, sugar and nutmeg.
Cauliflower is grown from seed and is available all year round. Hardy winter varieties tend to have leaves which curl over the curds to protect them from the frost, but the summer ones are more open.
Cauliflower curds vary in colour from the bright, white varieties such as *Flora Blanca* and *Armado* to cream-coloured ones, like *Roscoff*. All cauliflowers, even the very white ones, can turn yellow in very sunny or very frosty conditions. This does not spoil the quality, only the appearance, and if they're cheaper because of it, they are a good buy.
When choosing, look for tightly-packed heads and avoid damaged or spreading, "blown" ones. Check that the base of the stalk is clean, white and not slimy. Individual florets should snap off crisply. Avoid heads with black markings or yellow leaves. Many shopkeepers cut back the leaves, but cauliflowers last much longer if left intact. It is best to use cauliflowers within two days of purchase as they tend to dry out and become tasteless.
There are many different uses for cauliflower and this is undoubtedly why it is such as extremely popular vegetable. It is substantial and filling and can be made into a main meal quite easily. It can be eaten hot or cold, cooked or uncooked. Florets (or flowerets as they are also known) can be snapped off and added to salads or served with dips. Cold, steamed cauliflower, with vinaigrette, makes a pleasant salad.
To prepare, remove the toughest outside leaves, trim the bottom of the stalk and rinse in cold water. The small leaves around the head can be left on and eaten. Most commonly, cauliflower is boiled – the French call it *"choufleur à l'anglaise"*. Put it in a deep saucepan, stalk downwards (make a X in it if you like), with 1½ inches (4cm) of salted water, bring to the boil, cover and cook for 20 minutes. The stalk cooks in the water and the curds are steamed. It is quicker than steaming and helps keep flavour and texture. Florets take about 7 minutes in boiling salted water.
Cauliflower florets are sold fresh in packs in supermarkets and in freezer packs, which are a good standby.
To freeze your own, choose top quality, firm heads. Trim and wash carefully and break into florets. Blanch for 3 minutes, adding 1 tbsp (15ml) lemon juice per pint (560ml) of water to keep the cauliflower white. The florets can be stored for 6 months. The cauliflower is good news for the slimmer! It has only 4 calories per ounce (28g) when raw. And it has a high vitamin C content, making it a valuable winter vegetable.

Left: fresh cauliflower in peak condition – the creamy-white "curds" can be split up and served as individual florets

Above: Polish-style cauliflower – with chopped hard-boiled eggs and crispy paprika topping

Polish-style cauliflower

This vegetable dish is simple to prepare and delicious to eat

VEGETABLE Serves 4

Overall timing 35 minutes

Equipment 2 saucepans

Freezing Not recommended

INGREDIENTS

1	Small cauliflower	1
	Salt	
4	Eggs	4
4oz	Butter	125g
2 tbsp	Dried breadcrumbs	2×15ml
1 teasp	Paprika	5ml

METHOD

1 Trim cauliflower and cook whole in boiling salted water for about 20 minutes or until just tender.
2 Boil eggs for 10 minutes. Cool quickly in cold water, then shell and finely chop.
3 Drain cauliflower. Place on a serving dish and sprinkle with chopped hard-boiled egg. Keep warm.
4 Melt butter in saucepan. Add breadcrumbs and paprika and stir-fry until crisp. Sprinkle over cauliflower.

Crisp-topped cauliflower

Serve the cauliflower with its crispy topping surrounded by other vegetables – it looks splendid and is nourishing too

VEGETABLE Serves 4–6

Overall timing 30 minutes

Equipment 2 saucepans

Freezing Not recommended

INGREDIENTS

1	Cauliflower	1
	Salt	
½ teasp	Dried mixed herbs (optional)	2.5ml
	Grated nutmeg	
2oz	Butter	50g
3 tbsp	Mixed chopped nuts	3×15ml

METHOD

1 Remove leaves and trim cauliflower stalk. Cook cauliflower whole for 15–20 minutes in lightly salted boiling water with the mixed herbs and a pinch of nutmeg. Drain and keep warm.
2 Heat butter in a saucepan. Fry chopped nuts lightly till golden, then pour over cauliflower and serve.

Cauliflower and cress salad

The cress provides contrast in both colour and texture in this quickly prepared dish

SALAD Serves 4

Overall timing 15 minutes plus chilling time

Equipment Saucepan, salad bowl, bowl

Freezing Not recommended

INGREDIENTS

1	Cauliflower	1
	Salt	
	Dressing	
4 tbsp	Oil	4×15ml
3 tbsp	Vinegar	3×15ml
	Salt and pepper	
	Pinch of nutmeg	
1	Punnet of mustard and cress	1
2 tbsp	Chopped chives	2×15ml

METHOD

1 Remove any leaves and trim cauliflower stalk. Divide cauliflower into florets and cook for 7–10 minutes in boiling salted water. Drain, rinse in cold water, then place florets in salad bowl and leave them to cool.
2 To make dressing, mix together oil, vinegar, salt, pepper and nutmeg.
3 Wash cress and place in bowl, with chopped chives. Pour dressing over, toss salad, then chill for 20 minutes.

VARIATIONS

The Spaniards make a very similar salad to this one, but the cooked cauliflower florets are mixed with boiled diced potatoes and cocktail onions. They also add a pinch of cayenne to the dressing and sometimes finely chopped hard-boiled egg. If you prefer you can use watercress instead of mustard and cress. Wash it well, then remove larger stalks. Use as Step 3. Add extra goodness to the salad with chopped almonds, brazil nuts or raw peanuts. Mix in after the salad has been chilled for 20 minutes.

A TASTE FOR THE EXOTIC

The Caribbean Sea lies in the sickle-shaped curve of central America. The Sea is dotted with a chain of islands which run down from Cuba, due south of Florida, to Trinidad, just off the Venezuelan coast. These islands fall into two main groups called the Greater and the Lesser Antilles respectively. They attracted the attention of many conquerors – Spanish, British and French – during the late 15th and early 16th centuries, when the new world was being discovered – Columbus himself landed in the West Indies in 1492 and thought he had reached India.

Several of the islands are French-ruled (including Martinique, home of Napoleon's first wife, the Empress Josephine), a few are Dutch-owned, and Puerto Rico is an American protectorate. The island of Hispaniola comprises the two countries which have been independent the longest – Haiti, once French-ruled, and the Dominican Republic.

The Arawaks and Caribs were the original inhabitants of the islands, but not many survived the conquerors. Those who did married the black slaves imported from Africa. Later, Indians were brought in to improve the commercial life of the islands.

The Caribbean Sea is in the tropics, so the year-round warm sunshine and heavy rainfall produces abundant commercial crops of pineapples, coffee, bananas and sugar-cane. Many of the fruits and vegetables grown are imports, and flourish in the islands. They include nutmeg, Grenada's main crop, coffee and breadfruit which is now a staple and used as a substitute for potatoes, pasta or rice of cooler climes. There are plenty of root vegetables which also serve this purpose – sweet potatoes and yams, as well as the less tasty taro or dasheen (two very similar varieties of the same plant which grow in different islands). Both produce leaves called *callaloo* which are shaped like elephant's ears and taste like spinach. Callaloo soup in Jamaica contains crabmeat; in the French islands of Guadeloupe and Martinique, the soup is flavoured with peppers and cloves. Akee is a vegetable unobtainable outside the West Indies except in tins, whose latin name *Blighia sapida* is another reminder of Captain Bligh's connection with the agriculture of the Caribbean. Akees look and taste a little like scrambled egg, and in Jamaica they are eaten with salt fish. Other green vegetables available outside the islands, are okra (also known as ladies fingers, gombo or *bahmia*), little finger-shaped, green hairy vegetables, usually stewed with tomatoes and onions, and the various types of peppers and capsicums. Hot peppery dishes are popular and each island has its own fiery pepper sauce. The Indians brought curry sauces with them such as *Masala*, and these have been incorporated into local cuisine.

Another staple vegetable is the plantain, a large version of the banana, which is usually cooked and eaten in the green stage. Plantains are most often fried and eaten like chips, either savoury or with coconut and sugar as a dessert. In the Spanish-speaking islands, plantains are partly fried, beaten flat like an Austrian *schnitzel* and then fried again. This dish is called *Tostones de plátano*. In Haiti, a similar recipe is called *Banane pesé*. In Puerto Rico, plantains are stuffed with meat and called *Piononos*, a strange name which seems to imply that they are named after Pope Pius IX.

The cheapest and most easily available meat in the islands is pork and goat. Cattle are bred on the largest islands, Cuba and Jamaica, and there are a few sheep on the higher slopes of the French volcanic islands, but most beef and lamb are imported. Meat is usually barbecued (where fresh meat is easily available, such as Cuba and Martinique) or stewed. The most popular stew in the English-speaking islands is Pepperpot. It contains a mixture of meats flavoured with a condiment called *cassareep*, made from juice from the flesh of the cassava root mixed with cinnamon, cloves and molasses sugar. The Cuvans make a beef hash, usually of brisket or salt beef, called *Picadillo*. In Curaçao, an island in the Netherlands Antilles, there is a popular stew called *Keshy yena*. A Dutch Edam or Gouda cheese is hollowed out and pieces of meat and vegetable are cooked inside it. In Puerto Rico, there is a tripe stew called *Mondongo*; the tripe is cooked in orange and lemon juice, with salt pork, ham, tomatoes, peppers, pumpkin and fresh herbs. *Griots de porc*, glazed casseroled pieces of pork, are the Haitiian national dish, and are always served with *Banane pesé* and a peppery sauce called *Sauce ti-malice*. All the islanders make pasties of meat and vegetables which are eaten as snacks and sold from roadside stalls. Jamaican (or *Jamake*) patties are now commonly available in England in those areas with West Indian communities; the Puerto Rican equivalent of these patties is called *Pastellilos*.

Fish are plentiful and there is a huge variety, from common salt fish to the exotic flying fish and conch. There are wonderful shellfish, of which the king is undoubtedly the *langouste* or spiny lobster. Codfish fritters are popular throughout the Caribbean. In Martinique, they are called *Acras de morue*, in Puerto Rico *Bacalaitos* and in Jamaica they carry the picturesque name of "*Stamp and Go*". Pickled and marinated fish recipes abound. In the Dominican Republic, fish is marinated in lime juice, then fried and served in a sauce containing coconut milk. One of the most characteristic fish dishes of the French-speaking islands is *Poisson en blaff*, bream or grouper marinated in lime juice, then poached in wine and water with spices.

In the hot climate, people need plenty to drink, and there is a vast number of exotic long drinks, mostly based on rum. There is the famous Planters' punch, for which each island has a different recipe; Creole eggnog in Trinidad, Daiquiri in Cuba (rum, lime juice and sugar) and the heavenly *Piña colada* (pineapple, coconut milk, crushed ice and white rum) in Puerto Rico. The French-speaking islands have a drink called Shrub, made from their native dark rum and Seville oranges. In Trinidad, the sepals of a hibiscus flower are made into a cool refreshing drink.

Although sweet puddings, such as the chocolate pudding named after Trinidad's famous Pitch Lake, are popular, the most delicious and refreshing way of finishing a Caribbean meal is with one of the wonderful tropical fruits for which the islands are world-renowned. Some are well known: coconuts, loquats (medlars), guavas, the mangoes and pineapples praised by Colombus, bananas, limes, oranges, watermelon and melon. Then there are the Caribbean delicacies – the acerola (or Barbados cherry), the richest source of vitamin C, mamme apple, a type of yellow melon, the custard apples (sweetsops and soursops) and cashews.

Caribbean sunshine meal for six

PLANTERS' PUNCH

Ingredients 6 tbsp (6×15ml) caster sugar; 6 tbsp (6×15ml) water; 12 tbsp (12×15ml) lime juice; 1 pint (560ml) dark Jamaica rum; few drops Angostura bitters; ice cubes; sliced limes, lemons or oranges.

Method Heat sugar and water in small pan till sugar dissolves, stirring. Cool. Pour into cocktail shaker and add lime juice, rum and Angostura. Shake vigorously. Place ice cubes in a large jug and pour over punch. Add slices of citrus fruit. **Serves 6**

Dishes of the Caribbean from left to right: front – Banana cocktail, Pineapple, Guava and Mango ice creams (recipe page 357); centre – Griots de porc with Sauce ti-malice (recipe page 355) and Banane pesé, Planters' punch (recipe above), Pina colada (recipe page 355), Creole eggnog (recipe page 354)

Countdown

Creole eggnog
Shellfish cocktail
Griots de porc with Sauce ti-malice
Plantain chips Stewed okra
Exotic fruit ice cream

It's not so difficult to bring the taste of the Caribbean into your own home as the ingredients for these dishes are now far more widely available in this country. You can serve the eggnog alone or make a selection of Planters' punch, Pina colada and the egg cocktail

The day before Make sauce ti-malice and chill. Prepare pork and marinate overnight in fridge

4 hours before Make ice cream with chosen fruit and place in freezer

3 hours before Turn ice cream into a bowl, beat well, return to freezer

2 hours before Make shellfish cocktail and chill in fridge

1¾ hours before Beat ice cream again and return to freezer

1½ hours before Start cooking pork with marinade and stock. Simmer for about 1 hour

1 hour and 20 mins before Soak plantain. Prepare and soak okra. Then prepare tomato and onion for okra stew

¾ hour before Fry onions and add okra and tomatoes. Simmer until cooked then keep warm

35 mins before Dry plantain and fry for first time. Drain, flatten and leave. Prepare lime mixture

20 mins before Drain cooked pork and fry. Keep hot

10 mins before Prepare cocktails and **serve.** While your guests finish their cocktails, fry plantain for second time and keep hot

Serve Shellfish cocktail

Serve Pork, sauce and vegetables. Follow with ice cream

Since you have served cocktails, wine is not strictly necessary with your meal but a light Italian red wine could be served with the pork.

Creole eggnog

Exotic long drinks abound in the Caribbean, and this eggnog is no exception. Heavily laced with rum, it is a favourite "cooler" on the island of Trinidad. Also pictured is Pina colada, recipe page 355

COLD DRINK Serves 6

Overall timing 10 minutes

Equipment Bowl, 6 punch cups or glasses

Freezing Not recommended

Above: Creole eggnog and Pina colada — both Caribbean favourites

INGREDIENTS

3	Eggs	3
14oz	Can of condensed milk	397g
	Grated rind of a lemon	
	Angostura bitters	
½ pint	Trinidad rum	300ml
6	Ice cubes	6
	Decoration	
	Lemon slices	
	Cocktail cherries	

METHOD

1. Lightly beat the eggs in a bowl, then beat in the condensed milk. Add the lemon rind and a few drops of Angostura bitters and whisk in the rum.
2. Crush the ice and divide between punch cups or glasses. Pour the egg mixture over. Decorate with lemon slices and cocktail cherries and serve.

Shellfish cocktail

STARTER — Serves 6

Overall timing $1\frac{1}{2}$ hours including refrigeration

Equipment Saucepan, 2 bowls, 4 serving dishes

Freezing Not recommended

INGREDIENTS

6oz	Mint-flavoured frozen peas	175g
5 tbsp	Thick mayonnaise	5×15ml
3 tbsp	Mango chutney	3×15ml
$1\frac{1}{2}$ teasp	Vinegar	$1\frac{1}{2}$×5ml
	Salt	
	Freshly-ground black pepper	
3	Large bananas	3
$1\frac{1}{2}$ tbsp	Lemon juice	$1\frac{1}{2}$×15ml
9oz	Prepared shrimps	265g

METHOD

1 Cook the peas for 6 minutes in boiling, lightly salted water to which a pinch of sugar has been added. Drain and leave to cool.

2 Beat together the mayonnaise, mango chutney and vinegar. Season well with salt and freshly-ground black pepper.

3 Peel and slice bananas. Toss in lemon juice to prevent discoloration. Peel the shrimps and set aside a few for the garnish. Mix the rest with the bananas and peas.

4 Divide banana mixture between 6 individual serving dishes. Cover with mango mayonnaise and place in the fridge to chill for 1 hour. Garnish with reserved shrimps and serve with toast and butter.

drinks know-how

For a wonderfully refreshing pineapple drink, try Pina colada. Originally from the Caribbean, it's a favourite with Puerto Ricans in New York. A picture of Pina colada is on page 354 with the Creole eggnog.

Place in a blender $\frac{3}{4}$ pint (400ml) unsweetened pineapple juice *or* drained crushed pineapple from $15\frac{1}{2}$oz (439g) can. Add 7fl oz (200ml) each of canned coconut milk and white rum (Bacardi) and 6–8 ice cubes. Blend for 15–20 seconds, then pour into tall, chilled glasses. Decorate with a maraschino cherry or thin ring of fresh pineapple. **Serves 6**

Griots de porc with Sauce ti-malice

A superb pork dish from the Caribbean. If Seville oranges aren't available, use ordinary ones and add 1 tbsp (15ml) vinegar to the juice for bitterness

MAIN MEAL — Serves 6–8

Overall timing $1\frac{1}{4}$ hours plus overnight marination

Equipment Saucepan, 2 bowls, flameproof casserole

Freezing Not recommended

INGREDIENTS

	Sauce ti-malice	
2	Large onions	2
1	Garlic clove	1
1	Red capsicum	1
4	Green chillies	4
2	Limes	2
1 tbsp	Oil	15ml
	Salt	
	Freshly-ground black pepper	
$2\frac{1}{4}$oz	Can of tomato paste	63g
	Other ingredients	
3lb	Lean pork cut from shoulder or leg	1.4kg
1	Large onion	1
1	Green capsicum	1
1	Garlic clove	1
3	Seville oranges	3
	Salt	
	Freshly-ground black pepper	
$\frac{1}{2}$ pint	Light stock	300ml
4 tbsp	Oil	4×15ml

Below: Griots de porc with Sauce ti-malice. The peppery sauce is a speciality of Haiti

METHOD

1 To make the sauce, peel and thinly slice the onions and place in a saucepan with the peeled and crushed garlic. Wash, halve and deseed the red capsicum, slice and add to the onions. Deseed the chillies shred finely and add to the onions with the squeezed lime juice, oil and seasoning.

2 Cook over a low heat for 10 minutes, stirring frequently. Add the tomato paste and season to taste. Put into a bowl, cover and cool. Chill overnight to allow flavours to mingle.

3 Wipe and trim the pork, cut into 2 inch (5cm) cubes and place in a large bowl. Peel and finely chop the onion, wash, halve, deseed and slice the green capsicum and add to the pork with the peeled and crushed garlic.

4 Squeeze the juice from the oranges and pour over the pork. Add plenty of seasoning and mix well. Cover and marinate in the fridge overnight.

5 Next day, put the pork and marinade into the casserole and add the stock (made with a cube if necessary). Bring to the boil, cover and simmer for 1 hour till the pork is just tender.

6 Drain the pork thoroughly (reserve the stock and use for soup or gravy). Heat the oil in the rinsed and dried casserole and fry the pork a little at a time till crisp and golden.

7 Place in a warmed serving dish and keep hot till all the pork has been fried. Serve hot with the cold sauce, plantain chips (recipe page 356) and plain boiled rice and stewed okra.

Plantain chips

The plantain is a Caribbean vegetable, resembling a large banana, that can be served as a savoury or sweet. It is now available in many shops and markets

VEGETABLE Serves 6

Overall timing 35 minutes plus soaking

Equipment 2 bowls, large frying pan, greaseproof paper

Freezing Not recommended

INGREDIENTS

1½	Large plantains	1½
2	*or* small plantains	2
6 teasp	Salt	6×5ml
3 pints	Water	1.65 litre
9 tbsp	Oil	9×15ml
3	Limes	3

METHOD

1 Peel the plantain and cut diagonally into ½ inch (12.5mm) slices.
2 Put threequarters of the salt into a bowl with the water and stir till salt dissolves. Add plantain slices and leave to soak for 45 minutes.
3 Drain slices thoroughly and pat dry. Heat the oil in a large frying pan. Add plantain slices and fry very gently without browning for 10 minutes or until just tender. Remove from pan with a draining spoon and reserve oil.
4 Spread out plantain slices between 2 sheets of greased greaseproof paper. Using a rolling-pin, flatten slices until ¼ inch (6mm) thick.
5 Squeeze juice from limes into a bowl and add remaining 1½ teasp (1½×5ml) salt.
6 Reheat oil in frying pan. Dip each plantain slice into lime mixture, then fry for 3 minutes each side over a high heat until crusty and golden.
7 Remove from pan with draining spoon and drain on kitchen paper. Serve immediately sprinkled with salt.

TO SERVE

Plantain chips make an unusual accompaniment to cold roast meats or grilled chops or steak. Once you have tackled this menu you will find other opportunities to use this recipe.

Below: Plantain chips – slices of plantain are shallow fried, then flattened with a rolling-pin, dipped in lime juice and fried again until crisp and golden. Drain and sprinkle with salt before serving

Stewed okra

Soaking the okra in acidulated water and rinsing helps to remove some of the sticky juices, although enough remains to thicken the sauce slightly

STARTER OR VEGETABLE Serves 6

Overall timing 1¼ hours

Equipment Bowl, flameproof casserole

Freezing Pack into a rigid container, seal, label and freeze. Freezer life: 3 months. To use: place block in a saucepan, heat gently till thawed. Bring to the boil, and adjust seasoning to taste

INGREDIENTS

1lb	Okra	450g
6 tbsp	Vinegar	6×15ml
½ pint	Water	300ml
3	Large onions	3
1½lb	Ripe tomatoes	700g
6 tbsp	Olive oil	6×15ml
	Salt	
	Freshly-ground black pepper	
⅜ pint	Light stock	225ml
3 tbsp	Chopped parsley	3×15ml

METHOD

1 Wash, dry and top the okra. Place in a bowl and add the vinegar and water. Leave to stand for 30 minutes.
2 Meanwhile, peel and chop the onions. Blanch, peel and chop the tomatoes. Heat the oil in the casserole and fry the onions till golden.
3 Drain the okra, rinse and dry thoroughly. Add the tomatoes and okra to the pan with plenty of seasoning and the stock (made with a cube if necessary).
4 Bring to the boil, cover and simmer for 30 minutes. Taste and adjust the seasoning, stir in the parsley.

TO SERVE

To serve cold as a starter, cool, then chill and serve with warm pitta bread. To serve hot as a vegetable, sprinkle with freshly-ground black pepper and serve with Griots de porc or grilled lamb or chicken.

VARIATION

For a lunch or supper dish, follow Steps 1 to 3. Bring mixture to the boil, then pour half into an ovenproof dish. Sprinkle 6oz (175g) grated cheese over and cover with remaining vegetables. Top with 3oz (75g) grated cheese and 2oz (50g) fresh breadcrumbs. Bake in the centre of the oven at 375F (190C) Gas 5 for 25 minutes till the topping is bubbling and golden.

Exotic fruit ice cream

Here is a most attractive way of serving an ice cream dessert flavoured with exotic Caribbean fruit. Use only one of the variations below or serve a combination. Fold the flavour of your choice into 1 pint (560ml) of the basic ice cream mixture on the following page

DESSERT Serves 6

Overall timing 50 minutes plus freezing

Equipment Bowls, sieve, tray or mould, ice cream scoop

Freezing Freeze in tray or mould until firm, then make into scoops and arrange on plastic tray, cover, label and refreeze. Freezer life: 2 months. Before use: place scoops on tray in the fridge for 15 mins

INGREDIENTS

1 pint	Basic vanilla ice cream (see page 358)	560ml
	Fruit flavourings (see variations below)	
1	Fresh pineapple	1
	Ice cubes	

Peel and finely chop 8oz (225g) fresh pineapple or drain a 15½oz (439g) can of crushed pineapple. If using fresh fruit, fold 2oz (50g) caster sugar into basic mixture.

- For a banana flavour, mash 2 large bananas and mix with 2 tbsp (2×15ml) lemon juice. Stir into the basic mixture.
- Peel a ripe mango weighing about 12oz (350g). Remove stone and rub flesh through a sieve or chop finely. Stir into basic mixture with 2oz (50g) caster sugar.
- Drain a 15oz (425g) can of guavas. Rub pulp through a sieve and add to basic ice cream mixture.

TO SERVE

Place scoops in hollowed pineapple shell. Surround with ice cubes to keep the ice cream from melting.

Basic vanilla ice cream

A rich, creamy yellow ice made from a custard base. The added cream increases the fat content and gives the mixture a wonderfully smooth texture. It is beaten twice at the half-frozen stage so that the ice crystals are broken down

DESSERT Makes 1 pint (560ml)

Overall timing 40 minutes plus freezing

Equipment 3 bowls, 2 saucepans, sieve and muslin, freezer tray or mould

Freezing Freeze in tray or mould, cover and label. Freezer life: 2 months. To use: soften before serving by placing tray or mould in fridge for 30 minutes

INGREDIENTS

2	Egg yolks	2
2oz	Caster sugar	50g
½ pint	Milk	300ml
1	Vanilla pod *or*	1
1 teasp	Vanilla essence	5ml
¼ pint	Carton of double cream	150ml

METHOD

1 Put the egg yolks and sugar in a large bowl and beat until creamy.
2 Put milk and vanilla pod or essence into a pan and bring to just under boiling point. Remove from heat and take out vanilla pod if used.
3 Pour milk in a thin stream on to creamed mixture, stirring continuously. Place bowl over a pan of simmering water and cook for about 10 minutes without boiling, stirring continuously until mixture coats the back of the spoon.
4 Remove from heat and strain through a muslin-lined sieve into a bowl. Beat until cool to prevent skin forming. Now add any flavouring you wish to use or continue with step 5 for a plain vanilla ice cream.
5 Whisk the cream until it just holds its shape, then fold into cold custard. Pour into freezer tray or mould and freeze for about 1½ hours or until mushy.
6 Turn ice cream into a bowl and beat well. Pour back into container and return to freezer. Freeze till mushy.
7 Repeat beating process, then return to freezer and freeze till firm.

Above: Basic vanilla ice served in scoops.

1 *Put the egg yolks and sugar into a bowl and beat with a wooden spoon until creamy*

2 *Put milk and vanilla pod into a saucepan and bring to just under boiling point*

3 *Pour hot milk on to creamed mix in a thin stream, stirring continuously, then cook*

4 *Strain custard, beat until cool, fold in whipped cream. Pour into tray or mould*

Above: Apple and mincemeat tart – delicious served warm with a helping of ice cream

Apple and mincemeat tart

A delicious tart from France – you can use either the mincemeat you've made or a jar of the bought kind. The filling is juicy when served hot but is firmer when cold. As the tart freezes well, you can make it in advance, for Christmas, or to serve at any time

HOT OR COLD DESSERT Serves 6

Overall timing 1 hour

Equipment 9½ inch (24cm) fluted loose-bottom flan tin, bowl, baking tray

Freezing Cook and allow to go cold. Remove from tin, place on thick card and wrap in heavy foil. Label, seal and freeze. Freezer life: 3 months. To use: remove foil, replace tart in flan tin, cover over with foil and reheat at 350F (180C) Gas 4 for about 40 minutes until heated through

INGREDIENTS

7½oz	Frozen pastry	212g
14½oz	Jar of mincemeat	411g
1lb	Bramley apples	450g
3oz	Caster sugar	75g
½ teasp	Ground allspice	2.5ml
2oz	Butter	50g
1 tbsp	Plain flour	15ml

METHOD

1. Preheat the oven to 425F (220C) Gas 7.
2. Roll out the pastry and line flan tin.
3. Spread mincemeat evenly over pastry.
4. Peel and finely slice the apples. Mix with 2oz (50g) of sugar and allspice. Arrange in circles on mincemeat.
5. In a bowl, cut and fold the butter with remaining 1oz (25g) sugar and flour until the mixture resembles fine breadcrumbs Sprinkle evenly over the apples. Place flan on baking tray.
6. Bake in preheated oven for 15 minutes, then reduce to 375F (190C) Gas 5 for a further 30 minutes. Remove from oven and allow to cool. Lift tart from flan tin and place on serving plate. Spoon any topping from baking tray on to tart.

TO SERVE

Serve warm or cold, with whipped cream or vanilla ice cream.

Pear Suchard

Crisply set chocolate topping over an exquisitely light, fluffy centre

DESSERT Serves 6

Overall timing 1 hour plus setting

Equipment Blender, 4 bowls, 2 saucepans

Freezing Not recommended

INGREDIENTS

2×15oz	Cans of pear halves	2×425g
1 tbsp	Powdered gelatine	15ml
1 tbsp	Cornflour	15ml
¼ pint	Milk	150ml
3 tbsp	Caster sugar	3×15ml
1	Egg	1
¼ pint	Carton of double cream	150ml
	Plain dessert chocolate	
1 teasp	Arrowroot	5ml

METHOD

1. Drain the pears, reserving the syrup. Reserve 6 pear halves, put the remainder into a blender and purée till smooth, or press through a sieve. Put into a large bowl. Put 6 tbsp (6×15ml) of the reserved syrup into a small bowl. Sprinkle the gelatine over and leave it to sponge.
2. Put the cornflour into a small saucepan and gradually stir in the milk. Add the sugar and bring to the boil, stirring constantly. Cook for 3 minutes.
3. Separate the egg. Beat the yolk into the cornflour mixture and cook without boiling for 3 minutes, stirring constantly. Remove from the heat, add to the pear purée and mix well.
4. Stand the bowl of gelatine in a saucepan of simmering water and stir till dissolved. Allow to cool slightly, then trickle it into the pear mixture, stirring constantly. Chill till syrupy.
5. Whip the cream till it forms soft peaks, then fold into the pear mixture. Whisk the egg white till stiff but not dry and fold in. Pour into a shallow serving dish and chill till set.
6. Arrange the reserved pear halves on top of the mousse and return to the fridge. Break the chocolate into pieces.
7. Blend the arrowroot in a saucepan with ¼ pint (150ml) of the reserved pear syrup and bring it to the boil, stirring constantly. Remove from the heat and add the chocolate, beating till it melts.
8. Spoon the chocolate sauce over the pears and the surface of the mousse to cover completely and leave to set.

Above: Malaga dessert – quick to prepare with creamy cheese and lightly chilled

Malaga dessert

Soft cream cheese is combined with raisins – which come from Malaga grapes, hence the name. For best results, make just before serving

COLD DESSERT Serves 4

Overall timing 35 minutes

Equipment Saucepan, 2 bowls, 4 stemmed glasses

Freezing Not recommended

INGREDIENTS

3oz	Raisins	75g
1 tbsp	Water	15ml
2 tbsp	Rum	2×15ml
3oz	Flaked almonds	75g
12oz	Cream cheese	350g
3 tbsp	Caster sugar	3×15ml

METHOD

1 Put raisins and water in a pan, cover and heat for a few minutes until the water has evaporated. Remove lid and gently heat a little more until raisins are plump and dry. Put into small bowl with rum and leave for 15 minutes.
2 Meanwhile, toast almonds under a hot grill till golden.
3 Put the cheese, sugar and rum (drained from the raisins) into a bowl and beat till light and fluffy. Mix in raisins and two-thirds of the toasted almonds.
4 Divide mixture between serving glasses and sprinkle remaining almonds on top. Chill for 10–15 minutes before serving – not longer or the texture will be too firm.

VARIATION

To give a really pretty effect for a special occasion, cut 2 oranges in half by making deep zig-zag cuts to the centre right round the middle of each fruit. Remove flesh with a grapefruit knife and fill shells with cheese and raisin mixture, adding almonds.

Fried semolina cakes

For fruity cakes mould the mixture over halved plump prunes, chunks of banana or apple, then coat and fry

DESSERT Serves 4

Overall timing 1 hour

Equipment Saucepan, baking tray, deep-fryer, bowl, plate

Freezing After coating, open freeze. Pack in polythene, seal and label. Freezer life: 6 months. To use: deep fry from frozen

INGREDIENTS

1 pint	Milk	560ml
	Salt	
	Vanilla essence	
	Grated rind of 1 lemon	
4oz	Fine semolina	125g
2 tbsp	Caster sugar	2×15ml
½ teasp	Ground cinnamon	2.5ml
2oz	Butter	50g
2	Egg yolks	2
	Oil for deep frying	
1	Egg	1
2oz	Dried breadcrumbs	50g

METHOD

1 Put the milk into a saucepan with a pinch of salt, a few drops of vanilla essence and grated lemon rind. Heat till warm, then stir in semolina. Bring to boil and simmer for 5 minutes, stirring constantly.
2 Remove from the heat and stir in sugar, spice, threequarters of the butter and the egg yolks. Mix well. Cook over low heat for 5 minutes, stirring.
3 Grease a shallow baking tray with the remaining butter and pour in the semolina. Smooth the top with a wetted knife and press down till about ½ inch (12.5mm) thick. Leave to cool.
4 Heat oil in deep-fryer to 360F (180C). Cut the semolina into diamond shapes or squares. Lightly beat the whole egg in a bowl. Spread breadcrumbs on plate.
5 Coat the semolina cakes in the beaten egg, then in breadcrumbs, pressing them on lightly. Fry in the hot oil till golden on both sides. Remove with draining spoon, drain on kitchen paper. Sprinkle with caster sugar and serve very hot with custard.

VARIATION

To make croquettes, turn cooked mixture on to moistened work surface to cool. Form into croquette shapes, coat in egg and breadcrumbs and then deep fry. Dust with caster sugar and serve with hot jam sauce.

Above: Hazelnut steakburgers — a spicy-flavoured meat and nut mix topped with an egg

Hazelnut steakburgers

To enjoy the full flavour of these burgers, it's essential to use good quality meat. If you like, they can be returned to the oven for an extra 10 minutes at the end to cook the eggs lightly. Or you can serve the burgers without eggs

LUNCH OR SUPPER Serves 4

Overall timing 45 minutes

Equipment Frying pan, large bowl, baking tray

Freezing Not recommended

INGREDIENTS

1oz	Butter	25g
2oz	Shelled hazelnuts	50g
1	Large onion	1
1lb	Minced rump steak	450g
2 tbsp	Capers	2×15ml
	Grated rind of 1 lemon	
	Salt and pepper	
$\frac{1}{4}$ teasp	Paprika	$\frac{1}{4}$×5ml
$\frac{1}{2}$ teasp	Powdered mustard	$\frac{1}{2}$×5ml
2 tbsp	Brandy *or* stock	2×15ml
4	Egg yolks	4

METHOD

1 Melt butter in a frying pan. Chop shelled nuts and cook till golden in butter, stirring frequently.
2 Preheat oven to 375F (190C) Gas 5.
3 Peel the onion and cut into 4 thick slices. Remove 4 equal size inner rings of onion and reserve. Finely chop the remainder.
4 Put the minced steak in a large bowl with nuts, chopped onion, half the capers and the lemon rind. Add salt, pepper, paprika, mustard and brandy and mix well with a wooden spoon.
5 Divide the mixture into 4 portions. Shape into balls, place on a baking tray and flatten tops slightly with a wooden spoon, making a well in centre of each if you are serving with eggs. Bake in the centre of the oven for 25 minutes.

TO SERVE

Place each burger on a lettuce leaf on serving plate. Press an onion ring into each well, then carefully place a raw egg yolk in each ring and garnish with remaining capers. Serve with toast, or with French fried potatoes and a lightly tossed lettuce and tomato salad. Tinned sweetcorn is also easily and quickly heated through and goes well with this sort of meal.

Sweet and sour turkey

A spicy and unusual supper. Serve this memorable dish with chutney

LUNCH OR SUPPER Serves4–6

Overall timing 45 minutes plus marination

Equipment Bowl, 2 saucepans, frying pan

Freezing Not recommended

INGREDIENTS

$1\frac{1}{2}$lb	Turkey breasts	700g
2 tbsp	Oil	2×15ml
1 teasp	Salt	5ml
$\frac{1}{4}$ teasp	Finely-ground white pepper	1.25ml
	Tabasco sauce	
4oz	Butter	125g
8oz	Onions	225g
1 tbsp	Curry powder	15ml
1 teasp	Sugar	5ml
2	Dessert apples	2
1	Garlic clove	1
$\frac{3}{4}$ pint	Stock	400ml
3 tbsp	Lemon juice	3×15ml
1 inch	Piece of fresh ginger	2.5cm
$\frac{1}{4}$ pint	Carton of single cream	150ml
1	Banana	1
	Plain boiled rice	

METHOD

1 Slice the turkey breasts and cut into 1×2 inch (2.5×5cm) strips. Place in a bowl with the oil, salt, pepper and a few drops of Tabasco sauce. Turn till coated and marinate for 15 minutes.
2 Heat half the butter in pan, add turkey and marinating juices and cook over high heat till brown. Remove from heat and cover.
3 Peel and chop the onions. Heat $1\frac{1}{2}$oz (40g) of butter in a saucepan and fry the onions. Sprinkle in the curry powder and sugar and fry till the onions are transparent. Peel and finely chop 1 apple and add to the onions with the peeled whole garlic clove and salt. Add the stock (made with a cube if necessary) and bring to the boil. Simmer uncovered for 20 minutes.
4 Strain the sauce and pour over turkey. Add lemon juice, grated ginger and cream. Cook for 10 minutes till heated through but not boiling.
5 Lightly fry sliced banana and remaining apple. Serve turkey and sauce on rice and garnish with fruit.

Deep-fried eggs

This method of cooking eggs is like poaching them in fat. You'll need enough oil so that the egg is just covered, and because you baste it all the time and turn it a couple of times as well, the white forms a crisp brown coating for the yolk

LUNCH OR SUPPER Serves 4

Overall timing 15 minutes

Equipment Frying pan

Freezing Not recommended

INGREDIENTS

	Oil for frying (see Cook's know-how)	
8	Eggs	8
	Salt and pepper	
2	Tomatoes	2
	Fresh parsley	

METHOD

1 Half-fill a shallow frying pan with oil and heat to 370F (188C) or until a cube of bread browns in 1 minute.

2 Swirl fat round with a spoon. Break an egg into a cup and carefully slide into the hot oil. Cook for 1–2 minutes, basting with the hot oil all the time and turning the egg once or twice.

3 Remove from pan with a draining spoon and drain on kitchen paper. Sprinkle with salt and pepper and keep warm.

4 Garnish with tomato wedges and parsley sprigs and serve with toast.

cook's know-how

When frying eggs, a variety of fats can be used. In shallow frying, if the eggs are to be served with bacon, cook the bacon, then use the fat to cook the eggs, adding a little oil, butter or lard if necessary. On its own, butter can be a problem as it browns very quickly. Any oil can be used though corn, groundnut and the blended ones give little flavour.
In shallow frying, the heat should be moderate to low – not be so high that the fat spurts, nor so low that the fried egg is limp and greasy.
In deep frying, a hydrogenated fat or light cooking oil gives the best results. For a 5 inch (13cm) pan, use $\frac{3}{4}$ pint (400ml) oil; for a 6 inch (15cm) pan, 1 pint (560ml); correct temperature 370F (188C).

Above: Deep-fried eggs – crisp golden coating for the creamy yolks inside

When the temperature's right, add the egg and cook, basting and turning constantly

When the egg is cooked lift out and place on kitchen paper to drain. Fry other eggs

Lambs liver with basil

Crisp-fried bacon and tender slices of liver topped with aromatic basil

LUNCH OR SUPPER Serves 4

Overall timing 20 minutes

Equipment Frying pan

Freezing Not recommended

INGREDIENTS

8oz	Bacon rashers	225g
4 tbsp	Oil	4×15ml
1lb	Lambs liver	450g
4 tbsp	Plain flour	4×15ml
	Salt	
	Freshly-ground black pepper	
½ pint	Beef stock or red wine	300ml
2 tbsp	Chopped basil	2×15ml

METHOD

1 Derind bacon. Heat 1 tbsp (15ml) oil in a frying pan and fry bacon until crisp. Remove from pan and keep hot.

2 Wipe, trim and thinly slice liver. Coat lightly with seasoned flour. Add the remaining oil to frying pan and when hot fry the liver for 2–3 minutes each side. Remove from pan, arrange on serving dish with bacon and keep hot.

3 Stir remaining flour into pan and cook for 2 minutes till brown. Gradually add the stock (made with a cube if necessary) or wine and bring to the boil, stirring continuously. Boil for 3 minutes to reduce. Taste and adjust seasoning.

4 Spoon pan juices over liver. Sprinkle with chopped basil and serve immediately with creamed potatoes.

cook's know-how

For an unusual accompaniment to the liver why not serve leeks and carrots cooked together. The proportions can vary depending on what you have available. Prepare, wash and slice vegetables finely. Heat a little butter or oil in a pan and turn the vegetables briefly in it. This simply seals them and they should not colour. Add water to about half way up the leeks and carrots, bring to the boil and simmer for about 15 minutes. Drain, season and serve.

Milan-style macaroni salad

Two Italian favourites – pasta and salami – in a mayonnaise-topped salad

STARTER OR LUNCH Serves 8 or 4

Overall timing 30 minutes plus chilling

Equipment Saucepan, bowl

Freezing Not recommended

INGREDIENTS

8oz	Macaroni	225g
	Salt	
4oz	Frozen peas	125g
1	Onion	1
1	Red capsicum	1
4oz	Piece of salami	125g
4oz	Tongue	125g
4oz	Emmenthal	125g
½	Cucumber	½
	Dressing	
¼ pint	Thick mayonnaise	150ml
1 tbsp	Lemon juice	15ml
	Salt	
	Freshly-ground black pepper	
	Garnish	
2	Hard-boiled eggs	2
3	Tomatoes	3
1 teasp	Chopped parsley	5ml

METHOD

1 Place macaroni in saucepan of boiling salted water and cook till al dente. Drain in colander and rinse under cold water to cool. Place in large bowl.

2 Place peas in saucepan, cover with boiling water, bring to the boil and cook for 4 minutes. Drain and rinse under cold water. Add to the macaroni.

3 Peel and finely chop onion. Wash, deseed and cut capsicum into strips. Remove skin from salami and cut tongue, salami and Emmenthal into strips. Wash and thickly slice cucumber and quarter slices. Add all to macaroni and mix carefully.

4 Mix the mayonnaise, lemon juice and seasoning and pour over salad. Shell and quarter eggs. Blanch, peel and quarter tomatoes. Garnish salad with eggs and tomatoes and sprinkle parsley over. Chill for half an hour. Toss lightly at the table and serve with piping hot garlic bread.

Below: Milan-style macaroni salad – chill before serving to let the flavours develop

Veal Marengo

This dish which gets its name from a Napoleonic battle features a rich sauce made with white wine, tomatoes, herbs and vegetables

MAIN MEAL Serves 4

Overall timing 2 hours

Equipment Large pan or flameproof casserole

Freezing Cool quickly after cooking, seal in a foil container, label and freeze. Freezer life: 1 month. To use: thaw at room temperature for about 6 hours, heat on top of cooker until bubbling

INGREDIENTS

1lb	Stewing veal	450g
1oz	Butter	25g
1 tbsp	Oil	15ml
3	Shallots	3
1	Carrot	1
1oz	Plain flour	25g
4	Ripe tomatoes	4
4oz	Button onions	125g
1 teasp	Tomato paste	5ml
4fl oz	Dry white wine	120ml
4fl oz	Water	120ml
2	Garlic cloves	2
	Bouquet garni	
1 teasp	Salt	5ml
	Freshly-ground black pepper	
4oz	Mushrooms	125g

METHOD

1 Cut the veal into pieces. Heat the butter and oil in pan or flameproof casserole. Add the veal and brown on all sides over a high heat. Chop the shallots, scrape and slice carrots and add to pan.

2 Sprinkle with flour. Stir with wooden spoon until flour turns golden.

3 Blanch, peel and chop the tomatoes (or a small tin of tomatoes), peel the onions and add to the pan with tomato paste, white wine, water, crushed garlic, bouquet garni, salt and pepper. Cover and simmer for 1½ hours.

4 Wipe and slice mushrooms and add to pan. Cover and cook for a further 15 minutes, stirring occasionally.

5 Remove bouquet garni. Either serve in the casserole or transfer meat and sauce to a warmed serving dish. Serve with buttered noddles or plain, boiled rice and broccoli or green beans.

CHICKEN MARENGO

The original dish prepared by Napoleon's cook contained only the foods he could find in Marengo, in Northern Italy, at the time. Use 1½lb (700g) chicken pieces and follow the recipe for Veal Marengo. To make it truly traditional, steam crayfish above the chicken while cooking and serve it together with fried eggs as a garnish – rather hefty but obviously just the thing to follow a strenuous battle.

Casseroled chops

SUPPER Serves 4

Overall timing 1 hour

Equipment Casserole

Freezing Not recommended

INGREDIENTS

1	Onion	1
1	Garlic clove	1
4	Large spare-rib chops	4
1 tbsp	Tomato paste	1×15ml
¼ teasp	Ground allspice	¼×5ml
8fl oz	Dry cider	220ml
2 teasp	Brown sugar	2×5ml

METHOD

1 Chop onions, crush garlic and place in casserole with chops. Combine remaining ingredients, pour over chops, cover and cook in oven at 375F (190C) Gas 5 for 45 minutes.

Left: Veal Marengo – this dish is just as good made with chicken

Shepherds pie

Traditional English fare to use up the Sunday roast – it's also known as cottage pie. Bought and cooked minced beef will do just as well

LUNCH OR SUPPER Serves 4

Overall timing 1 hour

Equipment Large saucepan, frying pan, ovenproof dish

Freezing Not recommended

INGREDIENTS

2lb	Potatoes	900g
	Salt	
1	Large onion	1
3 tbsp	Oil	3×15ml
1	Garlic clove (optional)	1
1lb	Minced cooked lamb	450g
2oz	Butter	50g
¼ pint	Milk	150ml
	Salt	
	Freshly-ground black pepper	
3oz	Grated cheese	75g

Above: Shepherds pie – minced meat and a layer of potato with a crispy cheese topping

METHOD

1 Peel and halve potatoes. Place in a saucepan of cold salted water, bring to the boil and cook until tender.

2 Peel and finely chop onion. Heat oil in a frying pan, add onion and cook for about 10 minutes. Peel and crush garlic. Add garlic and meat and cook for about 5 minutes, stirring.

3 Preheat the oven to 425F (220C) Gas 7. Drain potatoes and mash with half the butter and the milk. Season to taste.

4 Grease overnproof dish. Cover base with the meat, then spread or pipe the potato on top.

5 Sprinkle with cheese, dot with remaining butter and bake on the top shelf of the oven for about 15 minutes till the top is browned. Serve with boiled carrots or Beans with herbs (see below).

Beans with herbs

An unusual but simple vegetable dish that would be delicious served with Shepherd's pie

VEGETABLE Serves 4–6

Overall timing 40 minutes

Equipment Heavy-based saucepan

Freezing Cook but don't add yogurt. Cool, pack in rigid container, cover, label and freeze. Freezer life: 3 months. To use: thaw by heating gently for 30 minutes, then mix in yogurt

INGREDIENTS

1lb	Fresh or frozen green beans	450g
2	Large onions	2
2 tbsp	Oil	2×15ml
2 tbsp	Butter	2×15ml
3 tbsp	Chopped parsley	3×15ml
pinch	Dried marjoram	pinch
1 tbsp	Chopped fennel tops (optional)	15ml
12oz	Fresh or frozen broad beans	350g
	Salt	
1	Garlic clove	1
5oz	Carton of natural yogurt	141g

METHOD

1 Wash fresh green beans and break or cut them into short lengths. Peel and slice the onions.

2 Heat oil and butter in pan and brown the onions. Add parsley, marjoram, fennel and broad beans. Sprinkle with salt and cook gently for 5 minutes, turning contents of pan over frequently. Add 3 tbsp (3×15ml) of water and green beans, reduce heat to very low and cook uncovered for 25 minutes.*

3 Peel and crush the garlic and stir into the yogurt. When the beans are cooked, stir in yogurt. Cook for 1 minute then serve.

*If using frozen green beans and broad beans, cook for only half this time.

Above: Lentils with courgettes and potatoes – aromatic herbs add flavour

Storecupboard pizza

As a standby for unexpected guests, this pizza takes some beating. It also freezes well, so make it for a time when you may not feel like cooking or do not have the time to shop

LIGHT LUNCH OR SUPPER Serves 4–6

Overall timing 1 hour 10 minutes

Equipment 2 mixing bowls, baking tray or flat ovenproof dish

Freezing When baked, cool and open freeze. Wrap in foil and then place in a polythene bag. Label and freeze. Freezer life: 3 months. To use: either thaw for 2 hours at room temperature and heat for 15 minutes at 400F (200C) Gas 6 or heat from frozen at same temperature for about 40 minutes

Below: Storecupboard pizza – super standby

Lentils with courgettes and potatoes

Flavoured with herbs and spices, this is a satisfying dish to serve on a cold winters day – and it will be easy on your budget as well

LUNCH OR SUPPER Serves 6

Overall timing 1½ hours

Equipment Large saucepan

Freezing Not recommended

INGREDIENTS

8oz	Continental lentils*	225g
2 pints	Water	1.1 litres
	Salt	
	Freshly-ground pepper	
2	Bay leaves	2
1	Onion	1
2 tbsp	Oil	2×15ml
12oz	Courgettes	350g
2 tbsp	Lemon juice	2×15ml
1	Garlic clove	1
5	Fennel leaves (optional)	5
pinch	Dried basil	pinch
pinch	Dried rosemary	pinch
1 teasp	Cumin seed	5ml
8oz	Potatoes	225g
1oz	Butter	25g
	Parsley for garnish	

METHOD

1 Wash and pick over the lentils and place in a large saucepan. Add water, seasoning and bay leaves. Bring to the boil and simmer for 5 minutes. Drain and reserve the liquid.

2 Peel and finely chop the onion. Heat oil in a large saucepan and fry onion. Top and tail and thickly slice the courgettes. Add to pan and stir-fry for 5 minutes. Add the lentils, lemon juice and peeled and crushed garlic.

3 Finely chop the fennel leaves and add to pan with dried basil leaves, rosemary, the cumin and the reserved lentil liquor.

4 Simmer for 45 minutes. Meanwhile, peel potatoes and cut into large chunks. Add to pan and simmer for a further 20 minutes or till the lentils are cooked.

5 Add the butter, taste and adjust seasoning. Sprinkle with chopped parsley and serve hot with a dish of grated cheese and some natural yogurt or slices of boiled bacon.

*Large brown lentils or small French lentils are found in health food shops.

INGREDIENTS

	Topping	
14oz	Can of tomatoes	396g
2	Garlic cloves	2
1	Small onion	1
½ teasp	Dried basil *or* mixed herbs	½×5ml
	Worcestershire sauce	
	Salt and pepper	
4oz	Can of sardines*	125g
	Base	
8oz	Self-raising flour	225g
	Pinch of salt	
3 tbsp	Oil	3×15ml
	Water to mix	
	Garnish	
6oz	Cheddar	175g
1	Small can of anchovy fillets	1
12	Small black olives	12
2 tbsp	Parmesan	2×15ml

*alternatives: 4oz (125g) of diced pork ring or salami; chopped streaky bacon

METHOD
1 To make topping, put mashed tomatoes and juice, crushed garlic, finely-chopped onion, herbs, a dash of Worcestershire sauce, seasonings and drained and chopped sardines into a bowl and mix lightly together.
Preheat oven to 450F (230C) Gas 8.
2 Meanwhile, make base: in another bowl place sieved flour and salt. Stir in oil and sufficient water to mix to a soft but not sticky dough.
3 Lightly oil a flat baking tray or oven-proof dish. Roll out dough to a large circle or rectangle as thick as you like. Pinch up the edge to make a ridge. Brush with oil.
4 Spread topping on to base. Cover with grated or sliced Cheddar and arrange anchovy fillets in a lattice shape on top. Garnish with olives and sprinkle with Parmesan.
5 Cook near top of oven at 425F (220C) Gas 7 for 15 minutes. Reduce heat to 375F (190C) Gas 5 and cook for about 20 minutes.

Creamed turnips

A piquant mash that makes a good accompaniment to a pheasant dish

VEGETABLE — Serves 4

Overall timing 45 minutes

Equipment Saucepan, potato masher

Freezing Omit cream. Cool, pack into a rigid container leaving 1 inch (2.5cm) headspace. Cover, label and freeze. Freezer life: 1 year. To use: place frozen block in pan, heat gently, beat in cream and adjust seasoning

INGREDIENTS

1½lb	Turnips	700g
½ pint	Milk	300ml
	Salt and pepper	
2oz	Butter	50g
4 tbsp	Single cream	4×15ml

METHOD
1 Peel the turnips and cut into chunks. Put into a pan with the milk and a little salt and bring to the boil.
2 Cover and simmer for about 25 minutes till tender and most of the liquid is absorbed.
3 Drain off any excess liquid and dry the turnips over a low heat for 1 minute, shaking the pan frequently.
4 Add the butter and mash over a low heat till smooth. Beat in the cream and season to taste.

Pheasant pie with sausages

A good recipe to make a pheasant go a little further, especially if you can buy local, inexpensive game

MAIN MEAL — Serves 4–6

Overall timing 1¾ hours

Equipment Flameproof casserole, frying pan, 2 pint (1.1 litre) pie dish, baking tray

Freezing Not recommended

INGREDIENTS

6	Small onions	6
1	Ovenready pheasant	1
	Salt and pepper	
4 tbsp	Plain flour	4×15ml
1½oz	Butter	40g
3 tbsp	Oil	3×15ml
½ pint	Red wine	300ml
2 tbsp	Tomato paste	2×15ml
1	Beef stock cube	1
1 teasp	Dried thyme	5ml
8oz	Cocktail sausages	225g
13oz	Packet of frozen puff pastry	375g
1	Egg yolk	1

METHOD
1 Peel the onions. Cut the pheasant into 6 neat joints, discarding as many of the bones as possible. Season the flour and toss the pheasant joints in it. Heat the butter and the oil in the casserole and fry the pheasant and onions till golden.
2 Sprinkle in any remaining flour and cook for 1 minute. Gradually add the wine and bring to the boil, stirring constantly. Add the tomato paste, stock cube, thyme and seasoning. Cover and simmer for 30 minutes.
3 Meanwhile, preheat the oven to 425F (220C) Gas 7. Fry the sausages over a high heat till golden.
4 Add the sausages to the casserole, then spoon the mixture into the pie dish and allow it to cool. (Reserve the extra gravy to serve separately.)
5 Roll out the pastry, wet the edge of the dish and cover with the pastry. Trim, knock up and crimp the edges. Brush top with the egg yolk.
6 Stand the pie on a baking tray and bake in the centre of the oven for 20 minutes. Reduce temperature to 350F (180C) Gas 4, place a sheet of greaseproof paper over the top of the pie and cook for a further 30 minutes. Serve hot with potatoes and creamed turnips (see left).

Cadogan

You could use bottled cooked mussels, and a little wine for the sauce, in this recipe when you can't find fresh mussels

LUNCH OR SUPPER Serves 4

Overall timing 40 minutes

Equipment Sieve, 2 saucepans, muslin, frying pan, baking tray

Freezing Not recommended

INGREDIENTS

8oz	Frozen spinach	225g
2 pints	Mussels	1.1 litres
5 tbsp	Dry white wine	5×15ml
1oz	Butter	25g
1oz	Plain flour	25g
$\frac{1}{4}$ pint	Milk	150ml
4oz	Grated cheese	125g
4 tbsp	Single cream	4×15ml
	Salt	
	Freshly-ground black pepper	
3 tbsp	Oil	3×15ml
8	Thick slices of bread	8

METHOD

1 Unwrap spinach, place in a sieve and leave to thaw. Scrub and wash the mussels. Put into a saucepan with the white wine and cook over a high heat till the shells open. Discard any that remain closed.
2 Remove the mussels from their shells and reserve. Discard shells. Strain the cooking liquor through a muslin-lined sieve and reserve.
3 Preheat the oven to 400F (200C) Gas 6.
4 Melt the butter in a saucepan, add the flour and cook for 1 minute. Gradually add the milk and the reserved cooking liquor and bring to the boil, stirring constantly. Remove from the heat and stir in the grated cheese and the cream. Season to taste.
5 Heat the oil in a frying pan and fry the slices of bread till golden on both sides. Arrange on the baking tray. Press the spinach till thoroughly drained and spread over the bread. Season.
6 Divide the mussels between the slices and spoon the sauce over. Bake in the centre of the oven for 10–15 minutes till golden. Serve immediately with a tomato and onion salad.

Left: Cadogan – bake in the oven till the top is golden or use hot spinach and finish off under a preheated grill

Above: Brill and vermouth envelope, and Brill pâté (see recipe page 380)

Brill and vermouth envelope

A lovely dish for a dinner party. Serve with lightly boiled vegetables and an Hollandaise sauce

MAIN MEAL Serves 6

Overall timing $1\frac{1}{4}$ hours plus overnight marination

Equipment Dish, ovenproof dish, bowl, frying pan, baking tray

Freezing Not recommended

INGREDIENTS

2lb	Brill fillets *or* sole fillets	900g
10 tbsp	Vermouth	10×15ml
14oz	Frozen puff pastry	397g
4oz	Mushrooms	125g
1	Onion	1
1oz	Butter	25g
1 tbsp	Chopped parsley	15ml
4oz	Cooked rice	125g
	Salt and pepper	
	Lemon juice	
1	Egg	1

METHOD

1 Put brill fillets in dish with vermouth. Cover and leave overnight.
2 The next day, thaw pastry. Preheat oven to 450F (230C) Gas 8. Put fish and vermouth into lightly greased dish and cook, covered, in centre of oven for 15 minutes. Drain fish, saving cooking liquor, and flake into a bowl.
3 Wipe and slice mushrooms. Peel and finely chop onion. Melt butter in frying pan and cook mushrooms and onion for 10 minutes. Drain, add to fish.
4 Stir parsley, rice, salt, pepper and lemon juice into flaked fish and moisten with reserved cooking liquor.
5 Roll out pastry to a large square. Trim edges and reserve trimmings. Place fish filling in centre of square and brush edges with water. Bring corners to middle to form an envelope and press edges together. Cut 16 small leaves from trimmings. Moisten undersides and place 4 on each pastry seam.
6 Place envelope on baking tray. Brush with beaten egg, bake for 40 minutes at 400F (200C) Gas 6. Serve hot.

Basic batters

1 To make the fritters, you will need the equipment shown here: 2 mixing bowls, a sieve, a wooden spoon and a whisk

2 Sift flour and salt (or sugar) into a bowl, making a well in the centre. Add egg and oil and start to mix with wooden spoon

3 Gradually add in liquid of choice to the mixture while beating with wooden spoon. An electric mixer can be used if you prefer

4 Just before use whisk 2 egg whites in a separate bowl until stiff then fold into flour mixture with a large metal spoon

5 Once the egg whites have been folded in use to coat sweet or savoury fillings and deep fry immediately. This batter mustn't stand

rules to remember

- Don't make fritter batter too thin. It's better to make it thicker and add more liquid later.
- If your deep-fryer doesn't have a thermostat and you don't have a suitable thermometer, drop a cube of stale white bread into the oil and if it rises to the top and becomes golden brown in 1 minute, the temperature is right.

Fritter

You can use this batter to coat vegetables (mushrooms, strips of courgette etc.), fruit (apple slices, banana pieces, canned fruit etc.) and cooked meats such as luncheon meat

SAVOURY/SWEET For 18–20 fritters

Preparation time 15 minutes

Equipment Mixing bowl, deep-fryer

INGREDIENTS

4oz	Plain flour	125g
$1\frac{1}{2}$ teasp	Salt *or* caster sugar	7.5ml
1	Whole egg	1
1 tbsp	Oil	15ml
4fl oz	Milk, beer, cider or water*	120ml
2	Egg whites	2

*You can use a mixture of liquids above in this and the recipe for crêpes.

TO COOK FRITTERS
Heat oil in a deep-fryer to 340F (170C) or until a cube of stale bread browns in 1 minute. Cook fritters until golden brown on both sides.

Pancake

Pancake batter can be made as shown in the pictures right, or put all the ingredients into a blender for a few seconds. The batter can be left to stand or placed in the fridge till needed but it isn't absolutely necessary. To prevent the pancakes becoming sodden during cooking, only add oil or butter to the pan after every 4 pancakes. And the pan mustn't get too hot – the secret is to let the pancakes brown evenly

SAVOURY/SWEET Makes 20

Overall timing 45 minutes

Equipment Mixing bowl, whisk, frying pan

INGREDIENTS

8oz	Plain flour	225g
$\frac{1}{4}$ teasp	Salt	1.25ml
2	Eggs	2
1 pint	Milk	560ml
2 tbsp	Cold water	2×15ml
	Oil or butter for frying	

1 To make the basic pancake batter, you will need a mixing bowl, sieve and whisk – or all the ingredients can be mixed in a blender

2 Sieve the flour and salt together and then add the eggs. Mix well, then add half the milk gradually, whisking all the time

3 Whisk in the cold water, rest of milk until a smooth batter is formed. Leave to stand for ½ hour, whisk again before using

TO COOK PANCAKES
Put a little oil or butter in a well-heated frying pan. Pour in 1 tbsp (15ml) batter and tilt the pan so batter spreads evenly. Let it brown underneath and then toss or turn it with a palette knife.

TO SERVE PANCAKES
As savoury: fill with spinach and cottage cheese; sliced ham and cheese, covered with a sauce; chopped mushrooms and parsley. As sweet: fill with jam, dust with icing sugar; sprinkle with brandy.

Crêpe

The famous light-as-air pancake of France. Traditionally cooked on a special flat hotplate, the batter is spread right to the edge with a palette knife before being flipped

SAVOURY/SWEET Makes 12

Overall timing 30 minutes

Equipment Bowl, 8 inch (20cm) omelette, heavy-based or non-stick frying pan

Freezing Cook crêpes and cool on a wire rack then stack them, interleaved with sheets of greaseproof paper. Overwrap in foil or polythene, label and freeze. Freezer life: 3 months. To use: remove from freezer, unwrap and separate crêpes. Leave at room temperature for ½ to 1 hour, then reheat quickly

INGREDIENTS

5oz	Plain flour	150g
¼ teasp	Salt	1.25ml
2	Eggs	2
½ pint	Milk, beer, cider or water	300ml
1oz	Butter (optional)	25g
	Oil or butter for frying	

TO COOK CRÊPES
Brush the pan with oil or melted butter, wait until it is very hot then pour in just enough batter to cover about two-thirds of the bottom of the pan. Tilt the pan from side to side to spread out the batter. Cook over a high heat until crêpe is golden brown underneath. With a palette knife loosen the edges and the middle, then flip the crêpe over. Cook the other side for half the time of the first. Turn out on to a clean cloth, cover with a second cloth or sugar, or greaseproof, or fill, or roll and sprinkle with sugar and lemon.

1 To make the basic crêpe batter, you will need bowl, sieve, whisk or electric mixer

2 Sift flour and salt into bowl and make a well in the centre. Add eggs and liquid

3 Melted butter is not essential, but if used should be well beaten in after liquid

rules to remember

- The first side of the crêpe always cooks more evenly in colour than the second so when you roll it, keep the second side inside.
- Brush the pan with oil or butter and heat well before cooking each crêpe.
- If the crêpes are to be used for dessert and you want to stack them as you make them, lightly sprinkle caster sugar over each one. Crêpes can be kept warm on a plate over a saucepan of boiling water – but don't keep them there too long.
- All the ingredients can go in together if using a blender but beat in melted butter later.
- Butter is optional in the basic recipe, but it is worth adding the amount suggested, or even more, if you like very soft crêpes.
- The true crêpe is as thin and light as the fabric which has the same name.
- Pour crêpe mixture into a measuring jug so you'll know how much batter to use for the number of crêpes you want.

Sweet yeast

The yeast adds a special taste to these pancakes, and there's a splendid "bready" smell as they cook. You can flavour and fill them as you like – see rules to remember below

SWEET Makes 24

Overall timing 2 hours

Equipment Bowl, saucepan, 8 inch (20cm) crêpe, heavy-based or non-stick frying pan

Freezing Cook pancakes and cool on a wire rack, then stack, interleaved with sheets of greaseproof paper. Wrap in foil or polythene, label and freeze. Freezer life: 3 months. To use: remove from freezer, unwrap and separate pancakes. Leave at room temperature for ½–1 hour, then reheat quickly in a hot, lightly greased frying pan

INGREDIENTS

½oz	Fresh yeast	15g
	or	
2 teasp	Dried yeast	2.5ml
27fl oz	Lukewarm milk	750ml
12oz	Plain flour	350g
3½oz	Icing sugar	100g
2	Eggs	2
½ teasp	Salt	2.5ml
½ teasp	Vanilla essence	2.5ml
	or	
2 tbsp	Rum	2×15ml
	Oil or butter for frying	

TO COOK PANCAKES

Brush the frying pan lightly with oil or butter, wait until it is hot then pour in just enough batter to cover two-thirds of the bottom of the pan. Tilt the pan from side to side to spread out the batter. Cook over a high heat until pancake is golden brown underneath. Use a spatula to lift up the sides and middle, then turn or toss pancake. Cook the other side until golden brown. As you turn it out flip pancake again so it is first-side-cooked downwards. Cover with a cloth and keep warm, or serve immediately. Continue until all the batter has been used.

TO SERVE

Either sprinkle with lemon juice or liqueur and a little caster sugar or add a spoonful of sweet filling: fruit purée, stewed fruit (thickened with arrowroot or cornflour), chocolate sauce with fruit or nuts or ice cream, and either roll up or fold.

1 Before you start get together all you need: a mixing bowl, sieve, whisk and saucepan

2 Add fresh yeast – or dried plus 1 teasp (5ml) icing sugar – to a third of the milk

3 Sift half the flour into bowl, making well in the centre. After 10 minutes, pour in yeast and mix till the flour absorbs the liquid

rules to remember

- Pancakes made with yeast are thicker, more substantial than crêpes.
- The yeast will have helped the batter to rise so, when you reach Step 6, stir the milk in gently with a wooden spoon so you won't knock all the air out again.
- Rather than being filled, yeast pancakes can have the seasonings mixed in – thin slices of apples, pears, plums or bananas can be added to the batter before cooking. Or you can stack the pancakes, American style, and pour over the syrup of your choice.

4 When all the liquid has been absorbed, add the eggs, salt and sifted icing sugar

5 Mix in rest of flour and beat till smooth. Cover and put in warm place for 30 minutes

6 The batter will have risen. Gently stir in rest of lukewarm milk and the flavouring

7 To turn, pancake is lifted in the centre, turned and "unrolled" with the palette knife

1 To make doughnuts, you'll need a saucepan, mixing bowl, doughnut cutter or pastry cutter and apple corer, draining spoon, deep-fryer

2 Sift flour and salt into bowl, then rub in butter with fingertips

3 Break in egg, then add yeast/milk mixture. Mix to soft dough. Leave to stand

Doughnuts

Favourites all round the world, doughnuts have a "bready" texture because of the yeast – use either fresh or dried

Overall timing 40 minutes plus cooking time

Equipment Saucepan, mixing bowl, doughnut cutter, deep-fryer

Freezing Cook but do not coat. Pack in polythene bags, exclude as much air as possible, seal and label. Freezing life: 2 months. To use: heat from frozen in oven (400F/200C/Gas 6) for 8 minutes. Sprinkle with sugar and cinnamon

INGREDIENTS

4fl oz	Milk	120ml
4 teasp	Caster sugar	4×5ml
1 tbsp	Dried yeast	15ml
1lb	Plain flour	450g
½ teasp	Salt	2.5ml
4oz	Butter	125g
2	Small eggs	2
	Oil for deep frying	
4oz	Caster sugar	125g
1½ teasp	Cinnamon	1½×5ml

METHOD

1 Heat milk to lukewarm, add caster sugar and, when dissolved, whisk in yeast. Leave for 20 minutes in a warm place till frothy.

2 Mix flour and salt together in a bowl and rub in the butter. Make a well in the centre and add the egg. Add yeast/ milk mixture and mix to a soft dough. Add a little more milk if necessary. Beat until smooth, then cover and leave to stand in a warm place for 15 minutes.

3 Place the dough on a floured board or work surface and lightly knead. Roll out to circular shape of about ½ inch (12.5mm) thickness. Cut into rounds with a doughnut cutter or use a pastry cutter and an apple corer for the hole in the middle.

TO COOK DOUGHNUTS

Heat oil in deep-fryer to 360F (180C) and cook doughnuts a few at a time (add at ½ minute intervals and lower them in with a draining spoon). Turn them over halfway through the cooking time (about 3 minutes). Lift out with draining spoon and roll immediately in sugar/cinnamon mixture.

4 Knead dough lightly and roll out. Cut out rounds as desired

5 Cook doughnuts a few at a time. Lift them out and coat them in sugar spice mix

Countdown

French onion soup
Caraway bread
Cheese board
Mixed vegetable salad
Fruit kebabs

When unexpected guests turn up you don't always have time or the opportunity to do much shopping. This simple meal for four people can mostly be made from the storecupboard. The only luxury touch is the homemade caraway bread. You can of course simply buy extra French bread or make soda bread (recipe page 293) which takes far less time. For the salad and fruit kebabs just use the vegetables and fruit you have to hand. The cheese selection can also be quite modest and you will still have a satisfying meal

During the afternoon Make the caraway bread

1½ hours before Prepare mixed vegetable salad and chill

1 hour before Prepare fruit kebabs to the end of Stage 2

45 minutes before Make onion soup

25 minutes before Lay out cheese board and cover while soup is simmering

10 minutes before Fry bread, place in individual bowls with the wine, seasonings, soup and Gruyère and put under a preheated grill to melt the cheese. Put salad, cheese board and extra board on the table

Serve piping hot soup. Follow with salad and cheese. When you are ready for the dessert reheat the grill, thread the fruit and bread cubes on to the skewers and grill for 10 minutes

Serve fruit kebabs hot with ice cream or whipped cream

Serve a light bodied claret with this meal or a local *Vins de Pays*. This is an official designation for a French country wine made to certain traditional standards and coming from a specified area. They represent excellent value for money. If you prefer a white wine a flavourful, fresh-tasting Riesling could be served too.

Caraway bread

A particularly rich bread made with a high proportion of fat and eggs. If you prefer, you can make the dough into 1 large loaf – cook it for 10 minutes more

BREAD — Makes 2 small or 1 large

Equipment Mixing bowl, baking tray, cooking rack

Freezing Wrap cooled loaves in a polythene bag, seal, label and freeze. Freezer life: 3–4 months. To use: thaw at room temperature for 3 hours, then refresh in a hot oven for 10 minutes

INGREDIENTS

1lb	Strong plain flour	450g
1 teasp	Sugar	5ml
1oz	Fresh yeast *or*	25g
4 teasp	dried yeast	4×5ml
5 tbsp	Lukewarm water	5×15ml
4fl oz	Lukewarm milk	120ml
1 teasp	Salt	5ml
1oz	Caster sugar	25g
2 tbsp	Caraway seeds	2×15ml
4oz	Softened butter	125g
2	Eggs	2
1 tbsp	Milk	15ml

METHOD

1. Mix together 4oz (125g) of the flour, the sugar, fresh or dried yeast and the warm water and milk in a large bowl. Cover with a polythene bag or tea towel and leave in a warm place until frothy, about 20 minutes.
2. Mix the remaining flour with the salt, caster sugar and caraway seeds. Add to the frothy yeast mixture with the butter and beaten eggs. Mix well to give a soft dough (add a little extra flour if the dough is too sticky).
3. Turn the dough on to a lightly floured surface and knead until smooth and elastic, about 10 minutes by hand or 2–3 with a mixer and dough hook.
4. Shape the dough into a roll and place inside a large greased bowl. Cover with a polythene bag or tea-towel and leave to rise until doubled in size, about 30 minutes in a warm place.
5. Turn the risen dough on to a lightly floured surface. Knead until the dough is firm again, about 2 minutes. Shape into 2 short rolls about 6 inches (15cm) long.
6. Grease and flour a baking tray and place loaves in the centre. Make 3 cuts across the top of each loaf with a very sharp knife. Brush with milk. Cover with a large polythene bag or damp tea-towel and leave to rise until loaves double in size, about 30 minutes in a warm place, longer in a cool one. During this time, preheat the oven to 400F (200C) Gas 6.
7. Bake in centre of oven for 30–35 minutes, until crusts are a rich golden brown and loaves sound hollow when tapped underneath. Cool on a cake wire.

Below: Caraway bread – caraway seeds are added to an enriched bread dough

French onion soup

In France this soup which is a speciality of the cafés of Paris is called either *soupe à l'oignon* or *soupe au fromage*. It's thick, tasty and warming and a great favourite with students, market porters – and, of course, tourists

HOT STARTER Serves 4

Overall timing 45 minutes

Equipment Large saucepan, ovenproof tureen, casserole or individual bowls

Freezing Add wine and seasoning before simmering. Freeze in container leaving a 1 inch (2.5cm) headspace. Freezer life: 3 months. To use: thaw, then reheat in saucepan. Proceed as Step 4 of method, right.

INGREDIENTS

1½lbs	Large onions	700g
2oz	Butter	50g
1 tbsp	Plain flour	15ml
½ teasp	Brown sugar	½×5ml
2½ pints	Water *or* stock	1.5 litres
8	Slices of French bread	8
4 tbsp	Dry white wine	4×15ml
	Salt and pepper	
2oz	Gruyère	50g

METHOD

1 Peel and slice onions. Melt half the butter in a large suacepan and cook onions over a gentle heat for 20 minutes. Don't let them turn brown.

2 Sprinkle onions with flour. Stir over heat until flour colours. Add sugar and pour in liquid a little at a time so soup keeps coming to the boil, then reduce heat and simmer for 20 minutes.

3 Preheat grill to high.

4 Fry bread in remaining butter. Place bread slices in bottom of individual bowls or ovenproof soup tureen. Add wine, salt and pepper then pour soup over bread. Grate Gruyère and sprinkle it into the bowls then put them under the grill to melt the cheese.

Above: French onion soup – a warming and filling dish for a wintry day

shape saver

A serving of this soup would make a very satisfying main meal for anyone trying to slim. Cut out the butter used for frying and grill the bread instead – wholemeal rather than a French loaf will not only be better for you but will add a different, nutty flavour to the dish.

preparing a cheese board

A cheese board gets its name from the wooden board traditionally used for serving cheese, but any dish or platter that has a cool, flat surface, and is portable, is equally good.
Plenty of variety is the secret of preparing a good cheese board. There's no need to go mad, though – some 5 or 6 different cheeses at the most should be sufficient to please even the most enthusiastic cheese eater.
Having decided on how many cheeses, next choose the varieties. One cheese from each principal family gives a sound balance of flavour and texture. So choose a hard and semi-hard, a blue, and two kinds of soft paste (for example, Brie and a stronger goats cheese).
Make sure the cheese is served at room temperature, so put it out 1–2 hours before serving and cover lightly. Always take a cheese out of its original wrapping, but keep it whole or in a large piece so the minimum amount of cut surface is exposed to the air. If a blue cheese is on the board, have 2 knives at hand to prevent cross-flavouring, and don't clutter up the board with garnishings. Biscuits, bread and butter should always be served separately.

Mixed vegetable salad

Exotic olives, artichoke hearts and capers with potatoes, carrots and peas are mildly spiced with coriander. This is a useful recipe as you can just as well use canned asparagus, cooked green beans or cauliflower florets, or tinned sweetcorn – depending on what you have in the storecupboard

LUNCH OR SUPPER Serves 4

Overall timing 25 minutes plus chilling

Equipment Bowl

Freezing Not recommended

INGREDIENTS

$1\frac{1}{2}$lb	Cooked waxy potatoes	700g
8oz	Cooked carrots	225g
3	Canned artichoke hearts	3
6oz	Cooked peas	175g
2 tbsp	Drained capers	2×15ml
12	Small black olives	12
12	Pitted green olives	12
4 tbsp	Olive oil	4×15ml
2 tbsp	Lemon juice	2×15ml
1 tbsp	Chopped parsley	15ml
$\frac{1}{4}$ teasp	Ground coriander	1.25ml
	Salt	
	Freshly-ground black pepper	

METHOD

1 Cut the potatoes and carrots into fine dice. Drain the artichokes and cut into quarters. Put all the vegetables into a serving dish with the capers and olives.
2 Whisk the oil and lemon juice together with the parsley, coriander and plenty of seasoning.
3 Pour the dressing over the salad and toss lightly. Chill for 30 minutes before serving with crusty bread.

Left: Mixed vegetable salad – deliciously rich in colour and Mediterranean flavour

Fruit kebabs

These are delightful for a barbecue or popped under the grill indoors. For a less filling version use just fruit and no bread

DESSERT Serves 4

Overall timing 20 minutes

Equipment Bowl, skewers

Freezing Not recommended

INGREDIENTS

2	Bananas	2
2	Small oranges	2
1	Small lemon	1
8oz	Can of pineapple chunks	227g
2 tbsp	Rum	2×15ml
3oz	Caster sugar	75g
1oz	Butter	25g
2	Thick slices of bread	2

METHOD

1 Peel the fruit. Divide oranges and lemon into segments; drain pineapple chunks, cut bananas into 1 inch (2.5cm) pieces. Place fruit in a bowl, pour rum over and sprinkle with $1\frac{1}{2}$ tbsp ($1\frac{1}{2}$×15ml) of the sugar. Preheat grill if using.
2 Butter the bread on both sides, cut into small cubes and roll in sugar to coat.
3 Thread fruit and bread cubes on to skewers. Cook over a barbecue or under the grill for 10 minutes, turning brochettes over from time to time and sprinkling them with any remaining sugar. Serve immediately with whipped cream or vanilla ice cream.

Below: Fruit kebabs – an unusual dessert for a summer day when you're having a barbecue, or for a winter pick-me-up when the sunny days seem a long way away

Avocados with horseradish

This dish, which comes from Israel, combines the "bite" of horseradish with the creaminess of mayonnaise and avocado flesh. Garnished with sprigs of fresh parsley it makes a most attractive dinner party starter or it could form part of a light buffet lunch

STARTER Serves 4

Overall timing 10 minutes

Freezing Not recommended

INGREDIENTS

1	Horseradish *or*	1
4 tbsp	bottled grated horseradish	4×15ml
2	Ripe avocados	2
1 tbsp	Lemon juice	15ml
8 tbsp	Thick mayonnaise	8×15ml
	Fresh parsley	
1	Slice of lemon	1

METHOD

1 If using fresh horseradish, wash or wipe it, then grate sufficient to make 4 tbsp (4×15ml).

2 Cut the avocados in half lengthways and lift out the stones. Sprinkle the flesh with lemon juice to prevent discoloration.

3 Divide the mayonnaise between each avocado shell, sprinkle with grated horseradish and garnish with parsley sprigs and a slice of lemon. Serve immediately.

VARIATION

To make the avocado filling even more piquant, mix in $\frac{1}{2}$ teasp (2.5ml) cayenne or a few drops of Tabasco sauce to the mayonnaise before spooning it on.

Below: Avocados with horseradish is an unusual combination of taste and texture

Above: Pork and garlic stuffed mushrooms – a treat for those who like a garlicky taste

Pork and garlic stuffed mushrooms

Stuffed mushrooms are a good way to start off a dinner party. They can be prepared and filled in advance, then put into the oven to cook while you have a drink with your guests when they arrive

STARTER Serves 4

Overall timing 40 minutes

Equipment Bowl, shallow ovenproof dish

Freezing Not recommended

INGREDIENTS

8	Large cup mushrooms	8
1oz	Fresh breadcrumbs	25g
6oz	Pork sausagemeat	175g
1 tbsp	Chopped parsley	15ml
	Salt	
4	Garlic cloves	4
$\frac{1}{4}$ teasp	Cayenne	1.25ml
1oz	Butter	25g
	Parsley sprigs	

METHOD

1 Preheat the oven to 375F (190C) Gas 5. Wipe and trim the mushrooms. Separate the stalks from the caps.
2 Finely chop the mushroom stalks and place in a bowl. Add the breadcrumbs, sausagemeat, parsley, salt, peeled and crushed garlic cloves and cayenne. Mash with a fork till evenly mixed.
3 Spoon the mixture into the mushroom caps and arrange in the greased ovenproof dish. Dot with the butter and bake on the centre shelf of the oven for 25 minutes.
4 Arrange on a warmed serving dish and garnish with parsley sprigs. Serve immediately with fresh toast fingers.

VARIATIONS

To serve with a sauce, press 14oz (397g) can of tomatoes through a sieve. Season to taste and spoon over the stuffed mushrooms before baking. Alternatively, coat with $\frac{1}{2}$ pint (300ml) thin cheese sauce and sprinkle with a mixture of 2oz (50g) grated cheese and 2 tbsp (2×15ml) fresh breadcrumbs for a crisp topping.

Mash 2 cans of sardines in tomato sauce with the mushroom stalks, breadcrumbs and parsley. Omit garlic and pork, add 2 tbsp (2×15ml) lemon juice and 4 finely diced gherkins and mix well. Divide between mushroom caps and bake as above.

Almond and cucumber salad

A well-flavoured salad that's cold, crisp and full of goodness

COLD STARTER OR SIDE SALAD Serves 6–8

Overall timing 10 minutes plus 30 minutes refrigeration

Equipment Glass dish or salad bowl

Freezing Not recommended

INGREDIENTS

1	Large cucumber	1
6oz	Flaked almonds	175g
3 tbsp	Oil	3×15ml
2 tbsp	Wine vinegar	2×15ml
3 tbsp	Lemon juice	3×15ml
1 teasp	French mustard	5ml
1 teasp	Brown sugar	5ml
	Salt and freshly-ground black pepper	

METHOD

1 Finely slice cucumber into a glass dish or salad bowl. Sprinkle almonds over.
2 Make dressing by mixing together oil, vinegar, lemon juice, mustard, sugar, salt and pepper.*
3 Pour over cucumber and almonds and mix well to distribute dressing. Place in fridge for 30 minutes.

TO SERVE

Remove from fridge and mix well again. Serve on individual plates as a starter or to accompany grilled meat or fish.

*A good way to make a dressing is to place the ingredients in a screwtop jar, screw down the lid and shake vigorously until combined.

cook's know-how

Flaked or crushed almonds can add crunch in simple ways. Mix just a tablespoon of either into a cold rice salad, for example, or sprinkle over the top of ice cream, bread-and-butter or rice puddings. For a different way to serve frozen whole green beans: melt butter in a frying pan, add flaked finely chopped almonds and gently brown. Add beans and cook for about five minutes, stirring constantly, then serve.

Brill pâté

This fish, because of its delicate fine flavour, makes an unusual creamy pâté – a very pleasant change from the more usual kipper or mackerel ones. Cream, and white breadcrumbs all contribute to the smooth texture and anchovy essence gives an extra accent to the taste. (See photograph on page 369)

STARTER Serves 4-6

Overall timing 15 minutes plus chilling time

Equipment Bowl, small saucepan, dish

Freezing When cold, wrap, label and freeze. Freezer life: 3 months. To use: thaw overnight in fridge or for 6 hours at room temperature

INGREDIENTS

$1\frac{1}{2}$lb	Poached brill	700g
4oz	Salted butter	125g
2	Lemons	2
2oz	Fresh white breadcrumbs	50g
3 teasp	Anchovy essence	3×5ml
$\frac{1}{4}$ pint	Carton of double cream	150ml
	Salt	
	Freshly-ground white pepper	
2oz	Unsalted butter	50g

METHOD

1. Remove skin and bones from brill. Flake the flesh into a bowl. Melt the salted butter in a small saucepan. Squeeze the lemons.
2. Add breadcrumbs, melted butter, lemon juice and anchovy essence to fish. Stir in lightly whipped cream and season to taste. Transfer mixture to dish, smooth top and chill for 30 minutes.
3. Melt unsalted butter, allow to cool slightly then pour over the firm pâté. Cool, then return pâté to fridge to set for 30 minutes. Garnish with a parsley sprig and serve the pâté with thin slices of toast and butter curls.

taste saver

Brill is delicious served cold, with thick mayonnaise. First let it cool in the cooking liquor, drain it well and place it on a bed of lettuce leaves, with sliced cucumber and hard-boiled eggs, or a mixture of cold diced vegetables.

Above: Thick celery soup – a creamy mixture served with crisp croûtons

Thick celery soup

A deliciously thick and filling soup that's just right for winter

STARTER OR LIGHT LUNCH Serves 4

Overall timing 35 minutes

Equipment Large saucepan, sieve and bowl or blender

Freezing Make soup, but don't add cream. When cold, ladle soup into rigid container, leaving $\frac{3}{4}$ inch (2cm) headspace. Cover, label and freeze. Freezer life: 3 months. To use: bring gently to boil, then add cream

INGREDIENTS

1lb	Celery	450g
2	Potatoes	2
2	Onions	2
2oz	Butter	50g
	Salt and pepper	
1	Bay leaf	1
1	Garlic clove	1
	Grated nutmeg	
$1\frac{3}{4}$ pints	Chicken stock	1 litre
$\frac{1}{4}$ pint	Single cream	150ml

METHOD

1. Cut off base of celery, then wash and chop stalks and leaves.
2. Peel and finely chop potatoes and onions. Heat butter in saucepan over a low heat. Add celery stalks and leaves, potatoes and onions, cover and cook for 5 minutes, stirring occasionally to prevent colouring.
3. Sprinkle with salt and pepper, add the bay leaf, peeled and crushed garlic, pinch of nutmeg and hot stock (made with 2 cubes if necessary). Cover and simmer for a further 20 minutes.
4. Remove bay leaf. Push soup through sieve into a bowl, or liquidize, then return to saucepan and add the cream. Heat through, without boiling. Adjust seasoning, then serve with croûtons (diced bread fried in oil till brown).

VARIATIONS

This soup will cost less to make if you use milk instead of stock and cream, and crumble in 2 chicken stock cubes. For a deep green soup, add $\frac{1}{2}$ a bunch of washed watercress at Step 3. As the potato is mainly in the soup as a thickener, it's a good way to use up leftover mash. Add at Step 4, then heat through.

Canadian cheese soup

European influence is strong in the cooking of Canada because of the numbers of immigrants. This cheese soup combines the famous cheeses from Italy and Switzerland and is like a Swiss fondue but is not as thick. If you prefer you could stir in 2 tbsp (2×15ml) dry sherry instead of the white wine, adding it just before serving

LUNCH OR SUPPER Serves 4–6

Overall timing 30 minutes

Equipment Saucepan

Freezing Not recommended

Below: Canadian cheese soup – serve with plain or garlic croûtons for contrast

INGREDIENTS

3oz	Butter	75g
1	Finely chopped onion	1
1½ pints	Light stock	850ml
¼ pint	Dry white wine	150ml
4 teasp	Cornflour	4×5ml
½ pint	Milk	300ml
	Salt	
	Freshly-ground white pepper	
4oz	Grated Emmenthal	125g
4oz	Grated Parmesan	125g

METHOD

1 Heat butter in a saucepan, add onion and fry till transparent. Stir in the stock and wine and bring to the boil slowly.
2 Blend the cornflour with a little water and add to the pan, stirring constantly. Bring to the boil, stirring, and cook for 3 minutes. Add the milk, salt, pepper and cheese. Stir over a very low heat till the cheese has completely melted.
3 Taste and adjust seasoning, then pour into a warmed tureen. Serve immediately with lots of croûtons.

Italian mixed salad

Radicchio leaves add a lively Italian touch to a simple mixed salad. Serve after the cheese soup for a nourishing and well balanced meal

ACCOMPANIMENT Serves 6

Overall timing 25 minutes plus chilling

Equipment Salad bowl, small bowl

Freezing Not recommended

INGREDIENTS

1	Small round lettuce	1
1	Head of radicchio *or*	1
¼	finely chopped red cabbage	¼
1	Large ripe tomato	1
1	Small onion	1
½	Cucumber	½
1	Garlic clove	1
1 tbsp	Lemon juice or white wine vinegar	15ml
3 tbsp	Olive oil	3×15ml
	Salt	
	Freshly-ground black pepper	

METHOD

1 Divide lettuce and radicchio into leaves. Wash and dry thoroughly, then tear into bite-size pieces. Put into a salad bowl.
2 Wash the tomatoes and cut each into 6 wedges. Peel and thinly slice the onion, separate into rings and add to the bowl with the tomato.
3 Wash the cucumber, peel off strips of skin lengthways to give a striped effect. Cut diagonally into thin slices and add to the bowl. Toss salad lightly and chill for 30 minutes.
4 Peel and crush the garlic into a bowl and add the lemon juice or vinegar, oil and seasoning. Mix well and pour over the salad. Toss lightly till ingredients are coated with dressing, then serve.

VARIATIONS

If you find radicchio (which looks like a red, leafy chicory) is hard to obtain, a similar effect will be given by substituting red cabbage. For a particularly distinctive flavour, make the dressing with lemon juice and add a pounded anchovy fillet instead of salt. Black olives and strips of yellow capsicum can also be added to the basic salad mixture.

Ham and veal parcels

Ham, veal and cheese sauce cooked in paper parcels – great for midweek as they can be prepared in advance

LUNCH OR SUPPER Serves 4

Overall timing 40 minutes

Equipment Saucepan, frying pan, greaseproof paper, baking tray

Freezing Not recommended

INGREDIENTS

4oz	Butter	125g
1 tbsp	Plain flour	15ml
½ pint	Milk	300ml
	Salt and pepper	
2oz	Grated Gruyère	50g
1 tbsp	Oil	15ml
2×8oz	Veal escalopes *or*	2×225g
4×4oz	boneless chicken breasts	4×500g
4	Slices of ham	4

METHOD

1 In a saucepan, melt 2oz (50g) of the butter. Stir in the flour and cook over low heat for 2–3 minutes. Remove from heat and gradually add the milk. Return to heat and stir until mixture has thickened. Season. Remove from heat and stir in the cheese.

2 Preheat oven to 425F (220C) Gas 7. In a frying pan, melt 1oz (25g) of butter with the oil. Add escalopes and cook on each side for 4 minutes. Season, then cut each one in half.

3 Cut 4 large heart shapes out of greaseproof paper and grease the edges with the remaining butter. In the centre of each heart (see picture) place a slice of ham, then half an escalope and a good layer of sauce. Fold ham over the filling. Close parcels securely and place on baking tray. Cook in oven for 15 minutes, then serve immediately.

Above: Escalopes en chemise – heart-shaped paper parcels with veal, cheese sauce and ham on the inside. Just the right size for a substantial meal

1 Grease edges of paper. Place ham, half escalope and some sauce in centre of paper

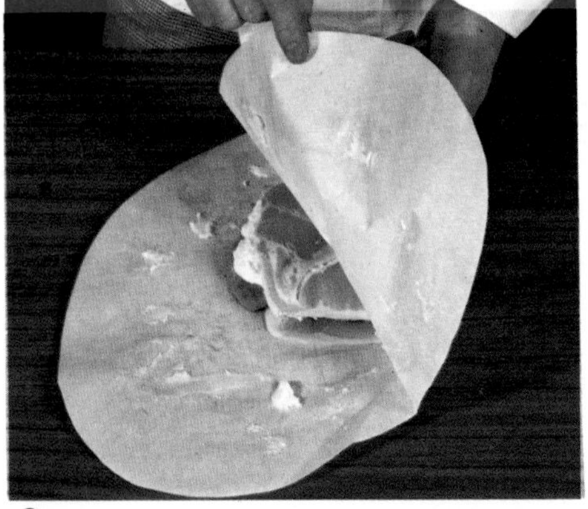

2 Fold the ham over the sauce and escalope, then fold the paper heart over it

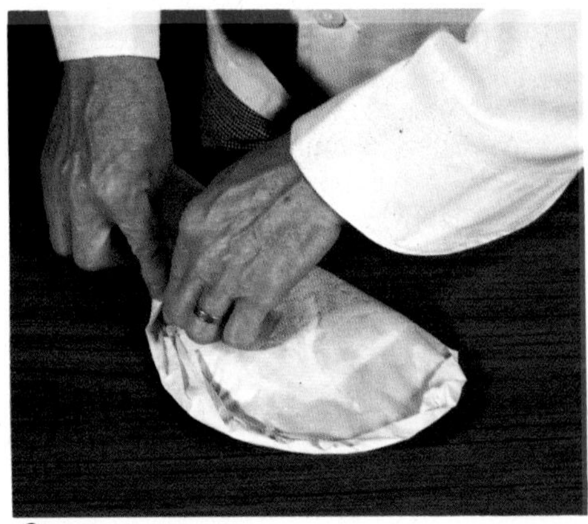

3 Fold heart-shape paper over and close edges to make a secure parcel, then bake

Quick chilli con carne

Famous Tex-Mex dish to make in double-quick time. The canned kidney beans make for speed of preparation while Tabasco gives vital "heat" to the flavour. This recipe is also good for an economical party dish – just give your guests a plate and fork and let them help themselves

LUNCH OR SUPPER Serves 4

Overall timing 40 minutes

Equipment Flameproof casserole

Freezing Cool, pour into a rigid container, leaving 1 inch (2.5cm) headspace. Cover, label and freeze. Freezer life: 3 months. To use: place block in pan, heat gently till thawed, then simmer for 5 minutes

INGREDIENTS

2	Large onions	2
2 tbsp	Oil	2×15ml
1lb	Minced beef	450g
1 tbsp	Plain flour	15ml
½ pint	Strong beef stock	300ml
14oz	Can of tomatoes	397g
1 teasp	Tabasco	5ml
	Salt	
	Freshly-ground black pepper	
14oz	Can of red kidney beans	397g

METHOD

1 Peel and chop the onions. Heat the oil in the casserole, add the onions and fry till golden. Add the minced beef and fry, stirring to break up any lumps, till browned all over.

2 Sprinkle in the flour and cook for 1 minute. Gradually add the stock (made with a cube if necessary) and bring to the boil, stirring constantly.

3 Add the canned tomatoes and juice, the Tabasco and seasoning. Cover and simmer for 10 minutes.

4 Drain the beans in a sieve and rinse under cold water. Drain thoroughly and add to the pan. Cover and simmer for a further 10 minutes.

5 Adjust the seasoning and serve immediately with boiled rice or noodles and a tossed green or mixed salad.

Above: Indian lamb fillets – finished with a chutney, cream and curry sauce

Indian lamb fillets

Curried apples are used well in this Indian dish to produce a tasty contrast to the quickly prepared leg of lamb fillets and vegetables

MAIN MEAL Serves 4

Overall timing 30 minutes

Equipment Frying pan, saucepan

Freezing Not recommended

INGREDIENTS

1lb	Aubergines *or* courgettes	450g
6 tbsp	Oil	6×15ml
4	Thick slices of lamb fillet *or*	4
4×8oz	Lamb steaks	4×225g
	Salt and pepper	
1oz	Butter	25g
2	Onions	2
8oz	Cooking apples	225g
1 tbsp	Mild curry powder	15ml
6 tbsp	Hot stock	6×15ml
4fl oz	Carton of single cream	113ml
2 tbsp	Mango chutney	2×15ml
	Pinch of sugar	

METHOD

1 Slice the aubergines and place in frying pan with half the oil. Fry very gently for 10 minutes, turning them over halfway. Remove from pan, drain, then arrange round edge of serving plate. Keep hot.

2 Remove any excess fat and gristle from meat. If at all tough, beat meat. Rub it with salt and pepper and cut each piece into 2.

3 Add rest of oil to frying pan and when hot, cook the meat for 5 minutes on each side. Remove meat and arrange on serving dish with aubergines. Keep hot.

4 Melt butter in a saucepan. Finely chop the onions and apples, add to the pan and cook, stirring, for 4 minutes until light brown.

5 Sprinkle in the curry powder and continue cooking. Place half of this mixture on the serving dish and stir stock and cream into the rest. Add the mango chutney and cook gently for a few minutes. Do not boil. Season with salt and sugar then pour into sauceboat and serve separately.

TO SERVE

With plain fluffy or saffron-flavoured rice, garnished with crisply fried onion rings, and a tomato or chicory salad dressed with vinaigrette sauce.

After basin is lined and flour-coated meat packed in, pour in the cold beef stock

Cover basin with foil or cloth, make a handle from string to make removal easy

Steamed steak and kidney pudding

One of the best known British dishes. During the long steaming the filling cooks to melt-in-the-mouth tenderness and the gravy is drawn into the suet, browning it

MAIN MEAL Serves 6

Overall timing 5¾ hours

Equipment Bowl, 3 pint (1.7 litre) pudding basin, greaseproof paper and foil or pudding cloth, string, saucepan, steamer

Freezing Complete to end of Step 7, remove covers from basin and cool quickly. Cover with clean wrappings and place in a polythene bag. Seal, label and freeze. Freezer life: 3 months. To use: steam from frozen for 2½–3 hours

Below: Steamed steak and kidney pudding – serve with boiled potatoes and carrots

INGREDIENTS

1½lb	Chuck or blade steak	700g
8oz	Ox kidney	225g
1	Large onion	1
	Salt	
	Freshly-ground black pepper	
3 tbsp	Plain flour	3x15ml
12oz	Self-raising flour	350g
6oz	Shredded suet	175g
	Water to mix	
½ pint	Cold beef stock	300ml

METHOD

1 Wipe and trim the meat and cut into 1½ inch (4cm) cubes. Wipe the kidney, removing any core, and cut into 1 inch (2.5cm) cubes. Peel and thinly slice the onion. Season plain flour and use to coat the steak, kidney and onion.

2 Sift the self-raising flour and 1½ teasp (7.5ml) salt into a bowl and stir in the suet and enough cold water to mix to a soft but not sticky dough.

3 Knead lightly till smooth. Roll out on a floured surface to a circle big enough to line the basin (about 14 inches/35cm in diameter). Cut out one quarter of the pastry and reserve.

4 Lift the large piece and place it in the greased basin so it fits neatly, and sealing the edges together. Place the meat mixture in the basin and add the cold stock (made with a cube if necessary) to come halfway up the meat.

5 Roll out the reserved pastry to a circle slightly larger than the top of the basin. Brush the top edge of the pastry lining with water and cover with the pastry lid. Seal the edges well.

6 Cover with greased, pleated greaseproof paper and pleated foil, or a pudding cloth and secure with string.

7 Stand the pudding in a steamer over a pan of boiling water. Cover and steam for 5 hours, topping up the pan with boiling water as required.

USING A PRESSURE COOKER

Prepare pudding and cover as above. Place trivet in pressure cooker and add 2 pints (1.1 litres) water and 1 tbsp (15ml) vinegar. Bring to the boil, cover and cook over a low heat till a steady jet of steam escapes from the vent. Reduce the heat and steam gently without weights for 15 minutes to allow the pastry to rise. Increase the heat till steady jet of steam can be seen, add the weights and bring to Low pressure. When the cooker makes a hissing noise, reduce the heat; when a gentle muttering sound can be heard start the timing. Cook for 1¼ hours. Reduce pressure at room temperature.

Potatoes and onions Irish style

Just one of the many ways the Irish have of treating their staple food! It's simple to prepare and can be served as an accompaniment or by itself for an economical family supper. To make it more substantial, add beaten eggs to the milk before pouring it over the potatoes and sprinkle grated cheese such as Cheddar or Parmesan on top

VEGETABLE Serves 8

Overall timing 1 hour

Equipment Large shallow ovenproof dish

Freezing Not recommended

INGREDIENTS

3lb	Waxy potatoes	1400g
4	Onions	4
4oz	Butter	100g
	Salt	
	Freshly-ground black pepper	
$1\frac{1}{2}$ pints	Milk	860ml
$\frac{1}{2}$ teasp	Freshly-grated nutmeg (optional)	$\frac{1}{2}\times$5ml

METHOD

1. Preheat the oven to 375F (190C) Gas 5.
2. Peel and thinly slice the potatoes and onions. Lightly grease the dish with half the butter.
3. Arrange the sliced potatoes and onions in the dish in layers, seasoning between each and finishing with a neat layer of potato. Press down well with the back of a spoon and dot with remaining butter.
4. Pour the milk over and sprinkle with nutmeg if liked. Bake at the top of the oven for 45 minutes till potatoes are tender and golden. Serve immediately.

Above: Honey-glazed bacon is served with apple rings fried in butter

Honey-glazed bacon

A tender, succulent joint that can be sliced thickly or thinly and served hot or cold. The fat is scored with a decorative diamond pattern and glazed with brown sugar and honey

MAIN MEAL 6–8 servings

Overall timing $1\frac{1}{2}$ hours plus overnight soaking

Equipment Large saucepan, small saucepan, roasting tin, frying pan

Freezing Not recommended

INGREDIENTS

4lb	Collar bacon	1.8kg
	Whole cloves	
2 tbsp	Clear honey	$2\times$15ml
3 tbsp	Soft brown sugar	$3\times$15ml
2	Granny Smith apples	2
2oz	Butter	50g

METHOD

1. Put bacon into a large saucepan. Cover with cold water and leave to soak overnight.
2. The next day, drain the bacon. Return it to the same pan and cover with fresh water. Bring to the boil. Remove any scum. Reduce heat, cover and simmer gently for an hour.
3. Preheat the oven to 375F (190C) Gas 5. Remove bacon from pan, allow to cool slightly then cut off the rind. Score fat in a lattice pattern and put a clove in the centre of each "diamond".
4. Gently heat honey and sugar in a small saucepan until melted. Brush over the surface of the bacon. Put joint in a roasting tin and cook in the bottom of oven for 20 minutes, basting from time to time.
5. Five minutes before the joint is cooked, peel, core and slice apples into $\frac{1}{4}$ inch (6mm) thick rings. Melt butter in a frying pan and fry the apple rings on both sides until lightly golden and tender.

TO SERVE

Serve bacon joint surrounded by apple rings with potato and onion dish (see left).

Crispy baked rabbit

Crisp coatings work with rabbit just as they do with chicken – but trim the portions well and remove as many small bones as possible

MAIN MEAL Serves 4–6

Overall timing 1¼ hours

Equipment 2 plates, frying pan, baking tray, bowl, piping bag, potato piping nozzle

Freezing Not recommended

INGREDIENTS

2lb	Young rabbit	900g
	Salt	
	Freshly-ground black pepper	
3 tbsp	Plain flour	3×15ml
½ teasp	Paprika	2.5ml
2	Eggs	2
2 tbsp	Milk	2×15ml
2oz	Dried breadcrumbs	50g
1oz	Butter	25g
4 tbsp	Oil	4×15ml
4 tbsp	Thick mayonnaise	4×15ml
1–2 tbsp	Horseradish sauce	1–2× 15ml
2 tbsp	Single cream	2×15ml
1 teasp	Lemon juice	5ml
	Hot creamed potato	
	Sprigs of parsley	

METHOD

1 Preheat the oven to 350F (180C) Gas 4.

2 Wipe and trim the rabbit, cut into small neat pieces, removing small bones. Season the flour, add paprika and toss the rabbit pieces in it till evenly coated.

3 Beat the eggs on a plate with the milk. Dip the rabbit into the egg mixture then into the dried breadcrumbs, pressing them on lightly.

4 Heat the butter and oil in a frying pan and fry the rabbit pieces over a moderate heat for 5 minutes, turning once. Place on baking tray and bake in centre of oven for about 40 minutes till tender.

5 Meanwhile, put the mayonnaise into a bowl and beat in the horseradish sauce, cream and lemon juice. Season to taste.

6 Arrange the rabbit pieces on a warmed serving dish and pipe hot creamed potatoes round them. Spoon the dressing over the rabbit or serve in a separate dish, garnish with parsley and serve with minted peas.

cook's know-how

Rabbit served with flavourful sauces makes a substantial meal for 4–6. Wipe, trim and cut 2½lb (1.1kg) rabbit into neat, boneless pieces. Season 2 tbsp (2×15ml) flour and toss rabbit in it. Heat 4 tbsp (4×15ml) oil in heavy-based casserole and fry rabbit for 10 minutes till brown. Remove rabbit from pan.

Mustard sauce Add any remaining seasoned flour to casserole with 1oz (25g) butter and fry, stirring, till golden. Gradually add ¾ pint (400ml) chicken stock (made with cubes if necessary) and bring to boil, stirring. Spike a peeled onion with 3 cloves, add to pan with rabbit, bouquet garni, salt and pepper. Cover and simmer for 45 minutes. Remove rabbit, place on serving dish and keep hot. Discard onion and bouquet garni, and boil sauce over moderate heat till reduced and thick. Mix 4 tbsp (4×15ml) single cream with 1 tbsp (15ml) prepared mustard, stir in. Reheat without boiling, spoon over rabbit and serve.

Sweet and sour sauce Peel a large onion and cut into 12 wedges. Add to pan with peeled and crushed garlic clove. Fry till transparent, then add remaining flour and cook for 1 minute, stirring. Gradually add ½ pint (300ml) chicken stock, ¼ pint (150ml) orange juice, contents of 8oz (227g) can of tomatoes, 1 tbsp (15ml) each of Worcestershire sauce, vinegar and demerara sugar. Bring to boil, stirring, add rabbit and simmer for 1 hour.

Left: Crispy baked rabbit

Duck with prunes

Pot roast duck with prunes, apples and bacon for added flavour. Cooked in this manner, with a small amount of liquid – in this case wine and water – added to produce enough steam, the duck flesh should be so tender it can be eaten with a fork

MAIN MEAL Serves 4

Overall timing 2½ hours

Equipment 2 bowls, flameproof casserole, poultry shears or kitchen scissors

Freezing Not recommended

INGREDIENTS

8oz	Pitted prunes	225g
¼ pint	Red wine	150ml
¼ pint	Water	150ml
4lb	Duck	1.8kg
	Salt and pepper	
3	Cooking apples	3
1 tbsp	Lemon juice	15ml
8oz	Thick bacon rashers	225g

METHOD

1 Place prunes in a bowl with wine and water and leave for 1 hour. Towards the end of this time, preheat the oven to 400F (200C) Gas 6.

2 Wipe and dry duck, then prick all over with a fork and sprinkle inside and out with salt and pepper. Place in lightly greased casserole and brown all over on a moderate heat to release some of the duck's fat. Discard fat and set the duck aside.

3 Wash, core and thickly slice apples. Sprinkle with lemon juice. Drain prunes and reserve marinade. Chop the bacon and mix with the apples and prunes in a bowl.

4 Place about a quarter of the mixture in the duck. Put the remaining apple mixture in the bottom of casserole and place the duck on top. Spoon the reserved marinade over, cover and cook for about 1¼ hours, basting from time to time, until the duck is tender.

TO SERVE

Cut duck into 4 with game or kitchen scissors. Serve with the apple and prune mixture and mashed potatoes and a green vegetable.

Above: Cheese and aubergine bake – a delicious combination

Fry aubergine slices on both sides till golden in colour

Add basil leaves to the tomato sauce in the frying pan

Spoon tomato sauce over aubergine and Mozzarella slices

Cheese and aubergine bake

A dish without meat but the cheese adds the protein – the aubergines are sliced in a different way to give an attractive look. If you like, as a variation, you can also add sliced hard-boiled egg, chopped leftover meat or even melted dark chocolate which will give a sweet-sour taste to the finished dish

LUNCH OR MAIN MEAL Serves 4

Overall timing 2¼ hours

Equipment Dish, large frying pan, sieve, shallow ovenproof dish

Freezing Prepare the dish in a foil container ready for cooking, cover, label and freeze. Freezer life: 3 months. To use: place in a preheated oven 350F (180C) Gas 4 for 45 minutes or until the Mozzarella has melted and the top begins to brown

INGREDIENTS

1¼lb	Aubergines	600g
	Salt	
2 tbsp	Plain flour	2×15ml
	Oil	
1	Small onion	1
2 tbsp	Olive oil	2×15ml
14oz	Can of tomatoes	397g
	Black pepper	
6	Fresh basil leaves	6
	or	
½ teasp	Dried basil	2.5ml
8oz	Mozzarella	225g
3oz	Grated Parmesan	75g

METHOD

1 Wash the aubergines, wipe dry and remove stalks. Cut lengthways into ½ inch (12.5mm) thick slices. Arrange in layers in a dish and sprinkle with salt. Leave for about 1 hour.

2 Rinse aubergines under running water, dry with a cloth then lightly flour. Preheat the oven to 350F (180C) Gas 4.

3 Heat some oil in a large frying pan and fry the aubergine slices on both sides till golden. Don't overcook them. Drain the slices on kitchen paper and keep them warm.

4 Peel and finely chop the onion. Cook for about 5 minutes in a frying pan with 1 tbsp (15ml) olive oil.

5 Mash the canned tomatoes and juice together with a fork or press through a sieve. Add to the frying pan and season with salt and pepper. Cook for 10 minutes over a moderate heat. Add the basil leaves or dried basil and simmer for a further 5 minutes.

6 Lightly brush an ovenproof dish with oil. Place a layer of aubergines on the bottom of the dish. Cover with slices of Mozzarella and spoon on a little tomato sauce. Sprinkle with grated Parmesan and a pinch of salt. Repeat the process, finishing with a Parmesan layer, until all the ingredients are used up. Sprinkle a little olive oil over the surface of the dish and bake in the oven for 15 minutes or until the Mozzarella has melted and the top begins to brown. Serve immediately with buttered noodles or a mixed salad.

Braised tuna steaks

Taste all the flavours of the Mediterranean in this easy braise, a cooking method ensuring moistness

MAIN MEAL Serves 6

Overall timing 1¼ hours

Equipment Flameproof casserole

Freezing Not recommended

INGREDIENTS

3×12oz	Tuna steaks *or*	3×350g
6	cod steaks	6
	Salt	
	Black pepper	
3 tbsp	Plain flour	3×15ml
1oz	Butter	25g
2 tbsp	Oil	2×15ml
2	Large onions	2
½ pint	Dry white wine	300ml
1 tbsp	Lemon juice	15ml
	Bouquet garni	
3	Large tomatoes	3
1 tbsp	Chopped parsley	15ml

METHOD

1 Preheat the oven to 400F (200C) Gas 6. Wash and dry the tuna steaks. Season the flour and coat the tuna lightly.

2 Heat the butter and oil in a casserole, add the tuna and fry for 3 minutes each side till browned. Remove from the pan and reserve.

3 Peel and slice the onions, add to the pan and fry till pale golden. Return the tuna to the pan, add the wine, lemon juice and bouquet garni and bring to the boil. Cover the pan, then bake in the centre of the oven for 40 minutes.

4 Wipe and quarter the tomatoes and arrange round the tuna. Cover and bake for a further 10 minutes till the tuna is tender.

5 Arrange the tuna and tomatoes on a warmed serving dish and keep hot. Boil the cooking liquor rapidly till reduced by half and pour round the tuna. Sprinkle with parsley and serve immediately with sauté potatoes and green salad.

cook's know-how

ROES ON TOAST

This makes a nourishing and quick supper snack.

Wash 12oz (350g) soft herring roes and pat dry with kitchen paper. Season 4 tbsp (4× 15ml) plain flour and dip roes into it. Heat 3oz (75g) butter in a frying pan, add roes and fry for about 5 minutes turning once. Divide between 4 slices of hot buttered toast, garnish with lemon slices and serve as a starter. **Serves 4**

Crab salad

Rich crab finds a perfect partner in cool, refreshing cucumber

LUNCH OR SUPPER Serves 6

Overall timing 20 minutes plus chilling

Equipment 2 bowls, salad bowl

Freezing Not recommended

INGREDIENTS

1	Cucumber	1
2×6oz	Cans of crabmeat	2×170g
2 tbsp	Lemon juice	2×15ml
3 tbsp	Olive oil	3×15ml
¼ teasp	Caster sugar (optional)	1.25ml
	Salt	
	White pepper	
1 tbsp	Chopped dill or chives	15ml
	Lettuce leaves	
1	Red capsicum	1
3	Hard-boiled eggs	3

METHOD

1 Wash the cucumber and cut in half lengthways. Slice thinly and put into a bowl. Drain the crabmeat and add to cucumber.

2 Mix the lemon juice and oil together in a bowl with the sugar and seasoning. Add chopped dill or chives and mix well. Pour over the salad, mix carefully and chill, covered, for 30 minutes.

3 Meanwhile, wash and dry lettuce leaves and use to line the salad bowl. Wash, deseed and slice the capsicum. Shell and slice the eggs.

4 Arrange salad in the bowl and garnish with capsicum and sliced eggs.

Below: Braised tuna steaks – thick slices of the fresh fish will serve two people

Above: Fried mackerel with mushrooms – garnished with thickly-sliced tomatoes

Fried mackerel with mushrooms

Italian treatment for mackerel fillets. The wine vinegar adds extra flavour – use dry white wine with a dash of lemon juice instead if you prefer

MAIN MEAL Serves 4–6

Overall timing 40 minutes

Equipment Small saucepan, large frying pan

Freezing Not recommended

INGREDIENTS

2lb	Mackerel fillets	900g
8oz	Button mushrooms	225g
2	Onions	2
5 tbsp	Oil	5×15ml
1	Garlic clove	1
	Salt	
	Freshly-ground black pepper	
2 tbsp	White wine vinegar	2×15ml
12oz	Tomatoes	350g
2 tbsp	Plain flour	2×15ml

METHOD

1 Wash mackerel fillets and pat dry. Wipe and slice mushrooms. Peel and finely chop onions.

2 Heat 2 tbsp (2×15ml) of the oil in a saucepan. Add onions, mushrooms and peeled and crushed garlic and fry for 10 minutes, stirring frequently. Season.

3 Stir in the vinegar and boil rapidly till it evaporates. Wash tomatoes and cut into ½ inch (12.5mm) thick slices.

4 Coat fillets with seasoned flour. Heat the remaining oil in a large frying pan, add the fillets and fry for 5 minutes on each side. Drain, arrange on warmed serving dish and keep hot.

5 Add tomato slices to frying pan and fry for 2 minutes. Spoon mushroom mixture over fillets. Season tomatoes and arrange on top. Serve immediately with minted peas.

Lemon thyme and plaice moulds

Plaice stuffed with prawns, poached and set in a herby, lemony jelly. Serve with fingers of brown bread

LUNCH OR STARTER Serves 6

Overall timing 1 hour plus chilling

Equipment Frying pan, string, muslin, sieve, bowl, saucepan, 6×¼ pint (150ml) dariole moulds

Freezing Not recommended

INGREDIENTS

6	Small plaice fillets	6
1 pint	Water	560ml
¼ pint	Dry white wine	150ml
3	Sprigs of lemon thyme	3
	Salt	
	White pepper	
6oz	Shelled prawns	175g
4 teasp	Powdered gelatine	4×5ml
6	Lemon slices	6
	Lettuce leaves	

METHOD

1 Wipe and skin the plaice fillets. Put the skins into a frying pan with the water and wine. Wash the thyme, reserve 1 sprig and add the rest to pan. Bring to boil. Cover, simmer for 10 minutes.

2 Meanwhile, place the fillets skin side up on a board and season. Divide the prawns between them and roll up tightly. Tie the rolls with fine string.

3 Add the rolled fillets to the pan, cover and poach for about 5 minutes, turning once. Remove the fish with a draining spoon, drain thoroughly and reserve.

4 Strain the liquor carefully through sieve lined with damp muslin and leave to cool. Put 3 tbsp (3×15ml) water into a bowl, sprinkle the gelatine over and leave till spongy. Stand bowl in a pan of simmering water. Stir till dissolved.

5 Remove from the heat, cool slightly, then fold into the fish liquor. Run moulds under cold tap and add 1 tbsp (15ml) of liquor to each. Chill till set.

6 Place a tiny sprig of thyme on each jelly, cover with a lemon slice and 3 tbsp (3×15ml) of the liquor. Chill till set.

7 Stand a rolled plaice fillet on end in each mould. Gently pour the remaining liquor over and chill till set.

8 Wash and shred the lettuce leaves. Divide between individual serving plates. Dip the moulds into hot water for 5 seconds then turn out on to the plates. Serve immediately.

Eggless chocolate and orange cake

A good standby cake that's especially useful if someone in the family is watching cholesterol levels. The golden syrup makes it deliciously moist and helps it to keep well, but eat it the same day you bake, to taste it at its best

TEA-TIME — Cuts into 8

Overall timing 50 minutes plus cooling

Equipment Two 8 inch (20cm) sandwich tins, large bowl, saucepan

Freezing Make as Steps 1–3. Wrap in polythene, seal, label and freeze. Freezer life: 4 months. To use: thaw for 2 hours, then decorate

INGREDIENTS

4oz	Butter	125g
4oz	Caster sugar	125g
½ teasp	Vanilla essence	2.5ml
2 tbsp	Golden syrup	2×15ml
10oz	Plain flour	275g
2oz	Cocoa	50g
2 teasp	Baking powder	2×5ml
½ teasp	Bicarbonate of soda	2.5ml
	Grated rind of 1 orange	
½ pint	Milk	300ml
	Filling	
1oz	Butter	25g
2 tbsp	Golden syrup	2×15ml
2 tbsp	Orange juice	2×15ml
8oz	Icing sugar	225g

METHOD

1 Preheat the oven to 375F (190C) Gas 5. Grease and base-line sandwich tins.
2 Cream butter, sugar, vanilla and syrup till fluffy and pale. Sift dry ingredients together, then fold into creamed mixture with grated orange rind and milk.
3 Divide mixture between prepared tins and bake just above the centre of the oven for 30–35 minutes till cake feels spongy to touch. Remove from tins and leave to cool on a wire rack.
4 To make the filling, put the butter, syrup and orange juice in a pan and stir over a gentle heat until the butter melts. Bring to just below the boil, then remove from the heat and beat in the sifted icing sugar. Beat until thick.
5 Sandwich cooled cakes together with the orange filling and dredge top with sifted icing sugar.

Chocolate fingers

Simple but delicious fare for family or fêtes. They are quick to make – with hardly any cooking!

TEA-TIME — Makes 24

Overall timing 20 minutes plus chilling and setting time

Equipment Saucepan, 2 bowls, 12×8 inch (30×20cm) swiss roll tin

Freezing Do not ice. Wrap, label and freeze in the tin. Freezer life: 6 months. To use: thaw at room temperature for 2 hours then ice and cut into slices

Storage Airtight container in a cool place, with greaseproof paper between layers

INGREDIENTS

	Base	
6oz	Granulated sugar	175g
4oz	Butter or margarine	125g
2 tbsp	Cocoa	2×15ml
8oz	Broken biscuits	225g
4oz	Salted, chopped peanuts	125g
1	Beaten egg	1
	Icing (optional)	
8oz	Icing sugar	225g
1 tbsp	Cocoa	15ml
3 tbsp	Boiling water	3×15ml
2 tbsp	Desiccated coconut	2×15ml

METHOD

1 To make the base, place sugar, butter or margarine and cocoa in saucepan, and heat gently. Crush biscuits and place with peanuts in a bowl. Mix in the egg, then beat in the near-boiling butter mixture until well combined.
2 Pour into greased tin and spread to edges with the back of a spoon. Leave to set in the fridge for 1 hour.
3 To make icing, sieve icing sugar into a bowl with cocoa. Mix in the boiling water, stirring with a knife, to form a thick consistency. Spread on base and smooth over. Sprinkle with coconut and leave to set. Slice when cold.

money saver

Though many recipes usually list digestive biscuits as the ones to use, you can use any broken biscuits – the ones that accumulate in the bottom of the biscuit barrel, or those sold in bulk at corner shops. If they have gone soft, it's because they have absorbed moisture. Just put them in a low to moderate oven to dry out for a little while.

Dublin fruit cake

A fruit cake for all year round, for tea-time or a special occasion. To make a simnel cake, put half the mixture in the tin, add thick layer of almond paste, then top with remaining mix. When cake is cold, stick another layer of almond paste on top with jam. Arrange 11 balls of toasted paste round edge to represent apostles. For Dundee cake, see below right

To make a Dublin or Dundee cake, cream butter and sugar. Fold in sifted flour and eggs alternately to mixture, beating well

When all the flour and eggs have been added, stir in the washed dried fruit, candied peel, chopped glacé cherries and lemon rind

Gradually add enough milk or whiskey to the bowl to give a soft but not sticky mixture. Turn into prepared tin and smooth surface

TEA-TIME Cuts into 10–12 slices

Overall timing 2½ hours

Equipment Sieve, 2 mixing bowls 4 inch (10cm) deep, 7–8 inch (18–20cm) round cake tin

Freezing See information below

Storage Airtight container

INGREDIENTS

8oz	Plain flour	225g
	Salt	
6oz	Softened butter	175g
6oz	Soft brown sugar	175g
3	Eggs	3
8oz	Sultanas	225g
8oz	Seedless raisins	225g
2oz	Mixed chopped candied peel	50g
2oz	Glacé cherries	50g
	Grated rind of 1 lemon	
3 tbsp	Milk or whiskey	3×15ml

METHOD

1 Line base and sides of tin with greased greaseproof paper. Preheat the oven to 325F (170C) Gas 3.

2 Sift the flour and a pinch of salt into a mixing bowl. Cream the butter and sugar together in another mixing bowl until light and fluffy. Then beat in the eggs, one at a time, adding a little of the flour between each egg.

3 Beat in the remaining flour, then stir in the dried and candied fruits, lemon rind and enough milk or whiskey to give a soft but not sticky mixture.

4 Spoon cake mixture into tin and smooth top with a flat-bladed knife or spatula.

5 Bake in the centre of the oven for about 2 hours or till a skewer inserted in the centre comes out clean. Remove from oven and leave to cool in tin. Turn out and remove greaseproof.

DUNDEE CAKE

The Dublin fruit cake mixture can be transformed very easily into a Dundee cake. Prepare cake as above, but use 4oz (125g) each of plain and self-raising flour, caster instead of brown sugar and milk rather than whiskey. Smooth surface and arrange 2oz (50g) whole blanched almonds on top in a decorative pattern. Brush with a little egg white and bake as above.

For a more economical cake, reduce the amount of butter and sugar to 5oz (150g) each, use 2 eggs only and sift 2 teasp (2×5ml) mixed spice with the flour. The dried fruit can also be cut down to 12oz (350g) overall. Bake for 1¾ hours.

Above: Dublin fruit cake – rich and fruity. Adapt the recipe to make a Dundee cake

HOW TO STORE AND FREEZE FRUIT CAKES

Most rich fruit cakes can be kept for 6 months (some say years!) if well wrapped in layers of greaseproof, overwrapped in foil and stored in a clean, dry airtight container. Alcohol added to completely cool, baked cakes lengthens storage time. If you don't mind them taking up freezer space, uniced fruit cakes can be wrapped as above and frozen. If the cake's large and can't be eaten quickly, it's best to freeze slices which can be taken out as required. Wrap slices in foil or greaseproof and pack in one or two rigid containers. Thaw cake slices in wrappings.

cook's know-how

If you wish to use the rich fruit cake recipe to make a three tiered cake, make 4½ times the quantity (use a preserving pan or new plastic washing up bowl) and divide between the tins. A 9 inch (23cm) round or 8 inch (20cm) square tin will take 1½ times the quantity of a 7 inch (18cm) round or 6 inch (15cm) square tin; an 11 inch (28cm) round or 10 inch (25cm) square tin will take twice the quantity. Fill the tins to equal depth so that the three tiers will be even. All large cakes being cooked for a long time need both a double lining and covering of greaseproof or brown paper.

Danish lunch
a sustaining meal for six

Denmark is the smallest of the Scandinavian countries. The mainland, Jutland, is joined to Germany, and separates the North Sea from the Baltic. Denmark also includes about 500 islands. Some, like Zealand, on which the capital, Copenhagen stands, are close by, while others, like the Faroes, are hundreds of miles away. Greenland is also a Danish possession. Denmark is a highly-developed and prosperous country, famous for her pork (pigs outnumber people by 2–1), bacon and dairy products.

The famous Danish open sandwich, *smørrebrød*, is eaten by virtually everyone for lunch at midday. It consists of thickly buttered bread, piled high with a variety of cold meats or fish, vegetables and garnishes.

Soup and porridge

Hot soups are a favourite dish, particularly during the long, hard Danish winter. The traditional pea soup, *gule aerter*, is made from split dried peas which are cooked with sliced gammon, salt pork and vegetables. At the end of the cooking time, the meat is removed and served as a separate course with pancakes.

Beer-bread, *øllebrød*, is popular with adults and children. Rye bread is soaked overnight in *lys* (non-alcoholic light beer), and then simmered with the rind and juice of a lemon until the mixture thickens. It is often served with whipped cream. Fruit soups, made with apples and berries, are eaten either as a starter or dessert.

Porridge is traditionally Danish, and in less affluent times was served as a filler or first course at the evening meal at about 6 o'clock. *Risengrød* or rice porridge is traditionally served at Christmas and the one who gets the hidden almond receives a present. Each region and island has its own special porridge recipe, and this can be made from buckwheat, ground rice, wheat flour and buttermilk, topped with treacle, butter, sugar or cinnamon.

Pork is the most popular meat by far. One dish, Passionate Love, *braendende kaerlighed*, consists of a ring or heart-shape of mashed potatoes and beetroot, enclosing fried onions and cubes of pork. Veal and poultry are also plentiful, but lamb and beef, which are mostly imported, are rather expensive.

The proximity of the sea has made the Danes a seafaring nation and great fish eaters. The fish market in Copenhagen is right at the water's edge and among the specialities are oysters, lump fish roe (mock caviare from lump fish caught off the shores of Greenland and Iceland) and shrimps. In the fishing port of Frederikshavn, "dry Jutlanders" or *tørre jyder* are a great favourite. Small, fresh plaice are gutted and tied in pairs and left for 2–3 hours covered in salt, before being hung to dry in a draughty place. The skin is removed before they are fried in butter (not unlike the "tied tailies" or Arbroath smokies of Scotland). Cod is treated with great reverence, and only eaten when there is an "r" in the month. Boiled cod is served for dinner on New Year's Eve. Eel is popular, fried, smoked, jellied or curried, and often used for *smørrebrød*. Herring is also high on the list, and appears pickled, soused, smoked, salted or fresh.

World-famous pastries

The world-famous Danish pastry tastes quite delicious in its homeland, unlike the heavy, doughy mixtures that are given the same name elsewhere. Danish flour is stronger and less finely milled than other white flour, and is specially imported by the USA for making the yeast-based, buttery Danish pastries called *Wienerbrød* (Viennese bread). "Hartshorn salt" (a rarely used leavening agent) also adds a light crispness to Danish baking. The Danes are fond of cakes and biscuits, mostly in mid-afternoon or late evening, and the major ingredient of them all is Danish butter. Much of their pâtisserie or *konditorkager* is of German origin, such as Vanilla wreaths, *vanillekranse*.

National drink

There are no home-grown grape wines in Denmark but supermarkets are well stocked with imported wines which tend to be drunk on formal or special occasions. Lager is the national drink, and the one that accompanies food. Danish lager is world famous, and the two largest brewers are Carlsberg and Tuborg. In sharp contrast to their fellow Scandinavians, the Danes are not heavy drinkers and social drinking tends to take place after the evening meal, not in pubs but at home where most entertaining is done. The favourite fire-water, *snaps*, is distilled from potatoes or grain (depending on the time of year), flavoured with caraway seed, and drunk ice cold at a gulp from tiny glasses.

Countdown

Danish beer soup
Open sandwiches
Rødgrød med fløde
Danish pastries

This meal for six would make a lovely lunch. The entire meal can be put on the table at once so you can enjoy the occasion with your guests. You can serve soup to start the meal. Very often the Danes will serve at least one hot item with the *smørrebrød*. For instance a simple fillet of fried plaice (see page 12) on rye. As an alternative to the pastries, offer a cold red berry dessert.

The evening before Soak the bread for the soup. Make the rødgrød med fløde and leave to cool

3 hours before Make the Danish pastries

1½ hours before Make beer soup to the end of Stage 3 and put to one side. Place rødgrød med fløde in fridge to chill

1 hour before Prepare the open sandwiches. Choose from the selection on page 395 and allow 2 or 3 per person. Start by preparing any cooked toppings. Then butter and halve all the bread and cover with toppings. If you are serving the plaice remember to butter some rye bread, cover with lettuce and put aside

30 mins before Prepare plaice and coatings. Heat oil

15 mins before Fry plaice, drain and keep hot

5 mins before Reheat soup and whip cream. Arrange sandwiches, cheese and pastries on the table. Decorate rødgrød med fløde with flaked almonds

Serve hot soup with cream. Follow with open sandwiches. When you clear the soup bowls place the hot plaice on the prepared bread, garnish and add to the platter

Offer both desserts to your guests with coffee

The best drink to serve is, of course, Danish lager.

A Danish lunch for six

This page: a Danish table set for an informal meal with much emphasis on neatness and tidiness. From front to back: Danish beer soup (recipe page 396); Danish lace biscuits; selection of smørrebrød (recipe page 395); Danish pastries (recipe page 397). On the cheeseboard are Danbo, Havarti with caraway, Samsoe, Danish blue and a Danish cream cheese flavoured with Grand Marnier and rolled in flaked hazelnuts

Open sandwiches

Smørrebrød, or Danish open sandwiches, are self-contained meals, eaten with a knife and fork. They are made up of four parts – the bread, butter, topping and garnish.
The bread should be fresh with a firm texture and a crisp crust. It can be dark or light rye, or white bread – mild flavoured toppings like shrimps, chicken and cheeses are generally used with white bread, and stronger ones such as pâté, meat and pickled herring with rye bread. Usually, slices are halved to make a base measuring about 2×4 inches (5×10cm), and about ¼ inch (6mm) thick. Crispbreads can be used as a base for open sandwiches but being crisp and crunchy they tend to break up easily. Once topped they have to be eaten quickly or they'll go soggy (never use them with hot toppings).
The butter should be spread on bread thickly. It acts as an anchor for the toppings and also prevents any moisture from them making the bread soggy. Danish butter is creamy and only mildly salted.
The topping can be hot or cold, sweet or savoury and should be used generously. Sliced meats and fish are often rolled to add height to the sandwich. A Danish lunch would probably include one hot topping – possibly fried fillet of plaice with lemon slices on a bed of lettuce, or ham with a fried egg on top.
The garnish gives an attractive finishing touch of colour and flavour. It should complement the flavour of the topping and look fresh rather than fussy. Radish roses, gherkin fans, tomato slices and cucumber or lemon twists are simple but effective.
The easiest way to make a quantity of sandwiches is to prepare any cooked toppings (such as hard-boiled eggs) and any cooked garnishes (such as fried onions) first. Butter and halve all the bread, then cover with toppings and garnish all the sandwiches at once. They should be arranged on a flat dish or tray and served one at a time. A mixture of fish, meat and cheese sandwiches, allowing 2 or 3 per person, makes a good lunch – follow with Danish pastries (recipe page 397) and coffee.

HANS ANDERSEN'S FAVOURITE
Thickly butter half a slice of rye bread and cover with a slice of chilled liver pâté. Top with a grilled rasher of bacon, a slice of tomato, a few fried mushrooms and a gherkin fan.

MASTER MARINER
Butter half a slice of rye bread. Roll up 3 pickled herring fillets and arrange on the bread. Garnish with 3 onion rings and a sprig of parsley.

CHEF'S SPECIAL
Arrange 2 gammon slices on half a slice of buttered rye bread. Add a spoonful of mayonnaise or scrambled egg and top with slices of tomato and cucumber, and chopped chives or a sprig of parsley.

EGG DELIGHT
Butter half a slice of rye bread and top with a lettuce leaf. Slice a hard-boiled egg and arrange on top. Spoon a little lumpfish roe along the centre.

BEEFEATER
Butter half a slice of rye bread and cover with 2 slices of cold roast beef. Top with a spoonful of mustard mayonnaise. Make this by beating ½ teasp (½×5ml) Dijon mustard into ¼ pint (150ml) mayonnaise. Garnish with a small lettuce leaf, a slice of tomato, a little grated horseradish and fried onion, and a gherkin fan.

CONTINENTAL
Roll 4 slices of Danish salami into loose horn shapes and arrange on half a slice of buttered rye bread. Garnish with fresh onion rings.

SHRIMP CRUSH
Butter half a slice of white bread and press a small lettuce leaf on to one end. Arrange shelled shrimps in 2 rows along the bread. Pipe or spoon mayonnaise between the rows and top with a twist of lemon and a sprig of parsley.

HAVARTI ON RYE
Arrange 2 slices of Havarti on half a slice of buttered rye bread. Tuck 2 small lettuce leaves under them and top with radish roses and mustard and cress.

OLIVER TWIST
Loosely roll 3 thin slices of pork luncheon meat and arrange on half a slice of buttered white bread. Top with a spoonful of canned cream flavoured with grated horseradish and garnish with a twist of orange, prunes and a sprig of parsley or small lettuce leaf.

PORK TOPPER
Cover half a buttered slice of rye bread with a slice of cold roast pork. Top with pickled red cabbage and garnish with a twist of orange, a prune and a crisp piece of pork crackling.

BLUE BOY
Arrange 2 slices of Danish blue cheese on half a buttered slice of rye bread and top with halved and seeded black grapes.

DANWICH INTERNATIONAL
Fold 2 slices of Danish ham in half and arrange on half a buttered slice of rye bread. Add a spoonful of Russian salad and garnish with tomato, twists of cucumber and a sprig of parsley or watercress.

CHICKEN CRUNCH
Top thickly buttered slices of dark rye bread with mixture of finely sliced, cooked chicken breast, finely chopped apples and gherkins combined with thick mayonnaise. Garnish with shredded cheese (Edam, Gruyère or Port Salut).

NUTTY CHEESIES
Mix together 4oz (125g) cream cheese and 2oz (50g) softened butter, then beat in ½oz (15g) finely chopped walnuts, 1 tbsp (15ml) finely chopped fresh parsley and plenty of salt and white pepper. Spread on 6 slices of well buttered white bread and garnish with walnut pieces.

OSLO'S OWN
Beat cream cheese with softened butter, then mix in sultanas and chopped nuts. Spread on buttered rye bread and garnish with pieces of crisp lettuce and twists of cucumber.

GREAT GORGONZOLA
Beat Gorgonzola with softened butter and a few drops of Worcestershire sauce. Mix in chopped parsley or basil, spread on white bread. Garnish with tomato slices.

PINEAPPLE POL
Mix together 1oz (25g) each of butter and brown sugar, and 1 teasp (5ml) Dijon mustard. Spread on 4 ham slices, grill for 3 minutes alongside 4 rings of pineapple. Place crisp lettuce on 4 slices of buttered rye bread, top with folded ham and then pineapple. Serve hot.

Left: Smørrebrød – the famous Danish open sandwiches. The selection shows, from the top and left to right: Chef's special, Egg delight, Master mariner, Havarti on rye, Beefeater, Hans Andersen's favourite, Shrimp crush and Continental, with Danish butter and thinly-sliced rye bread

Danish beer soup

A highly individual rich, thick soup, made with stout and lager and finished with cream

STARTER OR LIGHT LUNCH — Serves 6

Overall timing 30 minutes plus overnight marination

Equipment Saucepan with tight fitting lid, blender or sieve

Freezing Not recommended

INGREDIENTS

4oz	Pumpernickel or rye bread	125g
1	Small stick of cinnamon	1
	Grated rind of 1 lemon	
$\frac{1}{2}$ pint	Stout	300ml
$\frac{1}{2}$ pint	Lager	300ml
1 tbsp	Brown sugar	15ml
	Pinch of salt	
$\frac{1}{4}$ pint	Carton of double cream	150ml

METHOD

1 Dice the bread, cover with $\frac{1}{2}$ pint (300ml) of water and leave overnight.

2 The next day, place bread in a saucepan, add the cinnamon stick and finely grated lemon rind. Bring to the boil, then simmer for 15 minutes, tightly covered.

3 Remove cinnamon stick and place mixture in a blender or press through a sieve. Turn purée back into the saucepan, add both sorts of beer and the sugar and bring to the boil again. Add salt.

4 Whip cream lightly (it should be semi-liquid, not thick). Ladle soup into individual dishes and pour cream over the top of each. Serve with thin fingers of pumpernickel or rye bread.

Rødgrød med fløde

Delicious berry fruits of summer are combined in this delectable dessert from Denmark. As the fruits are gently cooked before being thickened, the dish could be made in winter with frozen fruit.

DESSERT — Serves 6

Overall timing 20 minutes plus cooling and chilling

Equipment Saucepan, measuring jug, serving dish

Freezing Do not decorate. Cool, pour into rigid container, cover, label and freeze. Freezer life: 3 months. To use: thaw overnight in fridge, then decorate and serve

INGREDIENTS

$1\frac{1}{2}$lb	Mixed soft fruit (raspberries, strawberries, blackcurrants, redcurrants, blackberries, loganberries)	700g
4oz	Caster sugar	125g
	Arrowroot	
1oz	Toasted flaked almonds (optional)	25g

METHOD

1 Wash and prepare fruit. Put into a saucepan and add enough water to just cover. Bring gently to the boil and simmer for about 5 minutes or until soft. Strain fruit and measure amount of juice. Place fruit in serving dish.

2 Return juice to pan, add sugar and heat gently till sugar dissolves.

3 Allowing 2 teasp (2×5ml) per pint (560ml) of fruit juice, measure out arrowroot and mix with a little cold water. Stir into pan and heat gently for 2 minutes, stirring constantly until slightly thickened and glossy. Do not boil.

4 Pour over fruit in serving dish, and leave to cool. Chill for 1 hour, then decorate with flaked almonds and serve with unsweetened whipped cream.

Below: Rødgrød med fløde – a red fruit jelly popular in Denmark. The fruits are cooked till soft but still whole, then the juice is strained off and thickened. The dessert should be served chilled

Above: Danish pastries — different shapes to make from one of several batches

1 Butter is enclosed in dough, then rolling and folding process begins

2 Dough is turned, rolled and chilled 3 times before shapes are cut and filled

Danish pastries

True Danish pastry is light, made with yeast, and slightly flaky. The amount in this recipe makes 15 cockscombs, envelopes or windmills, or 8 crescent shapes

TEA-TIME

Overall timing 2 hours including chilling time

Equipment Small bowl, large bowl, 2 baking trays

Freezing Cool, pack in foil containers, cover, label and freeze. Freezer life: 1 month. To use: thaw, wrapped, for 1–2 hours or in hot oven for 5 minutes

INGREDIENTS

3fl oz	Milk	90ml
1 teasp	Caster sugar	5ml
1 teasp	Dried yeast	5ml
9oz	Plain flour	250g
$\frac{1}{2}$ teasp	Salt	2.5ml
6oz	Butter	175g
1oz	Caster sugar	25g
1	Egg	1
4oz	Icing sugar	125g
2 tbsp	Water	2×15ml
1–2oz	Split almonds	25–50g
	Glacé cherries	

METHOD

1 Warm milk till hand hot. Place half of it in bowl and sprinkle on 1 teasp (5ml) of the sugar and the yeast. Leave in a warm place for 10 minutes until slightly frothy. Add rest of milk.

2 Sift together flour and salt, rub in $\frac{1}{2}$oz (15g) of the butter. Mix in yeast mixture with rest of sugar. Cover bowl and chill for 10 minutes. Shape remaining butter with a knife into an oblong.

3 Roll out chilled dough into an oblong twice the size of the butter. Place butter in centre and enclose it, overlapping edges across the middle. Seal sides by pressing lightly with rolling-pin.

4 Turn dough so folds are at sides. Roll into an oblong three times longer than it is wide. Fold bottom third up, top third down. Cover, chill for 10 minutes.

5 Repeat turning, rolling and chilling twice more. Roll out pastry into oblong 15×9 inches (38×23cm). Shape as desired (see instructions, right) and fill with almond paste (bought, if necessary) or confectioner's custard (you can buy packet mixes to make this).

6 Preheat oven to 425F (220C) Gas 7. Arrange shapes on baking trays and prove in a warm place for 20 minutes. Brush with beaten egg and bake for about 18 minutes. Toast almonds.

To make icing Stir icing sugar and water over gentle heat till glossy. Trickle icing over hot pastries and decorate.

To make the shapes shown above, cut the 15×9 inch (38×23cm) oblong of dough in these ways before cooking:

Cockscombs *Cut oblong into 15 squares — about 3 inches (7.5cm) each. Spread a "sausage" of almond paste in centre of each and fold in half, sealing with beaten egg. Make cuts in folded edge, almost to cut edges, spread out in a fan shape.*

Envelopes *Cut oblong into 15 squares — about 3 inches (7.5cm) each. Place a blob of almond paste in middle of each and fold opposite corners (2 or 4) to centre, securing tips with beaten egg.*

Windmills *Cut oblong into 15 squares — about 3 inches (7.5cm) each. Make diagonal cuts from each corner almost to centre. Place a touch of almond paste or confectioner's custard in centre and fold one corner of each triangle to it. Press down firmly to secure.*

Crescents *Cut oblong into two, each $7\frac{1}{2}$×9 inches (19×23cm). Turn each oblong so long side is facing. With a sharp knife, mark out a large W taking all lines to top and bottom of dough, with the centre peak coming half-way along the top edge. You will then have 3 equal triangles, and a fourth can be made by overlapping the two long edges of the 2 smaller triangles, and firmly pressing together before rolling.*

Irish lemon pudding

A moist, luscious sponge mixture with a golden brown sugar topping

DESSERT Serves 4–6

Overall timing 1 hour

Equipment 7 inch (18cm) soufflé dish, 2 bowls, roasting tin

Freezing Not recommended

INGREDIENTS

4oz	Butter	125g
6oz	Caster sugar	175g
4	Eggs	4
1	Lemon	1
3 tbsp	Plain flour	3×15ml
½ pint	Milk	300ml
1 tbsp	Icing sugar	15ml

METHOD

1 Preheat the oven to 400F (200C) Gas 6. Grease soufflé dish.
2 Cream the butter and sugar in a bowl till light and fluffy. Separate the eggs and add the yolks to the creamed mixture. Beat well.
3 Grate rind from lemon and squeeze out juice. Beat into the creamed mixture. Gradually stir in the flour, then the milk.
4 Beat egg whites till stiff, then carefully fold into mixture. Turn into prepared soufflé dish and sift icing sugar over.
5 Place dish in roasting tin containing 1 inch (2.5cm) hot water. Bake in the centre of the oven for 40–50 minutes till the pudding has risen and the top is golden. Serve hot or cold.

Below: Irish lemon pudding – serve it on its own, or top with a fresh raspberry or strawberry sauce for extra flavour

Cream the butter and sugar until light and fluffy, then beat in egg yolks. Grate lemon rind and squeeze out juice; add both to bowl

When the rind and juice have been beaten into the creamed mixture, gradually stir in the flour using a figure-of-eight motion

Continue to stir in flour making sure all lumps are removed, then stir in the milk a little at a time to obtain a smooth mixture

Beat egg whites till stiff, then carefully fold into creamed mixture. Turn into the prepared dish and sift icing sugar over

Meringue-topped apples

Delicious apple desserts, filled with almonds and currants or, if you prefer, sultanas. For fuel economy, bake them in the oven with your main meal

HOT DESSERT Serves 6

Overall timing 1 hour

Equipment 2 saucepans, ovenproof dish, bowl

Freezing Not recommended

INGREDIENTS

6	Apples	6
$\frac{1}{4}$ pint	Sweet or medium sweet white wine	150ml
3 tbsp	Caster sugar	3×15ml
1	Lemon	1
1 tbsp	Ground almonds	15ml
3 tbsp	Currants	3×15ml
	Custard	
1 tbsp	Cornflour	15ml
$\frac{1}{2}$ pint	Milk	300ml
1 tbsp	Caster sugar	15ml
	Pinch of salt	
1 teasp	Vanilla essence	5ml
2	Egg yolks	2
	Topping	
2	Egg whites	2
2 tbsp	Caster sugar	2×15ml

METHOD

1 Peel and core the apples, but leave whole. Put the wine and 2 tbsp (2×15ml) of the sugar in a wide saucepan. Finely grate rind from lemon and reserve. Squeeze juice into pan. Add apples and poach, turning, for 5 mins.

2 Preheat oven to 350F (180C) Gas 4. Grease ovenproof dish and arrange apples inside. Mix lemon rind, ground almonds, remaining 1 tbsp (15ml) sugar and currants. Divide mixture between apples, pressing down well into cavities.

3 To make the custard, blend the cornflour with a little milk in a pan. Add remaining milk, sugar, salt and vanilla. Bring to the boil, stirring, and simmer for 3–4 minutes.

4 Remove from heat and leave to cool slightly, then whisk egg yolks into custard. Pour over apples.

5 Whisk egg whites until stiff, then whisk in sugar. Spoon a little of the mixture over each apple and bake for 15 minutes in the centre of the oven. Serve hot.

Almond and cherry snowballs

The luscious sauce lifts this rice dessert into a special class

COLD DESSERT Serves 4

Overall timing $1\frac{1}{2}$ hours

Equipment 2 saucepans, bowl, small moulds

Freezing Not recommended

INGREDIENTS

$\frac{1}{2}$ pint	Milk	300ml
1oz	Butter	25g
2oz	Granulated sugar	50g
	Pinch of salt	
3oz	Pudding rice	75g
2 teasp	Gelatine	2×5ml
$\frac{1}{4}$ pint	Carton of double cream	150ml
$\frac{1}{4}$ teasp	Vanilla essence	1.25ml
2oz	Chopped almonds	50g
2 tbsp	Kirsch *or* brandy	2×15ml
$10\frac{1}{2}$oz	Can of red cherries	298g
3 tbsp	Lemon juice	3×15ml
2 teasp	Arrowroot	2×5ml
	Red food colouring (optional)	
$\frac{1}{4}$ teasp	Almond essence	1.25ml

Below: Meringue-topped apples – delicious

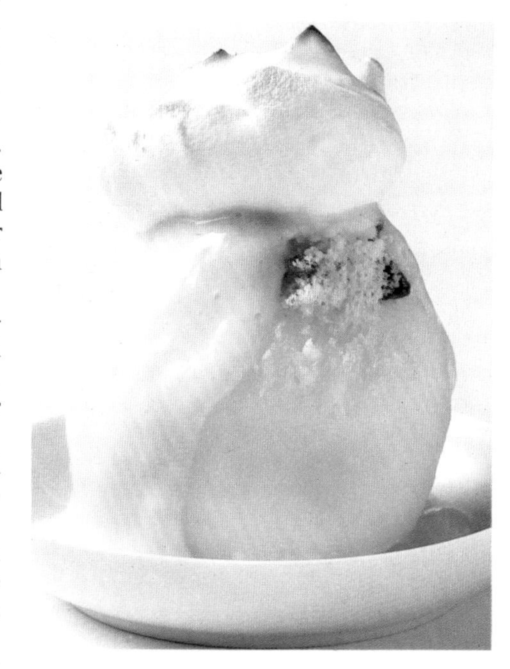

Above: Almond and cherry snowballs

METHOD

1 Put milk, butter, sugar and salt in a saucepan and bring to the boil. Stir in rice and simmer gently, uncovered, for 20–30 minutes till soft, creamy.

2 Meanwhile, sprinkle gelatine onto 2 tbsp (2×15ml) cold water. Leave to go firm, then put cup in saucepan of hot water and heat gently till gelatine dissolves. Whisk cream till stiff.

3 When rice is cooked, plunge pan into cold water to cool a little, then mix in gelatine, vanilla, almonds and half the Kirsch. Fold in cream.

4 Lightly oil moulds and fill with the rice mixture. Place in fridge to set (30 minutes to 1 hour).

5 Meanwhile, make the sauce. Drain the cherries and place juice in saucepan with lemon juice, arrowroot blended with a little water, a few drops of red colouring and almond essence. Bring to boil, stirring. Remove from heat, stir in cherries, rest of Kirsch. Cool.

6 Run knife round edges of rice, then immerse moulds up to rim in very hot water for few seconds. Invert on to individual serving dishes and spoon over the cooled cherry sauce.

Above: Chestnut charlotte – made with chestnut purée and marrons glacés

Chestnut charlotte

Definitely a superb dessert for chestnut lovers. It's very rich so the servings need only to be small. It's quite quick to make but needs chilling

DESSERT Serves 8

Overall timing 30 minutes plus 3 hours chilling time

Equipment 6 inch (15cm) charlotte mould or deep, round cake tin, 2 bowls, cup, saucepan

Freezing Complete to end of Step 6. Freeze the charlotte in the mould then unmould and wrap in foil and label. Freezer life: 1 month. To use: unwrap and place on serving dish, then loosely cover and thaw at room temperature. Decorate as in Step 7

INGREDIENTS

½oz	Butter	15g
4fl oz	Whisky	125ml
2fl oz	Water	50ml
20	Sponge fingers	20
1lb	Can of sweetened chestnut purée	450g
4 teasp	Gelatine	4×5ml
¾ pint	Double cream	420ml
7oz	Chopped marrons glacés	250g
8	Marrons glacés	8

METHOD

1 Grease charlotte mould or deep cake tin.
2 Place half the whisky and the water in a bowl. Quickly dip sponge fingers into the whisky mixture to absorb the liquid.
3 Line the base and sides of the mould or tin with the sponge fingers, placing the curved sides against the side of the mould or tin. Mix the chestnut purée with the remaining whisky.
4 In a cup mix the gelatine with 2 tbsp (2×15ml) cold water and leave to go firm. Place cup in a pan of hot water and heat gently until the gelatine has dissolved. Stir into the chestnut purée.
5 Whip the cream until thick. Fold two-thirds of it into the chestnut mixture, then half fill the lined mould. Sprinkle with the marrons glacés pieces. Add the remaining chestnut mixture.
6 Trim sponge fingers so they are level with the mould. Cover with a greased plate and a weight. Chill for at least 3 hours.
7 Put the mould into hot water for a few moments, then turn charlotte out on to a serving dish. Pipe or spread the remaining cream on top of the charlotte and serve decorated with halved glacé cherries or marrons glacés.

Pineapple and ginger flan

The crumb crust makes a crunchy contrast with the soft topping in this sweet and spicy fruit flan

DESSERT Serves 6

Overall timing 30 minutes plus chilling

Equipment Plastic bag, rolling-pin. saucepan, 8 inch (20cm) flan dish, 2 bowls

Freezing Not recommended

INGREDIENTS

	Crumb crust	
6oz	Ginger biscuits	175g
3oz	Butter	75g
	Filling	
14½oz	Can of pineapple tidbits	411g
14oz	Can of sweetened condensed milk	397g
1	Lemon	1
2	Egg yolks	2
1oz	Plain dessert chocolate	25g

METHOD

1 Put the biscuits into a plastic bag and crush with a rolling-pin. Melt the butter in a saucepan, stir in the crumbs and mix well. Press the mixture down firmly over the base and up the sides of the flan dish. Chill till firm.
2 To make the filling, drain the pineapple. Tip the condensed milk into a bowl. Wash the lemon and grate the rind into the milk. Squeeze out the juice and stir into the milk with the drained pineapple. Add egg yolks and stir over gentle heat till mixture thickens.
3 Pour filling into the crumb case, smooth the surface, cool, then chill till set.
4 Melt the chocolate in a bowl over a pan of simmering water and trickle from a teaspoon or greaseproof paper bag in a random pattern over the filling. Allow to set before serving.

Mixed grill

An easy meal to serve whether it's for a workday evening or a party in the garden. During the week you can put the meat in the marinade overnight or first thing in the morning

LUNCH OR SUPPER Serves 4

Overall timing 20 minutes plus marination

Equipment Bowl, barbecue or grill

Freezing Not recommended

INGREDIENTS

2	Lambs kidneys	2
4	Slices of lambs liver	4
2 tbsp	Oil	2×15ml
1 tbsp	Lemon juice	1×15ml
	Salt and pepper	
2	Large tomatoes	2
4	Sausages	4
4	Lamb cutlets	4
4	Smoked bacon rashers	4

METHOD

1 Prepare kidneys, removing outer membrane and core, and cut in half. Put into a bowl with the liver, all but 1 teasp (5ml) of the oil, the lemon juice, salt and pepper. Leave to marinate for at least 1 hour, but the longer the better.
2 Preheat the grill or barbecue.
3 Cut tomatoes in half and brush with the reserved oil.
4 Drain kidneys and liver and arrange on barbecue or lined grill pan with the sausages and cutlets. Grill for about 10 minutes, turning them over frequently. Add bacon and cook for the last few minutes until crisp. Serve with coarse grained mustard.

barbecue know-how

There's a cut of lamb to suit any type of barbecue. In New Zealand, they use a whole lamb for a celebration *hangi*. A pit is dug and the base covered with stones.
A fire is lit on it and when the coals and stones are glowing, the lamb is placed on them, covered completely with leaves and sacks and left for 24 hours. The lamb is then cooked perfectly, and the party can begin.
If you don't want to dig up your garden and prefer to use home-made or bought equipment, it's best to choose chops. Double and single loin, and double and single cutlets are the best bet. Chump chops can also be used, or breast riblets. Or buy the small lamb knuckles (now available) which are shaped like chicken drumsticks.
Barbecued lamb is aided by marination. It flavours and tenderizes the meat and cuts down cooking time. Red or white wine can be used on its own or combined with other ingredients, or use wine vinegar if you prefer (it makes a good substitute – increase the quantities if necessary so that the chops are almost covered by the marinade). Leave the chops for 8 hours, and turn them occasionally. Before barbecuing, remove them from the marinade, then strain it and boil till reduced. Taste and adjust seasoning and thicken if necessary to make a sauce for the chops.

Below: Tasty mixed grill

Above: Pork with mustard sauce – an exquisitely simple meal with a real French flavour

Pork with mustard sauce

The famous Dijon mustard adds a sharp rather than hot taste to a rich, creamy sauce – here served with tender pieces of pork cut from the fillet

LUNCH OR SUPPER Serves 4

Overall timing 25 minutes

Equipment Greaseproof paper, frying pan

Freezing Not recommended

INGREDIENTS

4	Pork escalopes or boneless chops	4
½oz	Butter	15g
	Salt	
	Freshly-ground black pepper	
1	Shallot or small onion	1
1 tbsp	White wine vinegar	15ml
2 tbsp	Dijon mustard	2×15ml
½ pint	Carton of double cream	284ml
4	Gherkins	4
	Watercress	

METHOD

1 Wipe and trim the pork escalopes. Place between damp sheets of greaseproof paper and bat out with a rolling-pin.
2 Heat butter in a frying pan. Cook the pork escalopes for about 8 minutes on each side till tender and golden. Season and remove from pan. Arrange on a warmed serving dish and keep hot.
3 Peel and chop the shallot or onion and add to the pan. Fry for 5 minutes. Add the vinegar to the cooking juices and cook, stirring with a wooden spoon, till any sediment dissolves. Boil for 2 minutes, stirring constantly.
4 Remove pan from heat and add the mustard and cream. Mix well. Drain and slice the gherkins and add to the pan. Heat through without boiling. Season to taste. Pour the sauce over the pork.
5 Garnish with watercress and serve immediately with French fried potatoes and a lightly tossed green salad.

Green bean purée

An unusual vegetable dish that's a meal in itself when served with crusty wholemeal bread. For more substantial fare this dish makes an excellent accompaniment to grilled meats and sausages

Top and tail beans, removing strings as necessary. Cook in boiling salted water

When beans are cooked – about 10 minutes – drain well and purée them in a food mill

Put purée into a clean saucepan and blend in already-mashed potatoes with a spoon

Add butter to vegetable mixture, then stir in grated cheese and heat through gently

LUNCH OR SUPPER Serves 4

Overall timing 40 minutes

Equipment 2 saucepans, blender or vegetable mill

Freezing Pack in rigid container. Cover, seal, label and freeze. Freezer life: 3 months. To use: put block into saucepan and heat through gently. Adjust seasoning

INGREDIENTS

1lb	Potatoes	450g
	Salt	
2 tbsp	Single cream (optional)	2×15ml
1lb	Haricots verts	450g
2oz	Butter	50g
3 tbsp	Grated Parmesan or Gruyère	3×15ml
	Freshly-ground black pepper	

METHOD

1 Peel potatoes and cook in boiling salted water until tender. Drain well and mash adding cream if liked.
2 Wash and top and tail beans and, if necessary, remove strings. Cook in boiling salted water for 10 minutes. Drain well.
3 Purée beans in a blender or vegetable mill. Pour purée into a saucepan and blend in the mashed potatoes.
4 Add butter and Parmesan or Gruyère and heat through, stirring gently. Add salt and pepper to taste and serve alone with bread or with grilled meats.

Welsh rarebit

Mace adds piquancy to the topping made with melted cheese and beer

SUPPER OR SNACK Serves 4–8

Overall timing 30 minutes

Equipment Baking tray, saucepan

Freezing Not recommended

INGREDIENTS

8	Slices of bread	8
3oz	Butter	75g
12oz	Cheddar cheese	350g
$\frac{1}{2}$ teasp	Ground mace	$\frac{1}{2}$×5ml
	Pinch of powdered mustard	
5 tbsp	Beer	5×15ml
	Freshly-ground white pepper	

METHOD

1 Preheat the oven to 400F (200C) Gas 6.
2 Toast the bread, and butter the slices while still hot. Place on baking tray.
3 Cut the cheese into small cubes and put in saucepan with mace, mustard and beer. Cook over a low heat, stirring with a wooden spoon, until cheese melts and is thick and creamy.
4 Spread mixture over toast. Sprinkle generously with pepper and cook just above centre of the oven for 10 minutes. Serve immediately.

Stir the beer into the cheese cubes, mace, mustard and seasoning and melt till creamy

Spread the butter right to the crusts of the freshly made hot toast

Top the toast with the melted cheese mixture before heating through in the oven

Below: Welsh rarebit – famous Welsh toasted snack with added spice

Above: Potage Réjane – named after a famous French actress called Gabrielle Réjane

Potage Réjane

This can be made with four chicken wings instead of turkey if preferred

LUNCH OR SUPPER Serves 6

Overall timing $1\frac{1}{4}$ hours

Equipment Saucepan, frying pan

Freezing Not recommended

INGREDIENTS

1	Large carrot	1
1	Large onion	1
1	Stalk of celery	1
2	Turkey wings	2
$2\frac{1}{2}$ pints	Water	1.5 litres
	Salt	
	Freshly-ground black pepper	
8oz	Waxy potatoes	225g
2	Leeks	2
4	Thick slices bread	4
$1\frac{1}{2}$oz	Butter	40g
3 tbsp	Oil	3×15ml

METHOD

1. Scrape and chop the carrot, peel and chop the onion. Wash, trim and chop the celery.
2. Wipe the turkey wings and put into a saucepan with the prepared vegetables, water, salt and pepper. Bring to the boil, skim off any scum, cover and simmer for 45 minutes.
3. Peel potatoes and cut into $\frac{1}{2}$ inch (12.5mm) cubes. Wash, trim and slice leeks.
4. Lift turkey wings out of pan with a draining spoon and leave to cool slightly. Add potatoes and leeks to the soup and simmer for 5 minutes till vegetables are tender.
5. Remove the skin and bones from the turkey wings and cut the flesh into strips. Add to the soup and reheat gently.
6. Meanwhile, remove the crusts from bread and cut into cubes. Heat the oil and butter in a frying pan, add the bread and fry till golden all over. Drain on kitchen paper.
7. Taste soup and adjust seasoning. Pour into a warmed tureen and sprinkle with croûtons. Serve immediately.

cook's know-how

Culinary history is littered with soups named after the famous. Impoverished Prince Condé goes with a soup of puréed haricot beans, Henry IV of France earned his place with his Petite Marmite, while his wife Marie and her cousin Catherine de Medici are remembered in the beef consommé garnished with a carrot purée. Madame Du Barry, of Cordon-bleu fame, has cream of cauliflower soup. Consommés were named after opera singer Adelina Patti (garnished with baked egg custard and puréed chestnuts) and Swedish nightingale Jenny Lind (game consommé with strips of quail and sliced mushrooms). Georges Sand, friend of Chopin and Liszt, gave her name to fish consommé garnished with quenelles, morels, prawn butter and croûtons topped with carp roe while Sarah Bernhardt is linked to chicken consommé with chicken quenelles, truffles, asparagus tips, poached beef marrow and prawn butter!

Bacon and egg pie

A simple closed pie that uses frozen shortcrust pastry – a dish easily made from storecupboard ingredients and just as good hot, or cold served with a salad

LUNCH OR SUPPER Serves 6–8

Overall timing 1 hour

Equipment 8 inch (20cm) pie plate, bowl

Freezing Cook pie in foil plate. Cool, open freeze, then wrap in polythene, seal and label. Freezer life: 4 months. To use: thaw for 4 hours then reheat in a hot oven for 10–15 minutes

INGREDIENTS

13oz	Frozen shortcrust pastry	368g
4oz	Streaky bacon	125g
4	Eggs	4
4 tbsp	Milk	4×15ml
3 tbsp	Single cream	3×15ml
½ teasp	Salt	2.5ml
¼ teasp	White pepper	1.25ml

METHOD

1 Thaw the pastry. Preheat the oven to 425F (220C) Gas 7. Use two thirds of the pastry to line the pie plate. Cut the bacon into 2 inch (5cm) lengths and arrange on top of pastry.

2 In a bowl, beat together the eggs, milk, cream, salt and pepper and then pour over the bacon. Roll out the remaining pastry and use to cover filling. Press pastry edges together. Brush top of pie with any remaining egg or a little top of the milk.

3 Bake in oven for 10 minutes then reduce the temperature to 350F (180C) Gas 4 and cook for a further 30 minutes.

4 To save time serve the pie with tinned sweetcorn which can be quickly heated through and garnish with grilled tomatoes for a splash of colour. Alternatively leave the pie to cool and serve it cold with a salad for lunch or supper, or as excellent picnic fare.

Casseroled hearts

A classic method of casseroling with button onions and bacon adding flavour and moisture. The potatoes turn it into a satisfying meal

SUPPER Serves 4

Overall timing 1¾ hours

Equipment Flameproof casserole, saucepan, frying pan

Freezing Not recommended

INGREDIENTS

4	Lambs hearts *or*	4
2	calves hearts	2
4oz	Butter	125g
1 pint	Beef stock	560ml
	Bouquet garni	
6oz	Streaky bacon	175g
8oz	Button onions	225g
2lb	Potatoes	900g
2 tbsp	Oil	2×15ml
	Salt and pepper	
2 tbsp	Redcurrant jelly	2×15ml
1 tbsp	Chopped parsley	15ml

METHOD

1 To prepare hearts, trim away any fat and gristle, snip out the blood vessels, turn inside out and wash thoroughly. Pat dry with paper and turn right way round again. Heat 2oz (50g) butter in casserole, add hearts and brown on all sides. Pour in stock (made with cubes if necessary), add bouquet garni, cover and simmer for 1½ hours until tender.

2 Meanwhile, cut the streaky bacon into fine strips. Peel onions. Peel potatoes and cut into cubes.

3 Bring a saucepan of lightly salted water to the boil, add the onions and cook for 5 minutes, add the potatoes and cook for a further 5 minutes. Drain.

4 In frying pan, heat remaining butter and oil. Add streaky bacon and fry gently till golden, add potatoes, onions, salt and pepper. Cook till golden brown, turning mixture occasionally.

5 Remove hearts from casserole and place on warm serving dish. Keep hot. Reduce liquid in casserole over high heat to about ¼ pint (150ml), then stir in redcurrant jelly.

6 Pour over vegetables in frying pan, cook for 2 minutes, then remove vegetables and arrange around hearts. Spoon over cooking juices and serve sprinkled with parsley and with a side salad of watercress.

Below: Casseroled hearts – a mixture of hearts, potatoes, bacon and onions

Salt beef

If you want to buy salt beef from your butcher you usually have to order it specially, giving him at least two weeks notice to prepare the meat for you, so why not have the satisfaction of salting the joint yourself? Buy the saltpetre from a chemist and select a joint of beef from the butcher – flank, silverside, ribs and brisket are the best cuts to use. Make sure the meat is well rolled and tied at intervals with string so it keeps a good shape

MAIN MEAL Serves 8–10

Overall timing 3½ hours plus 2 weeks salting

Equipment 2 large saucepans (one with lid), deep non-metallic bowl or bucket

Freezing Not recommended

INGREDIENTS

2lb	Coarse salt	900g
4oz	Sugar	125g
1 tbsp	Saltpetre	15ml
1oz	Pickling spice	25g
4	Bay leaves	4
1	Sprig of thyme	1
8 pints	Water	4.5 litres
5lb	Boiling beef	2.3kg
3	Large onions	3
5	Cloves	5
1	Stalk of celery	1
1 teasp	Black peppercorns	5ml
1lb	Medium-size carrots	450g
2	Medium-size turnips	2
1lb	Leeks	450g

METHOD

1 Put the salt, sugar and saltpetre into a large saucepan with pickling spices tied in muslin. Add bay leaves, thyme and water and heat gently, stirring, till sugar and salt have dissolved. Bring to the boil, then pour into bowl or bucket and leave to cool.

2 Add meat to the bowl, making sure that the salt solution completely covers it. Cover with clean tea-towel and leave to soak in the fridge or a cold larder for up to 2 weeks. Turn meat occasionally.

3 To cook salted beef, remove from pickle and wash thoroughly under cold running water. Put into a large saucepan with one of the onions peeled and spiked with cloves. Wash and chop the celery and add to pan with peppercorns. Cover with cold water and bring to the boil slowly. Skim, reduce heat, cover with lid and simmer for 2½ hours.

4 Meanwhile, scrape and wash carrots, cut in half lengthways then cut into 2 inch (5cm) pieces. Peel turnips and cut into quarters. Peel remaining onions and slice thickly. Trim leeks, cut into 2 inch (5cm) lengths and wash.

5 Add vegetables to pan, bring back to the boil and simmer for 30 minutes.

6 Remove beef and vegetables, arrange on a warmed dish, cover and keep hot.

7 Use ½ pint (300ml) of strained cooking liquor and ½ pint (300ml) milk to make a white, mustard, parsley or horseradish sauce. Serve with meat and vegetables.

cook's know-how

Leftover meats and vegetables in too small quantities to be served again are ideal for soups. With a blender as basic equipment you never need throw food away. A chicken carcass will make good stock (recipe page 313), and the meat can also be added. All leftover vegetables – potatoes, peas, carrots, spinach – can be puréed and added to stock for a thick tasty soup. Hard heels of cheese, finely grated, will convert into fondue-like soups, while leftover bread can be crumbled and used as a thickener.

Below: Salt beef – serve hot with the mixed vegetables, the sauce, and mashed potatoes and gherkins. Any leftovers can be sliced very thinly and served cold with salads or used in soup (see cook's know-how above)

Guinea fowl with lentils

Lentils and tomatoes make an unusual moist accompaniment for the fowl – chicken could be used instead

MAIN MEAL Serves 4

Overall timing $1\frac{1}{4}$ hours

Equipment 2 saucepans, pastry brush, roasting tin

Freezing Not recommended

INGREDIENTS

8oz	Continental lentils	225g
3	Onions	3
	Bouquet garni	
	Salt and pepper	
$2\times1\frac{1}{2}$lb	Prepared guinea fowl	2×700g
4 tbsp	Oil	4×15ml
2oz	Butter	50g
4oz	Bacon rashers	125g
$\frac{1}{2}$ pint	Hot stock	300ml
2	Tomatoes	2
2 tbsp	Tomato paste	2×15ml

METHOD

1 Preheat oven to 400F (200C) Gas 6.
2 Wash and pick over lentils. Put into a saucepan with enough water to cover. Peel 1 of the onions and add to lentils with bouquet garni and seasoning. Simmer for 1 hour.
3 Season the fowls and brush the insides with half the oil using a pastry brush. Put into a roasting tin and rub the outsides of the fowls with butter. Stretch the derinded bacon rashers and drape over fowls. Secure with cocktail sticks.
4 Roast in the hot oven for 30 minutes, then baste and add the hot stock (made with a cube if necessary). Cook for a further 15 minutes, basting frequently.
5 Drain the lentils and remove onion and bouquet garni. Peel and finely chop the remaining 2 onions; skin and finely chop the tomatoes. Heat remaining oil in saucepan, add onions and tomatoes, cook until the onions are transparent.
6 Pour in $\frac{1}{4}$ pint (150ml) water and bring to the boil. Stir in the tomato paste, the pan juices from the guinea fowl and the crispy bacon broken into pieces. Boil until the liquid is reduced by half, then add the drained lentils and reheat them in the sauce. Stir well.
7 Serve with guinea fowl and a lightly dressed watercress and lettuce salad.

Above: Lamb curry – good contrast from tomatoes, capsicum, potatoes and mushrooms

Lamb curry

Splendid mix of textures which can take any curry blend you like

MAIN MEAL Serves 6

Overall timing $1\frac{1}{2}$ hours

Equipment Large frying pan

Freezing Cook for only $\frac{3}{4}$ of time. Cool, pack in rigid container, leaving $\frac{1}{2}$ inch (12.5mm) headspace. Cover, label and freeze. Freezer life: 3 months. To use: reheat slowly from frozen

INGREDIENTS

$1\frac{1}{4}$ pints	Stock	700ml
3lb	Boned shoulder of lamb	1.4kg
1oz	Butter	25g
3 tbsp	Oil	3×15ml
2	Large onions	2
1 tbsp	Curry powder	15ml
	Salt and pepper	
1oz	Plain flour	25g
1 teasp	Tomato paste	5ml
	Bouquet garni	
1	Large tomato	1
1	Green capsicum	1
4oz	Button mushrooms	125g
1lb	New potatoes	450g

METHOD

1 Prepare stock with cubes if necessary and allow to cool. Cut meat into cubes.
2 Heat butter and oil in a frying pan over a low heat. Peel and chop onions and add to pan. Cook gently till transparent.
3 Add curry powder and cook, stirring, for 2 minutes. Add meat and cook till golden on all sides. Season with salt and pepper, sprinkle with flour and stir over a high heat for a few minutes.
4 Reduce heat and stir in cold stock and tomato paste. Add bouquet garni and bring to the boil, stirring all the time. Cover and cook gently for 40 minutes, stirring from time to time.
5 Skin, deseed and chop tomato; wash, deseed and slice capsicum; wipe mushrooms and halve or slice the larger ones. Wash potatoes but don't peel; cut into chunks. Add all of these to pan and cook until the potatoes are tender. Discard bouquet garni and serve with plain boiled rice.

Macaroni with seafood

A substantial dish that combines creamy seafood sauce with pieces of long macaroni – or indeed any pasta of your choice. The sauce is best made with fish stock (see page 312) but vegetable or a light chicken stock would do instead

MAIN MEAL Serves 4

Overall timing 30 minutes

Equipment 2 saucepans

Freezing Not recommended

INGREDIENTS

1	Large onion	1
4 tbsp	Oil	4×15ml
1oz	Plain flour	25g
½ pint	Fish stock	300ml
3½oz	Jar of smoked mussels	98g
4oz	Can of shrimps	113g
6oz	Shelled prawns	175g
¼ pint	Carton of single cream	150ml
	Worcestershire sauce	
1 teasp	Lemon juice	5ml
½ teasp	Dried sage	2.5ml
½ teasp	Dried tarragon	2.5ml
	Salt	
	Freshly-ground black pepper	
12oz	Long macaroni	350g
1 tbsp	Chopped parsley	15ml

METHOD

1. Peel and chop onion. Heat oil in a saucepan, add onion and fry till transparent. Stir in flour and cook for 2 minutes. Gradually add stock. Bring to the boil, stirring constantly, then simmer for 3 minutes. Remove from heat.
2. Drain mussels and add to sauce with shrimps, prawns, cream, a few drops of Worcestershire sauce, lemon juice, sage and tarragon. Mix well. Taste and adjust seasoning.
3. Break macaroni into 3 inch (7.5cm) pieces. Put into a pan of boiling salted water and cook till al dente. Drain thoroughly and add to sauce. Heat through, without boiling, for 5 minutes, stirring occasionally.
4. Transfer mixture to warmed serving dish and sprinkle with the parsley. Serve immediately with tomato and onion salad.

Below: Macaroni with seafood – a luscious mixture of prawns, shrimps and smoked mussels

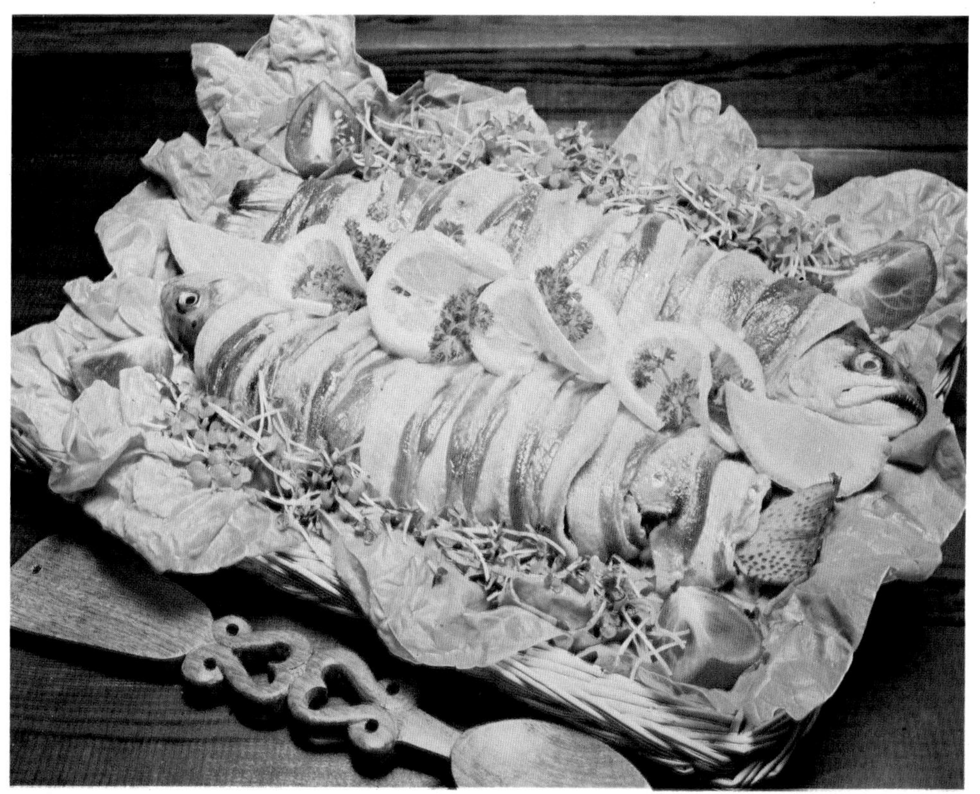

Above: Trout and bacon – streaky rashers replace mud which was once used in Wales when trout was cooked over an open fire

Trout and bacon

This colourful dish is a Welsh speciality. Streaky bacon and herb-flavoured butter keep the trout moist during baking. If you can't find the fresh herbs use a pinch of the dried varieties instead but do try to obtain fresh parsley – it does make a difference

LUNCH OR SUPPER Serves 2

Overall timing 45 minutes

Equipment Bowl, wooden cocktail sticks, shallow ovenproof dish, foil

Freezing Not recommended

INGREDIENTS

2×12oz	Trout	2×350g
1 teasp	Chopped sage	5ml
1 teasp	Chopped rosemary	5ml
1 teasp	Chopped thyme	5ml
1 tbsp	Chopped parsley	15ml
	Salt	
	Freshly-ground black pepper	
2oz	Softened butter	50g
4	Streaky bacon rashers	4

METHOD

1 Preheat the oven to 350F (180C) Gas 4.
2 Clean and wash the trout, pat dry on kitchen paper. Beat the herbs and seasoning into the butter and spread half inside each fish.
3 Derind and stretch the bacon. Wrap 2 rashers around each fish, securing with wooden cocktail sticks.
4 Place the trout in a greased ovenproof dish, cover with foil and bake in the centre of the oven for about 25 minutes till tender.
5 Remove the cocktail sticks, place the trout on a serving dish and garnish with lemon slices and sprigs of parsley. Surround with lettuce leaves, mustard and cress and tomato wedges and serve immediately. Plain boiled potatoes, cooked with their skins on if they are new potatoes, would be a good accompaniment.

Fish dumplings

Delicately-flavoured fish dumplings served in a creamy cheese sauce

LUNCH OR SUPPER Serves 4

Overall timing 45 minutes plus chilling

Equipment Blender, bowl, 2 saucepans, piping bag with plain nozzle (optional), ovenproof dish

Freezing Pack into rigid container, cover, label and freeze. Freezer life: 1 month. To use: reheat from frozen in oven at 350F (180C) Gas 4

INGREDIENTS

1lb	Mixed fish fillets	450g
2	Egg whites	2
	Salt and pepper	
	Cayenne pepper	
2 tbsp	Single cream	2×15ml
	Sauce	
$2\frac{1}{2}$oz	Butter	65g
1 tbsp	Plain flour	15ml
1 pint	Cold milk	560ml
2oz	Grated Gruyère	50g
1 tbsp	Single cream	15ml
	Salt and pepper	

METHOD

1 Skin and wipe fish fillets. Cut into small pieces and put into a blender for a few seconds to make a thick purée.
2 Turn mixture into a bowl and beat in egg whites with a wooden spoon. Season with salt, pepper and a pinch of cayenne, then beat in the cream. Place in fridge for at least 1 hour.
3 Preheat oven to 425F (220C) Gas 7. Bring a pan of salted water to the boil. Using 2 spoons, make egg shapes from the fish mixture and carefully lower them, one at a time, into the simmering water. Alternately, you can use a piping bag and then pipe mixture in short lengths into the water. Cook for 8–10 minutes, turning once. Remove from pan with a draining spoon, drain on kitchen paper and arrange in an ovenproof dish.
4 To make the sauce, melt 2oz (50g) of the butter in a pan. Stir in the flour and cook for 2 minutes. Gradually add the milk and bring to the boil, stirring. Cook over a low heat for 5 minutes. Remove from heat and stir in the cheese and cream. Season with salt and pepper.
5 Pour sauce into the ovenproof dish. Dot with remaining butter and bake in oven for about 10 minutes, or until the top is golden brown and bubbling.

Storecupboard sense

Canned, bottled and dried foods, apart from being major standbys, are also an investment on which you expect to draw when needed. This is especially true if you buy in bulk and, having saved money, you don't want to make the mistake of leaving foods too long on the shelf so they have deteriorated by the time you use them.

Modern preserving methods, along with strict hygiene regulations, ensure that most foods have a long shelf life. The only real problems occur with foods that don't have a "best by" or "eat by" date because you can't be sure how long they've been on the shop's shelves before you buy them. Pulses (dried beans, peas, lentils) age unnoticeably and if they have been around too long no amount of soaking and cooking is going to make them tender and tasty. Buying from shops with a quick turnover is a good rule for foods you intend to store. Label them immediately with date of purchase and, when you store them, bring existing stocks to the front.

Lengths of shelf life always vary and manufacturers err on the safe side because they cannot control storage conditions. Ideally cupboards should be cool (no warmer than 70F/21C) without any damp or moisture to rust cans and lids or spoil ingredients in paper packs.

Removing foods from their wrappings can extend the shelf life – staples such as flour, salt and sugar are best stored in moistureproof containers. Herbs and spices, often bought in too great a quantity for quick use, keep their aromas and flavours better in dark glass screw-top jars. Air and light also have an adverse effect on oil which needs the protection of a metal airtight container. When buying cans to store, avoid any with dents or rust on top or bottom rims. A raised surface at either end can mean that the contents have started to ferment – watch for this when buying acidic foods.

FOOD	STORAGE TIME	IDEAL STORAGE	SIGNS OF DETERIORATION
baked beans/spaghetti	1 year	DCP	dents, rust on can
baking powder/cream of tartar/bicarb of soda	1 year	CC, DCP	won't bubble when 1 teasp (5ml) is mixed with 3fl oz (90ml) hot water
biscuits, packet	6 months	DCP	musty smell, become soft/crumbly
bread mix	3 months	DCP	bag inflates
breadcrumbs	1 year	DCP, AC if opened	musty smell
cake mix	6 months	DCP	loss of flavour when cooked
chestnuts, purée	2 years	DCP	dents, rust on can
water, brined	1 year	DCP	lose crunchiness
chocolate, cooking	6 months	TW, DCP	bloom forms, becomes crumbly
powder	1 year	ST, DCP	dries out, loses flavour
cereals, breakfast	3 months	DCP, AC if opened	become soft, lose flavour
bran/wheatgerm	2–6 months	AC, DCP/fridge	rancid smell, weevils
rice/sago/semolina/tapioca	1 year	CC, DCP	stale smell, taste
cocoa	indefinitely	ST, DCP	loses volatile oil, flavour
coconut, creamed	6 months	DCP	rancid smell
desiccated	1 year	AC, DCP	becomes dry, tasteless
coffee, instant	2 years	AC, DCP	absorbs moisture
beans	6 months	AC, DCP	lose flavour
cream, sterilized	6 months	DCP	loses texture, becomes watery
custard, canned	6 months	DCP	loses texture
powder	1 year	ST, DCP	absorbs moisture
desserts/toppings, dried	6 months	TW, DCP	made-up dish not as intended
eggs	3–4 weeks	carton in fridge	become stale, bad
	2 weeks	room temperature	become stale, bad
pickled	indefinitely	DCP	liquid evaporates, changes colour
fats, hydrogenated	1 year	DCP	surface cracks from drying
margarine, tubs	6 months	CC in fridge	surface cracks from drying
block	3 months	TW in fridge	becomes darker, can dry
butter, salted	1 month	TW in fridge	can become rancid
unsalted	3 months	TW in fridge	loses flavour
suet, packet	2 years	DCP, CC if opened	becomes very greasy
fish, pastes	1 year	DCP	become over salty
anchovies/sardines/pilchards, in oil	indefinitely	DCP turn over every so often	not noticeable
in tomato sauce	1 year	DCP	lose texture
herrings/mackerel/salmon/tuna/roes	2 years	DCP	lose texture, become over salty
flour, white	6–9 months	CC, DCP	musty smell
wholemeal	2 months	CC, DCP	rancid smell, weevils
	6 months	fridge	rancid smell
cornflour/arrowroot	2 years	CC, DCP	musty smell
food colourings/essences	indefinitely	ST, DCP	evaporate, lose flavour
fruit, canned/bottled in syrup	2 years	DCP	loses flavour, texture
prunes/rhubarb	1 year	DCP	high acid may affect can
berries, canned	6 months	DCP	lose flavour, texture
citrus segments/juice	1 year	DCP	high acid may affect can
crystallized/glacé	indefinitely	DCP	hardness, stickiness (can be washed)
dried	1 year	CC, DDCP	may dry out/ferment
in spirits	indefinitely	CC, DDCP	may lose texture
gelatine, granules/sheets/strips	indefinitely	AC, DCP	absorb moisture; can absorb flavours from cupboard, other foods
aspic, sachet	6 months	DCP	loses quality
herbs	6 months	DGAC, DCP	musty smell, lose flavour
honey	indefinitely	AC, DCP	can crystallize, harden
horseradish, creamed	6 months	DCP	loses flavour
relish with vinegar	1 year	DCP	becomes sour tasting
ice cream mix, dried	6 months	DCP	absorbs moisture
jam/marmalade	2 years	ST, DCP	shrinks in jar

FOOD	STORAGE TIME	IDEAL STORAGE	SIGNS OF DETERIORATION
jellies, packet	1 year	TW, DCP	not noticeable
juices, concentrated	6 months	DCP	flavour alters, may change colour
lemon curd	3 months	DCP	separates, mould can form
opened	1 month	ST, fridge	separates
malt, powder	indefinitely	ST	dries out, becomes hard
marzipan (almond paste)	2 years	TW in AC	can become rancid
mayonnaise, bought	1 year	ST, DCP, in fridge if opened	dries out
meats, canned	18 months	DCP	dents, rust on can
ham	6 months	DCP/fridge	dents, rust on can
meringues, packet	6 months	CC, DCP	become crumbly, tasteless
milk, dried non-fat	1 year	ST, DCP	reconstitutes unevenly
condensed	6 months	DCP	loses texture
evaporated	6 months	DCP	darkens, becomes thick
sterilized	3 months	DCP	air causes souring
opened	3 days	fridge	air causes souring
longlife	6 months	DCP	air causes souring
opened	3 days	fridge	air causes souring
mincemeat, bottled	indefinitely	DDCP	shrinks in jar
mushrooms, dried	6 months	DDCP	become smelly, absorb moisture
mustard, ready mixed	18 months	ST, DCP	dries out, loses flavour
nuts, in shells	1 year	DDCP	mould can form
canned	1 year	ST, DCP	become soft
chopped/ground	6 months	AC, DCP	become rancid
oils, cooking/salad	1 year	MC, DCP	air and light cause "off" flavour
olives, canned	1 year	DCP	dents, rust on can
bottled	2 years	DDCP	evaporation of liquid
pasta	2 years	DCP	loses flavour
stuffed	1 year	AC, DCP	loses flavour
peanut butter	1 year	ST, DCP	develops off flavour
peppercorns, whole	2 years	DGAC	lose pungency
brined	2 years	ST, DDCP	colour bleaches out
pickles	indefinitely	ST, DDCP	liquid evaporates/contents shrink
popcorn	1 year	AC, DCP	won't pop, absorbs moisture
pulses (dried peas/ beans/lentils)	1 year	CC, DCP	won't soften when cooked
rennet, extract	4 months	ST, DCP	loses power
tablets	2 years	CC, DCP	lose power
salt	indefinitely	CC, DCP	absorbs moisture
sauces, bottled	1 year	DCP	lose flavour, thicken
shellfish, canned	1 year	DCP	rust on can
in oil/smoked	2 years	DCP	lose texture
in tomato sauce	1 year	DCP	lose texture
in vinegar, bottled	2 years	DCP	evaporation, cloudy liquid
soups, canned meat	6–9 months	DCP	lose flavour
canned vegetable	1 year	DCP	lose flavour
dried	18 months	DCP	lose flavour
spices	1 year	DGAC, DCP	lose effectiveness
stock cubes	6 months	AC, DCP	absorb moisture
stuffings, packet	1 year	TW, DCP	lose flavour
sugar	2 years	CC, DCP	absorbs moisture/hardens
syrups, canned/bottled	indefinitely	ST, DDCP	change in colour, flavour
tea, packets/tins	2 years	DCP	loses flavour
open	1 year	AC, DCP	loses flavour, becomes musty
tomatoes, canned	1 year	DCP	high acid may affect can
paste	1 year	ST, DCP	thickens, changes colour
vegetables, canned	2 years	DCP	loss of quality
bottled	3 years	DDCP	evaporation of liquid
dried, sachets	1 year	AC, DCP	loss of flavour
in brine	1 year	DDCP	loss of quality
vinegar	indefinitely	ST, DCP	sediment, strands in liquid (strain and rebottle)
yeast, dried	6 months	CC, DCP	won't froth

cook's know-how

Foods from the storecupboard can be used on their own for snacks, or combined with others to make meals. They also can be used with fresh foods (eg, canned soups as sauces for braised or steam roasted meat). When you're only cooking for yourself, or for two, smaller cans make more sense than larger, though larger ones can be used and half the dish saved for the next day. Canned vegetables bulk out left-over casseroles; drained and dressed with vinaigrette or mayonnaise (both storecupboard ingredients) they become quick salads. In terms of nutrition, we all need fresh foods and cannot live by cans alone – the simple addition of grated cheese adds substance to dried or canned soup; an egg beaten into instant mash, custard made with powder, or canned rice pudding, instantly enriches as does milk in jellies and soups. Fresh fruit mixed with canned makes an excellent fruit salad and you don't have to worry about making a syrup.

Abbreviations: CC covered container; AC airtight container; ST sealed tightly; TW tightly wrapped; DCP dry cool place; DDCP dark dry cool place; DGAC dark glass airtight container; MC metal airtight container

Chicken for the freezer

The flesh of chicken combines well with different ingredients, the bones give you a supply of chicken stock for soup or gravy, and the livers can be collected to be made into pâté at a later stage. The chickens should be fresh as frozen chicken cannot be thawed, then returned to the freezer uncooked. Four chickens plus a few vegetables and some storecupboard bits and pieces will give you six tasty dishes to store in the freezer to take out and serve over a period of 3 months and stock to last for 6 months

Preparing the chickens

Remove the giblets. Separate livers, place in small rigid container, cover, label and freeze. Freezer life: 3 months.

Wash rest of giblets and reserve. Wipe chickens inside and out. Cut through skin between leg and carcass and push legs away from body to expose joint. Sever and remove the legs, then divide into drumsticks for Spicy grilled drumsticks, and thighs for Chicken and pineapple curry. Cut through skin and flesh along breast-bone of each bird. Slip knife under flesh to one side of the bone and gradually detach breast from ribs and wings to give 8 boneless breasts – use 4 for Stuffed chicken breasts and 4 for Chicken and tarragon parcels.

Put remainder of chicken into large saucepan with giblets, peeled onion, scraped carrot, bay leaf and trimmed stalk of celery. Bring slowly to boil. Skim, then reduce heat and simmer for 45 minutes. Lift out carcasses, remove meat and reserve for Chicken and sweetcorn fricassée. Return bones to pan and simmer for 1 hour more. Strain stock, return to pan and boil till reduced to one-third. Cool quickly, pour into ice-cube trays and freeze. When frozen pack into polybag, seal and label. Freezer life: 6 months.

Stuffed chicken breasts

Ingredients 4 boneless chicken breasts; 4oz (125g) Roquefort cheese; 2 tbsp (2×15ml) single cream; 4 tbsp (4×15ml) plain flour; 2 eggs; 6oz (175g) fine breadcrumbs

Method Remove skin from chicken breasts (reserve to use in stock). Using a sharp knife, make deep horizontal cut along one side of each chicken breast to make a pocket. Beat Roquefort and cream till smooth and divide between each pocket. Close pockets with wooden cocktail sticks. Coat the chicken with flour. Beat eggs on a plate, spread breadcrumbs on greaseproof paper. Dip chicken into the egg to coat both sides, then press crumbs on firmly.

To freeze Place the coated chicken on a foil-lined baking tray, cover lightly and open freeze. Wrap each in foil, pack into polybag. Seal and label. Freezer life: 1 month.

To use Unwrap, place on baking tray and thaw in fridge for 4–6 hours. Heat oil in a deep-fryer to 320F (160C) and fry chicken breasts for about 10 minutes till golden. Drain on kitchen paper, remove cocktail sticks and serve. **Serves 4**

Chicken and sweetcorn fricassée

Ingredients 12oz–1lb (350–450g) cooked chicken; 1 large onion; 4oz (125g) button mushrooms; 2oz (50g) butter; 3 tbsp (3×15ml) plain flour; ½ pint (300ml) milk; ¼ pint (150ml) strong chicken stock; 8oz (225g) frozen sweetcorn kernels; salt; freshly-ground black pepper

Method Cut the chicken into neat pieces, removing any skin and bones (reserve them to use in stock). Peel and chop the onion, wipe, trim and slice the mushrooms. Heat the butter in a large saucepan and fry the onion gently till transparent. Add the mushrooms and fry for a further 3 minutes. Sprinkle the flour over and cook for 1 minute. Gradually add the milk and stock and bring to the boil, stirring. Add chicken and corn, mix well and season. Cool quickly.

To freeze Place a polybag inside a saucepan, pour the fricassée in, seal and freeze till hard. Remove, overwrap, label. Freezer life: 1 month.

To use Remove from bag, replace block in pan and heat gently, stirring occasionally. Stir in ¼ pint (150ml) single cream and 1 tbsp (15ml) chopped parsley. Garnish with grilled bacon rolls and serve. **Serves 4**

Chicken and tarragon parcels

Ingredients 1 onion; 4oz (125g) streaky bacon rashers; 4oz (125g) butter; 4 boneless chicken breasts; 1 tbsp (15ml) chopped tarragon; salt; freshly-ground black pepper

Method Peel and chop the onion, derind and dice the bacon. Heat 1oz (25g) of the butter in a frying pan and fry the onion and bacon till golden. Cut four 10 inch (25cm) squares of foil and sprinkle each with a quarter of onion and bacon. Arrange a chicken breast on top of each. Beat the remaining butter till soft, mix in the tarragon and seasoning, then spread over the chicken breasts. Bring two opposite sides of foil to centre and roll edges together to seal well.

To freeze Place in polybag, seal, label and freeze. Freezer life: 2 months.

To use Remove parcels from bag, arrange on baking tray and bake from frozen at 375F (190C) Gas 5 for about 45 minutes till chicken is tender. Serve chicken in the parcels with creamed potatoes, broccoli spears and carrot sticks. **Serves 4**

Spicy grilled drumsticks

Ingredients 8 chicken drumsticks; ½ teasp (2.5ml) each of curry powder, ground cumin, ground coriander and turmeric; juice of 2 lemons; wine vinegar; 4 tbsp (4×15ml) oil

Method Prick each chicken drumstick several times with a fork. Mix spices together and rub into chicken. Place in a shallow rigid container. Measure lemon juice in a jug and add equal quantity of vinegar and the oil. Mix well, then pour over the chicken to cover it. (If it doesn't, make up more marinade.)

To freeze Cover container, seal and label. Freezer life: 1 month.

To use Thaw overnight in fridge, then pour off two-thirds of the marinade. Add 5oz (141g) natural yogurt and 1 teasp (5ml) salt, turn chicken in it till coated, then leave for 20 minutes. Preheat grill, line grill pan with foil. Arrange drumsticks on pan, grill for about 10 minutes, turning frequently till browned all over. Serve immediately with boiled rice and mango chutney. **Serves 4**

Chicken and pineapple curry

Ingredients 2oz (50g) butter; 2 tbsp (2×15ml) oil; 8 chicken thighs; 2 large onions; 1 tbsp (15ml) Madras curry powder; 1 tbsp (15ml) plain flour; ½ pint (300ml) chicken stock; 8oz (227g) can of pineapple pieces; 2 tbsp (2×15ml) mango chutney

Method Heat the butter and oil in a large saucepan. Fry the chicken thighs, a few at a time, turning frequently till browned all over. Remove from pan and reserve. Peel and thinly slice the onions. Add to the pan and fry gently till transparent. Sprinkle the curry powder and flour over and fry for 1 minute. Gradually stir in the stock and bring to the boil, stirring. Return chicken to pan with the pineapple and juice and the chutney. Bring to the boil and simmer for 20 minutes.

To freeze Cool quickly. Line saucepan with polybag, pour curry in, push meat down into the sauce. Seal and freeze till hard. Remove from pan, label. Freezer life: 3 months.

To use Remove bag, replace block in pan and stir over low heat till boiling. Adjust seasoning, serve immediately with boiled rice. **Serves 4**

Countdown

Potted liver
Lobster Thermidor
Boiled rice
Venetian-style green beans
Melon on the rocks
Macaroons

Just occasionally there's a good reason for a really special dinner. However, you don't want to spend too much time in the kitchen so this menu needs very little last-minute work except for the lobster. The beans would be just as good served cold as a salad and as such could be prepared well in advance. The potted liver makes a delicious spread for toast or canapés so you could make double the quantity and keep half for another day

The morning before or earlier Make the macaroons. Once cool, store in an airtight tin. Make the potted liver and chill in fridge

2 hours before Prepare melon and chill in the fridge

1¼ hours before, or much earlier if you wish to serve the bean dish cold, prepare green beans and cook over a low heat for 1 hour

35 mins before Start preparing and cooking lobster

20 mins before While lobster sauce is simmering put rice on to boil

10 mins before Wash and dry lobster shells, fill with sauce and place under a hot grill

5 mins before Test beans to see if cooked, remove from heat and keep warm

Serve potted liver while lobster is under the grill. Alternatively fill the shells with the sauce and put aside. Then grill when the first course is finished

Serve lobster with plain boiled rice and green beans or serve the vegetable dish, hot or cold, after the lobster, as they do in France. Finish melon dish (Step 2) just before serving with macaroons

A full-bodied dry white wine should be served with this meal. A white Côtes du Rhône or a Graves would be a good choice and of course it needs to be well chilled.

Potted liver

A well-flavoured pâté made with tender lambs or calves liver and baked in individual ramekins. The mixture is enriched with brandy and cream, and the anchovy fillet is added to provide a subtly piquant taste. This pâté freezes well so you could double the quantities and freeze half for later

STARTER — Serves 2

Overall timing 1 hour plus chilling

Equipment Mincer, bowl, 2 ramekins, roasting tin, foil

Freezing Make liver paste in foil-lined ovenproof dish, cook for 1½ hours. When cold, turn out, wrap in foil, put in polythene bag, seal, label and freeze. Freezer life: 1 month. To use: unwrap, return to dish and thaw overnight in fridge or 6–8 hours at room temperature

INGREDIENTS

½lb	Lambs *or* calves liver	225g
1oz	Lean bacon	25g
1	Small bay leaf	1
1	Desalted anchovy fillet	1
1	Small onion	1
1	Egg	1
2 tbsp	Fresh breadcrumbs	2×15ml
	Salt	
	Freshly-ground black pepper	
1 tbsp	Single cream	15ml
1 tbsp	Brandy	15ml

METHOD

1 Preheat the oven to 400F (200C) Gas 6. Trim, wipe and chop the liver. Derind and dice bacon. Soak anchovy in milk or water for 15 minutes to desalt, then pat dry. Finely mince the liver, bacon, bay leaf, peeled onion and anchovy twice into a bowl.
2 Add the egg, breadcrumbs, seasoning, cream and brandy to the mixture and mix well.
3 Divide the mixture between the ramekins and smooth surface. Cover each ramekin with foil and place in roasting tin containing 1 inch (2.5cm) water. Cook in the centre of the oven for about 45 minutes.
4 Remove from oven and leave to cool at room temperature. When cool, place in fridge to chill for 2–3 hours. When ready, serve potted liver in individual ramekins with toast or fresh bread.

Lobster Thermidor

Though the French revolutionaries' name for November didn't catch on, it lives on in this classic and probably most famous lobster dish

SUPPER — Serves 2

Overall timing 35 minutes

Equipment Kitchen scissors, 2 saucepans

Freezing Not recommended

INGREDIENTS

1×1½lb	Cooked lobsters	1×700g
1oz	Butter	25g
1 tbsp	Plain flour	15ml
5 tbsp	Double cream	5×15ml
¼ pint	Fish stock (recipe page 312)	150ml
	Salt	
	Pinch of paprika	
	Pinch of celery salt	
	Pinch of cayenne	
	Topping (optional)	
1oz	Butter	25g
1 tbsp	White wine	15ml
1½oz	Fresh breadcrumbs	40g
1oz	Grated Parmesan	25g

METHOD

1 Use kitchen scissors or a sharp knife to cut centrally through the underside of the lobster (or cut in half if you prefer). Remove the flesh from the body and legs and chop it into ½ inch (12.5mm) pieces.
2 Melt butter in saucepan and when frothy, stir in flour and cook for 1 minute. Gradually add cream and stock, stirring constantly over gentle heat till well combined. Add lobster flesh, salt, paprika, celery salt and cayenne. Simmer for 10 minutes stirring frequently. Remove from heat.
3 Preheat grill.
4 Wash and dry lobster shells, fill with lobster sauce and place under hot grill for 10 minutes. Alternatively, heat butter and wine, stir in breadcrumbs and Parmesan and when all liquid is absorbed, sprinkle over lobster mixture. Grill till crisp and golden. Serve with plain boiled rice.

Right: Lobster Thermidor – delicious with or without the cheese and crumb topping

Above: Venetian-style green beans – dressed with a luscious tomato and herb sauce

Venetian-style green beans

A bean dish from Northern Italy with a sauce made from fresh tomatoes, onion and a delicious mixture of herbs. Luckily, when tomatoes are expensive in the winter, the sauce can be made from canned tomatoes. This dish can be served equally well hot, or cold as a salad

VEGETABLE Serves 2–3

Overall timing 1¼ hours

Equipment Flameproof casserole

Freezing Cook, cool quickly then pack, label and freeze. Freezer life: 3 months. To use: turn into a pan and heat through gently or serve cold

INGREDIENTS

12oz	Runner or French green beans	300g
½lb	Fresh tomatoes *or*	225g
8oz	can of tomatoes	227g
1	Small onion	1
1oz	Butter	25g
1 tbsp	*or* oil	1×15ml
1	Small garlic clove	1
	Bouquet garni	
	Pinch dried oregano *or* marjoram	
	Salt and pepper	

METHOD

1 Wash beans. Top and tail them and remove strings. If using fresh tomatoes, blanch in boiling water then peel and chop them (or chop canned tomatoes). Peel and chop the onion.
2 Heat the butter or oil in the casserole and lightly brown the onion.
3 Add beans, tomatoes, crushed garlic, bouquet garni, oregano or marjoram, and salt and pepper to taste. Cover and simmer over a very low heat for 1 hour. If necessary add a little boiling water during cooking to prevent sticking.

Macaroons

Almond flavoured biscuits that can be eaten on their own or as an accompaniment to a dessert. The recipe makes a quantity but this isn't a problem as the biscuits store well

TEA-TIME OR DESSERT Makes 28

Overall timing 2½ hours

Equipment Mixing bowl, baking trays, rice paper

Freezing Not recommended

Storage Airtight tin

INGREDIENTS

2	Egg whites	2
6oz	Caster sugar	175g
5oz	Ground almonds	150g
	Grated rind of 1 small orange	
	Grated rind of 1 small lemon	
	Small pinch of salt	
½ teasp	Ground cinnamon	½×5ml
	Pinch of ground cardamom (optional)	
	Flour for dusting	

Below: Macaroons – make a batch for storing

METHOD
1 Preheat the oven to 275F (140C) Gas 1.
2 Beat the egg whites in a bowl until stiff. Gradually beat in caster sugar, a little at a time. Stir in the almonds, orange and lemon rind, salt and spices.
3 Cut out 28 small circles about 2 inches (5cm) in diameter from the rice paper and place on floured baking trays. Alternatively, line trays with whole sheets of rice paper.
4 Place a heaped teaspoonful of mixture on to each circle leaving a margin all round, or place spoonfuls at intervals.
5 Put on the middle and lower shelves of the oven and leave for 1½–2 hours – the macaroons are dried rather than actually cooked. Halfway through, swap trays round.
6 When done, remove from oven and leave to cool on baking trays. Break paper from around each macaroon if using rice paper sheets.

VARIATION
For a nuttier and fruitier version, reduce the caster sugar to 3oz (75g), replace the ground almonds with 4oz (125g) finely chopped almonds and the fruit rind and spices with 2oz (50g) chopped dried figs and 2oz (50g) seedless raisins. Beat the egg whites with the salt, stir in the caster sugar and fold in the dried fruit and almonds. Place on rice paper as above then cook on middle shelf of oven heated to 300F (150C) Gas 2 for 30 minutes. Leave to cool on tray and dust with icing sugar before serving.

Melon on the rocks

The simplest of desserts that can be prepared in advance. Serve it on crushed ice for best effect

DESSERT Serves 2

Overall timing 15 minutes plus chilling

Equipment Glass bowl

Freezing Not recommended

INGREDIENTS

1	Ripe cantaloup melon	1
1 tbsp	Caster sugar	1×15ml
2 tbsp	Rum, Kirsch *or* Maraschino	2×15ml
	Crushed ice	

Above: Melon on the rocks – the cantaloup in the picture is also known as rockmelon or netted melon because of the skin pattern

METHOD
1 Cut the melon into quarters and discard the seeds. Remove the flesh and cut into neat chunks. Put into a glass bowl and sprinkle with sugar. Mix gently and chill in the fridge for at least 2 hours.
2 Pour the rum, Kirsch or Maraschino over and mix well. Divide between individual glass dishes and sink each into a larger dish containing the crushed ice. Prepare this by crushing the ice cubes, placed in a polythene bag, with a rolling pin. Serve immediately.

VARIATION
In Australia, rockmelon is served very simply as a dessert. Cut the rockmelon in half widthways (allow 1 half for each person) and remove and discard the seeds, being careful to leave behind the juices in the bowl of the melon. Sprinkle with caster sugar and chill for 2 hours. To serve, pile scoops of ice cream into each melon half.

Left: Potato gnocchi – tiny buttered dumplings with Parmesan and a sprinkling of nutmeg

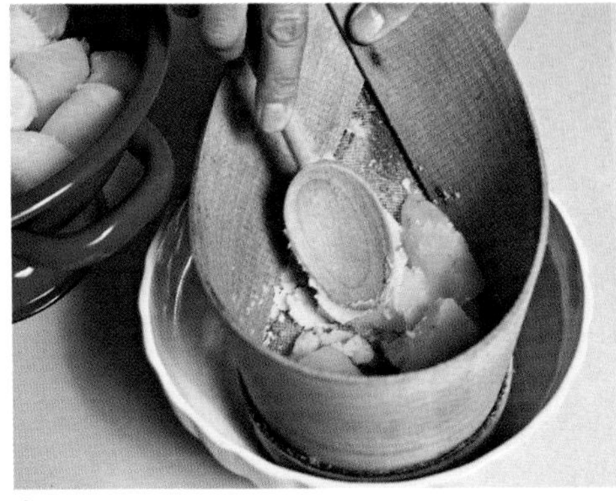

1 Drain and peel the cooked potatoes and press through a sieve into a large bowl

2 Add sifted flour and baking powder and mix together well with a wooden spoon

3 Beat in the eggs and seasoning, then spread mixture on plate and chill till firm

4 Drop small amounts into simmering salted water and cook till they rise to the surface

Potato gnocchi

Gnocchi are small savoury dumplings made from flour, semolina or potato and poached for a few minutes in simmering salted water till they rise to the surface. Potato gnocchi with butter, Parmesan and nutmeg make a delicious hot starter – they can also be served as a vegetable

STARTER Serves 6

Overall timing $1\frac{1}{2}$ hours plus chilling

Equipment 3 saucepans, sieve, large bowl, plate

Freezing Not recommended

INGREDIENTS

2lb	Floury potatoes	900g
	Salt	
8oz	Plain flour	225g
1 teasp	Baking powder	5ml
2	Eggs	2
	Freshly-ground black pepper	
2oz	Butter	50g
3 tbsp	Grated Parmesan	3×15ml
	Freshly-grated nutmeg	

METHOD

1 Scrub the potatoes and put into a saucepan of cold salted water. Bring to the boil and simmer for about 30 minutes till tender. Drain, peel and press through a sieve into a large bowl.
2 Sift the flour and baking powder together, add to the potatoes and mix in with a wooden spoon. Beat in the eggs and seasoning. Spread out on a plate and chill for 2–3 hours till firm.
3 Bring a large pan of salted water to the boil, reduce heat till simmering. Put teaspoonfuls of the mixture into the water and cook for about 4 minutes or till they rise to the surface.
4 Remove with a draining spoon, pile in a serving dish and keep hot while you cook the rest.
5 Melt the butter in a small saucepan and trickle over the gnocchi. Sprinkle with Parmesan and nutmeg and serve immediately.

VARIATIONS

If liked, layer cooked dumplings in an ovenproof dish with slices of cheese and a little butter and brown them under a hot grill or in the oven for 5–10 minutes at 425F (220C) Gas 7. You can serve gnocchi with meat or tomato sauce as the Italians do, or top them with a cheesy Béchamel sauce.

Bortch

One of the many versions of the famous soup which originated in Russia. In this one, meat makes the soup a substantial meal

STARTER OR LUNCH Serves 6

Overall timing $2\frac{1}{4}$ hours

Equipment Large casserole, small saucepan

Freezing When cold, ladle soup into a rigid container, allowing $\frac{3}{4}$ inch (2cm) headspace. Cover, label and freeze. Freezer life: 3 months. To use: turn into a saucepan and gently bring to the boil

INGREDIENTS

1	Onion	1
3	Carrots	3
4	Stalks of celery	4
1	Leek	1
1lb	Braising steak	450g
6oz	White cabbage	175g
1oz	Butter	25g
1 tbsp	Plain flour	15ml
2 tbsp	Vinegar	2×15ml
2	Tomatoes	2
6oz	Cooked beetroot	175g
2 tbsp	Chopped parsley	2×15ml
4 tbsp	Soured cream	4×15ml

METHOD

1 Peel and roughly chop the onion. Scrape the carrots, then cut into matchstick lengths. Roughly chop the celery. Wash and chop the leek.

2 Place the vegetables in a large saucepan with the beef and $1\frac{3}{4}$ pints (1 litre) water. Cover and cook for $1\frac{1}{2}$ hours over a medium heat.

3 Meanwhile, wash and shred the cabbage and place in a small saucepan. Cook with the butter over a low heat until the cabbage softens, then stir in the flour and vinegar. Mix cabbage into the soup.

4 Blanch tomatoes, remove skins then peel and chop. Peel and dice beetroot. Remove the meat from the soup. Cut it into large cubes, discarding any fat. Return the meat to the soup with the tomatoes, beetroot and parsley.

5 Cover and simmer gently for a further 30 minutes. The bortsch may be served with or without soured cream and chopped parsley.

Right: Bortsch – famous Russian soup made from beetroot and cabbage

Above: Buckling and potato salad – an attractive and tasty mixture

Buckling and potato salad

There's more to this dish than meets the eye! The strong flavour of the buckling – smoked herring – combines well with the bland potato, and crunch and colour comes from dessert apples, eggs and tomatoes. It's a dish that looks attractive with little effort.

STARTER OR LIGHT LUNCH Serves 4–6

Overall timing 30 minutes

Equipment 2 bowls

Freezing Not recommended

INGREDIENTS

3	Buckling	3
8oz	Cooked potatoes	225g
8oz	Red apples	225g
	Dressing	
4 tbsp	Olive oil	4×15ml
3 tbsp	Lemon juice	3×15ml
	Salt and pepper	
	Garnish	
2	Tomatoes	2
2	Hard-boiled eggs	2
	Sprigs of dill or fennel	

METHOD

1. Slice buckling along back-bone. Skin and fillet, then blanch in boiling water for 3 minutes. Break fish into large pieces and place in serving bowl. Cut the potatoes into cubes and add to bowl.
2. Mix the olive oil, lemon juice, salt and pepper together to make a dressing.
3. Wash and core apples and chop into fine chunks. Add to fish and potatoes. Pour dressing over the salad. Toss salad carefully and leave for 15 minutes for the flavours to develop.
4. Wash tomatoes and cut into eighths. Slice eggs and arrange with the tomatoes and herbs around the salad. Serve with hot, crusty bread.

Cream of chicken soup

There are various different ways of making chicken soup, such as using just the carcass, or utilizing the leftovers from a roast chicken, but this recipe, which calls for a whole bird, is in a completely different class. Quite simply, the flavour is superb.

STARTER Serves 6–8

Overall timing 2½ hours

Equipment 2 saucepans

Freezing Complete Step 3, then cool. Pour into rigid container, leaving ¾ inch (2cm) headspace, cover, label and freeze. Freezer life: 3 months. To use: put block in saucepan and reheat gently till thawed. Complete Step 4

INGREDIENTS

1	Onion	1
2	Carrots	2
1	Stalk of celery	1
2½lb	Boiling chicken	1.1kg
3 pints	Water	1.7 litres
	Bouquet garni	
6	Peppercorns	6
2oz	Butter	50g
3 tbsp	Plain flour	3×15ml
¼ pint	Milk	150ml
1 tbsp	Lemon juice	15ml
¼ teasp	Grated nutmeg	¼×5ml
¼ pint	Single cream	150ml
	Salt and pepper	

METHOD

1. Peel the onion. Wash and trim the carrots and celery. Put into a large saucepan with the chicken and water, bouquet garni and peppercorns. Bring to the boil, skim off any scum, then cover and simmer for 1½–2 hours till the chicken is tender.
2. Remove the chicken from the pan. Strain the stock and reserve. Remove the flesh from the chicken, discarding skin and bones, and cut into tiny pieces.
3. Heat the butter in a saucepan. Stir in the flour and cook for 1 minute. Gradually add the milk and the strained stock and bring to the boil, stirring constantly. Add the chicken flesh, lemon juice and nutmeg and simmer for 5 minutes.
4. Remove from the heat and stir in the cream. Taste and adjust seasoning, then heat through gently without boiling. Serve immediately with croûtons or toast, or French bread.

Sautéed kidneys with macaroni

The combination of kidneys and macaroni makes this dish filling as well as appetizing. The bland flavour of the pasta contrasts well with the savoury sauce

SUPPER Serves 4

Overall timing 30 minutes

Equipment Saucepan, frying pan

Freezing Not recommended

INGREDIENTS

1lb	Lamb kidneys	450g
2oz	Streaky bacon rashers	50g
1	Onion	1
12oz	Long macaroni	350g
	Salt	
2oz	Butter	50g
1 tbsp	Plain flour	15ml
1 pint	Beef stock	560ml
1 tbsp	Tomato paste	15ml
	Pepper	
½ teasp	Dried sage	2.5ml

Below: Rognons sautés aux macaroni – an economical and nourishing dish

METHOD

1 Prepare and wash kidneys, cut into thin slices. Derind and dice bacon. Peel and chop onion. Put macaroni into a pan of boiling salted water and leave to cook for 15 minutes or until al dente.

2 Meanwhile, heat butter in frying pan and fry kidneys for 3 minutes, stirring from time to time. Remove from pan.

3 Add diced bacon and onion to pan and cook gently till golden. Sprinkle flour over and cook, stirring, for 2 minutes.

4 Remove from heat and gradually stir in the stock (made from cubes if necessary), tomato paste, salt, pepper and sage. Bring to the boil, stirring, then return kidneys to pan, reduce heat and simmer for 15 minutes.

TO SERVE

Drain macaroni and arrange in serving dish. Spoon kidneys and sauce over and serve immediately with crisp lettuce and cucumber salad dressed with herb vinaigrette (see below).

cook's know-how

Fresh herbs added to a vinaigrette give a lovely flavour to your salads. Use whatever herbs you have to hand. For a good basic recipe mix together 8 tbsp (8×15ml) oil and 3 tbsp (3×15ml) wine vinegar. Season with salt and pepper and add a pinch of sugar. Stir in 1 teasp (5ml) each of finely chopped fresh parsley, chives, chervil and tarragon. Serve immediately as the herbs will become strong and unpleasant if left in the oil for too long. For a creamier taste and a tablespoon (15ml) of single cream (or use the top of the milk) or plain yoghurt and mix in well.

Left: Sautéed kidneys with macaroni – an economical and nourishing dish

Lamb with beans and croûtons

Succulent lamb steaks, sprinkled with a hot seasoning mix, are served on crisply fried bread slices and a bed of tender green beans. Ask your butcher to cut the steaks from a leg of lamb or buy ready-prepared lamb steaks now more easily available from a good supermarket. As an alternative, flash-fry beef steaks are good served in this way

LUNCH OR SUPPER Serves 4

Overall timing 45 minutes

Equipment Saucepan, frying pan

Freezing Not recommended

INGREDIENTS

1½ lb	Green beans	700g
2oz	Butter *or* margarine	50g
	Salt	
4fl oz	Stock	120ml
2 tbsp	Chopped parsley	2×15ml
5 tbsp	Oil	5×15ml
2	Slices of white bread	2
1	Garlic clove *or*	1
¼ teasp	garlic salt	1.25ml
4	Lamb steaks	4
2 teasp	Freshly-ground black pepper mixed with ground coriander seed *or*	2×5ml
2 teasp	prepared pepper for steak	2×5ml
2	Tomatoes	2
	Fresh parsley	

Above: Lamb with beans and croûtons – a quick and easily prepared mid-week meal

METHOD

1 Wash beans, then top and tail them and remove strings. Break or cut into short lengths.
2 Melt the butter or margarine in a saucepan. Add the beans and cook for a few minutes. Season with salt and pour in the stock (made up with a cube if necessary). Cook for 10–15 minutes or until just tender.
3 Mix in the chopped parsley. Cover and keep warm.
4 To make the croûtons, heat half the oil in a frying pan. Halve the slices of bread and lightly brown them on both sides in the oil. Remove from pan and keep warm.
5 Add rest of oil to pan with peeled and crushed garlic. If using garlic salt instead, sprinkle over the steaks. Cook the steaks for 5 minutes on each side.
6 Sprinkle with salt, then with pepper and coriander mixture or prepared pepper for steak.

TO SERVE

Cover the bottom of a serving dish with the beans. Put the lamb steaks on to the croûtons and place on top of the beans. Garnish with tomatoes, cut into eighths, and a few parsley sprigs.

Creamed potatoes

A basic accompaniment that's the perfect complement for many dishes. For extra flavour add egg yolks and freshly-grated nutmeg or Parmesan. Cream can be used instead of milk

VEGETABLE Serves 4

Overall timing 40 minutes

Equipment Saucepan, potato masher

Freezing Not recommended

INGREDIENTS

2lb	Floury potatoes	900g
	Salt	
2oz	Butter	50g
$\frac{1}{4}$ pint	Milk	150ml
	Freshly-ground black pepper	

METHOD

1 Peel and cut the potatoes into even-size pieces. Wash, then put into a saucepan and cover with cold salted water. Bring to the boil, cover and simmer over a gentle heat for 15–20 minutes till tender when pierced with a knife.

2 Drain thoroughly in a colander. Place butter and milk in the saucepan and return to a very low heat. Bring almost to the boil, add the potatoes and mash.

3 Remove from the heat and beat with a wooden spoon till soft and fluffy. Taste and adjust seasoning, put into a warmed serving dish and serve immediately.

cook's know-how

A gravy can be made by adding $\frac{1}{2}$ pint (300ml) stock or leftover wine to the frying pan in which you have cooked the rissoles. Bring the liquid to the boil, scraping the pan to mix in the remaining meat juices. To thicken add beurre manié made by mashing equal amounts of butter and flour together. Whisk small pieces at a time into the gravy until the right desired consistency is reached.

Right: Mustard rissoles – a variation on the hamburger theme. The well-flavoured patties can be made large for a filling lunch or supper, or small to serve at parties or as appetizers with drinks

Mustard rissoles

Freshly-ground mustard seed gives a piquant flavour to a simple recipe for beef patties – delicious served with creamed potatoes and a tasty gravy. With a little extra time and effort a more sophisticated dish with an unusual mustard sauce may be prepared (see the variation below)

LUNCH OR SUPPER Serves 4

Overall timing 25 minutes

Equipment Bowl, mortar and pestle or pepper mill, frying pan

Freezing Cool completely, pack into rigid container, cover, label and freeze. Freezer life: 2 months. To use: fry from frozen for about 15 minutes

INGREDIENTS

2	Large onions	2
1	Carrot	1
1lb	Minced beef	450g
1 tbsp	Chopped parsley	15ml
1	Egg	1
2 teasp	Mustard seeds	2×5ml
	Salt	
	Freshly-ground black pepper	
3 tbsp	Plain flour	3×15ml
4 tbsp	Oil	4×15ml
	Parsley sprigs	

METHOD

1 Peel and finely chop the onions. Scrape, wash and finely grate the carrot. Put into a bowl with the minced beef, parsley and egg.

2 Roughly grind the mustard seed in a mortar or pepper mill and add to the beef with plenty of salt and pepper.

3 Mix with a fork till the ingredients are well blended. Shape into 12 balls and coat with seasoned flour.

4 Heat the oil in a frying pan and fry the meatballs for about 10 minutes till crisp and golden. Drain on kitchen paper and arrange on a warm serving plate. Garnish with sprigs of parsley. Serve with creamed potatoes and gravy made from the meat juices (see left).

VARIATION

Prepare the meatballs as above using beef that's been minced twice. Divide into 24 pieces and shape into small balls. Coat the meatballs in beaten egg and fresh breadcrumbs and shallow fry in oil for about 10 minutes till crisp and golden. Meanwhile, heat 1oz (25g) butter in a saucepan. Add 3 tbsp (3×15ml) plain flour and cook, stirring, for 1 minute. Gradually add $\frac{1}{4}$ pint (150ml) each of beef stock (made with a cube if necessary) and milk and bring to the boil, stirring. Beat in 1 tbsp (15ml) prepared mustard and 1 teasp (5ml) vinegar and season to taste. Pour into a warmed sauce boat and serve hot with the fried meatballs. The minced beef can be replaced with 12oz (350g) pork sausagemeat and 4oz (125g) fresh breadcrumbs if liked. Serve meatballs as a cocktail snack to dip into mustard or a tomato sauce.

Texan stew

There are still more cattle than people in Texas and lean, tender beef is the heart of Texan cooking. Here it's combined with sweetcorn in a stew robust enough to have kept an old-style cowboy going

MAIN MEAL Serves 4

Overall timing $2\frac{1}{4}$ hours

Equipment Saucepan or flameproof casserole

Freezing Pour cooled mixture into rigid container. Cover, label and freeze. Freezer life: 3 months. To use: reheat gently from frozen, stirring from time to time

INGREDIENTS

$1\frac{1}{2}$lb	Braising beef	700g
1oz	Butter	25g
1 tbsp	Oil	15ml
1 pint	Stock	560ml
2	Capsicums	2
4	Tomatoes	4
$11\frac{1}{2}$oz	Can of sweetcorn kernels	326g
10oz	Can of peas and carrots	280g
	Salt	
	Freshly-ground black pepper	
2 teasp	Cornflour	2×5ml

METHOD

1 Chop meat into 1 inch (2·5cm) cubes. Heat butter and oil in saucepan or casserole, add meat and cook for 10 minutes till brown all over. Pour in stock (made with 2 stock cubes if necessary) and cook, covered, for $1\frac{1}{2}$ hours over a gentle heat.

2 Wash, deseed and cut capsicums into strips. Blanch, peel and chop tomatoes. Drain corn and peas and carrots.

3 Add vegetables, capsicums and tomatoes to meat and season well with salt and pepper. Cook, covered, for 15 minutes over a moderate heat. Blend cornflour with a little water in a cup. Stir into saucepan or casserole, then bring to boil again, uncovered. Serve stew in warmed bowls.

Left: Texan stew – braised beef with sweetcorn, peas, carrots, capsicums and tomatoes

Poached capon

Capon remains succulent and tender after poaching, and is served with a well-flavoured mustard sauce

MAIN MEAL Serves 6

Overall timing $1\frac{3}{4}$ hours

Equipment Large flameproof casserole, saucepan

Freezing Cooked capon, without the potatoes, may be frozen either whole or portioned in the stock. Pack in plastic container, cover, label and freeze. Freezer life: 3 months. To use: thaw overnight in fridge and then heat

INGREDIENTS

5lb	Oven-ready capon	2.3kg
2	Leeks	2
1	Stick of celery	1
1	Small carrot	1
2	Cloves	2
1	Medium-size onion	1
	Pepper	
$1\frac{1}{2}$lb	Potatoes	700g
	Gherkins	
	Mustard sauce	
$2\frac{1}{2}$ tbsp	Flour	$2\frac{1}{2}\times15$ml
1 tbsp	Dry mustard	1×15ml
1oz	Butter	25g
1 tbsp	Lemon juice	15ml
2 tbsp	Cream	2×15ml
	Salt and pepper	

METHOD

1 Place the capon in casserole, cover with cold salted water and bring slowly to boil over medium heat. Skim surface.

2 Wash the vegetables and peel or scrape. Slice the leeks, celery and carrot, stick the cloves in the peeled onion, and when the water is boiling add them to the casserole. Season with pepper. Bring to boil again, then reduce heat and leave to simmer for 30 minutes.

3 Peel and quarter potatoes. Add to the casserole, cook 30 minutes longer.

4 To make mustard sauce: combine flour, mustard and butter in saucepan and stir over low heat until butter has melted and flour and mustard are smoothly blended. Remove pan from heat and gradually stir in $\frac{1}{2}$ pint (300ml) of hot stock from the cooking capon. Add lemon juice. Stir sauce over medium heat until it begins to thicken, then add cream, and season to taste.

5 To serve, place capon on serving dish and surround it with the vegetables. Serve with mustard sauce and gherkins.

Leek pie

Sliced leeks, bacon and single cream baked in a shortcrust case

LUNCH OR SUPPER Serves 4

Overall timing 1 hour

Equipment 2 frying pans, shallow pie dish, bowl

Freezing Open freeze baked pie. Wrap well, put in polythene bag, seal and label. Freezer life: 3 months. To use: thaw for 3 hours at room temperature then reheat in oven at 350F (180C) Gas 4 for 30 minutes

INGREDIENTS

$1\frac{1}{2}$lb	Leeks	700g
2	Onions	2
2oz	Butter	50g
	Salt	
	Freshly-ground white pepper	
8oz	Streaky bacon rashers	225g
12oz	Shortcrust pastry	350g
1 tbsp	Cornflour	15ml
$\frac{1}{4}$ pint	Carton of single cream	150ml
1	Egg	1

METHOD

1 Preheat the oven to 400F (200C) Gas 6. Wash, trim and slice leeks. Peel and slice onions.

2 Melt butter in a frying pan and fry onions till golden. Add sliced leeks, salt and pepper and cook gently for 5 minutes.

3 Meanwhile, derind and lightly fry bacon rashers in another pan.

4 Roll out two-thirds of the pastry and line base and sides of the pie dish. Cover with leek mixture and arrange bacon rashers on top. Mix cornflour with the cream and pour over.

5 Roll out remaining pastry and cover filling. Seal and crimp edges, using any pastry trimmings to decorate top. Glaze with beaten egg. Bake for 45 minutes until golden brown.

Fry sliced onions in butter until golden, then add the sliced leeks, salt and pepper and cook gently for a further 5 minutes

Spread leek mixture in a pastry-lined dish and arrange derinded and fried bacon on top

Vegetable croquettes

Make in flattish shapes rather than round and you have vegetarian hamburgers. Serve in hot sesame baps

LUNCH OR SUPPER Serves 4

Overall timing $1\frac{1}{4}$ hours plus chilling

Equipment Saucepan, frying pan, potato masher, deep-fryer

Freezing Open freeze at end of Step 6, pack in polythene bags, seal and label. Freezer life: 3 months. To use: spread out on a baking tray to thaw, then complete Steps 7 and 8 but make sure that the croquettes are well dried before dropping into the hot oil to avoid any risk of spluttering

Below: Vegetable croquettes – nutritious mix formed into balls or rounds and deep fried

INGREDIENTS

$1\frac{1}{2}$lb	Floury potatoes	700g
1	Large parsnip	1
	Salt	
2	Large leeks	2
1	Stalk of celery	1
2	Large carrots	2
2oz	Butter	50g
2 tbsp	Chopped parsley	2×15ml
$\frac{1}{4}$ teasp	Freshly-grated nutmeg	1.25ml
	Freshly-ground black pepper	
2	Eggs	2
4 tbsp	Plain flour	4×15ml
	Oil for deep frying	
	Sprigs of parsley	

METHOD

1 Peel and quarter the potatoes. Peel the parsnip and cut into chunks the same size as the potatoes. Put into a saucepan, cover with cold lightly salted water and bring to the boil. Simmer for 15–20 minutes till tender.

2 Meanwhile, wash, trim and finely shred the leeks and celery. Scrape, wash and finely grate the carrots and reserve. Heat the butter in a frying pan, add the leeks and celery and fry for about 10 minutes, stirring frequently, till golden.

3 Drain the potatoes and parsnip, return to the pan and shake over a low heat to dry throughly.

4 Remove from the heat and mash to a smooth purée. Stir in the fried vegetables and any pan juices. Add the carrots, parsley and nutmeg and season to taste.

5 Add the eggs to the mixture and beat in thoroughly. Spread the mixture on a plate and leave to cool, then chill for 2–3 hours till firm.

6 Divide the mixture into 20 pieces and shape each into balls between floured hands.

7 Heat the oil in a deep-fryer to 340F (170C), add the croquettes and fry, a few at a time, for 5–6 minutes, till crisp and golden. Drain on kitchen paper and keep hot while the rest are cooked.

8 Arrange on a serving dish, garnish with parsley sprigs and serve immediately with home made tomato sauce (recipe page 121) and wholewheat spaghetti or in hot sesame baps with tomato sauce and Turkish salad (see right).

Turkish shepherds salad

Presentation is all in this salad from Turkey. Remove the skin from the tomato in the same way as you would peel an orange – in one strip – so that it can be curled into a rose. This attractive and tasty salad would make an excellent accompaniment to any vegetarian meal

SALAD Serves 4–6

Overall timing 20 minutes

Equipment Serrated knife, bowl

Freezing Not recommended

INGREDIENTS

1	Cos lettuce	1
½	Cucumber	½
4	Large tomatoes	4
1	Onion	1
3 tbsp	Olive oil	3×15ml
2 teasp	Tomato paste	2×5ml
1 tbsp	Lemon juice	15ml
3 tbsp	Chopped parsley	3×15ml
	Salt	
	Freshly-ground black pepper	

METHOD

1 Wash and dry the lettuce, cucumber and tomatoes. Shred lettuce, finely chop cucumber, peel and slice the onion.

2 Using a serrated knife, cut skin and a thin layer of flesh from 1 tomato in a long strip. Reserve. Chop the flesh and the other tomatoes.

3 Mix oil, tomato paste, lemon juice, parsley and seasoning in bowl. Add vegetables and toss lightly till coated and glistening.

4 Arrange on serving dish and coil tomato skin into a rose shape on top. Garnish with pickled chillies, black olives and cucumber slices and serve.

Above: Corned beef hash – cooked with lots of chunky potato and sliced onions

Corned beef hash

Best known of all hashes – literally chopped up mixtures – is the American corned beef hash, which always includes potatoes and onions. Any kind of cooked meat or poultry, cut up or diced, can be made into hash

LUNCH OR SUPPER Serves 4

Overall timing 1 hour

Equipment Saucepan or flameproof casserole

Freezing Not recommended

INGREDIENTS

2	Medium-size onions	2
6 tbsp	Oil *or*	6×15ml
2oz	dripping	50g
1	Stalk of celery	1
1	Large carrot	1
1lb	Corned beef	450g
	Salt and pepper	
½ teasp	Powdered mustard	2.5ml
1lb	Potatoes	450g
1 pint	Beef stock	560ml

METHOD

1 Peel and thinly slice onions lengthways. Heat oil or dripping in saucepan or casserole. Add the onions and cook gently till transparent.

2 Finely chop celery. Wash and scrape carrot, then grate or dice. Cut corned beef into 1 inch (2.5cm) cubes. Add all of these to onions and cook for a few minutes, then season with salt, pepper and mustard (add more if a stronger taste is preferred). Cook gently, uncovered.

3 Meanwhile, peel potatoes and cut into chunks. Add to pan with boiling stock (made with 2 stock cubes if necessary) and cook for 20 minutes. Serve in warm bowls topped with fried or poached eggs, and with lots of fresh bread to mop up the juices.

Minted eel and peas

An unusual combination – eels braised with mint and peas

MAIN MEAL Serves 4

Overall timing 1¼ hours

Equipment Flameproof casserole

Freezing Not recommended

INGREDIENTS

1	Onion	1
2 tbsp	Oil	2×15ml
2lb	Prepared eels	900g
	Salt and pepper	
½ pint	Fish stock, white wine *or* water	300ml
2	Sprigs of fresh mint	2
8oz	Frozen peas	225g
	Sugar	
1oz	Butter	25g
2 tbsp	Chopped fresh mint	2×15ml

METHOD

1 Peel and chop the onion. Heat the oil in a flameproof casserole and fry the onion until golden.

2 Cut the eels into 2 inch (5cm) lengths. Add to the casserole and fry for 10 minutes, turning them frequently. Season and add fish stock, wine or water, and sprigs of mint. Cover and cook gently for about 40 minutes or until tender.

3 Add the peas, a pinch of sugar and butter to the casserole, cover and cook for a further 5–8 minutes or until peas are tender.

4 Stir in the finely chopped mint. Taste and adjust seasoning if necessary.

Above: Prawn pilaf – rice, fish and vegetables combined in one flavourful dish

Prawn pilaf

Dry and spicy pilafs are popular in the Middle East and the Balkans. The rice absorbs the meaty tomato stock as it cooks and then juicy prawns are stirred in for additional texture

MAIN MEAL Serves 4

Overall timing 1 hour plus 1 hour thawing time if using frozen prawns

Equipment Heavy-based casserole with tight-fitting lid

Freezing Not recommended

INGREDIENTS

1lb	Prawns*	450g
2	Large onions	2
2	Fresh green chillies	2
2	Garlic cloves	2
8oz	Long-grain rice	225g
1 tbsp	Oil	15ml
8oz	Streaky bacon rashers	225g
14oz	Can of tomatoes	397g
	Salt	
¾ pint	Chicken stock	400ml
2 tbsp	Chopped parsley	2×15ml
2 tbsp	Grated Parmesan	2×15ml

METHOD

1 If using frozen prawns, thaw. Peel and slice onions. Wash, deseed and slice chillies. Peel and crush garlic.

2 Heat the oil in the casserole. Derind bacon, chop and fry in the oil until well browned on both sides. Add the onion, chillies and garlic to the casserole. Cook over a medium heat for a few minutes until onion is soft and transparent but not brown, stirring occasionally.

3 Add the rice and stir for 2–3 minutes until grains are coated with oil. Add the canned tomatoes with their juice, salt and chicken stock. Bring rapidly to the boil, then reduce heat, cover and simmer for 15 minutes on a very low heat. Stir and add the prawns. Cover and cook for a further 5 minutes.

4 Turn mixture into deep serving dish, and mix well. Sprinkle with chopped parsley and grated Parmesan and serve immediately.

*If using fresh prawns, 1½–2lb (700–900g) will give you approximately 1lb (450g) of prawn meat after peeling.

Baked mackerel with lemon

Mackerel at its very easiest– the lemon and wine combine to add extra flavour in the baking

LUNCH OR SUPPER Serves 4

Overall timing 35 minutes

Equipment Shallow ovenproof dish, saucepan

Freezing Not recommended

INGREDIENTS

2lb	Mackerel fillets	900g
	Salt	
	Freshly-ground black pepper	
2oz	Butter	50g
1	Large lemon	1
2 teasp	Oil	2×5ml
5 tbsp	Dry white wine	5×15ml
2 tbsp	Chopped parsley	2×15ml

METHOD

1 Preheat the oven to 400F (200C) Gas 6.
2 Grease ovenproof dish. Wash fillets, pat dry and arrange in dish. Season.
3 Melt the butter in a saucepan. Halve lemon, squeeze the juice from 1 half and add to the pan, stirring, with oil and wine. Pour sauce over mackerel and bake in the centre of the oven for 20 minutes or till tender.
4 Slice the remaining lemon half and arrange around mackerel. Sprinkle the chopped parsley over and serve immediately with buttered new potatoes.

cook's know-how

Some easy ideas for canned mackerel.
Mackerel potatoes Drain 15oz (424g) mackerel in oil and mash. Add to scooped-out centres of jacket-baked potatoes with 2oz (50g) butter and 4oz (125g) grated cheese. Pile into potatoes and bake till golden.
Mackerel tomatoes Mix 15oz (424g) mackerel in tomato sauce with 4oz (125g) cream cheese, 1 tbsp (15ml) lemon juice, salt and pepper, then use to fill 4 hollowed-out tomatoes.
Mackerel in pastry Drain 15oz (424g) can of mackerel in oil and stir into ½ pint (300ml) Béchamel sauce (see page 77), with 3 sliced hard-boiled eggs and 2 tbsp (2×15ml) chopped parsley. Fill pastry envelope (see page 369), bake.

Hearty fish soup

With all the makings of a meal in itself, this soup is cooked in a casserole. Its looks alone will demand attention and its irresistible flavour is sure to bring great compliments for the cook

MAIN MEAL Serves 6

Overall timing 50 minutes

Equipment Flameproof casserole

Freezing Cool, then turn into a rigid container leaving 1 inch (2.5cm) headspace, cover, label and freeze. Freezer life: 1 month. To use: reheat slowly from frozen

INGREDIENTS

2lb	Mixed fish	900g
2	Onions	2
1	Garlic clove	1
2	Tomatoes	2
3	Medium-size potatoes	3
8oz	White cabbage	225g
2	Green capsicums	2
6 tbsp	Oil	6×15ml
4oz	Long grain rice	125g
1¾ pints	Fish stock or water	1 litre
1 tbsp	Tomato paste	15ml
8oz	Frozen prawns	225g
¼ teasp	Dried oregano	1.25ml
	Salt and pepper	

METHOD

1 Remove skin and bones and cut fish into bite-size pieces. Peel and chop onions and garlic. Blanch, peel and chop tomatoes. Peel potatoes and cut into small chunks. Wash and shred cabbage. Deseed and dice capsicums.
2 Heat the oil in a casserole and fry the onions and garlic till golden. Add the rice, then the fish and fry for 5 minutes, stirring all the time.
3 Add prepared vegetables and stock or water. Bring to the boil. Mix tomato paste with a little hot water and stir into the casserole. Cook for 15 minutes. Add prawns, oregano, salt and pepper and cook for a further 10 minutes. Serve immediately with hot, crusty bread.

Below: Hearty fish soup – it tastes as good as it looks. Serve with crusty rolls or bread

Baking with mustard

As well as bringing out the flavour of other ingredients, mustard is also an aid to digestion as it helps to emulsify fatty foods such as cheese and meat. Powdered mustards can be sieved with the flour in many baked savoury dishes. Prepared mustards should preferably be cooked only for short periods of time as the essential flavouring oils are quickly lost at high temperatures

Baked mustard toasts

Bread slices spread with a mustard and parsley butter mix to use as a topping for stews and casseroles

ACCOMPANIMENT Serves 4

Overall timing 35 minutes

Equipment Bowl

Freezing Not recommended

INGREDIENTS

3oz	Softened butter	75g
2 teasp	Prepared mustard	2×5ml
1 tbsp	Chopped parsley	15ml
	Salt and pepper	
12	Slices of French bread	12

METHOD

1 Preheat the oven to 400F (200C) Gas 6.
2 Beat the butter in a bowl till smooth. Add the mustard, parsley and seasoning and mix well. Spread over the slices of bread.
3 Arrange slices in a circle on top of a casserole or stew so that the gravy can soak up into the bread. Bake for 25 minutes till crisp and golden on top.

VARIATION

Beat 2oz (50g) grated cheese into the butter with the other ingredients. Cook as above or spread onto slices of bread placed on a baking tray and cook for 15–20 minutes. Serve with soups or salad.

Mustard and cheese bread

Mustard releases the full flavour of the cheese in this easy-to-make loaf

BREAD Makes 1 loaf

Overall timing 1¾ hours

Equipment Mixing bowl, 1lb (450g) loaf tin, polythene

Freezing Cool completely, pack in polythene bag, seal, label and freeze. Freezer life: 3 months. To use: foil-wrap frozen loaf and reheat at 400F (200C) Gas 6 for about 30 minutes

INGREDIENTS

10oz	Packet of brown bread mix	283g
2 teasp	Powdered mustard	2×5ml
1 teasp	Prepared mustard	5ml
3oz	Grated cheese	75g
1	Egg	1

METHOD

1 Put the bread mix into a large bowl and stir in the powdered mustard. Add enough hot water to make a soft but not sticky dough.
2 Knead on a floured surface till smooth and glossy. Divide the dough into 18 pieces. Knead each piece and shape into a ball.
3 Grease the loaf tin and arrange 6 of the balls in the bottom, flattening them slightly. Brush half the prepared mustard over the dough and sprinkle with one third of the cheese.

4 Repeat the layering once and cover with the remaining bread dough. Cover with oiled polythene and leave in a warm place to rise till doubled in size.
5 Preheat the oven to 425F (220C) Gas 7.
6 Beat the egg and brush over the bread. Bake in the centre of the oven for 25 minutes. Sprinkle with the remaining cheese and return to the oven for a further 10–15 minutes, or till the base of the loaf sounds hollow when tapped.
7 Serve hot, cut into thick slices, with soups, casseroles or salads.

VARIATIONS

Make up a 10oz (283g) white bread mix as instructed on the packet. Knead and roll out on a floured surface to a large rectangle. Spread the surface with prepared mustard. Peel and chop 1 onion and fry in 1oz (25g) butter till transparent. Sprinkle over the dough with 4oz (125g) grated cheese, then roll up the dough. Curl dough roll into a circle, brush the ends with beaten egg and secure the join. Place, join down, on a floured baking tray. Slash sides at 2 inch (5cm) intervals and twist each section slightly so that it lies at an angle. Cover with oiled polythene and leave to prove in a warm place till doubled in size. Glaze with beaten egg and bake at 425F (220C) Gas 7 for 25–30 minutes. Or, fill and roll loaf as above but place the roll, join down, in a 2lb (900g) loaf tin. Make several deep slashes in the top with a sharp knife or kitchen scissors. Leave to prove in a warm place, then glaze with beaten egg and bake as above.

Mustard and cheese pastry

A delicious savoury pastry to use instead of ordinary shortcrust in your favourite recipes or in quiches

Overall timing 15 minutes

Equipment Mixing bowl, baking trays

Freezing Wrap uncooked pastry in cling film or foil, label and freeze. Freezer life: 3 months. To use: thaw for about 8 hours in fridge

INGREDIENTS

8oz	Plain flour	225g
2 teasp	Powdered mustard	2×5ml
½ teasp	Salt	2.5ml
4oz	Butter or block margarine	125g
4oz	Grated cheese	125g
1	Egg	1

METHOD

1 Sift the flour, mustard and salt into a mixing bowl. Rub in the fat till the mixture resembles breadcrumbs.
2 Stir in the cheese and make a well in the centre. Add a little beaten egg and mix with a palette knife to a soft but not sticky dough.
3 Knead lightly till smooth, roll out on a floured surface and use as required.

CHEESE STRAWS

Roll out the pastry to ¼ inch (6mm) thickness. Cut into strips about 3 inches (7.5cm) wide and place on a greased baking tray. Cut into straws about ¼ inch (6mm) wide, separating them as you cut. Shape several of the straws into rings, wetting the ends to make them stick. Repeat till all the pastry is used. Bake just above the centre of the oven for about 10 minutes, till crisp and golden. Allow to cool completely on the tray before transferring to a wire rack to cool completely. Thread several of the cheese straws through the rings before serving.

BELTED SAUSAGES

Preheat the oven to 400F (200C) Gas 6. Roll out the pastry to ¼ inch (6mm) thickness. Cut into strips about 6 inches (15cm) long and ½ inch (12.5mm) wide. Dip the strips into beaten egg and wind round the middle of uncooked sausages. Arrange on a lightly-greased baking tray and bake just above the centre of the oven for 25–30 minutes till crisp and golden.

Below: a selection of baked goods made with mustard. From left to right: Baked mustard toasts to top casseroles and stews; Mustard and cheese bread, which can be baked as a loaf, roll or ring; Asparagus and cheese quiches, made with mustard and cheese pastry; Belted sausages and Cheese straws – the sticks should be threaded through the pastry rings for an attractive finish

Dinner Alsatian style

A French meal with a German flavour

Alsace-Lorraine is the most easterly province of France and because it shares a border with Germany, both countries have had a considerable influence. For nearly 50 years (between 1871 and 1919) Alsace and Lorraine were part of Germany but before and since they have been considered French.

The Alsatians speak a dialect which sounds very much like German spoken with a French accent and their dishes tend to be French with a German flavour. Best known of these in France is the Alsatian version of sauerkraut, *choucroute à l'alsacienne.* The sauerkraut is cooked with bacon, sausages, gammon, carrots, onions, bouquet garni and juniper berries (see the recipe opposite). It is often served as an accompaniment to other dishes. Another adaptation from German cookery is *Beckenoffe,* a hearty stew based on pork, beef and lamb.

Famous for flavour

Situated in the beautiful Rhine Valley, Alsace has mild summers which make the land ideal for viniculture. The Riesling is different though not inferior to the neighbouring German and the Alsatian Gewürztraminers with their individual bouquet are highly regarded. All should be chilled before serving, and are especially refreshing when the weather's hot.

The Alsatians are full of approval for their wines and there is hardly a main dish, whether fish or meat, that does not require at least one glass of Riesling in the cooking. Chicken cooked with Riesling, *poulet sauté au Riesling à l'alsacienne,* and trout with Riesling, *truite au Riesling,* speak for themselves. The trout come from the streams of the lower slopes of the Vosges mountains, the natural dividing line between Alsace and Lorraine.

There is good agricultural land for market gardens and for the rearing of pigs and poultry. Chicken and turkey are eaten a lot, and goose is as popular as it is over the border in Germany. Goose dripping is a major ingredient in many dishes.

Potatoes are generally the most common accompaniment to a meal. The Alsatians have a distinctive recipe called *Pflütten.* The potatoes are boiled and mashed, mixed with flour or semolina, beaten egg, parsley, butter, nutmeg, salt and pepper, shaped into balls or croquettes and either fried or grilled.

Horseradish is popular for flavouring meat dishes; pork chops with horseradish, *côtes de porc au raifort,* is a nourishing everyday dish which helps see Alsatians through their bitter winters. Of course, the crowning glory of Alsace which has made the regional capital of Strasbourg world famous is *pâté de foie gras.* This goose-liver delicacy is often mixed with truffles from Perigord in south-west France and packed into tins and terrines. In Lorraine it is encased in a pastry shell (*en croûte*) a rather rich dish.

This easterly province not only produces splendid liqueurs (Kirsch, cherry brandy, for example) but is also the beer-brewing centre of France. The beers which come from both Alsace and Lorraine are of the lager and pilsener types, but they are lighter than their German counterparts.

Accent on desserts

Both regions enjoy the same taste in desserts and cakes. Both bake a version of the yeast-dough cake called *Kugelhopf* which is of Austrian origin. Tarts are also popular, made with the profuse fruits and berries of the area. Again there is a language combination as with black plum tart. In Lorraine it's called *tarte aux quetsches* which is half French and quetsche is the local version of the German Zwetschen – black plum. Also popular are yellow plum tarts, *tarte aux mirabelles* and cherry tart, *tarte aux cerises.* The Alsatians also produce *pouding aux cerises,* a base of sweet buns covered in hot cherry sauce. The most elaborate dessert from Lorraine is *vacherin dames blanches* – three layers of meringue with cream, strawberry ice cream and fruit salad sandwiched between.

Poteé Lorraine – a mixture of leeks, onions, potatoes, a whole cabbage and

bacon – is more of a meal than a soup and is characteristic of the Lorraine cuisine. Probably the best known dishes of the area are *quiche Lorraine* and *tourte à la Lorraine*. Both of these are pastry based, and have the most delicious creamy, and meaty, fillings. Lorraine has certain historic links with Poland, in that one of the Dukes of Lorraine, Stanislas Leczinski, was an ex-king of Poland (and father-in-law of Louis XV). He rebuilt Nancy, famous for *boudin noir* (black pudding), in Polish style and is believed to have had much to do with local cuisine. Red cabbage, which is frequently served with apples as an accompaniment to a pork dish, is certainly as popular in Poland as it is in Lorraine. Veal chops, *côtelettes de veau Lorraine*, are also often eaten in Poland.

By taking something from each of those who came to stay, Alsace and Lorraine together have established a cuisine that's unique within a country that itself has had such influence all over the world.

CHOUCROUTE A L'ALSACIENNE

Ingredients 4oz (125g) thick streaky bacon rashers; 2oz (50g) thin streaky bacon rashers; 1lb (450g) can sauerkraut; 4 bay leaves; 4 juniper berries; 6 cloves; 2 onions; 2 garlic cloves; $\frac{1}{2}$ teasp (2.5ml) salt; 5oz (150g) belly pork rashers; 4 large frankfurters; 4 large potatoes; 9fl oz (250ml) stock; 5fl oz ($\frac{1}{4}$ pint) red wine.

Method Preheat the oven to 350F (180C) Gas 4. Line a fairly deep ovenproof dish with bacon rashers. Cover with a layer of sauerkraut and sprinkle on half the bay leaves, juniper berries and cloves. Finely chop remaining bacon and put in pan to slowly brown and crisp. Peel and finely chop the onions. Crush the garlic and combine with salt. Mix into the onions. Spread half of this mixture over the dish. Place the belly pork and frankfurters on top and cover with a layer of sauerkraut then with a layer of peeled and sliced potatoes. Finally, cover with remaining sauerkraut, bay leaves, juniper berries and cloves. Pour in the stock and red wine. Sprinkle bacon pieces over top, cover and bake in the middle of the oven for 1 hour 20 minutes. **Serves 4.**

Below: some dishes from Alsace. Left to right: Choucroute à l'alsacienne (recipe above); Poulet au Riesling (recipe page 434) and Alsatian apple flan (recipe page 436)

Countdown

Salade Alsacienne
Poulet au Riesling
Boiled new potatoes
Deep-fried cauliflower
Alsatian apple flan
Bilberry tart

This meal, based on the cuisine of the Alsace-Lorraine region of France, should be a success with those who love the rich food of Germany as well as fans of the French style of cooking

The morning before Make bilberry tart and cool. When cold decorate with sieved icing sugar

2½ hours before Make pastry for apple pie

2 hours before Roll out pastry, line flan case and bake blind. Add apple and bake for a further 10 minutes. Prepare creamy mixture for tart and put to one side

1½ hours before Prepare chicken, brown with bacon and onions. Add wine and cook for 35 mins

1 hour before Wash and trim cauliflower. Divide into florets and cook in boiling salted water for 7–10 minutes. Drain and leave to cool

¾ hour before Boil potatoes and egg for salad. Prepare new potatoes. Add mushrooms to chicken

½ hour before Put new potatoes on to boil. Take chicken out of pan and keep hot. Make sauce, keep hot but do not allow to boil

¼ hour before Finish Salade Alsacienne. Drain new potatoes and keep hot. Pour creamy mixture on apple flan and bake

10 mins before Prepare egg mixture and breadcrumb coating while oil is heating up. Deep fry cauliflower, drain and keep warm

Serve Salade Alsacienne Follow with chicken and vegetables.

Serve choice of hot and cold desserts

The perfect wine to serve with this meal is a Riesling from the Alsace region. These wines are similar to the white wines of Germany – light, flowery and fragrant – but with a slightly dryer, fresher flavour.

Salade Alsacienne

A simple but typically Alsatian starter for a special meal

STARTER Serves 6

Overall timing 15 minutes

Equipment Serving dish, small bowl

Freezing Not recommended

INGREDIENTS

2	Dessert apples	2
3	Boiled, peeled potatoes	3
1	Small cooked beetroot	1
2	Frankfurters	2
1	Onion	1
1	Hard-boiled egg	1
2 teasp	Chopped parsley	2×5ml
	Sprigs of parsley	
8	Walnuts	8
3 tbsp	Olive oil	3×15ml
1 tbsp	Wine vinegar	15ml
1 teasp	Powdered mustard	5ml
	Salt	
	Freshly-ground black pepper	

METHOD

1 Peel, core and chop the apples. Dice the potatoes, peel and dice beetroot. Slice the frankfurters, peel the onion and cut into rings. Shell the egg and cut into 6 wedges.
2 Arrange in rows in a serving dish and sprinkle with chopped parsley. Garnish with parsley sprigs and walnuts.
3 To make the dressing, put the oil, vinegar and mustard into a bowl, mix well, then season. Pour dressing over the salad and serve immediately.

Poulet au Riesling

This dish combines many of the good foods of Alsace – chicken, pork, fresh vegetables and tender young herbs. The rich sauce is typical of the region and is made with superb local wine (you can use any dry white as a substitute) and cream for a velvety smoothness. Arrowroot is a useful thickener, as it takes less time to cook than ordinary flour, and doesn't mask the delicate flavour of the sauce

MAIN MEAL Serves 4–6

Overall timing 1½ hours

Equipment Large, heavy-based casserole with tight-fitting lid

Freezing Not recommended

Below: Poulet au Riesling – a chicken dish for a special occasion

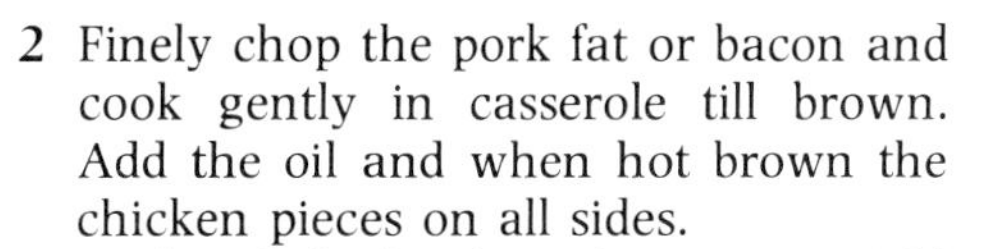

INGREDIENTS

3lb	Chicken, jointed *or* chicken legs and wings	1.4kg
8		8
1	Garlic clove	1
2oz	Pork fat *or* streaky bacon rashers	50g
4 tbsp	Oil	4×15ml
2	Onions	2
4fl oz	Dry white wine	120ml
4oz	Mushrooms	125g
2	Bay leaves	2
2 tbsp	Chopped parsley	2×15ml
2 tbsp	Chopped chives	2×15ml
	Freshly-ground salt and black pepper	
	Sauce	
1 tbsp	Arrowroot	15ml
4fl oz	Dry white wine	120ml
¼ pint	Carton of single cream	150ml
	Sprigs of fresh parsley	

METHOD

1 Wash and dry the chicken. Rub the skin with a cut garlic clove.
2 Finely chop the pork fat or bacon and cook gently in casserole till brown. Add the oil and when hot brown the chicken pieces on all sides.
3 Peel and finely chop the onions. Add to the casserole and brown. Pour in the white wine, cover and cook over medium heat for 35 minutes.
4 Slice mushrooms finely and add to the casserole with the bay leaves, half the chopped parsley and chives, salt and pepper. Cover and cook for a further 10 minutes.
5 Remove pan from heat, lift out bay leaves and discard. Take out chicken pieces with a draining spoon and place on a serving dish. Cover and keep warm.
6 If there's a lot of liquid in the pan place over a high heat till reduced by half. Remove from heat.
7 Mix arrowroot with a little of the wine and stir into the pan juices. Place pan over a low heat and stir until sauce thickens, then gradually stir in the cream. When hot (it must not boil) pour sauce over the chicken.

TO SERVE

Sprinkle over remaining chopped parsley and chives and garnish with parsley sprigs. Serve with boiled new potatoes and a crisp green salad.

Deep-fried Cauliflower

Crispy, golden cauliflower florets – a vegetable dish to impress guests

VEGETABLE Serves 6

Overall timing 25 minutes

Equipment Saucepan, 3 bowls, deep-fryer

Freezing Not recommended

INGREDIENTS

1	Large cauliflower	1
	Salt	
1	Egg	1
1	Egg white	1
2oz	Plain flour	50g
4oz	Dried breadcrumbs	125g
	Oil for frying	
	Grated Parmesan	
	Chopped parsley	

METHOD

1 Wash and trim cauliflower. Divide into 25–30 florets. Put into boiling salted water and cook for between 7 and 10 minutes or until just tender. Drain and allow to cool.
2 In a bowl, beat together the egg, egg white and a pinch of salt till frothy.
3 Dip each floret into flour, then beaten egg, then roll in breadcrumbs till well coated.
4 Heat oil to 320F (160C) and cook cauliflower till golden brown and crisp.
5 Remove cauliflower from pan with a draining spoon and drain on kitchen paper. Serve sprinkled with salt and a little grated Parmesan and chopped parsley mixed together.

Above: Apple flan from Alsace – an unusual variation on an old favourite

Alsatian apple flan

Though the ingredients are simple, this speciality of Alsace is no ordinary dessert. The rich smooth custard topping contrasts well with the apple halves and makes a satisfyingly sweet way to end a meal

WARM DESSERT Serves 6–8

Overall timing 1½ hours including refrigeration

Equipment 2 mixing bowls, 9 inch (23cm) flan dish, baking tray

Freezing Not recommended

INGREDIENTS

	Pastry	
8oz	Plain flour	225g
4oz	Butter	125g
2 tbsp	Caster sugar	2×15ml
1	Egg	1
	White wine to mix	
	Filling	
4	Golden Delicious apples	4
1 tbsp	Caster sugar	15ml
½ pint	Carton of double cream	284ml
2	Eggs	2
2×1oz	Sachets of vanilla sugar	2×25g
1	Lemon	1
2oz	Caster sugar	50g

METHOD

1. Make pastry then roll into a ball and put in the fridge for 30 minutes.
2. Remove pastry from fridge, roll out on lightly floured surface and line flan dish, easing the pastry up at the sides. Place on baking tray and bake blind near top of oven at 400F (200C) Gas 6 for 20 minutes (see page 38).
3. Peel the apples, cut them in half and remove the cores. Arrange apple halves on top of the pastry, rounded side up, and sprinkle lightly with sugar. Bake for 10 minutes in the middle of the oven.
4. Meanwhile, whip the cream and beat in the eggs, vanilla sugar, grated rind of lemon and caster sugar until creamy. Spread the creamed mixture on top of the apples. Reduce heat to 350F (180C) Gas 4 and cook tart for 20 minutes.

Bilberry tart

In France these small, dark fruits with a grape-like bloom and delicious, tangy flavour are known as *myrtilles*. They form the filling for this luscious tart in which biscuit crumbs are cleverly used to soak up the rich, fruity juice

COLD DESSERT Serves 6–8

Overall timing 1½ hours

Equipment 2 bowls, 11 inch (28cm) loose-bottom flan tin

Freezing Cool quickly, wrap in foil or cling film, label and freeze. Freezer life: 3 months. To use: thaw for 2 hours

INGREDIENTS

	Base	
12oz	Plain flour	350g
½ teasp	Salt	2.5ml
1 tbsp	Caster sugar	15ml
6oz	Butter	175g
6 tbsp	Water	6×15ml
	Filling	
5	Digestive biscuits	5
1lb	Fresh or bottled bilberries	450g
2	Eggs	2
2oz	Caster sugar	50g
¼ pint	Carton of double cream	150ml
1oz	Icing sugar	25g

METHOD

1. To make the base, mix flour, salt and sugar in a bowl and make a well in the centre. Melt the butter and pour in, add water and knead to smooth dough. Cover and chill for 30 minutes.
2. Preheat oven to 425F (220C) Gas 7. Crush biscuits with a rolling pin. If using bottled bilberries, drain them. If using fresh, wash and remove stalks.
3. Roll out pastry on a floured board and line well greased flan tin. Cover with crushed biscuit crumbs, pressing firmly into place, then top with bilberries. Bake in oven for 15 minutes.
4. Meanwhile, put eggs and sugar in a bowl and beat until pale and thick. Add cream gradually, whisking all the time.
5. Remove tart from oven. Reduce oven temperature to 400F (200C) Gas 6. Cover tart with creamed mixture and return it to oven. Bake for a further 15–20 minutes or till golden brown.
6. Remove tart from tin and place on a wire rack to cool. When cold, remove lining paper and decorate top with sieved icing sugar (cut paper circles for shape).

Below: Bilberry tart – a fruity centre with a creamy topping

cook's know-how

Bottled fruit is a very useful standby to keep in the larder, especially during the winter months when fresh fruit is hard to come by. Most fruits can be bottled but plums, cherries, bilberries and blackcurrants are particularly good preserved this way. You can use them in pies and tarts, under a crumble topping or simply served with fresh cream or ice cream. If you do not want to bottle your own fruit, some of the best and least expensive brands come from Eastern Europe. Bottled fruit from countries such as Poland and Rumania is now widely available and is well worth trying.

Above: Coconut milk jelly – an unusual flavour for a family favourite

Coconut milk jelly

A milk jelly made with coconut milk sets a lovely creamy white colour and it looks good whatever shape of jelly mould you choose to use

DESSERT Serves 6–8

Overall timing 1 hour plus overnight chilling

Equipment Measuring jug, grapefruit knife, grater, bowl, saucepan, 2 pint (1.1 litre) decorative mould

Freezing Not recommended

INGREDIENTS

1	Fresh coconut	1
$1\frac{3}{4}$ pints	Milk	1 litre
	Pinch of salt	
7oz	Caster sugar	200g
$\frac{1}{2}$ teasp	Vanilla essence	2.5ml
5 teasp	Powdered gelatine	5×5ml

METHOD

1 Use clean nail and hammer to pierce black "eyes" of coconut. Drain any milk inside into a measuring jug. Remove white flesh, but not inner rind, with grapefruit knife and grate.

2 Add sufficient milk to the coconut milk to make up the required amount. Bring milk to the boil in a saucepan, together with the salt, sugar and grated coconut. Remove pan from heat, stir in vanilla essence and leave to cool. Meanwhile, mix the gelatine with 3 tbsp (3×15ml) cold water in a small bowl and leave to firm.

3 Place bowl in a saucepan of simmering water and stir until gelatine dissolves. Cool slightly, then stir into coconut mixture. Cool completely before pouring mixture into the wetted decorative jelly mould.

4 Leave in fridge overnight. To turn out, dip mould bottom into hot water for a few seconds, then invert jelly on to serving plate, tap sharply so it slides out intact. Serve with coconut macaroons or biscuits.

Jam layer pudding

A great favourite with children, who enjoy seeing all the different colours in the jam layers. Use a good clear red, such as strawberry, and apricot or peach for the yellow layer. You can ring the changes by employing other jams to introduce other colours – such as greengage

DESSERT Serves 6

Overall timing 3 hours

Equipment Bowl, 2 pint (1.1 litre) pudding basin, greaseproof paper, steamer or large saucepan, foil

Freezing Not recommended

INGREDIENTS

8oz	Self-raising flour	225g
2 tbsp	Caster sugar	2×15ml
$\frac{1}{4}$ teasp	Salt	1.25ml
4oz	Shredded suet	125g
$\frac{1}{4}$ pint	Cold water	150ml
2 tbsp	Red jam	2×15ml
3 tbsp	Yellow jam	3×15ml
4 tbsp	Blackcurrant jam	4×15ml

METHOD

1 Grease the pudding basin. Mix together the flour, sugar, salt and suet in a bowl. Add enough cold water to give a light elastic dough and knead lightly till smooth.

2 Divide dough into 4 pieces graded in size. Roll smallest piece out to 1 inch (2.5cm) larger than the bottom of the basin. Add red jam.

3 Roll out next smallest piece of pastry to fit the bowl neatly. Cover with the yellow jam. Repeat layering, finishing with last piece of pastry. Cover with a piece of pleated greased greaseproof paper, then with pleated foil. Tie in place with string.

4 Bring water to boil in steamer or saucepan. Cover and steam for $2\frac{1}{2}$–3 hours, topping up with boiling water when necessary.

5 Remove from heat and turn pudding out on to a warm plate. Serve hot with fresh cream or custard.

Fruity apple dessert with rice

A full-of-goodness pudding that's perfect for a family meal

HOT DESSERT Serves 6–8

Overall timing 1¼ hours

Equipment 2 saucepans, ovenproof dish, 2 mixing bowls

Freezing Not recommended

INGREDIENTS

1¼ pints	Milk	700ml
	Salt	
4	Strips of lemon rind	4
5oz	Round grain rice	150g
1½lb	Apples	700g
2	Bananas	2
1oz	Butter	25g
4oz	Sugar	125g
1 teasp	Ground cinnamon	5ml
4oz	Bottle of sweet cocktail cherries	110g
2oz	Shelled walnuts	50g
3	Eggs	3

Below: Fruity apple desert – subtle flavours, light and airy texture

METHOD

1 Put the milk, pinch of salt and strips of lemon rind into a saucepan and bring to the boil. Add the rice. Cover and cook for 40 minutes on a low heat, stirring occasionally.
2 Preheat oven to 350F (180C) Gas 4.
3 Meanwhile, peel and slice the apples and bananas.
4 Heat the butter and 2oz (50g) of the sugar in a saucepan until golden brown. Add the apples and cook for 5 minutes, then add the bananas and cook for 2–3 minutes more. Sprinkle on the cinnamon, then stir in drained cherries and chopped walnuts.
5 Remove from heat and put mixture into a greased ovenproof dish and smooth over. Work quickly to prevent caramel setting.
6 Separate the eggs. Cream together the yolks and 1oz (25g) sugar in one bowl. In another, beat the whites and remaining sugar together until they are very stiff.
7 Fold both mixtures into the cooked rice (take out the lemon peel first) then pour over the fruit. Cook for 30 minutes on the middle shelf of the oven.
8 Remove from oven and serve pudding immediately with pouring cream.

Frangipane flan

For best results make this dessert well in advance and serve chilled

COLD DESSERT 8–10 servings

Overall timing 1½ hours plus cooling and chilling time

Equipment Mixing bowl, 10 inch (25cm) flan ring, baking tray, 2 saucepans, double saucepan

Freezing Place flan in rigid container, wrap, label and freeze. Freezer life: 3 months. To use: thaw at room temperature for about 2 hours

INGREDIENTS

	Pastry	
8oz	Plain flour	225g
4oz	Butter	125g
3oz	Caster sugar	75g
	Water to mix	
	Filling	
1 pint	Milk	560ml
	Vanilla pod	
2	Whole eggs	2
4	Egg yolks	4
	Pinch of salt	
4oz	Caster sugar	125g
3oz	Plain flour	75g
3½oz	Ground almonds	100g
1 tbsp	Orange flower water	15ml
4 tbsp	Strawberry jam	4×15ml
3 tbsp	Apricot jam	3×15ml
2 tbsp	Kirsch or water	2×15ml
	Flaked almonds	

METHOD

1 Make pastry and roll out. Grease flan ring and place on a baking tray. Line ring with pastry and bake blind for 10 minutes at 400F (200C) Gas 6 (see page 38). Remove from oven.
2 To make filling, put milk and vanilla pod into a saucepan. Bring to the boil and remove from heat. Take out pod.
3 Put whole eggs, yolks, salt, sugar and flour into a bowl and whisk well. Put into top of a double saucepan.
4 Over low heat, slowly mix warm milk into egg mixture. Stir until mixture starts to boil. Remove from heat.
5 Mix ground almonds with orange flower water. Spread strawberry jam over flan. Mix together custard and almond mixture. Spread on top of jam.
6 Cook in oven just above centre for about 30 minutes. Allow to cool.
7 To make topping, heat apricot jam and Kirsch gently in a small saucepan, then sieve over flan. Sprinkle with flaked almonds. Chill well before serving.

Above: Rhubarb pie – a spicy rhubarb tart to serve with cream or pouring custard

Bread and butter pudding

Probably the most satisfying and filling of puddings especially when the weather's not so warm. The bread combines with the egg custard as well as forming a crisp layer on top

DESSERT Serves 6–8

Overall timing 50 minutes

Equipment Saucepan, large shallow 2 pint (1.1 litre) ovenproof dish, bowl, roasting tin

Freezing When cold, wrap, label and freeze. Freezer life: 3 months. To use: thaw at room temperature, or place in cold oven and heat to 350F (180C) Gas 4 for 1 hour

INGREDIENTS

10–12	Slices of bread	10–12
4oz	Butter	125g
1 pint	Milk	560ml
	Pinch of salt	
1	Vanilla pod *or*	1
5–6	drops of vanilla essence	5–6
4	Eggs	4
4oz	Caster sugar	125g

METHOD

1 Preheat oven to 425F (220C) Gas 7.
2 Butter slices of bread with 3oz (75g) of the butter. Grill with buttered side up, then cut into triangles.
3 Bring milk to the boil with salt and vanilla. Remove from heat and lift out pod if using.
4 Grease ovenproof dish and place bread triangles in it so that they overlap. In a bowl, whisk the eggs and sugar until creamy. Pour in the hot milk and whisk well.
5 Slowly pour egg/milk mixture over the bread, holding the bread down with a spatula to stop it floating to the surface.
6 Place ovenproof dish in a roasting tin of warm water and then in the oven. Cook for 30 minutes, but after 10 minutes check that the bread hasn't floated to the top. If it has, press it down with a spatula again. Serve hot or cold.

VARIATIONS

You can sprinkle 2–4oz (50–125g) of currants or sultanas over the bread triangles in the dish, before pouring the egg and milk mixture over.
Or, for a tangy change, add 2oz (50g) candied peel and grated rind of 1 orange.

Rhubarb pie

A traditional pie from Wales – the generous helping of rhubarb in the centre was much appreciated by the hard-working Welsh farmers who favoured really king-size portions

DESSERT Serves 6–8

Overall timing $1\frac{3}{4}$ hours

Equipment 3 bowls, baking tray, 9 inch (23cm) pie plate

Freezing Not recommended

INGREDIENTS

9oz	Plain flour	250g
	Salt	
$\frac{1}{4}$ teasp	Mixed spice	1.25ml
$\frac{1}{2}$ teasp	Ground cinnamon	2.5ml
5oz	Butter	150g
2 tbsp	Caster sugar	2×15ml
	Water to mix	
2lb	Rhubarb	900g
6oz	Granulated sugar	175g
1	Egg yolk	1

METHOD

1 Sift flour, pinch of salt and spice into a bowl. Rub in the butter till the mixture resembles fine breadcrumbs. Stir in the caster sugar and enough water to make a soft but not sticky dough. Knead lightly till smooth, wrap and chill for 30 minutes.
2 Meanwhile, wash and trim the rhubarb and cut into 1 inch (2.5cm) lengths. Put into a bowl with all but 1 tbsp (15ml) of the granulated sugar and mix well.
3 Preheat the oven to 400F (200C) Gas 6. Place a baking tray on the shelf just above the centre to heat up.
4 Roll out half the pastry on a floured surface and use to line the pie plate. Brush the edge with water. Pile the rhubarb into the pie in a dome shape. Roll out remaining pastry and cover the pie, sealing and crimping the edges.
5 Beat the egg yolk and brush over top of pie. Stand pie on hot baking tray and bake for 20 minutes. Reduce the temperature to 350F (180C) Gas 4 and cook for a further 25 minutes till crisp and golden.
6 Remove from the oven, sprinkle remaining sugar over and serve immediately with cream or pouring custard.

Above: Courgettes with tomato and Mozzarella – a tasty starter or lunch

Layer the drained and seasoned slices of fried courgettes in an ovenproof dish

Cut Mozzarella into thin slices and layer into dish with remaining courgettes

Ladle over the tomato, onion and garlic dressing and chill for 1 hour

cook's know-how

Mozzarella is a soft white cheese from Italy. The cheese available outside Italy is always made from cow's milk although south of Rome you can often see 'Mozzarella di bufalo' for sale beside the road. It is made in an irregular round shape and is wrapped in plastic or paper. It should always be stored in water or whey. A cheaper version comes from Denmark and this is made into a rectangular shape. Danish Mozzarella is good for cooking but for this recipe it would be better to buy the Italian variety.

Courgettes with tomato and Mozzarella

Courgettes layered with Mozzarella, one of Italy's best cooking cheeses, in a fragrant, herby tomato sauce. Instead of basil, a good pinch of dried oregano gives extra flavour. To make this a main meal, add minced cooked meat or chopped ham between the layers of courgettes

LUNCH OR STARTER — Serves 4

Overall timing 30 minutes plus chilling

Equipment Frying pan, ovenproof dish

Freezing Not recommended

INGREDIENTS

1	Onion	1
1	Garlic clove	1
3 tbsp	Oil	3×15ml
1oz	Butter	25g
1lb	Fresh tomatoes *or*	450g
14oz	canned tomatoes	397g
4	Basil leaves *or*	4
½ teasp	dried basil	½×5ml
6	Courgettes	6
3 tbsp	Flour	3×15ml
	Salt and pepper	
8oz	Mozzarella	225g

METHOD

1. Peel and finely chop onion. Peel and crush garlic. Heat 1 tbsp (15ml) oil and the butter in a frying pan. Cook onion and garlic till onions are transparent.
2. Blanch, peel and chop fresh tomatoes or drain can of tomatoes. Add to pan with chopped basil and cook over a low heat for 20 minutes. Purée mixture in a blender or push through a sieve.
3. Heat rest of oil in pan. Wash courgettes and trim ends, then slice. Coat slices with flour and fry in oil till lightly golden and tender. Drain on kitchen paper and season with salt and pepper.
4. Thinly slice Mozzarella. Place in dish layers of courgettes, Mozzarella, then tomato dressing. Place in the fridge and chill for 1 hour. Serve with hot garlic bread or toast and butter curls.

Spicy lamb cutlets

Marinate by day and enjoy these lamb cutlets for a spicy supper. So as to lose none of the piquancy, the marinade, which includes vinegar, Worcestershire sauce and mustard, is boiled to reduce and thicken it, then served with the meat

LUNCH OR SUPPER — Serves 4

Overall timing 20 minutes plus 1 hour marination

Equipment Large bowl, saucepan

Freezing Not recommended

INGREDIENTS

8	Lamb cutlets	8
5 tbsp	Tomato soup	5×15ml
1 tbsp	Worcestershire sauce	15ml
2 tbsp	Wine or cider vinegar	2×15ml
1 teasp	English mustard powder	5ml
	Salt and pepper	
1	Onion	1

METHOD

1 Place the cutlets in a mixing bowl.

2 Mix together the tomato soup*, Worcestershire sauce, vinegar, mustard, salt and pepper. Peel and chop the onion and add, then pour marinade over the cutlets. Leave to marinate for about 1 hour or put in the marinade the morning before.

3 Preheat the grill. Drain the cutlets, saving the marinade. Cook under a hot grill for 3–4 minutes on each side. Arrange the cutlets on a serving dish and keep in a warm place.

4 Pour the marinade into a saucepan and boil for 2–3 minutes, stirring constantly with a wooden spoon. Pour it over the cutlets.

*The tomato soup can be any canned kind – reserve the rest for a starter. Or you can use packet soup, making up as much as necessary.

Above: Bashed neeps – a simple dish of boiled swede mashed till smooth with lots of butter and a sprinkling of black pepper

Bashed neeps

Swedes or "neeps" are a favourite vegetable in Scotland and, along with mashed potatoes (Chappit tatties) and plenty of neat whisky, are the traditional accompaniment to haggis at Burns Night dinners. Prepared this way swedes make a delicious addition to any supper. Or they can become a meal on their own when eggs are added and served with bacon (see the variation below)

VEGETABLE — Serves 4–6

Overall timing 35 minutes

Equipment Saucepan

Freezing Not recommended

INGREDIENTS

2lb	Swedes	900g
	Salt	
3oz	Butter	75g
	Freshly-ground black pepper	

METHOD

1 Peel the swedes thickly, wash and cut into 1 inch (2.5cm) chunks. Put into a saucepan of lightly salted cold water and bring to the boil.

2 Reduce the heat, cover and simmer for 15–20 minutes till tender. Drain thoroughly.

3 Mash well till smooth with two-thirds of the butter. Season to taste.

4 Arrange in a warmed serving dish, top with the remaining butter and grind a little pepper over. Serve immediately.

VARIATIONS

"Clapshot" is a traditional mixed swede and potato dish from the Orkney Islands, off the north coast of Scotland. Cook equal quantities of swedes and floury potatoes, 1lb (450g) of each, in separate pans till tender. Drain well, then mash together with butter and seasoning and 1 small very finely chopped onion or 2 tbsp (2×15ml) chopped chives. Any leftovers can be fried in butter.

To turn Clapshot into a tasty lunch or supper dish, spread the hot mashed swede, potato and onion mixture into a shallow ovenproof dish. Make 4 hollows with the back of a spoon and break an egg into each one. Season and dot with butter, then bake in the centre of the oven, preheated to 425F (220C) Gas 7, for 8–10 minutes till the eggs are lightly set. Serve immediately with rashers of crispy fried bacon.

Steak with mushrooms

A popular dish that's easily prepared and good served with a selection of steamed vegetables and melted butter if you want to avoid the more traditional though calorific accompaniment – chips

LUNCH OR SUPPER Serves 4

Overall timing 35 minutes

Equipment Large frying pan

Freezing Not recommended

INGREDIENTS

12oz	Button mushrooms	350g
2oz	Butter	50g
2 tbsp	Oil	2×15ml
4	Steaks	4
4fl oz	Dry white wine	120ml
½ teasp	Dried thyme	½×5ml
¼ teasp	Garlic salt	¼×5ml
	Freshly-grated nutmeg	
	Black pepper	

METHOD

1 Wipe and thickly slice mushrooms. Heat butter in frying pan and add mushrooms. Fry, stirring over a moderate heat for 5 minutes till mushrooms are golden, then remove from pan and reserve.

2 Add oil to pan and heat till hazing. Add steaks and cook for 2 minutes each side to seal them. Reduce heat and cook for a further 2–4 minutes each side according to taste. Remove from pan, arrange on warmed serving dish and keep hot.

3 Pour off any excess fat from the pan, retaining cooking juices. Return pan to high heat, add wine, thyme and bring to the boil, stirring to dissolve sediment.

4 Boil steadily till reduced by half then add mushrooms, garlic salt, freshly-grated nutmeg and black pepper to taste. Cook till mushrooms are heated through, then arrange around steaks. Pour pan juices over and serve.

Below: Steak with mushrooms – nutmeg, thyme and white wine flavour the cooking juices

Creamed pork escalopes

A rich creamy sauce with a touch of tanginess enhances the thin, pre-cooked escalopes. The same treatment can be used for veal escalopes, or boned turkey or chicken breasts, which can easily be bought from a supermarket

LUNCH OR SUPPER Serves 4

Overall timing 25 minutes

Equipment Large frying pan

Freezing Not recommended

INGREDIENTS

1	Onion	1
4×5oz	Pork escalopes	4×150g
4 tbsp	Plain flour	4×15ml
	Salt and pepper	
2oz	Butter	50g
1 tbsp	Oil	15ml
3 tbsp	Dry white wine	3×15ml
¼ pint	Carton of double cream	150ml
2 tbsp	Lemon juice	2×15ml
	Cayenne pepper	
	Parsley	
1	Lemon	1

METHOD

1 Peel and finely chop the onion. Rinse pork and dry on kitchen paper. Mix 2 tbsp (2×15ml) of the flour, salt and pepper on a plate and use to coat escalopes on both sides.

2 Heat butter and oil in a frying pan. Cook escalopes for 2–3 minutes on each side over a moderately high heat, then remove from pan and keep warm.

3 Add chopped onion to frying pan and cook gently for 5 minutes. Sprinkle remaining 2 tbsp (2×15ml) flour over onions and cook for 1 minute, stirring all the time.

4 In a bowl, mix together the wine and cream. Then stir into pan and heat through gently for 4 minutes.

5 Stir in lemon juice and a pinch of cayenne. Return escalopes to pan. Heat gently for 2 minutes, then transfer to warmed serving plate. Garnish with parsley sprigs and slices of lemon. Serve with buttered noodles and a crisp lettuce or chicory and mandarin salad.

Stewed breast of veal

Economical breast of veal made superbly tender by long slow cooking in a rich wine flavoured stock

MAIN MEAL Serves 6

Overall timing 2 hours

Equipment Bowl, flameproof casserole, frying pan

Freezing Not recommended

INGREDIENTS

4oz	Button onions	125g
3lb	Chopped breast of veal	1.4kg
8oz	Streaky bacon rashers	225g
1	Garlic clove	1
2oz	Lard	50g
3 tbsp	Plain flour	3×15ml
¾ pint	White stock	400ml
½ pint	Red wine	300ml
	Bouquet garni	
	Salt	
	Freshly-ground black pepper	
4oz	Button mushrooms	125g
2oz	Butter	50g
2 tbsp	Oil	2×15ml
6	Slices of French bread	6
1 tbsp	Chopped parsley	15ml

METHOD

1 Put onions into a bowl and cover with boiling water. Leave to soak for 10 minutes to loosen skins.
2 Wipe and trim the veal, discarding any excess fat and loose bones. Derind the bacon and cut across the rashers into strips. Peel the garlic.
3 Heat the lard in the casserole, add the bacon and veal and fry for 10 minutes till browned all over.
4 Sprinkle the flour over and cook for 1 minute. Gradually add the stock and bring to the boil, stirring constantly.
5 Add the red wine, bouquet garni, crushed garlic and seasoning. Cover and simmer for 1¼ hours, or cook in the centre of the oven preheated to 350F (180C) Gas 4 for 1¼ hours.
6 Meanwhile, peel the onions. Wipe, trim and quarter the mushrooms. Heat the butter in frying pan, add the onions and fry for 5 minutes till just golden. Add the mushrooms and fry for 3 minutes.
7 Lift the vegetables out of the pan with a draining spoon and add to the veal. Cover and cook for a further 15 minutes.
8 Add the oil to the frying pan and fry the bread till crisp and golden on both sides. Drain on kitchen paper.
9 Remove the bouquet garni from the stew. Adjust seasoning to taste, pour into a warmed serving dish. Dip one end of the croûtons into the parsley and arrange round the stew. Serve with buttered rigatoni or macaroni.

Watercress salad

Influenced by the Orient, this salad has a tanginess and crunchiness well suited to meat or fish with little texture. The watercress must be chilled so that it crisps. Serve it as a refreshing contrast to a rich casserole such as stewed breast of veal

SALAD Serves 6

Overall timing 15 minutes plus chilling

Equipment Screw-top jar, salad bowl

Freezing Not recommended

INGREDIENTS

2	Bunches of watercress	2
18	Small radishes	18
4	Stalks of celery	4
1 inch	Piece of green ginger *or*	2.5cm
¼ teasp	ground ginger	¼×5ml
6 tbsp	Oil	6×15ml
3 tbsp	Orange juice	3×15ml
2 teasp	Soy sauce	2×5ml
	Coarse salt	
	Freshly-ground black pepper	

METHOD

1 Wash watercress and remove stalks. Dry sprigs well, place in covered bowl in fridge for 1 hour.
2 Wash, trim and slice radishes. Wash, trim and chop celery. Finely chop ginger.
3 Put ginger in screw-topped jar with oil, orange juice, soy sauce, salt and pepper to taste. Shake well.
4 Put watercress, celery and radishes in salad bowl, add dressing and toss. Chill for 15 minutes before serving.

Above left: Stewed breast of veal – enhanced with mushrooms, bacon and onions. Serve with crisp croûtons for contrast

Swiss cream of barley soup

A perfect meal-in-itself soup to serve with crusty bread and Swiss cheese – or buy some tasty smoked ham from your delicatessen or supermarket

LUNCH OR SUPPER Serves 4–6

Overall timing 2¾ hours

Equipment 2 saucepans

Freezing Not recommended

INGREDIENTS

2	Large onions	2
3	Cloves	3
1	Pigs trotter *or* meaty veal bone	1
4oz	Pearl barley	125g
	Bay leaf	
3 pints	Water	1.7 litres
	Salt	
	Black pepper	
12oz	Carrots	350g
4	Stalks of celery	4
2	Small leeks	2
4oz	Smoked streaky bacon rashers	125g
2oz	Lard	50g
2	Egg yolks	2
¼ pint	Carton of single cream	150ml
1 tbsp	Chopped chives	15ml

METHOD

1 Peel 1 of the onions and spike with cloves. Wash pigs trotter or veal bone, chop in half and put into a saucepan with the barley, spiked onion and bay leaf. Add the water, season, then bring to the boil. Skim off any scum, cover and simmer for 2 hours.

2 Meanwhile, scrape and dice the carrots. Peel and chop the remaining onion. Wash, trim and chop the celery and leeks. Derind and dice the bacon. Heat the lard in a large saucepan. Add the bacon and vegetables and fry for 10 minutes till golden.

3 Remove spiked onion and bay leaf from stock and discard. Lift trotter or veal bone out of stock and remove the meat, discarding skin and bone.

4 Add meat to the vegetables with the stock. Bring to the boil and simmer for 10 minutes till vegetables are tender.

5 Put the egg yolks and cream into a tureen and beat together with a fork. Season the soup to taste and gradually pour into tureen, stirring constantly.

6 Sprinkle soup with chives and serve with bread and cheese or cold meat.

Below: Swiss cream of barley soup – fabulously creamy and packed with vegetables and meat

time saver

Nourishing soups with a distinctive home-made flavour can be produced in minutes rather than hours in a pressure cooker. Basic stocks can be made in the cooker, then extra ingredients added and cooked in it too. Meat and vegetables can also be fried in the open cooker and stock added. When boiling stock or soup in the open pan, remove any scum with a draining spoon before pressure cooking. Use High pressure (15lb/1kg) and calculate cooking time by that of the main ingredient. The base of the cooker must never be more than half full when all the ingredients have been added. This allows room for the liquid to boil up and for steam to form, and ensures that the vent doesn't become blocked. As a general rule, if you're going to need more soup than the cooker will hold, increase solid ingredients and reduce liquid. The soup can be thinned with hot water, milk or stock after pressure cooking. Cream or eggs, included for richness, should also be added after cooking but don't boil if reheating. For soups made with fresh vegetables, meat and fish, reduce pressure with cold water: for dried vegetables, reduce at room temperature.

Paprika chicken

A beautifully savoury Spanish-style dish. The chicken is well-seasoned with a mixture of paprika, salt and pepper, fried gently in butter till browned, then stewed whole with tomatoes, shallots and parsley. The cooking liquid is thickened and flavoured with wine before serving. Chicken portions can be used but should be cooked for just 40 minutes before the vegetables are added

MAIN MEAL Serves 6

Overall timing 1¾ hours

Equipment Bowl, flameproof casserole

Freezing Not recommended

INGREDIENTS

3½lb	Ovenready chicken	1.6kg
	Salt	
2 teasp	Paprika	2×5ml
	Freshly-ground black pepper	
2oz	Butter	50g
¾ pint	Chicken stock	400ml
3	Shallots	3
1lb	Small tomatoes	450g
1 tbsp	Chopped parsley	15ml
1 tbsp	Cornflour	15ml
3 tbsp	White wine	3×15ml

METHOD

1 Preheat the oven to 400F (200C) Gas 6. Wipe the chicken. Mix ½ teasp (½×5ml) salt with the paprika and plenty of pepper. Sprinkle half the mixture inside the chicken and rub the rest into the skin.

2 Heat the butter in the casserole, add the chicken and fry gently till browned all over. Add the stock (made with cubes if necessary), cover and cook in the centre of the oven for 1 hour.

3 Peel and finely chop the shallots. Blanch and peel the tomatoes. Arrange shallots and tomatoes round the chicken and sprinkle with parsley. Cover and cook for a further 20 minutes till the juices of the chicken run clear when the thickest part of the thigh is pierced with a skewer.

4 Lift the chicken out of the casserole and cut into 6 portions. Arrange on a warmed serving dish with tomatoes and shallots. Blend cornflour with wine, add to casserole. Bring to the boil, stirring constantly, then simmer for 3 minutes.

5 Adjust the seasoning to taste, then pour over the chicken. Serve immediately with jacket baked potatoes.

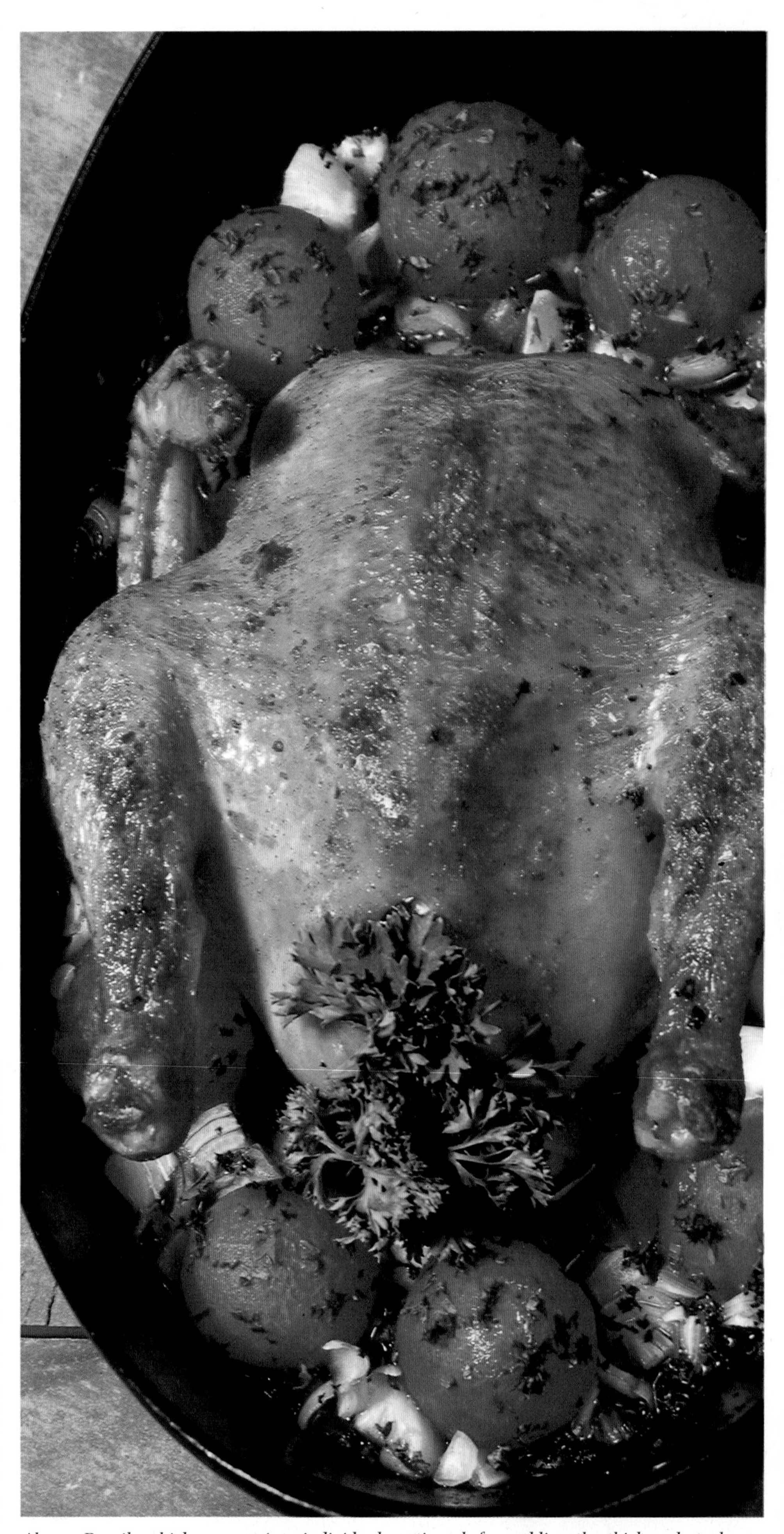

Above: Paprika chicken – cut into individual portions before adding the thickened stock

Sweet-sour roast lamb

The garlic spiked lamb absorbs the sweet-sour flavours of the marinade, then it's cooked so that the sugar caramelizes on the surface. Ask the butcher to chine the joint

MAIN MEAL Serves 6

Overall timing 1¾ hours plus overnight marination

Equipment Large bowl, roasting tin, saucepan, sieve

Freezing Not recommended

INGREDIENTS

2lb	Best end of neck of lamb	900g
2	Large garlic cloves	2
	Salt	
1	Onion	1
1	Carrot	1
1	Stalk of celery	1
2 tbsp	Oil	2×15ml
½ pint	Dry white wine	300ml
2 tbsp	Vinegar	2×15ml
4 tbsp	Soft brown sugar	4×15ml
	Freshly-ground black pepper	

METHOD

1 Wipe and trim the lamb. Make several deep incisions in the fat with a thin-bladed knive. Peel the garlic cloves and cut into slivers. Toss in salt and insert into the cuts in the meat.

2 Peel and chop the onion, scrape and chop the carrot, trim and chop the celery. Put into a large bowl with the oil, wine, vinegar and half the sugar. Add the meat, turning till coated, then leave to marinate overnight.

3 Next day, preheat the oven to 350F (180C) Gas 4. Remove the meat from the marinade and place fat side up in a roasting tin.

4 Put the marinade into a saucepan, add the remaining sugar and bring to the boil. Boil steadily till reduced by half. Season to taste.

5 Strain through a sieve over the lamb. Bake in the centre of the oven for 1–1¼ hours, basting several times so the lamb is coated with a sticky glaze.

6 Remove the lamb from the oven and place on a warmed serving dish. Cut between the ribs and serve immediately with rice and stewed fennel with tomatoes (see right).

Above: Stewed fennel with tomatoes – cooked so they still have a "bite"

Stewed fennel with tomatoes

This delicious mixture of fennel bulbs and tomatoes is a favourite with the Italians. It will make an unusual accompaniment to sweet-sour roast lamb

VEGETABLE Serves 6

Overall timing 1 hour

Equipment Bowl, saucepan, flameproof casserole, potato peeler

Freezing Not recommended

INGREDIENTS

6	Saffron strands *or* pinch of turmeric	6
3	Bulbs of fennel	3
	Salt	
2	Large onions	2
3 tbsp	Olive oil	3×15ml
3	Large ripe tomatoes	3
1	Orange	1
¼ pint	Dry white wine	150ml
1 teasp	Caster sugar	5ml
	Freshly-ground white pepper	

METHOD

1 Put the saffron into a bowl with 2 tbsp (2×15ml) hot water and leave to soak for 10 minutes.

2 Wash and trim the fennel and cut each bulb into quarters. Blanch in boiling salted water for 5 minutes, then drain.

3 Peel and slice the onions. Heat the oil in the casserole, add the onions and fry till transparent.

4 Blanch, peel and chop the tomatoes. Remove the zest from the orange with a potato peeler and shred finely. Squeeze the juice from the orange. Add to the pan with the fennel, saffron and soaking water or turmeric and 2 tbsp (2×15ml) of water, wine and sugar. Bring to the boil and season.

5 Cover tightly and simmer for about 30 minutes till vegetables are tender.

6 Adjust seasoning to taste and serve immediately.

Fried scampi

Scampi as it is most commonly known, especially in Britain, deep fried in a crisp batter. You can freeze fresh (but not frozen) scampi in the batter after cooking for 1 minute

MAIN MEAL Serves 4

Overall timing 30 minutes

Equipment Bowl, deep-fryer

Freezing Cook for 1 minute, drain on kitchen paper and cool. Spread on baking tray and open freeze, then pack in polythene. Freezer life: 2 months. To use: deep fry from frozen for 6–10 minutes

INGREDIENTS

	Savoury fritter batter (recipe page 370)	
	Oil for deep frying	
1¼lb	Shelled fresh scampi	600g

METHOD

1. Make a fritter batter according to the instructions on page 370, but do not add egg whites.
2. Heat oil in a deep-fryer to 340F (170C).
3. Fold whisked egg whites into batter. Dip scampi into batter and cook a few at a time for 5–6 minutes till golden. Drain well on kitchen paper and serve with lemon wedges and tartare sauce, sauté potatoes or plain boiled rice and mixed salad.

Coley with mustard

An unusual treatment of fish but one that gives fried coley a delightful fillip. The bite of the mustard is tempered by the breadcrumb coating and the cream

MAIN MEAL Serves 4

Overall timing 20 minutes

Equipment 2 bowls, frying pan

Freezing Not recommended

INGREDIENTS

1¾lb	Coley fillets	750g
2 tbsp	Strong prepared mustard	2×15ml
	Dried breadcrumbs	
2 tbsp	Oil	2×15ml
	Salt and pepper	
4 tbsp	Single cream	4×15ml

METHOD

1. Wash and dry fillets on kitchen paper. Spread them with mustard, then dip then into a bowl of breadcrumbs. Press the breadcrumbs on to the fish.
2. Heat oil in a frying pan. Cook fillets for 5 minutes on each side. Season with salt and pepper.
3. In a bowl, mix a little salt and pepper into the cream and warm. Remove fillets from pan and place on a warm serving dish. Pour seasoned cream over and serve.

cook's know-how

The term "à la meunière" comes from the French word for miller and applies to a method of cooking fish in which the fish is coated with seasoned flour, then fried in butter. **To make** Coley à la meunière, wash 4 coley fillets and dry on kitchen paper. Coat lightly with 2 tbsp (2×15ml) seasoned flour. Heat 2oz (50g) butter in a frying pan. When it begins to foam, add the coley fillets and cook on both sides over a moderate heat for a total of 5–7 minutes. Remove fish carefully from pan with a fish slice and put on a warmed serving dish. Season with salt and pepper and garnish with lemon slices. Sprinkle with 2 tbsp (2×15ml) lemon juice and 1 tbsp (15ml) chopped parsley. Serve piping hot with side dishes of French fries and broccoli or French beans.

Cold red mullet with mint

A dish to serve on summer days with a bottle of chilled dry white wine. If you don't have a blender, pound all the sauce ingredients except the oil in a mortar with a pestle, then add the oil, drop by drop, as for mayonnaise (see page 237), pounding well between additions

LUNCH OR SUPPER — Serves 4

Overall timing 45 minutes plus chilling

Equipment Frying pan, serving dish, bowl, blender, sauce boat

Freezing Not recommended

INGREDIENTS

4×8oz	Cleaned and scaled red mullet	4×225g
3 tbsp	Plain flour	3×15ml
8 tbsp	Olive oil	8×15ml
½ pint	Water	300ml
2 tbsp	White wine vinegar	2×15ml
8oz	Fresh breadcrumbs	225g
1 tbsp	Chopped parsley	15ml
3 tbsp	Chopped mint	3×15ml
1 tbsp	Capers	15ml
1	Egg	1
1 teasp	Sugar	5ml
1 tbsp	Anchovy essence	15ml
	Salt	
	Freshly-ground black pepper	

METHOD

1 Wipe the fish and toss in the flour till lightly coated. Heat half the oil in the frying pan and fry the mullet for about 10 minutes each side till tender.
2 Remove from the pan, drain on kitchen paper and arrange on a serving dish. Allow to cool, then chill for 3 hours.
3 Meanwhile, put the water into a large bowl and add the vinegar and breadcrumbs. Leave to soak for 10 minutes.
4 Squeeze excess moisture out of the breadcrumbs and place in a blender. Add the parsley and mint, capers, egg, sugar and anchovy essence. Blend till fairly smooth.
5 Remove the centre cap from the blender lid and continue to blend while slowly pouring remaining oil in through the hole in the lid to make a smooth purée.
6 Season to taste and chill for 2 hours. Serve the mullet and sauce separately with boiled new potatoes and a tomato and onion salad.

Italian marinated sprats

Fried sprats take on a tangy taste in a cooked marinade which includes sliced onion, vinegar and sage leaves

STARTER — Serves 6

Overall timing 45 minutes plus overnight marination

Equipment Deep frying pan, shallow dish

Freezing Not recommended

INGREDIENTS

2lb	Sprats	900g
	Salt	
	Freshly-ground black pepper	
3oz	Plain flour	75g
	Oil for frying	
1	Large onion	1
8	Sage leaves *or*	8
½ teasp	dried sage	½×5ml
6 tbsp	Vinegar	6×15ml
4 tbsp	Water	4×15ml

METHOD

1 Rinse and drain the sprats thoroughly. Season the flour and use to coat the fish.
2 Heat 1 inch (2.5cm) oil in a deep frying pan and fry the floured sprats, a few at a time, for about 4 minutes till crisp and golden. Drain on kitchen paper, then put into a shallow serving dish.
3 Peel and slice the onion. Heat 2 tbsp (2×15ml) oil in frying pan, add the onion and fry gently till transparent.
4 Add the sage leaves, vinegar and water and bring to the boil. Boil for 3 minutes, remove from the heat and season.
5 Pour the hot marinade over the sprats. Cover and leave to marinate in a cool place overnight.
6 Serve cold with crusty bread and butter.

Coat the fish in seasoned flour then fry in oil a few at a time till crisp and golden

Fry sliced onion gently till transparent. Add the vinegar, water and sage leaves, bring to the boil and boil for 3 minutes

Season and pour over the sprats, turning them carefully till they are all coated. Cover and leave in a cool place overnight

Below: Italian marinated sprats – a tasty and unusual way to serve these small fish

Family tree of sauces

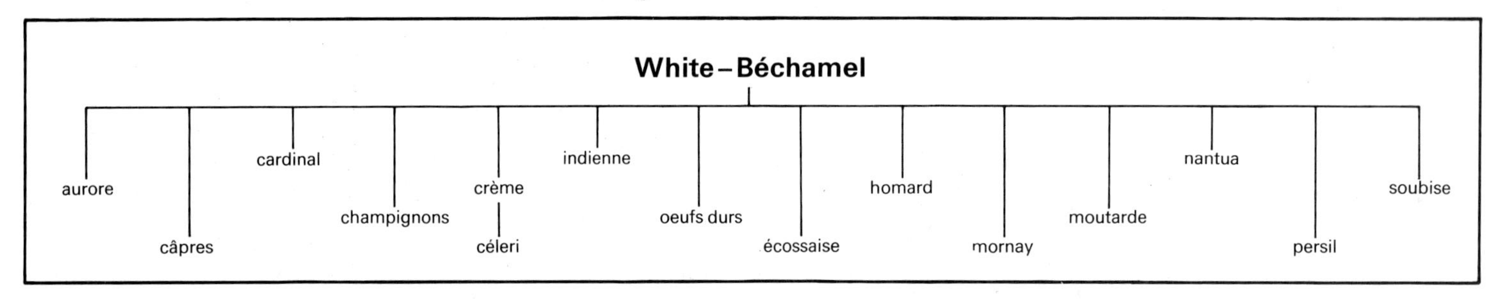

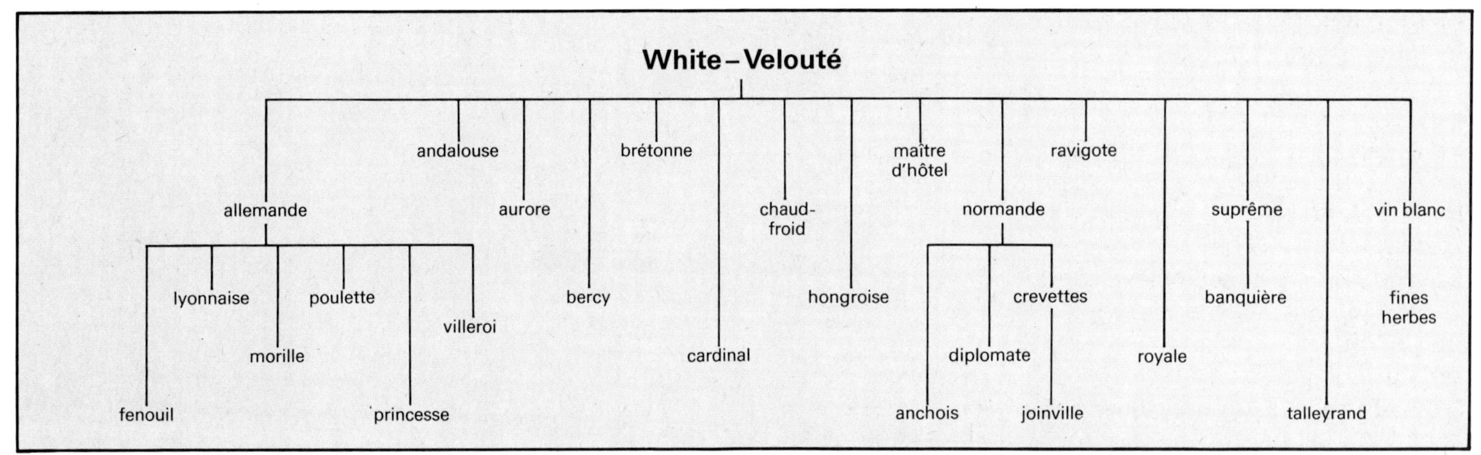

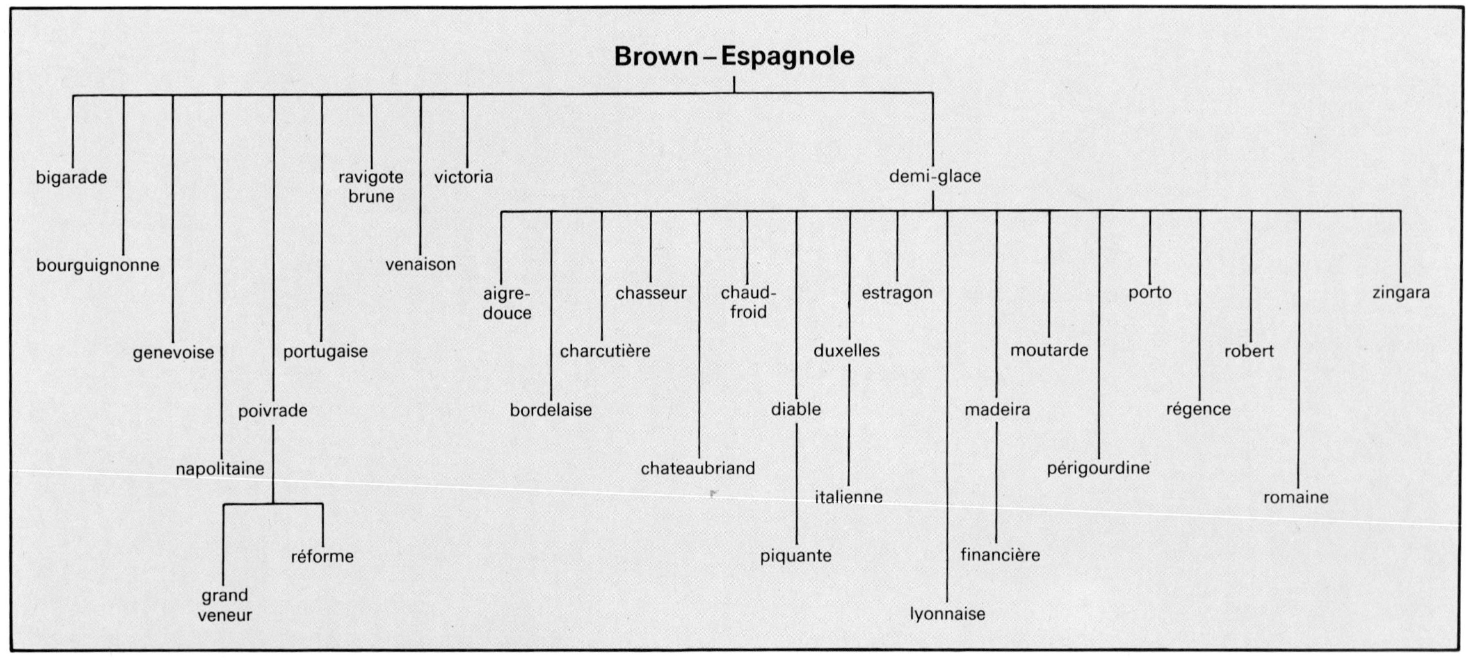

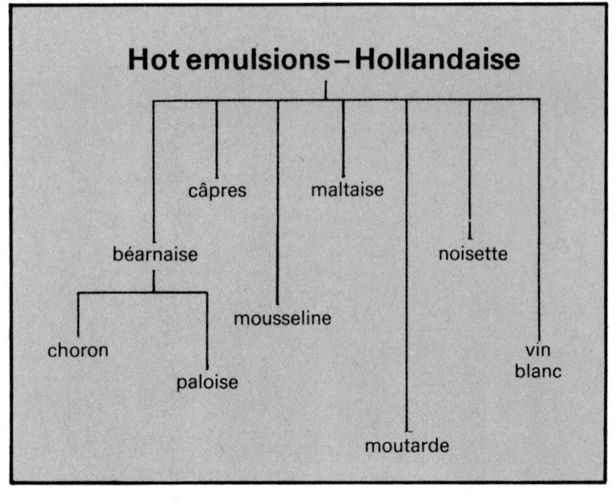

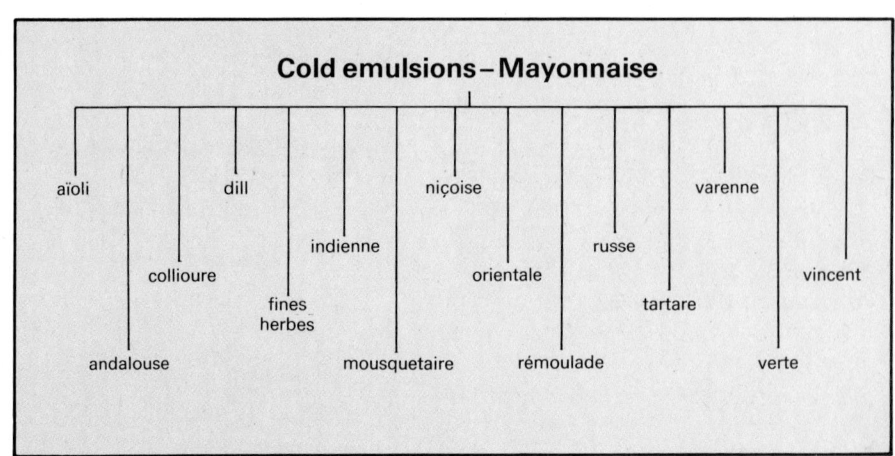

Colourful coats

Sauces are liquid or semi liquid preparations that add colour and flavour to food and make it more palatable. They can be hot, cold, savoury or sweet. Sauces fall into three categories: uncooked vinegar-based sauces (mint and vinaigrette); sauces that come in bottles and should correctly be called condiments; and the roux or egg-based classic sauces of French cooking. It is this last group which this section concentrates on, and in detail shows how basic techniques are used to make a wide range of sauces.

Many of the sauces as we know them in recipes and on menus were the creations of the famous 19th century chefs Carême and Escoffier which is why they have French names.

The mother (or *grandes*) sauces are Béchamel (named after the Lord Steward at the court of Louis XIV), Velouté (named after its velvety texture) and Espagnole (nothing to do with Spain). The two egg-based mother sauces are Hollandaise (its origin is Dutch) and Mayonnaise (its origin is uncertain). Espagnole and Hollandaise will be dealt with on pages 490–495.

Roux-based sauces Keep the pan on the heat once the flour has been added. It has to cook properly so the starch grains will burst and thicken the sauce. If not cooked long enough the sauce will taste raw. Liquid should be warm or at room temperature so it combines better with the roux. If lumps do form, it isn't a disaster – they can easily be whisked out (professional sauce makers always make their sauces with whisks), or the sauce can be sieved.

Egg-based sauces need slow, gentle cooking and constant whisking. If the mixture curdles through overheating, whisk it gradually into another egg yolk.

White sauce – Béchamel

A classic, rich white sauce which, by varying the proportions of the ingredients, you can make in three different consistencies – pouring (for sauces to be served separately), coating (for foods to be cooked further), and panada (for binding mixtures like croquettes, stuffings). A simple white sauce is Béchamel without the infused, flavoured milk

Place 1 pint (560ml) milk, ½ peeled onion, ½ chopped carrot and ½ chopped stalk of celery in pan with bay leaf. Bring to boil, remove from heat and leave for 15 minutes. In another pan, melt butter without browning, stir in flour and cook for 1 minute

Gradually stir in strained milk. Bring to the boil, then simmer for 3 minutes, stirring. Add salt, pepper and nutmeg. For 1 pint (560ml) milk use 1½oz (40g) each of butter and flour for pouring sauce; 2oz (50g) each for coating sauce; and 4oz (125g) each for binding sauce

Below: Béchamel – the most popular basic sauce, and suited to all types of food

Béchamel-based sauces

These are the sauces the cook can use to enhance everything from pasta to poultry

Quantities given are for adding to Béchamel sauce made with 1 pint (560ml) milk.
BECHAMEL AURORE Add 2oz (50g) tomato paste, 1 teasp (5ml) sugar and 1oz (25g) butter to **Béchamel sauce.**
Serve with eggs, poultry, sweetbreads
BECHAMEL CARDINAL To **Béchamel sauce** add 6 tbsp (6×15ml) single cream, 3 tbsp (3×15ml) lobster butter, made from powdered lobster shell and 4oz (125g) melted butter with the roe and liver of the lobster beaten in. Strain through a muslin-lined sieve and add 1 tbsp (15ml) finely chopped truffles.
Serve with fish
CHAMPIGNONS Thinly slice 4oz (125g) button mushrooms and fry in 1oz (25g) butter till golden. Add to **Béchamel sauce** with 4 tbsp (4×15ml) single cream and 1 teasp (5ml) chopped chervil.
Serve with fish, poultry
CREME Add 6 tbsp (6×15ml) single cream and 2oz (50g) butter to **Béchamel sauce.**
Serve with eggs, fish, poultry, vegetables
CELERI Wash, trim and finely chop 1 celery heart and simmer in ¼ pint (150ml) light stock with 1 clove-studded onion. Drain and purée. Add to **crème sauce.**
Serve with fish, poultry
ECOSSAISE Shell 3 hard-boiled eggs and reserve 1 of the yolks. Chop the rest and add to **Béchamel sauce.** Press the yolk through a sieve, mix with 1 tbsp (15ml) chopped parsley and sprinkle over sauce.
Serve with white fish, eggs, poultry
HOMARD Dice 4oz (125g) lobster flesh and add to **Béchamel sauce** with 1 teasp (5ml) anchovy essence and pinch cayenne.
Serve with fish, vol-au-vents, omelettes
INDIENNE Peel and finely chop 1 small onion and sweat in 1oz (25g) butter till transparent. Add 1 teasp (5ml) curry powder and fry for 3 minutes, stirring. Add to **Béchamel sauce** with 1oz (25g) butter.
Serve with hard-boiled eggs
MOUTARDE BLANCHE Add 2 teasp (2×5ml) prepared mustard and 1 teasp (5ml) vinegar to **Béchamel sauce.**
Serve with fish, pork
NANTUA Add 3 tbsp (3×15ml) each of crayfish cooking liquor and crayfish butter (made by taking 8oz (225g) crayfish meat and blending it with 4oz (125g) butter) with 2 tbsp (2×15ml) single cream, 2 tbsp (2×15ml) brandy and a pinch of cayenne to **Béchamel sauce.**
Serve with eggs, fish, shellfish
OEUFS DURS Shell and finely chop 2 hard-boiled eggs. Add to **Béchamel sauce** with ¼ teasp (¼×5ml) freshly-grated nutmeg. *Serve with poached fish*
PERSIL Add 3 tbsp (3×15ml) chopped parsley with 1 teasp (5ml) lemon juice to **Béchamel sauce.**
Serve with eggs, fish, ham, vegetables

Câpres

A piquant sauce to serve with mutton, lamb or rabbit

Beat 3oz (75g) butter in hot Béchamel sauce then heat gently till melted

Drain and finely chop 4 tbsp (4×15ml) capers, add to sauce, adjust seasoning

Mornay

Smooth cheese sauce to serve with vegetables, pasta or fish

Beat 3oz (75g) butter into hot Béchamel sauce and heat till melted

Remove from heat, stir in 4 tbsp (4×15ml) single cream, heat gently

Remove from heat, add 2–4oz (50–125g) grated cheese. Stand pan in simmering water to melt cheese if necessary

Soubise

Traditional onion sauce to serve with lamb, grilled meats, offal (especially good with liver) and vegetables (particularly carrots)

Peel and chop 1 large onion, blanch in boiling water for 1 minute. Drain thoroughly. Put into pan with 1oz (25g) butter, cover and sweat for 10 minutes without browning. Add to Béchamel sauce, cook for 5 minutes

Remove from heat and rub the sauce through a sieve. Reheat gently. Add a pinch of freshly-grated nutmeg and ½ teasp (½×5ml) sugar, then taste and adjust seasoning

White sauce – Velouté

The second of the white "mother" sauces, Velouté is rich and must be made with the best quality stock from fish, poultry or veal according to the food with which it is to be served, and should be both smooth and velvety

2 Gradually add 1 pint (560ml) light stock and bring to the boil, stirring

1 Heat 2oz (50g) butter in saucepan, add 2oz (50g) plain flour and cook for 1 minute, stirring constantly

3 Simmer the sauce for 5 minutes, then season to taste. Strain through a sieve into a clean saucepan and reheat

Below: Velouté sauce – serve with (or over) chicken or other poultry or fish

Velouté-based sauces

Quantities given below are for Velouté sauce made with 1 pint (560ml) light stock.

ANDALOUSE Add 2 tbsp (2×15ml) tomato paste, 1 teasp (5ml) sugar and 1 chopped canned red capsicum to **Velouté sauce** with 1 tbsp (15ml) chopped parsley. *Serve with eggs, fish, poultry*

HONGROISE Peel and finely chop 1 onion and fry gently in 1oz (25g) butter till transparent. Add 1 tbsp (15ml) paprika, ¼ pint (150ml) dry white wine and a bouquet garni and boil till reduced by half. Add to **Velouté sauce,** simmer for 5 minutes. Strain and add 1oz (25g) butter. *Serve with fish, poultry, meats, eggs*

MAITRE D'HOTEL Add 2oz (50g) maître d'hôtel butter (made by beating 1 tbsp (15ml) parsley and 2 teasp (2×5ml) lemon juice into 2oz (50g) butter) to **Velouté sauce.** *Serve with fish, poultry*

NORMANDE Add 6 tbsp (6×15ml) strong fish stock and 2 tbsp (2×15ml) mushroom cooking liquor to **Velouté sauce.** Boil steadily till reduced by a quarter. Add 2 egg yolks, 4 tbsp (4×15ml) single cream and 2oz (50g) butter. *Serve with fish*

ANCHOIS Add 1 tbsp (15ml) anchovy essence to **normande sauce.** *Serve with hard-boiled eggs, fish*

DIPLOMATE Omit extra butter from **normande sauce.** Add 4 tbsp (4×15ml) lobster butter (see facing page) and 2 tbsp (2×15ml) brandy, pinch of cayenne and 1 tbsp (15ml) each of chopped lobster and truffles. *Serve with fish*

ROYALE Add 4 tbsp (4×15ml) single cream, 2oz (50g) butter, 1 tbsp (15ml) chopped truffles and 2 tbsp (2×15ml) sherry to **Velouté sauce.** *Serve with eggs, poultry*

SUPREME Add ½ pint (300ml) home-made chicken stock to **Velouté sauce** and boil till reduced by half. Beat in 2oz (50g) butter and ¼ pint (150ml) single cream. *Serve with eggs, poultry, offal, vegetables*

BANQUIERE Add 6 tbsp (6×15ml) Madeira and 2 tbsp (2×15ml) chopped truffles to **suprême sauce.** *Serve with eggs, poultry, offal, vol-au-vents*

TALLEYRAND Add ¼ pint (150ml) home-made chicken stock to **Velouté sauce** and boil till reduced by a quarter. Add 4 tbsp (4×15ml) each of Madeira and single cream and 1oz (25g) butter. Stir in 2 tbsp (2×15ml) each of mirepoix (diced vegetables such as carrots, onions and celery sweated in butter or baconfat), truffles and tongue. *Serve with poultry, offal*

VELOUTE CARDINAL Add 3 tbsp (3×15ml) lobster butter (as Béchamel cardinal, left), 6 tbsp (6×15ml) single cream and a pinch of cayenne to **Velouté sauce.** *Serve with fish, omelettes, hard-boiled eggs*

Allemande

An attractive yellow Velouté sauce given smoothness with egg yolks and butter or cream. It can also be called sauce blonde or parisienne

ALLEMANDE Put 2 egg yolks into a large saucepan and whisk in ½ pint (300ml) each of light stock and **Velouté sauce.** Cook gently, stirring constantly, without boiling till sauce coats the back of a spoon. Beat in 2oz (50g) butter or 4 tbsp (4×15ml) single cream.
Serve with eggs, poultry, offal, vegetables
FENOUIL Add 2 tbsp (2×15ml) chopped fennel fronds, 1 tbsp (15ml) lemon juice and ¼ teasp (¼×5ml) freshly-grated nutmeg to **allemande sauce.**
Serve with grilled oily fish, vegetables
LYONNAISE BLANCHE Peel and chop 2 large onions and cook in 2oz (50g) butter till transparent. Add to **allemande sauce** with 1 teasp (5ml) each of chopped tarragon and lemon juice and a little nutmeg.
Serve with poultry, offal, vegetables
MORILLE Simmer 4oz (125g) morels, a type of mushroom (see page 252), in court-bouillon till tender. Drain and add to **allemande sauce** with 2 tbsp (2×15ml) each of lemon juice and chopped chervil, and 1oz (25g) butter.
Serve with fish, poultry, offal
POULETTE Add 3 tbsp (3×15ml) chopped parsley and 2 teasp (2×5ml) lemon juice to **allemande sauce.**
Serve with offal, vegetables
PRINCESSE Add 2 tbsp (2×15ml) each of chopped parsley and jellied chicken stock, 1oz (25g) butter, 2 teasp (2×5ml) lemon juice and a little grated nutmeg to **allemande sauce.**
Serve with poultry, offal, vegetables
VILLEROI Add ¼ pint (150ml) chicken stock flavoured with mushroom trimmings to **allemande sauce.** Boil steadily but carefully till reduced by half.
Use as coating sauce for chops and poultry which are then fried

Ravigote blanche

Highly seasoned sauce for poultry, offal

1 Put 2 tbsp (2×15ml) each white wine and wine vinegar, 1 chopped shallot in pan

2 Boil till reduced to one-third. Add to Velouté sauce, bring to boil, stirring

3 Add 2 teasp (2×5ml) dried thyme and 1 bay leaf, simmer for 5 minutes. Strain

4 Beat in 1oz (25g) butter, 4 tbsp (4×15ml) cream, 1 teasp (5ml) parsley

Velouté aurore

Serve with eggs, poultry, offal

Add 8oz (227g) peeled sieved tomatoes to Velouté sauce. Simmer for 10 minutes

Press through sieve into pan, bring to boil and beat in 2oz (50g) butter

Crevettes

A shrimp sauce to accompany fish. Adding truffles makes it into joinville

Replace butter in normande sauce with 4 tbsp (4×15ml) shrimp butter (as crayfish butter page 452). Rub through sieve

Return to pan and reheat sauce. Stir in 4oz (125g) shelled shrimps, 1 teasp (5ml) anchovy essence and a pinch of cayenne

Taste and adjust seasoning. To make joinville sauce, add 2 tbsp (2×15ml) shredded truffles to shrimp sauce

Vin blanc

Distinctively flavoured sauce for fish, veal, poultry, vegetables

Make up Velouté sauce and transfer to a large clean saucepan

Add 6 tbsp (6×15ml) white wine, reduce by one-third. Cool slightly

Whisk in 2 egg yolks and stir over a low heat for 2 minutes – do not boil

Remove from heat, beat in 2oz (50g) butter cut into small pieces

Fines herbes Simmer 1 shallot in vin blanc sauce, strain. Add 1 tbsp (15ml) each parsley and chervil

Chaud-froid blanc

Coating sauce for chicken or hard-boiled eggs to be served cold

Add ½ pint (300ml) jellied light stock to Velouté sauce in pan

Boil till reduced by half and sauce coats back of spoon. Reduce heat, stir in 4 tbsp (4×15ml) single cream

Brétonne

A delicate sauce to enhance eggs or fish, poultry or offal

Fry leek, celery, mushrooms in 1oz (25g) butter. Add Velouté sauce

Purée, then add 2oz (50g) butter, simmer for 5 minutes. Add 2 tbsp (2×15ml) each white wine, double cream

Bercy

A sauce for fish, usually made from the fish cooking liquor

Add 5 tbsp (5×15ml) each fish stock and white wine, 1 fried shallot to Velouté sauce. Reduce by half. Add 1oz (25g) butter and 1 tbsp (15ml) chopped parsley

Countdown

Cheeseburgers

Coleslaw

Banana splits

Children are notoriously conservative about food. They seem quite happy to eat the same favourite meal day after day. However much you may struggle to interest them in a wider range of food for most of the year, a birthday tea is the time to offer what all children love best – cheeseburgers. A crunchy coleslaw salad will provide some vitamins in a tempting form, and be sure to serve a variety of chutneys and relishes. Banana splits look spectacular but they're actually very easy to prepare and can be adapted to the time of year

The morning before Make the lemonade (see below) and then chill

1½ hours before Soak the white cabbage for the coleslaw

1 hour before Drain and shred the cabbage and make the coleslaw. If you like, add freshly grated carrot or apple and sultanas or caraway seeds. Chill

45 minutes before Prepare fruit for banana splits and chill in fridge

30 minutes before Start preparing cheeseburgers

15 minutes before While burgers are cooking lay the table with an assortment of relishes and heat the buns in a moderate oven

Serve cheeseburgers in warm buns with the coleslaw. While the children are enjoying this course finish making the banana splits

Serve banana splits

Children are very fond of fizzy drinks of all sorts even if they aren't very nourishing. For a change you could serve your own homemade lemonade. To make 2½ pints (1.5 litre) of lemonade pare the rind and squeeze the juice from 4 lemons. Put rind into a large saucepan with 2 pints (1.1 litre) water and 8oz (225g) sugar. Heat through, stirring occasionally until the sugar is dissolved. Bring to the boil and add lemon juice, allow to cool and strain before serving.

Cheeseburgers

Becoming the top family favourite round the world, hamburgers taste even better with melted cheese

LIGHT LUNCH OR SUPPER Serves 4

Overall timing 30 minutes

Equipment Large bowl

Freezing Not recommended

INGREDIENTS

1	Large onion	1
1lb	Minced beef	450g
3 tbsp	Fresh breadcrumbs	3×15ml
4 tbsp	Milk	4×15ml
	Salt	
	Paprika	
1 teasp	Powdered mustard	5ml
	Oil	
4	Small tomatoes	4
4	Slices of Cheddar	4
4	Buns	4

METHOD

1 Heat the grill. Peel and finely chop onion. In a large bowl, mix together the onion, minced beef, breadcrumbs and milk. Season with salt, a pinch of paprika and mustard. Leave for 10 minutes.

2 Make 4 hamburgers from the mixture. Brush with oil. Cook for 5 minutes on each side under the grill.

3 Remove from heat. Top with slices of tomato and strips of cheese. Put hamburgers back under the grill till the cheese melts. Serve in warm buns.

cook's know-how

Children sometimes need to be encouraged to eat vegetables and salads. Try serving coleslaw – an American salad of shredded white cabbage dressed with mayonnaise – with the cheeseburgers. It's sure to be a favourite with the younger generation and tastes so much better when it's homemade. To make, soak the cabbage in iced, lightly sugared water for 30 minutes, then drain and shred. Mix in the mayonnaise, chill for 30 minutes, then serve. Freshly grated carrot and/or apple, sultanas or caraway seeds can also be added. For a lighter version of this salad dress the cabbage with a mixture of plain thick yogurt and mayonnaise.

Below: Cheeseburger – a hamburger dressed up with slices of cheese and tomato and grilled

Above: Banana split — each serving includes a whole banana, scoops of ice cream, fruit, sauce, cream and tiny, ready-made meringues

Banana split

A delicious dessert which gets its name from the way the banana is cut

COLD DESSERT Serves 4

Overall timing 30 minutes

Equipment 3 mixing bowls, piping bag

Freezing Not recommended

INGREDIENTS

8oz	Strawberries*	225g
4oz	Grapes	125g
1	Orange	1
1	Kiwi fruit	1
4 tbsp	Milk shake syrup *or* homemade fruit sauce (see right)	4×15ml
2 teasp	Arrowroot	2×5ml
$\frac{1}{4}$ pint	Double cream	150ml
4	Bananas	4
1	Small block of vanilla ice cream	1
8	Little meringues	8

METHOD

1 Hull strawberries and cut them in half. Halve grapes and remove pips. Peel orange (be careful to remove pith) and divide into segments. Peel and slice kiwi fruit. Place all the fruits in a bowl, and put in fridge for 15 minutes.

2 Remove fruits from fridge — they should be really cold. If milk shake syrup is not thick enough, mix arrowroot with a little cold water and blend into syrup over gentle heat and bring to boil to thicken. Whip cream to piping consistency.

3 Peel bananas. "Split" in half lengthways and place halves down each side of 4 serving dishes.

4 Arrange fruit between bananas and place scoops of ice cream on top. Pour over a little syrup, pipe on cream swirls and top with meringues. Serve immediately with crisp fan wafers.

*This is a recipe that can be adapted to the time of year because you can use canned fruit when the selection of fresh is not large. Make the sweet sauce from the syrup in the can, using arrowroot to thicken it and a little red food colouring.

cook's know-how

Fruit sauces, served hot or cold, are a quick and impressive way of dressing up desserts. They are delicious poured over ice cream and topped with a few nuts, spread over sponge puddings, brushed over hot scones, pancakes or waffles.

Melba sauce (see page 59), most used with Peach Melba, is one of the very famous.

Apricot sauce Put $\frac{1}{2}$ pint (300ml) water and 4oz (125g) sugar in a pan. Heat gently, without stirring, until sugar dissolves. Bring to the boil and simmer gently for about 10 minutes. Leave to cool. Place in blender with 8oz (225g) stoned ripe apricots and blend for a few seconds till reduced to a purée. Serve cold or heat gently for 5 minutes and serve.

Berry sauce Make as for apricot sauce above, using 1lb (450g) fresh or frozen hulled strawberries, blackberries or raspberries instead of the apricots.

Above: Marinated mushrooms – a simple but exquisite starter to serve warm or cold

Marinated mushrooms

A lemon and oil based marinade makes the mushrooms succulent and juicy. A good dish for making well in advance of your dinner party

STARTER OR SALAD Serves 4–6

Overall timing 25 minutes plus cooling

Equipment Frying pan

Freezing Not recommended

INGREDIENTS

1lb	Mushrooms	450g
5 tbsp	Oil	5×15ml
1	Garlic clove	1
¼ teasp	Ground cumin	¼×5ml
¼ pint	Water	150ml
1	Bay leaf	1
	Salt	
	Freshly-ground black pepper	
4 teasp	Finely chopped parsley	4×5ml
3 tbsp	Lemon juice	3×15ml

METHOD

1 Wipe and trim the mushrooms and cut into large chunks. Heat the oil in the frying pan. Add the mushrooms, the peeled and crushed garlic and cumin and fry for 5 minutes.

2 Add the water, bay leaf and plenty of seasoning and bring to the boil. Lower the heat and simmer for 10 minutes.

3 Stir in the parsley and lemon juice, then taste and adjust seasoning. Pour into a serving dish and leave till warm before serving, or allow to cool completely and serve cold. Serve with French bread.

cook's know-how

This method of preparing mushrooms can be adapted for other vegetables which will make equally delicious starters. Leeks, courgettes, carrots and small button onions may all be used. Clean and chop the vegetables finely, or peel the onions and proceed as in the main recipe. Some vegetables may need to be simmered a little longer than the mushrooms. A selection of two or three marinated vegetables prettily arranged in a dish could also be served.

Ramekins savoyards

This recipe for a light, individually served starter comes from Savoy, formerly in the Kingdom of Sardinia in Italy, but now in southern France

STARTER Serves 4

Overall timing 25 minutes

Equipment 4 ramekins, bowl, baking tray

Freezing Not recommended

INGREDIENTS

1oz	Butter	25g
4	Slices of bread	4
4oz	Grated cheese	125g
3	Eggs	3
½ pint	Milk	300ml
¼ pint	Carton of single cream	150ml
½ teasp	Freshly-grated nutmeg	2.5ml
	Salt	
	Freshly-ground black pepper	

METHOD

1 Preheat the oven to 400F (200C) Gas 6. Grease the ramekins.

2 Butter the bread and cut into cubes. Divide between the ramekins and sprinkle with the cheese. Beat the eggs in a bowl with the milk, cream, nutmeg, salt and pepper. Pour mixture over the bread and cheese.

3 Place the ramekins on a baking tray and bake for about 15 minutes till lightly set and golden. Serve immediately.

VARIATIONS

Soak 8oz (225g) fresh breadcrumbs in 1 pint (560ml) hot milk. Pour half the soaked breadcrumbs into a greased 2 pint (1.1 litre) soufflé dish, cover with 3oz (75g) grated cheese then add the remaining soaked crumbs. Beat 3 eggs in a bowl with 1oz (25g) grated cheese, ½ teasp (2.5ml) grated nutmeg, salt and pepper. Pour over the crumbs and bake at 400F (200C) Gas 6 for 30 minutes till set.

To make more filling individual dishes to serve for a light lunch, use 8oz (225g) leftover boiled potatoes instead of the slices of bread. Cut the potatoes into slices, then layer them with the cheese in the greased ramekins. Cover with the egg mixture (as Step 2 above) and bake. Serve with a mixed salad.

cook's know-how

If you grow your own mint, it can be harvested for winter use just before the plants bloom. Pick the leaves, wrap in foil or cling film and freeze, or cut the stems near the base of the plant, tie loosely in bundles and hang upside down in an airing cupboard. Or, dry in a cool oven (250F/130C Gas $\frac{1}{2}$) with the door ajar. When dry but still green, strip the leaves from the stem and store in an airtight container. Dried mint can be used when fresh isn't available – use 1 teasp (5ml) for every 1 tbsp (15ml) of the fresh herb called for in a recipe. The flavour of dried mint is concentrated and keeps for a long time.
Mint sauce and mint jelly are famous accompaniments for roast lamb, but the fresh or dried leaves can be rubbed on to any joint or poultry before roasting. Fresh mint is essential in Mint julep, the iced Bourbon whisky drink of the southern states of America, but fresh or dried mint can be used to flavour tea.

Chilled cucumber and mint soup

Ideal for a summer dinner party, this really delectable cold soup is light and refreshing and enhanced by the tang and fragrance of fresh mint leaves. Serve in chilled bowls

STARTER Serves 4

Overall timing 10 minutes plus maceration

Equipment Potato peeler, bowl, blender

Freezing Not recommended

INGREDIENTS

1	Large cucumber	1
$\frac{1}{2}$ pint	Milk	300ml
1	Garlic clove	1
$1\frac{1}{2}$ pints	Natural yogurt	850ml
	Salt	
	Freshly-ground pepper	
12	Fresh mint leaves	12

METHOD

1. Peel the cucumber with a potato peeler, then cut in two. Slice one half lengthways into 4 and cut each quarter into thin slices. Put slices in a bowl. Chop remaining half and place in blender with milk. Blend till smooth.
2. Peel and crush the garlic and put into blender with the yogurt and seasoning. Blend for 2 seconds, then pour over the cucumber.
3. Wash, pat dry and roughly chop mint leaves. Sprinkle over the cucumber and yogurt mixture. Leave to macerate in fridge for 2 hours.
4. Stir in the mint, taste and adjust the seasoning. Serve immediately with breadsticks.

VARIATION

To make this soup in the winter months, don't use dried mint but try a teaspoon (5ml) of mint sauce concentrate stirred into the yogurt instead. It makes a very acceptable substitute.

Below: Chilled cucumber and mint soup – its delicate colour is as pleasing as its flavour

Sausage brioche

A variation on that old favourite the sausage roll. The steam from the simmering sausage will help the brioche dough to rise

STARTER Serves 6–8

Overall timing 2½ hours plus proving

Equipment 2 large bowls, baking tray

Freezing Not recommended

INGREDIENTS

1lb	Sausage meat	450g
2 tbsp	Fresh mixed herbs	2×15ml
1	Clove of garlic	1
1	Onion	1
8oz	Strong flour	225g
¼ teasp	Salt	¼×5ml
½oz	Fresh yeast *or*	15g
1½ teasp	dried yeast	1½×5ml
2 tbsp	Warm water	2×15ml
1 tbsp	Caster sugar	15ml
2	Eggs	2
2oz	Melted butter	50g
1	Egg yolk	1

METHOD

1 Finely chop the herbs (sage, parsley and thyme). Crush the garlic clove. Mix the herbs and garlic into the meat and roll into a sausage shape.

2 Meanwhile, sift the flour and salt into a large bowl. Cream the fresh yeast and the water and add to the flour with the sugar. Or, sprinkle dried yeast on to the water, add a pinch of the sugar and mix well. Leave in a warm place till frothy, then add to the flour with the remaining sugar.

3 Add the eggs and melted butter to the flour and mix to a soft dough. Knead till glossy, wrap in oiled polythene and leave in a warm place to prove.

4 Preheat the oven to 425F (220C) Gas 7.

5 Roll out the dough on a floured surface to a rectangle large enough to enclose the sausage. Brush the edges with cold water. Place the sausage meat along the centre and fold the dough round it, pinching the edges to seal.

6 Place, join down, on a greased baking tray. Cover with oiled polythene and leave to prove for 15 minutes.

7 Brush with the egg yolk and bake in the centre of the oven for about 25 minutes till crisp and golden.

8 Place on a warmed serving dish and serve immediately, cut into thick slices.

Below: Sausage brioche – traditionally served by itself without accompaniment

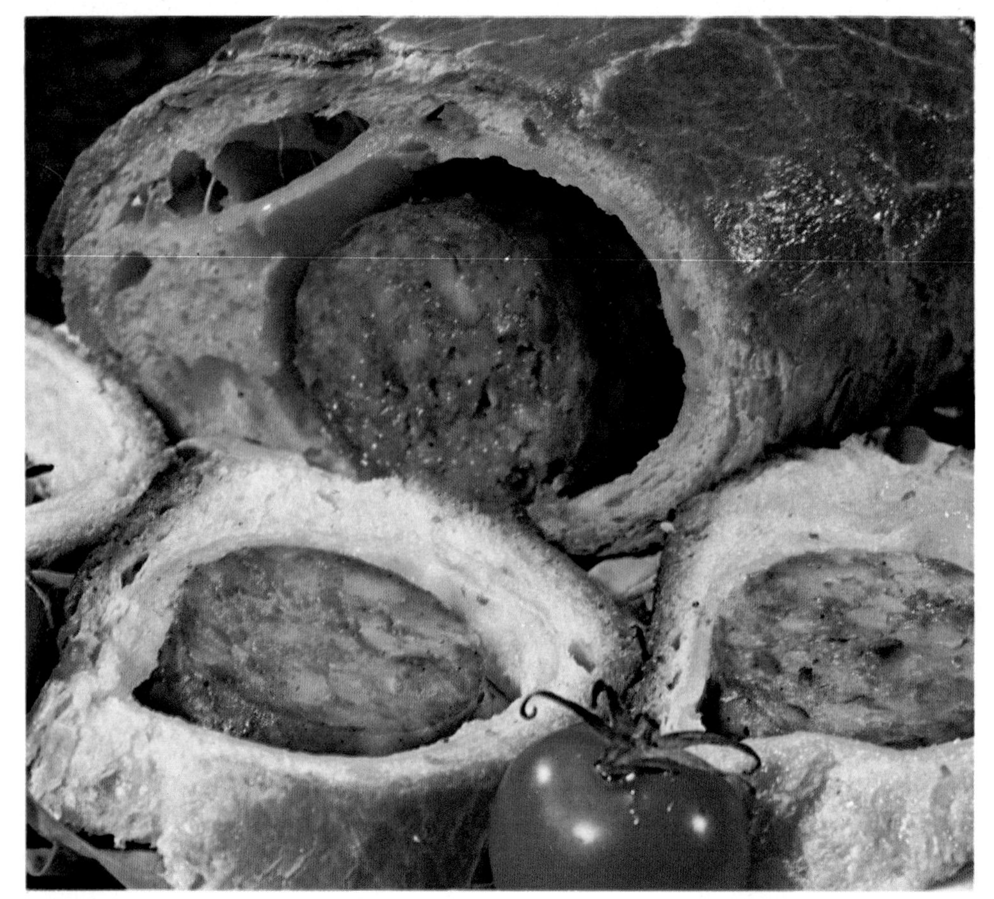

Potato and vegetable soup

Perfect heart-warming fare, this soup originates from south-western Poland, an area which used to be known as Silesia. The thickening agent is grated potato which makes for a soup that's quite substantial

STARTER Serves 6

Overall timing 1 hour

Equipment Saucepan, tureen

Freezing Prepare soup to end of Step 3. Cool, then pour into rigid container, leaving 1 inch (2.5cm) headspace, cover, label and freeze. Freezer life: 1 month. To use: place block of soup in a pan, heat gently till thawed, complete Step 4

INGREDIENTS

1	Large onion	1
2	Medium-size carrots	2
1	Large leek	1
2	Stalks of celery	2
4oz	Lean bacon rashers	125g
2 tbsp	Oil	2×15ml
3 pints	Hot chicken stock	1.7 litres
12oz	Floury potatoes	350g
¼ teasp	Dried marjoram	1.25ml
1 tbsp	Finely chopped parsley	15ml
	Salt	
	Freshly-ground black pepper	
2	Egg yolks	2
4oz	Finely grated cheese	125g

METHOD

1 Peel and finely chop the onion, scrape and dice the carrots. Wash, trim and thinly slice the leek and celery. Derind and dice the bacon.

2 Heat the oil in a saucepan and fry the bacon till golden. Add the vegetables, cover and sweat over a low heat for 10 minutes.

3 Add the stock, bring to the boil. Scrub potatoes well, then coarsely grate and stir into the stock. Bring to the boil and simmer for 20 minutes, then add the marjoram, chopped parsley and seasoning.

4 Put the egg yolks into the tureen, add the grated cheese and mix well. Pour the soup in a thin stream on to the egg and cheese, whisking constantly. Serve immediately with chunks of fresh rye or black bread.

Pasta omelette

An Italian dish in which eggs, grated cheese, garlic and herbs are mixed with cooked spaghetti, then fried in butter to form a moist savoury cake. It's economical to make as spaghetti left over from another meal can be used

LUNCH OR SUPPER Serves 4

Overall timing 30 minutes

Equipment Saucepan, 2 bowls, large frying pan

Freezing Not recommended

INGREDIENTS

8oz	Spaghetti	225g
	Salt	
4	Eggs	4
2oz	Grated Parmesan	50g
1	Garlic clove	1
1 tbsp	Chopped parsley	15ml
6	Basil leaves	6
½ teasp	*or* dried basil	½×5ml
	Freshly-ground black pepper	
2oz	Butter	50g

METHOD

1 Put the spaghetti into a pan of boiling salted water and cook till al dente. Meanwhile, put the eggs, cheese, peeled and crushed garlic, parsley and chopped basil into a bowl with seasoning and mix well with a fork.

2 Drain the spaghetti and put into a large bowl. Pour the egg and cheese mixture over and mix well.

3 Heat 1oz (25g) butter in frying pan. Add spaghetti mixture and press down well with the back of a spoon to form a cake. Fry over a low heat for about 5 minutes, pressing down to keep the cake flat.

4 Run a knife round the edge of the pan to loosen the mixture, then turn it out on to a board. Add remaining butter to the pan and, when melted, slide the cake, opposite way up, back into the pan. Fry for 3–5 minutes till the mixture is firmly set. Place on a warmed serving dish and serve immediately, cut into wedges. A salad will be all you need to accompany the omelette.

Above: Pasta omelette – cut into wedges and serve with a crisp green salad

Beat the eggs with the cheese, garlic and herbs, then pour over the cooked, drained spaghetti and mix thoroughly with a fork

Pour the mixture into pan and fry till the base is cooked. Turn the cake out of the pan, then return it to cook the other side

cook's know-how

It's well worth growing your own fresh basil in the garden or in a pot on the window sill. You can grow it from seed of course, but it's much easier to buy seedlings from a nursery or garden centre.

Fresh basil is especially good with salads, when you want to garnish a dish or for making the classic pesto, a mixture of basil oil, garlic and parmesan for adding to soups (see page 485).

Spinach dumplings

These tasty little spinach dumplings, topped with butter and cheese, are for serving with meat stews and casseroles

ACCOMPANIMENT Serves 6

Overall timing 40 minutes plus setting

Equipment 2 saucepans, bowl, frying pan

Freezing Arrange uncooked dumplings on a tray and open freeze till firm. Pack in plastic bags, seal and label. Freezer life: 2 months. To use: cook frozen dumplings in boiling salted water for 12–15 minutes, then complete Step 6

INGREDIENTS

2lb	Fresh spinach*	900g
½	Chicken stock cube	½
5 tbsp	Warm milk	5×15ml
12oz	Plain flour	350g
	Salt and pepper	
3	Eggs	3
4oz	Butter	125g
8oz	Fresh breadcrumbs	225g
¼ teasp	Grated nutmeg	¼×5ml
1 tbsp	Chopped parsley	15ml
1 tbsp	Snipped chives	15ml
4oz	Grated cheese	125g

METHOD

1 Wash and pick over the spinach and drain thoroughly. Put into a saucepan with only the water that clings to it. Bring to the boil, cover and cook for 5 minutes.

2 Put the stock cube and milk into a saucepan and heat gently, stirring, till stock cube dissolves. Allow to cool slightly. Sift the flour, salt and pepper into a bowl, add the eggs and milk and mix to a soft dough.

3 Drain the spinach thoroughly and chop finely. Melt half the butter in a frying pan, add the breadcrumbs and fry till crisp and golden. Add to the dough with the nutmeg, parsley and chives. Add the spinach and mix to a stiff dough.

4 Roll the dough between floured hands into long sausage-shapes about ½ inch (12.5mm) in diameter. Leave to set.

5 Cut across the dough into 1 inch (2.5cm) lengths. Bring plenty of lightly salted water to the boil. Add the dumplings, and simmer for about 10 minutes till they float to the surface.

6 Lift out with a draining spoon, drain thoroughly and arrange in a warmed serving dish. Melt the remaining butter, pour over the dumplings and sprinkle with the grated cheese.

*Or use 1lb frozen spinach. Drain and chop when thawed.

Above: Leftover meat stew – don't simmer for too long or the beef will become dry

Leftover meat stew

A favourite in Scotland, where it is called Inky Pinky and is often served with triangles of hot toast

LUNCH OR SUPPER Serves 6

Overall timing 50 minutes

Equipment Saucepan, bowl

Freezing Not recommended

INGREDIENTS

1lb	Onions	450g
3oz	Dripping *or* butter	75g
1½lb	Piece of cold roast beef	700g
1lb	Carrots	450g
¾ pint	Strong beef stock	450ml
	Salt	
	Freshly-ground black pepper	
1½ teasp	Cornflour	1½×5ml
1 tbsp	Vinegar	15ml
2 tbsp	Water	2×15ml
1 tbsp	Chopped parsley	15ml

Left: Spinach dumplings – serve with grilled meats, or pop into stews and casseroles

METHOD

1 Peel and thinly slice the onions. Heat the fat in a saucepan, add the onions and fry gently for about 10 minutes till golden brown.
2 Meanwhile, trim the beef, discarding any fat, and cut into small cubes. Scrape and slice the carrots.
3 Add to the pan and fry, stirring, for 5 minutes. Add the stock (made with cubes if necessary) and seasoning and bring to the boil. Reduce the heat, cover and simmer for 20 minutes.
4 Blend the cornflour with the vinegar and water and stir into the stew. Bring to the boil, stirring constantly, and simmer for 3 minutes.
5 Adjust seasoning to taste, place on a warmed serving dish and sprinkle with parsley. Serve immediately with lightly tossed spinach dumplings.

finishing touches

There are many toppings for stews that transform their appearance, provide a contrasting texture and make them more substantial.
Dumplings are soft, suety dough balls that partially absorb the gravy. They can be given extra flavour by the addition of grated cheese, powdered mustard, or herbs. Bacon, crisply grilled and crumbled, can be sprinkled on top to add contrast.
French bread slices can be spread with herb butter or mustard and arranged on the top of stews for the last 30 minutes of baking. (See recipe for mustard croûtes, page 430.)
Breadcrumbs, mixed with an equal quantity of grated cheese can be sprinkled over stews to crisp in the heat.
Savoury scones or "cobblers" make a crisper topping than dumplings. Bake them in an overlapping circle on top of the stew for 15 minutes at 425F (220C) Gas 7.
Puff pastry trimmings can be cut into fancy shapes, glazed with egg and baked on a baking sheet at 425F (220C) Gas 7 for 10 minutes. Serve the hot "fleurons" on the stew.
Saucy topping for thicker stews can be quickly prepared by mixing together 5oz (141g) natural yogurt, 1 egg, 2oz (50g) grated cheese and plenty of seasoning. Pour over the stew 30 minutes before the end of cooking time.

Israeli liver with sultanas

An unusual sweet and sour dish of lambs or calves liver browned in butter then coated with a sauce made from the pan juices, wine vinegar and sultanas

LUNCH OR SUPPER — Serves 4

Overall timing 20 minutes

Equipment Frying pan, draining spoon

Freezing Not recommended

INGREDIENTS

1lb	Lambs *or* calves liver	450g
2 tbsp	Oil	2×15ml
1oz	Butter	25g
2oz	Sultanas	50g
1 tbsp	Plain flour	15ml
1 tbsp	Red wine vinegar	15ml
	Salt	
	Freshly-ground black pepper	

METHOD

1 Cut the liver into 8 slices or ask your butcher to slice it. Heat the oil and butter in a frying pan, add liver and fry for 3–4 minutes each side till tender. Remove from pan with draining spoon and arrange on warmed serving dish. Keep hot.
2 Toss the sultanas in the flour and add to the frying pan. Fry, stirring, for 3 minutes. Add vinegar, $\frac{1}{4}$ pint (150ml) water and seasoning to taste. Cook for a further 3 minutes, stirring continuously. Pour the juices over the liver and serve with chopped boiled potatoes.

Above: Israeli liver with sultanas – arrange diced boiled potatoes around the liver and pour the sauce over the top. Or, if preferred, serve with plain boiled rice

Above: Beef and dhal curry – use tamarind water sparingly till you find the strength you prefer

Beef and dhal curry

Dhal – puréed lentils – with beef and tamarind water in a spicy curry

MAIN MEAL Serves 4

Overall timing 2¼ hours

Equipment Saucepan, flameproof casserole

Freezing Not recommended

INGREDIENTS

4oz	Egyptian lentils	125g
¾ pint	Water	400ml
2	Dried chillies	2
1½lb	Chuck or blade steak	700g
2	Medium onions	2
1	Garlic clove	1
2oz	Ghee or butter	50g
2	Cardamom pods	2
2	Cloves	2
2 inch	Piece of cinnamon stick	5cm
1 tbsp	Curry powder	15ml
1 tbsp	Tomato paste	15ml
¼ pint	Tamarind water*	150ml
	Salt	

METHOD

1 Wash and pick over the lentils. Put into a pan with the water and deseeded chillies. Bring to the boil and simmer for 10 minutes.

2 Meanwhile, wipe and trim the meat and cut into large cubes. Peel and finely chop the onions, peel the garlic.

3 Drain the lentils, reserving the liquid. Discard the chillies.

4 Melt the ghee or butter in the casserole, add the onions and crushed garlic and fry for 3 minutes. Lightly crush the cardamom pods and add to the pan with the cloves, cinnamon and curry powder. Fry gently for 3 minutes.

5 Stir in the tomato paste and the meat and fry till coated with the spice mixture. Add cooking liquor from the lentils. Bring to the boil, cover and simmer gently for about 1½ hours till the beef is tender.

6 Add the lentils and tamarind water and simmer, uncovered, for a further 15 minutes till the lentils become mushy and absorb the liquid.

7 Discard the cinnamon, cardamom and cloves. Add salt to taste, then serve immediately with plain boiled rice.

*Alternatively use ¼ pint (150ml) of water with 1–2 teasp (1–2×5ml) of lemon juice.

Bacon and barley cake

A savoury cake that makes a deliciously different lunch dish. For unusual mini-starters or appetizers, simply divide the ingredients between 12 deep bun tins

LUNCH OR SUPPER Serves 4–6

Overall timing 2¼ hours

Equipment Saucepan, colander, 8 inch (20cm) sandwich tin or deep bun tray

Freezing Not recommended

INGREDIENTS

4oz	Pearl barley	125g
6	Long back bacon rashers	6
2	Large eggs	2
1 teasp	Dried yeast	5ml
¼ teasp	Dried basil	¼×5ml
1 tbsp	Chopped parsley	15ml
	Freshly-ground black pepper	

METHOD

1 Place barley in saucepan, cover with water and cook for 1½ hours. Drain some but not all of the moisture by holding the lid over the pan to keep back the barley. Mix all the other ingredients (except the pepper and bacon) into the barley.

2 Butter sandwich or deep bun tins. Derind bacon and stretch rashers slightly. Arrange them on base of tin or tins so they overlap at the bottom and hang over the rim – it may look untidy but they will shrink back during cooking. For the bun tins you will need to cut the bacon to size.

3 Spread barley mixture over and top with ground black pepper. Bake just above the middle of the oven for 35 minutes (large tin) or 20 minutes (small tins).

TO SERVE

Turn out on to plate and serve hot, cut into portions like a cake, with a tomato and onion salad.

Put cooked rice into a bowl with egg yolk, cream, lemon juice and seasoning. Mix well

Spread pastry base with half the rice and spinach, the salmon and hard-boiled eggs

Top with spinach and rice, brush pastry edge with egg white then cover with pastry

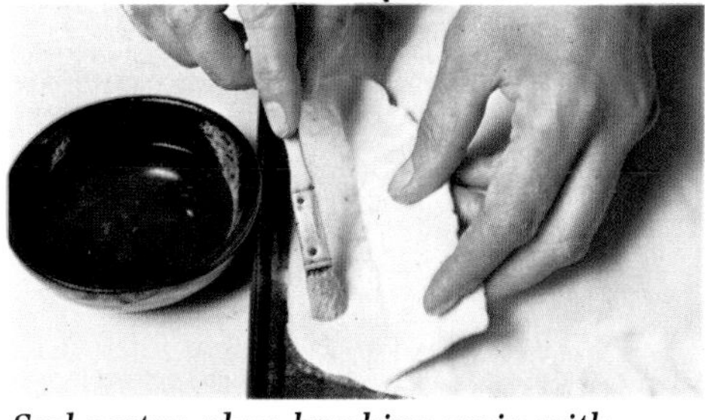

Seal pastry edges brushing again with egg white if necessary, decorate and bake

Shellfish au gratin

An impressive and highly-flavoured dish for a dinner party. The combination of a variety of seafoods baked in a cream-enriched tomato sauce thickened with bread, makes it a very special dish indeed

LUNCH OR SUPPER Serves 8

Overall timing 1 hour

Equipment Saucepan, bowl, blender, sieve, ovenproof dish

Freezing Not recommended

INGREDIENTS

$1\frac{3}{4}$ pints	Mussels	1 litre
2 tbsp	Lemon juice	2×15ml
8oz	Bread	225g
$\frac{1}{4}$ pint	Milk	150ml
2	Onions	2
14oz	Can of tomatoes	397g
1 teasp	Paprika	5ml
	Salt	
	Freshly-ground black pepper	
8oz	Sliced scallops	225g
8oz	Shelled scampi	225g
8oz	Shelled prawns	225g
2oz	Grated cheese	50g
4fl oz	Carton of double cream	113ml
3oz	Butter	75g

METHOD

1 Put the mussels into a saucepan with lemon juice and $\frac{1}{4}$ pint (150ml) water, cover and cook over a high heat till the shells open, shaking pan frequently. Remove flesh from shells. Strain and reserve the cooking liquor.

2 Soak the bread in the milk. Drain and squeeze out the moisture. Peel and chop the onions and place in blender with tomatoes and juice, paprika, salt, pepper and reserved cooking liquor. Blend till smooth, then rub through a sieve.

3 Preheat the oven to 400F (200C) Gas 6.

4 Stir shellfish, bread, cheese and cream into the tomato mixture. Grease ovenproof dish with half the butter, then pour in shellfish mixture. Dot top with remaining butter and bake above centre of oven for 25 minutes. Serve immediately with plain boiled rice and broccoli.

Above: Shellfish au gratin – you can make the shellfish go further by halving the quantities given and adding the equivalent amount of chopped fillets of hake or monkfish, first poached in milk

Meringues

Meringue is a mixture of egg white and sugar combined in different ways to give different results, depending on how you want to use it. The Swiss meringue mix is the one made into shells or layers and is the most difficult to get right; meringue cuite is similar to Swiss but is "set" by heat before baking. Italian meringue mix, easier to do than Swiss, is made with hot sugar syrup and is used as a dessert topper; this type never dries out. Although the ingredients are simple, making perfect meringues is one of the biggest challenges in cooking. The various schools of thought on the subject don't even agree on what can go wrong, or why it does. For example, a "weeping" meringue which oozes syrup is variously attributed to an oven that's too cool, a damp kitchen, or overbeating before the sugar is added. In fact, lack of crispness could result from any or all three of these. There's no doubt that some people have the knack of making meringues successfully time after time, but for those who have been disappointed there are certain guidelines to follow: moisture or humidity in the air will cause sugar to absorb water which is fatal for dry, light meringues; yolk in the white introduces fat – as disastrous to perfect meringues as grease in the bowl or on the blades of the whisk or even on the pan in which the sugar was weighed.

Eggs which are 1–3 days old, or ones thawed from a freezer produce the greatest quantity and volume but only if at room temperature when whisked. Ideally they should be broken into a bowl and left for 24 hours at room temperature before whisking so that some of the moisture will evaporate and the albumen (the protein which stretches and expands) becomes more concentrated.

Sugar has two roles in meringue making: to sweeten the mix and to stabilize the foam. Usually 2oz (50g) is added per medium or large egg white for meringues and 1½oz (40g) for meringue toppings. All sugar should be left to dry in a warm place before using in meringues. The best texture and yield of Swiss meringues comes from caster or half caster/half icing sugar – mix together in weighing, and sift over before whisking and folding in. Half caster/half granulated won't give as many or as white meringues. The largish crystals of granulated and demerara sugar give meringues an attractive crunch, but cream of tartar or vinegar must be added to increase the volume of the whites before these sugars are folded, rather than whisked, in. Granulated sugar is best used when making Italian meringues.

Cream of tartar, vinegar and lemon juice are all acids which produce a better volume and stable foam in whisked whites.

Equipment needs to be scrupulously grease-free – if in doubt, quickly wipe the bowl out with a cut lemon. Choose a wide shallow bowl for balloon type whisks, narrow and deep for rotary or electric mixers. Copper, steel, glass and pottery bowls should always be used in preference to plastic. A hand balloon whisk takes longer but, especially in conjunction with a copper bowl, produces more meringues.

Shaping can be done in many ways. For stars or rosettes use a star nozzle to pipe to required size; pull the pipe away quickly to form peaks. Pipe fingers with a plain or star nozzle; cut off lengths with a knife. For nests, pipe a circle spiralling outwards, then pipe on top of the outside edge to required depth. To make layers, pipe or spoon into circles; pipe top circle in six or eight wedges for easier serving. Or pipe a trellis for top and fill holes with fruit and cream.

Below: Swiss meringue – can be shaped into shells, then baked and sandwiched together

Swiss meringue

Preheat the oven to 250F (130C) Gas ½, so it is hot enough initially to set the egg whites. Put 2 egg whites in a wide, grease-free mixing bowl. Add a pinch of cream of tartar or salt and whisk till whites are stiff, moist and glossy – they should not slip in the bowl, and you should be able to invert the bowl without the whites falling out. Add 2oz (50g) sifted caster/icing sugar or just caster sugar and whisk again till the mixture is satin-like, smooth, close-textured and forms stiff peaks. Use a metal spoon to fold in another 2oz (50g) sifted caster/icing sugar or caster sugar, and work around the edge of the bowl, then under the mixture, bringing the bottom to the top. The mixture should immediately be spooned or piped on to lightly oiled foil or non-stick baking paper on baking trays prepared well in advance so the meringues are not left waiting. To shape shells, use 2 same-size spoons. Scoop up a rounded spoonful of the meringue mix, then use the other spoon to push the meringue gently on to the baking tray with domed side up. Or, fill a piping bag with the mix and pipe rosettes or shapes as wished. Dredge the meringues with caster sugar. If nuts are added to whites, toast them beforehand and fold in with final sugar – allow 1oz (25g) nuts per egg white. Work quickly and evenly so oil cannot come out of the nuts. Place the meringues on the lowest shelf of the oven and bake for 20 minutes, then reduce temperature to 225F (110C) Gas $\frac{1}{4}$ (or lowest setting if you like) and dry out meringues for 3–4 hours. Once cold, put immediately in an airtight container or freeze in a rigid container.

Meringue cuite

A form of Swiss meringue, meringue cuite is "cooked" or set by heat before baking. To each medium or large egg allow $2\frac{1}{4}$oz (57g) icing sugar. Put the sugar and egg whites in a bowl over a pan containing 1 inch (2.5cm) hot water. Whisk well till thick enough to stand in stiff peaks. Turn off the heat when the water reaches simmering point. Use for making shells or meringue baskets, or piping rosettes, then cook on the lowest shelf of the oven, preheated to 300F (150C) Gas 2, for 45 minutes–1 hour till crisp and dry. Meringue cuite can also be used for topping desserts (see page 498). Dredge caster sugar over to give a crisp top and soft inside and cook at 400F (200C) Gas 6 for about 20 minutes till golden. The meringue will not dry out if made in this way.

serving suggestions

Keeping a store of meringues in the freezer or an airtight tin means you can produce a dessert or tea-time treat in minutes.
Meringue nests make individual cases for many different fillings. Arrange drained canned fruits such as apricots, mandarins or cherries in each nest, then top with whipped cream. Fresh strawberries or raspberries, or mixed black and white grapes can be arranged in an attractive pattern on top of nests filled with cream or custard. Or, fold puréed fruit, crushed pineapple or passionfruit pulp into the cream or custard and spoon into the nests. Don't fill till just before serving or the meringue will start to dissolve.
Tiny meringue stars or rosettes make pretty dessert toppers. Arrange them on mousses or trifles – they'll look like fresh cream but will surprise everyone by being crisp. Ice cream sundaes can be topped with rosettes at the last minute. To serve at tea-time, sandwich the meringues together with piped cream and sprinkle with chocolate vermicelli. Or, dip the base of each meringue in melted chocolate and sandwich together in pairs before it sets. You can also arrange rosettes on iced cakes for a contrasting texture.
Crisp meringue fingers also make an attractive cake decoration. Trim the ends till they are all the same size, dip the tips in melted chocolate and stand the meringues on end round the side of a butter-iced coffee or chocolate sponge – tie a ribbon round to keep them in position – an elegant finish for a celebration cake. Serve meringue fingers with or in cold desserts instead of wafer biscuits.
Crisp meringue layers sandwiched with luscious fillings make spectacular desserts. Prepare the filling in advance (use a mixture of fruit and cream, or coffee, chocolate or chestnut buttercream, or custard), but don't fill till the last minute. Sprinkle with chopped toasted nuts or icing sugar, or pipe cream in whirls and top with whole fruit, nuts or chocolate squares.
Meringue topping is a favourite for lemon pies – try it on orange, lime or grapefruit pie made in the same way. Milk pudding becomes less like nursery food when topped with meringue – beat the egg yolks into the pudding to enrich it. Sprinkle with flaked almonds or coconut to toast as the topping browns. Baked apples, pears or peaches are extra special when their stuffing is concealed by soft peaks of meringue. To give a Victoria sandwich an unusual icing, spread uncooked meringue mix over the cakes in their tins, then bake in the usual way. To serve, put one cake with topping upwards on a plate and spread with jam; cover with the second cake – also topping up.

Italian meringue

A thick, light and snowy meringue that can be used to complete elaborate desserts which only need browning in a hot oven before serving. It cannot be used for shells or layers but because it is "cooked" during the making, it can be made in advance, covered and stored in the fridge till needed. Put 8oz (225g) granulated sugar in a saucepan with $\frac{1}{4}$ pint (150ml) water and stir over a low heat till sugar dissolves. Brush round inside of pan above the liquid with cold water to dissolve any sugar crystals. Bring to the boil and boil steadily without stirring. Keeping an eye on the thermometer, whisk 4 egg whites to a stiff snow with an electric beater. When the syrup reaches hard ball stage (250F/121C), remove from heat and pour slowly in a thin stream into the egg whites, whisking all the time. Whisk till all the syrup is absorbed and the meringue is stiff and very white. Use as required, and bake at 425F (220C) Gas 7 for 5-10 minutes.

Below: Meringue cuite – good for topping desserts such as Banana split (recipe page 457)

A Pharaoh's feast for six

Egypt, the land of the Pharaohs, was conquered by the Arabs in the seventh century AD and has been Moslem ever since. It was ruled by the caliphs during the Middle Ages, as part of the Moslem empire whose heart was in Baghdad; after the Turkish military conquest of 1517, Egypt fell under Ottoman rule, which ended with the Napoleonic invasion of 1798. Napoleon's defeat in the Battle of the Nile was the beginning of British influence in Egypt, culminating in British occupation of the country in 1882. There has been a sizeable foreign population and they have made their mark on the customs and cuisine of Egypt, often introducing new foods and dishes.

Lentils are popular

The national dish, *ful medames*, was almost certainly eaten in the days of the Pharaohs. *Ful* are small brown beans which are stewed in salt water and served with crushed garlic, olive oil, lemon wedges and hard-boiled eggs. *Ful medames* is eaten by the poor at the roadside, where it is boiled in large pots, but it is equally popular in wealthy homes, where it is usually an appetizer or first course.

The *meze*, brought to the Arab world by the Greeks and Turks, usually consists of fried vegetables and meats served separately in tiny dishes and they are eaten between lunch and dinner as an appetizing snack.

Pulses and rice are the Egyptian staples, and Egyptian lentils are popular the world over. Rice is the main food as well as export crop. In Cairo, a mound of plain white rice is served at the end of the meal to refresh the palate, but elsewhere it is eaten as part of the main course.

Vegetables which, like fruit, are in plentiful supply throughout the year, are added to meat stews, especially okra (*bamia* or ladies fingers) and aubergines (eggplant), though also popular are onions, capsicums, tomatoes, small fat marrows and cucumbers.

Savoury pastries, stuffed with meat or pulses, are to be found throughout the Middle East. They probably originated in Turkey or Persia, but are now universal in Moslem countries. The Egyptian version of these pastries is called *sanbusak* – crescent shapes made with wheat flour dough, oil and clarified butter (*samna*), or from *filou* pastry dough (the flaky oily pastry of the Greeks and Turks). The fillings include spinach, ground meat, brains or white cheese. Pastries are only one of the variety of food and drinks sold in the streets. Street sellers also do a brisk trade in *falafel* (little balls of ground chickpeas fried in oil), water and refreshing drinks such as *soos*, made from liquorice root.

Cheese and yogurt (called *laban zabadi*) are also sold in the streets. Some form of preserving milk without refrigeration is essential in a hot climate. Hard and soft cheeses are fermented from goats, sheeps and cows milk.

The only animal raised for meat in Egypt is the sheep. Beef cattle are highly uneconomical in a dry climate, and pork is forbidden both to the Moslem majority and the coptic (oriental Christian) minority. On festive occasions, a whole sheep is roasted on a spit. Spit roast meat, in the form of tasty kebabs (called *meshwi*) is popular at other times. Those who cannot afford a whole roast sheep on festive occasions eat chicken or goose which are relatively low-priced.

Spices and herbs are widely used in Egyptian cooking. Saffron, cinnamon, rose water, orange flower water, cardamom, cumin seed, caraway and allspice are all used in cooking. Allspice is used to flavour hard-boiled eggs, cinnamon and mint are added to tea, and aniseed is used to add interest to milk puddings.

Savoury and sweet preserves

Spices and herbs preserve food, so does pickling, and the Egyptians make large quantities of pickled vegetables to serve as condiments and appetizers. Beetroot, turnips, cauliflower, cucumber and carrots are all preserved in salt and vinegar. Sweet preserves are eaten with strong Egyptian coffee.

Pâtisserie throughout the Arab world is based on *filou* – *baklava*, with its honey and nut filling, *ma'amoul* (meaning "stuffed"), little, filled pastries, and *zelebia*, runny yeast dough boiled in oil like doughnuts, are universally eaten in the East, from Egypt to as far away as India.

Egyptian cooking is exotic and sophisticated, and most of the ingredients available abroad are relatively low priced, well worth trying at home.

Left: a selection of dishes from Egypt. Clockwise from top – Bamia or ladies fingers (recipe page 475); spicy Dukkah with olive oil and pitta bread (recipe page 477); Ful medames with Hamine eggs and lemon wedges (recipe page 474), and Khoshaf – dried fruit salad (recipe page 476)

Countdown

Ful medames with Hamine eggs
Egyptian bamia
Rice
Egyptian fruit salad
Ma'amoul

Egyptian food has a marvellously rich, earthy quality. Many dishes take some time to prepare, so you need to think about the meal a day or two before. However there's very little last-minute work and the ingredients for a typically Egyptian meal can mostly be found very reasonably priced in our shops. If you like you can serve Dukkah (recipe page 477) as an appetizer with drinks

48 hours before Prepare the Egyptian fruit salad and chill in fridge

The evening before Soak the beans for Ful medames. Make Ma'amoul. When cool store in and airtight container

5¼ hours before Start cooking eggs with onions for Ful medames

2½ hours before Start cooking soaked beans

1¼ hours before Prepare the lamb stew. Simmer for about one hour. Then prepare okra to the end of Step 4.

30 mins before Fry okra and keep hot. Put rice on to boil

15 mins before Drain and dress beans. Peel hard boiled eggs, add to beans with other garnishes. Drain rice and keep warm.

Serve Ful medames with warmed pitta bread if liked

Serve Egyptian bamia, having added cooked okra to lamb stew as shown. Accompany with plain rice

Serve chilled fruit salad with cream. Follow with Arabian coffee (recipe page 175) and Ma'amoul

In Egypt no alcohol would be served but a robust red wine from the Côtes du Roussillon would be a good accompaniment to this meal. Why not try some Mint tea too to give a truly Middle Eastern touch to the meal.

Ful medames with Hamine eggs

Two Egyptian favourites of ancient origin. During the long cooking time, the onion skins give the eggs a wonderfully deep mahogany colour

MAIN MEAL Serves 6

Overall timing 5¼ hours plus overnight soaking

Equipment 2 large saucepans

Freezing Not recommended

INGREDIENTS

1lb	Ful medames (Egyptian brown beans)	450g
4	Eggs	4
4	Brown onions*	4
2	Garlic cloves	2
6 tbsp	Olive oil	6×15ml
3 tbsp	Chopped parsley	3×15ml
	Salt	
	Freshly-ground black pepper	
	Lemon wedges	
	Flat-leaf parsley	

METHOD

1 Wash the beans and soak in plenty of cold water overnight.

2 The next day, place the whole eggs and all layers of onion skins in a large saucepan and carefully cover with cold water so the eggs don't crack. Bring to the boil, cover, and simmer as slowly as possible for 5 hours, topping up with boiling water as necessary. The dye from the onion skins turns the shells a dark brown, and the egg white pale beige. If cooking eggs this way for Easter, you can cook for less time if you like so that the eggs are just coloured.

3 After the eggs have been cooking for 2½ hours, drain the beans and discard the soaking water. Place in a large saucepan and cover with plenty of fresh cold water. Bring to the boil, cover and simmer for about 2½ hours till tender, but not overcooked.

4 Drain well and add the peeled and crushed garlic, the olive oil, chopped parsley and seasoning. Toss lightly till the beans are evenly coated with the dressing.

5 Pile the beans on to a serving dish. Shell the eggs and cut into quarters lengthways. Garnish the beans with the egg, lemon wedges and parsley. Or, serve in soup bowls with the halved egg on top and pass round extra oil, parsley and seasoning.

*As skinned onions do not keep well, use up quickly. To freeze, lightly sauté slices in butter or oil, pack in rigid container, seal and freeze.

Below: Ful medames with Hamine eggs – an unusual dish that's traditional in Egypt. Try colouring eggs this way for Easter

Egyptian bamia

Bamia (the Arabic name for okra) is commonly used in a great variety of Egyptian meat stews. Traditionally lamb, fried with vegetables in rich clarified butter, is used in these dishes, but nowadays, beef and veal are becoming popular, and oil or ordinary butter are used for frying

MAIN MEAL Serves 6

Overall timing $1\frac{1}{4}$ hours

Equipment Large saucepan, large frying pan

Freezing Not recommended

INGREDIENTS

2lb	Boned shoulder of lamb	900g
1lb	Onions	450g
2	Garlic cloves	2
4 tbsp	Oil	4×15ml
$\frac{1}{2}$ teasp	Ground coriander	$\frac{1}{2}$×5ml
1lb	Tomatoes	450g
$\frac{1}{2}$ pint	Stock	300ml
	Salt	
	Freshly-ground black pepper	
1lb	Okra	450g
1oz	Butter	25g
2 tbsp	Lemon juice	2×15ml

METHOD

1 Wipe lamb and trim off excess fat. Cut meat into 1 inch (2.5cm) chunks. Peel and chop the onions. Peel garlic.

2 In a large saucepan, heat half the oil and add the onions and crushed garlic. Fry until just beginning to brown.

3 Add coriander and lamb and brown on all sides. Blanch, peel and chop tomatoes. Add to pan with stock (made with a cube if necessary). Season, cover and simmer for about 1 hour.

4 Meanwhile, wash, dry and top the okra. Cook in boiling salted water for 5 minutes. Drain well and dry.

5 Heat remaining oil and the butter in a large frying pan and fry the okra, without browning, until tender. Add the lemon juice and season to taste.

Above: Egyptian bamia – arrange two thirds of okra around the edge of a serving plate. Add remaining okra to lamb, pour into centre and serve immediately with rice

Above: Egyptian fruit salad – a simple but delicious mixture

Egyptian fruit salad

A delicious mix of dried fruit makes this unusual dessert called *khoshaf* which is popular in Egypt

DESSERT Serves 6

Overall timing 15 minutes plus 48 hours soaking

Equipment Shallow dish, bowl

Freezing Not recommended

INGREDIENTS

8oz	Dried apricots	225g
4oz	Stoned prunes	125g
2oz	Seedless raisins	50g
4oz	Dried figs	125g
2oz	Flaked almonds	50g
1oz	Pistachio nuts	25g
2oz	Amardine*	50g
$\frac{1}{2}$ pint	Water	300ml
1oz	Caster sugar	25g
1 tbsp	Orange flower water	15ml
2 teasp	Rose flower water	2×5ml

METHOD

1 Place the dried fruit in a shallow dish, halving the figs if very large. Sprinkle nuts over.
2 Soften the amardine in the water and add the sugar and flower waters. Pour over fruit.
3 Place in fridge for 48 hours, stirring occasionally. Serve very cold* with crisp biscuits or single cream.

*If you cannot find amardine replace with a further 2oz of dried apricots.

Ma'amoul

These stuffed pastries are popular all over Africa. Serve them after dinner with Arabian coffee

CONFECTIONERY OR DESSERT Makes 32

Overall timing $1\frac{1}{2}$ hours

Equipment Bowl, saucepan, baking trays

Freezing After Step 7, cool, pack in rigid foil container, cover, label and freeze. Freezer life: 3 months. To use: thaw uncovered for 4 hours, then refresh in oven preheated to 400F (200C) Gas 6 for 10 minutes. Sift icing sugar over

Storage 1 month in airtight container

INGREDIENTS

	Pastry	
1lb	Plain flour	450g
8oz	Unsalted butter	225g
1 tbsp	Orange-flower water	15ml
2 tbsp	Water	2×15ml
	Filling	
1lb	Dried dates	450g
1 teasp	Orange-flower water	5ml
4 tbsp	Water	4×15ml
4 tbsp	Icing sugar	4×15ml

METHOD

1 Sift the flour into a large mixing bowl and rub in the butter till the mixture resembles fine breadcrumbs. Make a well in the centre and add the orange-flower water and water. Mix with a palette knife to make a soft but not sticky paste. Wrap and chill for 20 minutes.

2 Meanwhile, prepare filling. Stone and chop the dates. Place in a saucepan with the orange-flower water and water and simmer for about 15 minutes till mushy, stirring frequently. Allow to cool.

3 Preheat the oven to 325F (170C) Gas 3. Roll out half the pastry on a floured surface till very thin. Cut into 16 rectangles about $3\frac{1}{2}\times4$ inches (9×10 cm). Brush edges lightly with water.

4 With the short side of a rectangle facing, place a spoonful of filling in a line across the centre of pastry, leaving $\frac{1}{2}$ inch (12.5mm) space at each side.

5 Fold the long sides of the pastry in over the filling. Fold the pastry edge nearest you over the filling, then roll it so the join is underneath.

6 Repeat till all the pastry and filling is used, and arrange the rolls on greased baking trays. Bake for about 25 minutes without browning.

7 Remove the pastries, which will still seem soft, and place on a wire rack to cool and become firm.

8 Sift the icing sugar over. After dinner, serve with fresh dates if liked; for dessert, with a jug of pouring cream.

cook's know-how

Mint tea is a lovely refreshing drink – a great favourite throughout the Middle East. You could serve it to visitors between meals with a snack such as Ma'amoul, or after dinner for those who do not like coffee. To make, pour a little boiling water over 4 teasp (4×5ml) green tea leaves, swirl round and pour out the water, leaving tea in the pot. Add 1 tbsp (15ml) dried mint and 4oz (125g) caster sugar. Pour $1\frac{1}{2}$ pints (850ml) boiling water over and leave for 5 minutes. Add extra sugar to taste, if desired, and serve in glasses. **Serves 6**

DUKKAH

Ingredients 2oz (50g) sesame seeds; 1oz (25g) coriander seeds; 2 teasp (2×5ml) ground cumin; 4oz (125g) chickpeas; 1oz (25g) hazelnuts; 1 teasp (5ml) salt; $\frac{1}{2}$ teasp (2.5ml) freshly-ground black pepper; pitta bread and olive oil to serve.

Method Preheat oven to 400F (200C) Gas 6. Spread sesame seeds, coriander seeds, cumin, chickpeas and hazelnuts on a baking tray. Place in centre of oven and roast for about 10 minutes, or until crisp and golden. Place in a blender or crush to a coarse powder (don't over-blend or a paste will form). Remove from blender and add salt and pepper. Serve in a small dish, with fingers of pitta bread and a bowl of olive oil. To eat, first dip bread in oil, then in spices.

Left: Ma'amoul – tiny Egyptian pastries with a filling of dates fragrantly flavoured with orange-flower water

Salade niçoise

One of the most famous salads which mixes together an abundance of fresh produce. It takes its name from Nice on the Côte d'Azur and a variety of different recipes can be found all over France

SALAD OR STARTER Serves 4

Overall timing 25 minutes

Equipment 2 saucepans, 2 bowls

Freezing Not recommended

INGREDIENTS

1lb	Waxy potatoes	450g
	Salt	
8oz	Green beans	225g
4oz	Large black olives	125g
2 tbsp	Drained capers	2×15ml
1	Garlic cloves	1
4 tbsp	Olive oil	4×15ml
1 tbsp	Tarragon vinegar	15ml
1 teasp	Lemon juice	5ml
	Freshly-ground black pepper	
1 tbsp	Chopped parsley	15ml
1	Large firm tomato	1
6	Anchovy fillets	6

METHOD

1 Peel the potatoes and cut into neat dice. Cook in boiling salted water for about 5 minutes, or till just tender. Top, tail and string the beans and cut into 1 inch (2.5cm) lengths. Cook in boiling salted water for 5 minutes, or till tender.
2 Drain the vegetables and rinse under cold water. Drain thoroughly and put into a salad bowl. Add half the olives and the capers.
3 Peel and crush the garlic clove into a bowl. Add the oil, vinegar and lemon juice and mix well. Add the pepper and parsley, then pour over vegetables. Toss lightly till evenly coated.
4 Wash the tomato and cut into thin wedges. Arrange on the salad with the remaining olives.
5 Cut the anchovies into strips and arrange in a lattice on top of the salad. Serve immediately with French bread.

VARIATIONS

Strips of crisp green capsicum, tiny new potatoes, artichoke hearts (either canned or fresh), wedges of hard-boiled egg or chunks of tuna can be added. The juicy black olives, however, are essential.

Pheasant terrine

A rich pâté containing some unusual flavours – serve as a starter or snack

STARTER Serves 8–10

Overall timing 2¾ hours plus overnight pressing

Equipment Frying pan, mincer, ovenproof dish, foil, roasting tin

Freezing Cool the terrine but do not pour butter over. Wrap in foil, overwrap, label and freeze. Freezer life: 1 month. To use: remove wrappings and thaw overnight in fridge. Complete Step 7

INGREDIENTS

1lb	Cooked pheasant	450g
4oz	Streaky bacon	125g
4oz	Lambs liver	125g
3oz	Butter	75g
1	Garlic clove	1
8oz	Pork sausagemeat	225g
4oz	Fresh breadcrumbs	125g
	Grated rind of 1 orange	
1 tbsp	Pastis, Pernod *or* brandy (optional)	15ml
½ teasp	Dried thyme	½×5ml
	Salt and pepper	
	Bay leaf	

METHOD

1 Trim the pheasant and cut into small chunks. Derind and dice the bacon.
2 Wipe and chop the liver. Fry in 1oz (25g) of butter for 2–4 minutes. Peel and crush the garlic, add to the pan and cook for 1 minute.
3 Add the contents of the pan to the sausagemeat, diced bacon and breadcrumbs and push through a mincer.
4 Add the pheasant, orange rind, pastis and thyme with salt and pepper. Mix well and press into ovenproof dish.
5 Cover the dish with foil and stand it in a roasting tin containing 1 inch (2.5cm) of hot water. Bake at 325F (170C) Gas 3 for 2¼ hours till firm.
6 Remove the dish from the tin and place a weight on the foil. Cool completely then chill overnight.
7 The next day, remove the foil and melt the remaining butter. Put a bay leaf on pâté, pour butter over and leave to set.

Left: Salade niçoise – a colourful salad with a delightful mixture of flavours

Above: Potage Crécy, a nourishing carrot soup that is thickened with rice

1 *Gently cook sliced carrots and onion in butter for 15 minutes, then stir in rice*

2 *Add seasonings, half the stock, simmer for 45 minutes. Pass through food mill*

3 *Put carrot purée back in pan with rest of stock, and butter. Cover and simmer*

4 *Work soup through a sieve, if liked, for a very fine texture. Check seasoning*

Potage Crécy

Dishes bearing the name Crécy usually contain carrots or a carrot purée as in this soup. The term is derived from the French town of Crécy, renowned for the excellent quality of its carrots

STARTER Serves 6

Overall timing 1 hour 40 minutes

Equipment Large saucepan, food mill or blender, sieve (optional)

Freezing Cool, then pour into rigid container. Cover, label and freeze. Freezer life: 3 months. To use: thaw for 1 hour. Turn into pan and heat gently

INGREDIENTS

1lb	Carrots	450g
1	Large onion	1
2oz	Butter	50g
3oz	Long grain rice	75g
$2\frac{1}{2}$ pints	Chicken stock	1.5 litres
$\frac{1}{4}$ teasp	Thyme	$\frac{1}{4}\times$5ml
	Salt and pepper	
2 tbsp	Chopped parsley	2×15ml

METHOD

1 Scrape and trim root and stem ends of carrots, then wash and slice them thinly. Peel and finely chop the onion.

2 Melt 1oz (25g) of the butter in saucepan over medium heat. Add the carrots and onion. Cook, covered, for 15 minutes over low heat, stirring from time to time.

3 Add the rice, half the stock, thyme, salt and pepper. Cover and simmer for 45 minutes.

4 Pass the mixture through a food mill, or place in a blender. Pour purée back into the saucepan. Add remaining stock and butter, cover and simmer for 15 minutes.

5 Remove pan from heat and pass soup through sieve (optional). Season with salt and pepper and pour into soup tureen. Sprinkle with parsley and serve.

VARIATION

Traditionally rice is used as the thickening agent in Crécy soup but oatmeal works equally well with carrot soup. Thickening with oatmeal takes less cooking time than rice and gives a delicious nutty flavour to the soup.

Complete recipe to step 2 then add all but 4fl oz (120ml) of the stock and simmer gently until the carrots are really tender. Purée the vegetables in a food mill or blender and put liquid back in the saucepan with the butter. Mix to a paste $1\frac{1}{2}$oz (40g) fine oatmeal with the remainder of the stock, add to this a little of the puréed soup, then pour the oatmeal mixture into the rest of the soup. Simmer over a low heat, while stirring, for 10 minutes.

Above: Mock caviare vol-au-vents – adding a touch of class to the party

Mock caviare vol-au-vents

Tiny little appetizers for a special occasion. The crisp puff pastry cases are topped with Danish lumpfish roe, easily available and a fraction of the price of real caviare but looking just like the roe from the most expensive beluga sturgeon

APPETIZER OR PARTY SNACK Makes 16

Overall timing 40 minutes

Equipment 2½ inch (6.5cm) and 1 inch (2.5cm) cutter, baking tray

Freezing Open freeze uncooked, unfilled cases. When hard, pack in polythene bags, seal and label. Freezer life: 3 months. To use: proceed as Steps 4 and 5, lengthening cooking time to 20–25 minutes

INGREDIENTS

13oz	Packet of frozen puff pastry	370g
2oz	Danish lumpfish roe	50g
1	Egg white	1
1 tbsp	Water	15ml
1 tbsp	Lemon juice	15ml

METHOD

1 Thaw pastry. Open jar of lumpfish roe and place in fridge. Preheat oven to 425F (220C) Gas 7.

2 Roll out pastry very evenly on a floured surface. Cut out 32 circles, 2½ inches (6.5cm) across, dipping cutter into hot water and shaking off the excess moisture each time. Cut a 1 inch (2.5cm) circle out of the centre of 16 of the circles making ring shapes. The very small circles you have cut out can be used for lids.

3 Sprinkle baking tray with cold water and arrange large pastry circles on it. Wet undersides of pastry rings and place on top of pastry circles. Gently move a rolling-pin across them to make sure the tops are even and in place. Put small lids separately on tray.

4 Lightly beat together the egg white and water and brush over pastry cases. Bake at the top of the oven for 10 minutes, then turn tray (so front is to back of oven) and bake cases for a further 10 minutes.

5 Remove from oven, leave till completely cold, then fill cases with roe and lightly sprinkle with lemon juice. Top with lids or leave open.

cook's know-how

Unless the ideal conditions of the Black or Caspian seas or Russian rivers can be reproduced in other parts of the world, caviare will go on being *the* de luxe food. However there is the lumpfish from Denmark. Less pretty in looks and name, and without the glamour of the beluga (top class), sevruga, sterliad and sterlet sturgeons from Russia that produce caviare, its roe makes an excellent inexpensive substitute. Both lumpfish roe and caviare taste best when chilled, served with a little lemon and sliced toast.

Curried apple and cider soup

In this unusual soup apples accentuate the fruity flavour of the cider, and cream mellows its sharp bite. It can be served hot, but is rather special cold

HOT OR COLD STARTER Serves 4

Overall timing 15 minutes

Equipment Saucepan, electric blender, bowl

Freezing Make soup as Steps 1–3. Cool, pour into rigid container, cover, label and freeze. Freezer life: 3 months.
To use: reheat gently from frozen in a pan, then proceed as Step 4

INGREDIENTS

1	Onion	1
1½oz	Butter	40g
1 tbsp	Curry powder	15ml
2 tbsp	Cornflour	2×15ml
¾ pint	Chicken stock	400ml
2	Dessert apples	2
2	Egg yolks	2
¼ pint	Carton of double cream	150ml
½ pint	Dry cider	300ml
1 tbsp	Lemon juice	15ml

METHOD

1 Peel and chop the onion. Heat the butter in a pan and fry the onion till transparent. Sprinkle in the curry powder and cook for 1–2 minutes.

2 Add cornflour to pan, blending it in well. Slowly stir in stock (made up with 1 stock cube if necessary). Bring back to the boil and simmer for 5 minutes, stirring constantly. Remove from heat and leave to cool slightly.

3 Peel, core and finely chop 1½ of the apples. Put into the blender with the soup and blend till smooth. Return to pan and bring back to the boil.

4 Remove from heat. Blend egg yolks and cream together in a bowl and slowly stir into the soup. Add cider, allow fizzing to subside, then taste and adjust seasoning if necessary. Reheat gently.

TO SERVE

Slice remaining ½ apple into wafer-thin strips and toss in the lemon juice. Drain and add to soup just before serving. Garnish with a swirl of cream or plain yogurt if desired. The soup can also be served cold – it's particularly good before a rather hot and spicy main course or as a cooling summer soup.

Above: Canadian bacon and potato salad – simple to prepare on those busy days

Canadian bacon and potato salad

Fried onions in a piquant mustard and vinegar sauce are mixed with crispy bacon and boiled potatoes, topped with fresh chives and served piping hot

LUNCH OR SUPPER Serves 6–8

Overall timing 55 minutes

Equipment Saucepan, frying pan, foil

Freezing Not recommended

INGREDIENTS

2lb	Medium-size waxy potatoes	900g
	Salt	
8oz	Streaky bacon rashers	225g
1	Large onion	1
4 tbsp	White wine vinegar	4×15ml
4 tbsp	Water	4×15ml
	Freshly-ground black pepper	
1 teasp	Powdered mustard	5ml
1 tbsp	Chopped chives	15ml

METHOD

1 Scrub the potatoes, cover with cold salted water and bring to the boil. Cook for about 30 minutes till tender.

2 Meanwhile, derind and dice the bacon and fry over a moderate heat till crisp and brown. Lift out of the pan with a draining spoon and put into a warmed serving dish. Cover with foil to keep hot.

3 Drain the potatoes and cut into about ½ inch (1cm) thick slices. Add to the bacon and cover with foil.

4 Peel and roughly chop the onion, add to the pan and fry over a moderate heat till golden. Add the vinegar, water, salt, pepper and mustard and bring to the boil.

5 Pour over the potatoes and bacon, turning them carefully till coated. Sprinkle with chives and serve immediately with fresh crusty bread.

cook's know-how

When buying potatoes for boiling, waxy ones are best. There are a number of varieties to choose from – King Edward, Desirée or Maris Piper being the most widely available. New potatoes, when in season, are also excellent for boiling. 'White' potatoes are better for chips, sauté and roasting. Choose firm potatoes with smooth skins. Do not select ones with withered, green or damaged skins, or if they are sprouting.
Store potatoes in a cool, dark place or brown paper bag, as green patches may develop on those kept in the light. Any green parts should be cut off.

Spicy green beans

Cumin, often used in Portuguese, Indian and Mexican cuisine, adds an extra spiciness to this filling vegetable dish, which may also be served as a starter

VEGETABLE Serves 4

Overall timing 45 minutes

Equipment 2 saucepans

Freezing Not recommended

INGREDIENTS

$1\frac{1}{2}$lb	Fresh or frozen green beans *or*	700g
2×14oz	cans of cut green beans	2×397g
4	Firm tomatoes	4
1 tbsp	Oil	15ml
4oz	Unsmoked bacon rashers	125g
	Salt and pepper	
$\frac{1}{4}$ teasp	Cumin	$\frac{1}{4}$×5ml
1 tbsp	Chopped parsley	15ml

METHOD

1. If using fresh beans, wash, top and tail and remove strings. Break or cut into short lengths if necessary. Blanch them for 5 minutes in boiling water. Drain.
2. Blanch the tomatoes in boiling water. Drain, peel and chop.
3. Heat the oil in a saucepan and brown the diced bacon for a few minutes.
4. Add beans, tomato, salt, pepper and cumin to pan. Cover and simmer very gently for about 15 minutes until beans are tender. If using drained canned beans, cover and simmer for 5–8 minutes only to heat through and absorb flavours.
5. Transfer mixture to warmed serving dish. Sprinkle with chopped parsley.

cook's know-how

Cumin, a light aromatic spice, is available ground or as whole seeds from most supermarkets. It is an essential ingredient in chilli powder and curry powders. Cumin is also used in pickles and chutneys, mixed into mince or rubbed on lamb before roasting. It's especially good sprinkled on salads, dips, breads and pastry, or added to the cooking water of cabbage, potatoes and green beans.

Below: Spicy green beans flavoured with cumin

Turkish lamb chops

Lamb is the most popular meat in Turkey – this is one of their simpler recipes

MAIN MEAL Serves 4

Overall timing 25 minutes

Equipment Saucepan, frying pan with lid

Freezing Not recommended

INGREDIENTS

3	Tomatoes	3
1	Garlic clove	1
3 tbsp	Oil	3×15ml
1 tbsp	Chopped fresh basil	15ml
1 tbsp	Chopped parsley	15ml
	Salt and pepper	
8	Lamb chops	8
3fl oz	Dry white wine	90ml
	Dried oregano or thyme	
$\frac{1}{2}$ pint	Hot stock	300ml

METHOD

1. Blanch, peel and chop the tomatoes. Peel and crush the garlic. Put them in a saucepan with 2 tbsp (2×15ml) of the oil, the basil and parsley. Season with salt and pepper and simmer, uncovered, for 10 minutes.
2. Season the chops with salt and pepper. Heat oil in frying pan, add chops and brown on both sides. Pour off the fat.
3. Pour the wine over the chops and simmer gently, uncovered, until it evaporates. Add a pinch of oregano or thyme and the stock (made with a stock cube if necessary), cover and simmer for a further 5 minutes.
4. Arrange the chops on a warm serving dish. Add the tomato sauce to the meat juices and heat through, stirring. Pour sauce over chops and serve with rice and a green vegetable.

Dutch sausage with mashed vegetables

This is a typical Dutch winter dish. The smoked sausage rings are quite different to British sausages as they contain almost all meat. They can also be served cold, sliced and added to salads and sandwiches. If kale is not available, use broccoli or cabbage

LUNCH OR SUPPER Serves 4

Overall timing 35 minutes

Equipment 2 saucepans

Freezing Not recommended

INGREDIENTS

$1\frac{1}{2}$lb	Floury potatoes	700g
	Salt	
2lb	Curly kale	900g
2×8oz	Dutch smoked pork rings	2×225g
2oz	Butter	50g
$\frac{1}{4}$ pint	Milk	150ml
$\frac{1}{4}$ teasp	Grated nutmeg	$\frac{1}{4}$×5ml
	Freshly-ground black pepper	

METHOD

1 Peel the potatoes and cut into quarters. Put into a saucepan, cover with cold salted water and bring to the boil. Simmer for 10 minutes.

2 Meanwhile, wash the kale, remove any damaged leaves and tough stalks and shred finely. Bring a large pan of water to the boil, add the sausages and simmer for 10 minutes.

3 Add the kale to the potatoes and cook for a further 10 minutes till the potatoes are tender. Drain the vegetables thoroughly in a colander. Melt the butter in the saucepan with the milk. Return the vegetables to the pan and mash till smooth. Add the nutmeg and salt and pepper to taste.

4 Spread on a warmed serving dish with a fork and add the drained sausages.

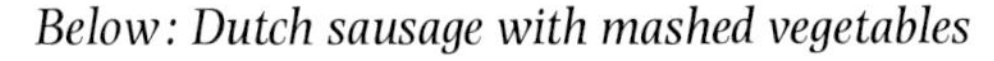

Below: Dutch sausage with mashed vegetables

Buttered pasta with Parmesan

The Italians like their pasta and this dish, which is favoured because it is so simple to prepare, combines it with butter and Parmesan. Use any type of pasta – spaghetti, macaroni (long or short) or shells. Adding a little oil to the cooking water will stop the pasta sticking together

LUNCH OR SUPPER Serves 4

Overall timing 15 minutes

Equipment Large saucepan

Freezing Not recommended

INGREDIENTS

14oz	Pasta	400g
1 teasp	Salt	5ml
1 tbsp	Oil	15ml
4oz	Unsalted butter	125g
3oz	Grated Parmesan	75g

METHOD

1 Three quarters fill a saucepan with water, bring to the boil and add salt and oil. Add pasta a little at a time (the water must not stop boiling). Do not cover. Stir frequently until cooked. Drain thoroughly and set pasta aside for the moment.

2 Add butter to pan over a medium heat. When hot, but not coloured, add pasta. Remove from heat and mix well using 2 forks, adding cheese a little at a time until pasta is well coated. Pour on to serving dish and serve immediately with a tomato and onion salad.

Asparagus quiche

The quiche (or *kiche* as it is sometimes called in Alsace-Lorraine where it originated is a rich and creamy savoury custard that can be flavoured in different ways. In this one the delicate asparagus combines well with the filling which is cooked in two stages to give special taste and texture

LUNCH OR SUPPER Serves 4

Overall timing 1¼ hours

Equipment 10 inch (25cm) flan ring or dish, small saucepan, baking tray

Freezing Either cook quiche in foil plate or remove from ring and place on cardboard. Wrap in polythene bag. Seal tightly, excluding air. Freezer life: 6 months. To use: thaw overnight in fridge and refresh in hot oven for 10 minutes

INGREDIENTS

8oz	Frozen shortcrust pastry	227g
2 tbsp	Butter	2×15ml
4 tbsp	Plain flour	4×15ml
¾ pint	Milk	400ml
1 teasp	Salt	5ml
	Pepper	
	Pinch of nutmeg	
2	Eggs	2
4oz	Gruyère	125g
12oz	Can of asparagus	340g

METHOD

1 Allow pastry to thaw. Preheat the oven to 425F (220C) Gas 7 and grease flan ring or dish (or foil plate if you intend freezing the quiche).

2 Roll out the pastry to ¼ inch (6mm) thick and line ring or dish. Prick pastry with fork. Bake blind for 5 minutes.

3 To make the sauce, melt the butter in a small saucepan. Stir in flour. Remove pan from heat and gradually stir in ½ pint (300ml) of the milk. Season with salt, pepper and nutmeg. Return to heat and bring to the boil, stirring constantly. Cook for 2 minutes. Remove pan from heat. Separate the eggs and stir one yolk into pan. Grate the Gruyère and add to the sauce.

4 Pour the sauce over the pastry. Return to the oven and cook for 15 minutes.

5 Remove quiche from oven. Drain asparagus, cut into small lengths and arrange evenly over surface. Mix together the rest of the milk, the remaining egg yolk and 2 egg whites and pour this over quiche. Bake for 30 minutes more at 375F (190C) Gas 5.

Lamb with figs

Over-ripe figs can be used just as well in this casserole. Simply cook the meat for 30 minutes before adding figs

MAIN MEAL Serves 4

Overall timing 1½ hours

Equipment Flameproof casserole

Freezing Cool, turn into rigid container, cover, label and freeze. Freezer life: 4 months. To use: reheat slowly from frozen

INGREDIENTS

1lb	Fresh figs	450g
2lb	Breast of lamb	900g
1	Large onion	1
4 tbsp	Oil	4×15ml
1 tbsp	Plain flour	15ml
½ pint	Dry white wine	300ml
	Salt and pepper	
	Chopped parsley	

METHOD

1 Wipe figs and cut in half. Chop breast of lamb into shortish pieces. Peel and chop onion.

2 Heat the oil in a casserole and brown the meat on all sides. Add the onion and cook until golden.

3 Sprinkle flour over casserole and cook over a high heat until flour begins to brown. Gradually stir in the wine and bring to the boil.

4 Reduce heat, add figs and season with salt and pepper. Stir gently. Cover and simmer over a low heat for about 1 hour or until the lamb is tender. Garnish with chopped parsley and serve.

VARIATION

A stuffing can be made for breast of lamb or belly of pork. Chop 8oz (225g) of dried figs and place in a bowl with a finely chopped onion, 2oz (50g) fresh white or brown breadcrumbs, salt and freshly-ground black pepper and ½ pint (300ml) medium sweet cider. Leave until all liquid has been absorbed, then use to stuff the meat. Roll up, secure with string at intervals, then roast. Serve cold, sliced, with salad.

Above left: Asparagus quiche, a variation of the classic egg and pastry flan, makes the most of the more economical can of asparagus

Minestrone with pesto

The most famous of the Italian soups, minestrone is made with a variety of vegetables and some pasta. In this version, pesto is added as well to make it even more rich and filling. A similar soup is made in Nice, in France, and is called *soupe au pistou*

MAIN MEAL Serves 8

Overall timing 2½ hours plus soaking time

Equipment Bowl, frying pan or flameproof dish, large casserole or saucepan with a lid, pestle and mortar

Freezing Cook but do not add pesto. Cool quickly, pack in plastic containers leaving ¾ inch (2cm) headspace. Cover, label and freeze. Freezer life: 3 months. To use: thaw for 6 hours, then heat to simmering point. Add pesto

Below: Minestrone with pesto – Italy's favourite vegetable soup, flavoured with basil

INGREDIENTS

4oz	Dried pinto* beans	125g
1	Onion	1
1	Garlic clove	1
1	Celery stalk	1
3 tbsp	Oil	3×15ml
2 tbsp	Chopped parsley	2×15ml
8oz	Head of celery	225g
4oz	Spinach	125g
4oz	Cabbage	125g
4oz	Carrots	125g
12oz	Tomatoes	350g
4oz	Courgettes	125g
11oz	Potatoes	325g
7½oz	Can of red kidney beans	213g
8oz	Fresh or frozen peas	225g
1 tbsp	Salt	15ml
6oz	Vermicelli or spaghetti	175g
	Pesto	
4 tbsp	Chopped fresh basil	4×15ml
2	Garlic cloves	2
4 tbsp	Olive oil	4×15ml
4oz	Parmesan	125g
	Pinch of salt	

METHOD

1. Place the pinto beans in a bowl and cover with boiling water. Soak for 2 hours.
2. Peel and chop onion, peel and crush garlic, wash and finely chop celery stalk. Sprinkle some of the oil over the prepared vegetables and mix in the chopped parsley. Place rest of oil in frying pan or flameproof dish and fry mixture for a few minutes. Set aside.
3. Wash and chop head of celery and spinach. Wash and shred the cabbage. Scrape and slice carrots. Scald, then peel tomatoes. Set one aside and peel and chop the rest. Wipe and dice courgettes, peel and dice potatoes. Drain kidney beans. If using fresh peas, shell them.
4. Bring 4½ pints (2.5 litres) water to the boil in a large saucepan. Add the salt and all the vegetables. (If using frozen peas do not add till next step.) Add the already cooked onion and celery mixture, cover the pan and simmer gently for 1½ hours.
5. Break the vermicelli or spaghetti into short lengths and add to the soup with the frozen peas, if used. Stir, then continue cooking for a further 15 minutes.
6. Meanwhile, prepare pesto: sieve reserved tomato flesh and place in mortar with the basil and the peeled and chopped garlic. Pound with the pestle, gradually adding the oil, then 1oz (25g) of the grated Parmesan. Add a little salt.
7. Spoon pesto into soup and stir in well so that basil flavours other ingredients. Simmer for a few minutes. Adjust seasoning. Serve with grated Parmesan.

*You could also use borlotti or cannelini beans.

Celery in yogurt sauce

Yogurt is combined with soured cream in a very tasty sauce to make this dish a versatile vegetable accompaniment to meat roasts, pies and pasties

VEGETABLE Serves 4–6

Overall timing 45 minutes

Equipment Saucepan, large frying pan, measuring jug, flameproof dish

Freezing Not recommended

Choose the thick outer stalks, wash and dry them, then cut into equal lengths

The chopped onions are fried, then the blanched celery is added, and the stock

Sauce, made from cooking liquor, cream, yogurt, is spooned over celery and heated

INGREDIENTS

2lb	Green celery	900g
	Salt	
1	Onion	1
1oz	Bacon fat or pork dripping	25g
2oz	Butter	50g
	Pepper	
1 pint	Chicken stock	560ml
	Sauce	
$\frac{1}{2}$ oz	Butter	15g
$\frac{1}{2}$oz	Plain flour	15g
$\frac{1}{2}$ pint	Stock	300ml
$\frac{1}{4}$ pint	Carton of soured cream	150ml
5oz	Carton of plain yogurt	141g
	Salt and pepper	
	Grated nutmeg	

METHOD

1 Trim and wash celery. Cut into short lengths, blanch for 5 minutes in boiling salted water, then drain well.

2 Peel and chop onion. Heat bacon fat or dripping and butter in large frying pan. Add onion and cook till transparent – do not allow to brown too much.

3 Add the celery and sprinkle with pepper. Cover with stock (made up with 2 cubes if necessary) and cook over a low heat for 20–30 minutes, covered.

4 Remove from heat and drain liquid into a measuring jug. There should be $\frac{1}{2}$ pint (300ml) – make up to this amount with a little extra stock if necessary.

5 To make the sauce, melt the butter in a saucepan. Stir in the flour and cook for 1 minute. Remove from the heat and gradually stir in measured stock. Return to the heat and bring to the boil stirring. Add soured cream, yogurt, salt, pepper and a pinch of nutmeg. Stir till smooth and creamy, then remove immediately from heat.

6 Transfer celery to flameproof dish. Pour sauce over and heat through gently on top of the stove for a few minutes.

Below: Celery in yogurt sauce – a vegetable dish for all occasions

Empanadas

Delicious meat pasties from Brazil with raisins providing a contrast to the minced beef and pork

LUNCH OR SUPPER Makes 8

Overall timing 50 minutes

Equipment Mincer, frying pan, bowl, baking tray

Freezing Omit the hard-boiled eggs. Open freeze at end of Step 6. Pack into rigid containers, cover, label and freeze. Freezer life: 2 months. To use: arrange frozen on baking tray, glaze and bake at 425F (220C) Gas 7 for about 30 minutes

INGREDIENTS

13oz	Packet of frozen puff pastry	375g
1	Onion	1
4oz	Belly pork rashers	125g
1oz	Butter	25g
8oz	Minced beef	225g
3 tbsp	Seedless raisins	3×15ml
	Pinch of ground cloves	
	Salt	
	Freshly-ground black pepper	
¼ teasp	Paprika	1.25ml
2	Hard-boiled eggs	2
8	Pitted green olives	8
1	Egg	1

METHOD

1 Thaw the pastry. Roll out on a floured board to form a rectangle 8×16 inches (20×40cm). Cut into 8 even-sized squares (4 inch/10cm).
2 Preheat oven to 400F (200C) Gas 6.
3 Peel the onion and chop finely. Derind and mince the belly pork rashers. Heat the butter in the frying pan and fry the onion and pork till golden. Add the minced beef and fry for 10 minutes over high heat, stirring frequently, till brown.
4 Remove from heat and add the raisins and ground cloves, salt, pepper and paprika. Mix well.
5 Shell and coarsely chop the hard-boiled eggs, chop the olives and add to the pan with the eggs and mix well.
6 Beat the egg in a small bowl. Place one eighth of the meat mixture on to half of each pastry square. Brush the edges with a little of the egg and fold pastry over to enclose the filling. Crimp the edges together to seal.
7 Arrange on a wetted baking tray and brush tops with the beaten egg. Bake near the top of the oven for about 25 minutes till well risen and golden. Serve hot with green vegetables. The fresh taste of celery in yogurt sauce (see left) would make a refreshing accompaniment to these pasties.

Above: Empanadas – filling and tasty pasties, easily prepared in advance. They are ideal for a warming meal after a family outing on a cold wintry day

Rabbit with mushrooms

This cooking method ensures both excellent flavour and tenderness. Try a fresh bouquet garni using stronger herbs like rosemary and sage plus a strip of orange peel

MAIN MEAL Serves 4–6

Overall timing 1¾ hours

Equipment Flameproof casserole

Freezing Not recommended

INGREDIENTS

2½lb	Rabbit	1.1kg
4oz	Streaky bacon	125g
8oz	Button mushrooms	225g
2	Shallots	2
2	Large tomatoes	2
2oz	Butter	50g
2 tbsp	Plain flour	2×15ml
½ pint	Dry white wine	300ml
1 tbsp	Tomato paste	15ml
	Salt	
	Freshly-ground black pepper	
	Bouquet garni	
1 teasp	Chopped parsley	5ml

METHOD

1 Wipe and trim the rabbit and cut into neat pieces, removing any small bones.
2 Derind and dice the bacon. Wipe and trim the mushrooms and slice thickly. Peel and chop the shallots, blanch, peel and chop the tomatoes.
3 Heat the butter in the casserole and fry the mushrooms and bacon for 3 minutes. Add the shallots and chopped tomatoes and fry for 5 minutes.
4 Add the rabbit pieces to the pan and fry for about 10 minutes till browned on all sides. Sprinkle with flour and cook, stirring, for 1 minute.
5 Gradually add the wine and bring to the boil, stirring constantly. Stir in the tomato paste, seasoning and bouquet garni. Cover and simmer for 1 hour.
6 Discard the bouquet garni. Adjust the seasoning and sprinkle with parsley. Serve the rabbit from the casserole with sauté potatoes and a green vegetable such as spinach.

VARIATION

Use a can of tomatoes instead of fresh tomatoes, add to the pan at Step 5 and stir well to break them up. After 40 minutes, stir in 4oz (125g) long grain rice. Cover and simmer for 20 minutes.

Skate with black butter sauce

A dish from Brittany, where fish are always treated simply but well. The black butter sauce, cooked till nut brown and not black, is flavoured with vinegar, pepper, parsley and capers

MAIN MEAL Serves 4

Overall timing 30 minutes

Equipment Saucepan, frying pan

Freezing Not recommended

INGREDIENTS

4	Slices of skate	4
½ teasp	Salt	2.5ml
6 tbsp	Vinegar	6×15ml
4oz	Butter	125g
	Freshly-ground black pepper	
2 tbsp	Chopped parsley	2×15ml
2 tbsp	Capers	2×15ml

METHOD

1 Wash the skate and place in a saucepan. Cover with cold water and add salt and 5 tbsp (5×15ml) of the vinegar. Bring to the boil slowly over medium heat. Remove from heat, cover and leave to poach for 10 minutes.
2 Meanwhile, make black butter sauce: melt butter in pan over medium heat until nut brown but not black. Stir in remaining vinegar, pepper, parsley and capers.
3 Drain the skate well, then place on warmed serving plates. Pour over black butter sauce, garnish with parsley sprigs and serve with boiled potatoes.

cook's know-how

Clarified butter is best in all butter sauces, and it's easy to prepare. Place the butter in a saucepan and melt over a low heat. Allow to stand for 5 minutes. Gently pour off the crystal clear butter, leaving the sediment in the pan, or strain through fine muslin into a bowl.

Left: Skate with black butter sauce

Clam soup

Clams in their shells, cooked Italian-style with wine, tomatoes and herbs. Though described as a soup, it is really a well-flavoured sauce into which clams are mixed

HOT STARTER OR LIGHT LUNCH Serves 4

Overall timing 45 minutes

Equipment 2 saucepans, sieve, muslin

Freezing Not recommended

INGREDIENTS

8oz	Can of tomatoes	227g
2 tbsp	Olive oil	2×15ml
1	Garlic clove	1
3 tbsp	Fresh chopped basil *or*	3×15ml
1 teasp	dried basil	5ml
1 tbsp	Fresh chopped parsley	15ml
	Salt and pepper	
1¼ pints	Dry white wine	700ml
3lb	Clams	1.4kg
2fl oz	Water	60ml

METHOD

1 Put the contents of the can of tomatoes into a saucepan with the olive oil, peeled and crushed garlic, herbs, salt and pepper and half the wine. Bring to the boil and simmer, uncovered, for about 15 minutes until reduced by about half the quantity.
2 Meanwhile, wash and scrub clams well under running cold water. Place in a large saucepan with the remaining wine. Bring to the boil, cover and cook about 5 minutes or until the shells open. Discard any that do not open.
3 Strain the cooking liquor through a muslin-lined sieve and return it to the saucepan with the clams still in their shells.
4 Add the water to the clams, heat gently, then add the hot tomato mixture. Spoon into individual bowls and serve with toasted french bread.

VARIATION

Other bivalve molluscs such as cockles or mussels may be cooked in the same way. Cook the shellfish as Step 2, then take out of their shells and add them to the sauce. Pour it over spaghetti, noodles, rice – or any pasta. Or reduce the liquid, then add the shellfish and use as a topping for pizza.

Below: Clam soup – clams cooked in wine and tomatoes. Scoop up the juice with the shells

Brown sauce-Espagnole

The third major "mother" sauce in classic French cooking (see pages 450–455) has nothing to do with Spain, but the colour has obvious links with the sunshine. For a true, rich flavour use garden-fresh vegetables and stock made from beef bones, not from cubes

2 Add 2oz (50g) flour, brown. Stir in 1 pint (560ml) beef stock, 4 tbsp (4× 15ml) tomato paste. Simmer 45 minutes

1 Chop 2 streaky bacon rashers, small onion, carrot, 2oz (50g) mushroom stalks. Fry for 10 minutes in 2oz (50g) butter

3 Strain sauce and discard flavourings. Stir in 3 tbsp (3×15ml) dry sherry, salt and pepper to taste. Reheat, stirring

Below: Espagnole – brown sauce for meats, with flavour improved by long cooking

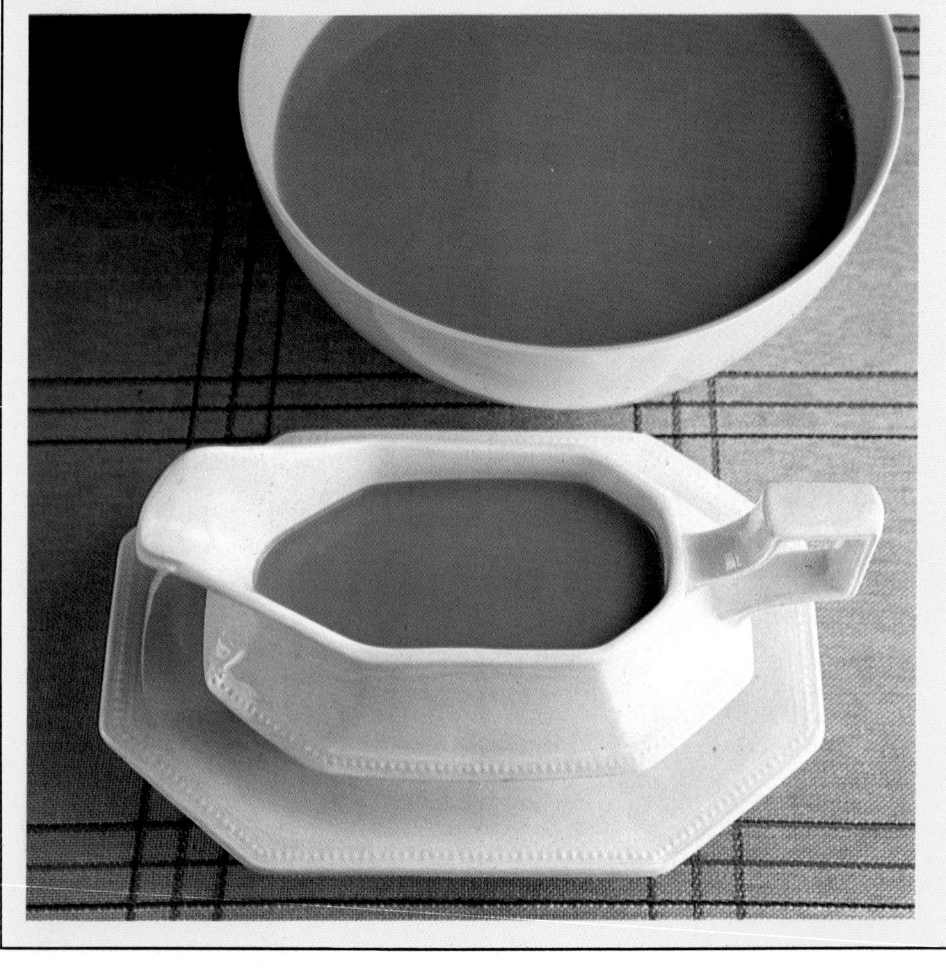

Espagnole-based sauces

Apart from genevoise which is always served with fish, these complement stronger-flavoured meats and game

Quantities given are for Espagnole sauce made with 1 pint (560ml) beef stock.

BOURGUIGNONNE Cook 1 small chopped onion in 1oz (25g) butter till transparent. Add ½ pint (300ml) red wine and a bouquet garni and boil till reduced to one-third. Add to **Espagnole sauce,** strain and stir in 1oz (25g) butter.
Serve with eggs, poultry, meat

GENEVOISE Make a mirepoix au maigre from an onion, a celery stalk and 4oz (125g) carrots. Dice the vegetables and add to 2oz (50g) melted butter in a saucepan. Fry gently for 10 minutes. Add to this fish trimmings and ½ pint (300ml) red wine, and boil till reduced by half. Add to **Espagnole sauce** and simmer for 30 minutes. Strain and add 1oz (25g) butter and 1 teasp (5ml) anchovy essence.
Serve with fish, especially salmon or trout

NAPOLITAINE Add 1 tbsp (15ml) each of grated horseradish and chopped lean ham to **Espagnole sauce** with 4 tbsp (4×15ml) each Madeira and consommé and a bouquet garni. Simmer for 30 minutes, strain and add 2 tbsp (2×15ml) redcurrant jelly. *Serve with game or venison*

PORTUGAISE Add one strip each of orange and lemon rind to **Espagnole sauce** with 1 teasp (5ml) each of coriander seeds and sugar and 4 tbsp (4×15ml) consommé. Simmer for 30 minutes, strain and add 4 tbsp (4×15ml) Malaga wine, a few drops lemon juice and 1oz (25g) butter.
Serve with braised or roast beef, ham

RAVIGOTE BRUNE Fry 1 chopped onion in 1oz (25g) butter. Add to **Espagnole sauce** with a peeled and crushed garlic clove, 6 tbsp (6×15ml) Chablis, 1 tbsp (15ml) each of capers and consommé and 1 teasp (5ml) crushed peppercorns. Simmer for 30 minutes, strain and add 1 teasp (5ml) Dijon mustard. *Serve with beef, poultry, veal*

VENAISON Put ¼ pint (150ml) Burgundy into a saucepan with 2 tbsp (2×15ml) each of vinegar and sugar, 4 tbsp (4×15ml) redcurrant jelly and the flesh of ½ a lemon. Simmer for 10 minutes, strain and add to **Espagnole sauce.** *Serve with venison*

VICTORIA Add ¼ pint (150ml) port, 3 tbsp (3×15ml) redcurrant jelly and a strip of orange rind to **Espagnole sauce** with 3 cloves, 6 peppercorns and a cinnamon stick. Simmer for 30 minutes, and add juice of 1 orange. Strain and add pinch of cayenne.
Serve with braised or roast duck, ham

Poivrade

Sauces to serve with meat can be made with the meat as it cooks. The meat is fried to develop the flavour and the sauce flour is fried in the same pan so that all the meat juices are retained. Liquid is added gradually, brought to the boil and simmered till the meat is tender. The meat is removed so the sauce can be strained and final adjustments made to the consistency and flavour, according to taste

1 Fry 2oz (50g) each bacon, onion and carrot with game. Add 1 garlic clove, 2 tbsp (2×15ml) each white wine, flour

2 Fry, stirring, over a moderate heat till golden brown, then gradually stir in ½ pint (300ml) of game marinade

3 Add 1 pint (560ml) game giblet stock, bring to boil, stirring constantly. Add salt, bouquet garni. Simmer till tender

4 Strain the cooking liquor through sieve into a clean saucepan. Remove the game, place on warmed serving dish and keep hot

5 Rub the flavouring vegetables through sieve into the strained sauce, discarding the bouquet garni

6 Add 2 teasp (2×5ml) roughly crushed white peppercorns, reduce by half. Strain. Add 2 tbsp (2×15ml) Cognac

Grand veneur Add 2 tbsp (2×15ml) gooseberry jelly or sieved gooseberry jam to **poivrade sauce.** Simmer for 5 minutes. Remove from heat, stir in 4 tbsp (4×15ml) single cream.
Serve with venison, hare

Réforme Cut 1oz (25g) cooked tongue, the white of 1 hard-boiled egg and 1 small cooked truffle into fine strips. Add to **poivrade sauce** with 2 sliced button mushrooms fried in ½oz (15g) butter. Reheat.
Serve with lamb or mutton cutlets

Bigarade

Fragrant orange sauce, best with fatty meats like duck

Blanch shredded rind of 1 orange and ½ lemon, drain. Add to Espagnole sauce with juice of 1 orange. Bring to boil, simmer 5 minutes. Beat in 1oz (25g) butter

Demi-glace

Espagnole sauce with the addition of a rich, brown stock and Madeira. Using a good bone stock ensures full strength of flavour and a gelatinous quality which is lacking in stock made with cubes. Poultry carcasses, together with a few giblets, can be used as can game trimmings

Wipe and chop 1lb (450g) marrow bone or knuckle of veal. Wipe 1lb (450g) shin of beef, cut into cubes. Heat 1oz (25g) dripping in large pan, add bones, meat, 1 sliced carrot and 1 sliced onion and fry, stirring, till the meat is browned all over

Add 2 pints (1.1 litres) water, bay leaf, bouquet garni and seasoning. Bring to the boil, cover and simmer for 2 hours. Pour off stock into large pan, boil rapidly till reduced by half. Sprinkle 1 tbsp (15ml) plain flour over meat in pan

Fry, stirring, for 2 minutes, then gradually add reduced stock. Bring to boil, stirring. Remove from heat and lift out bones. Rub through a sieve into Espagnole sauce. Boil till reduced by half. Add 4 tbsp (4×15ml) Madeira, then season to taste

Demi-glace-based sauces

Quantities given below are for 1 pint (560ml) demi-glace sauce.

AIGRE-DOUCE Dissolve 1 tbsp (15ml) sugar in 3 tbsp (3×15ml) wine vinegar and boil till pale golden. Add to **demi-glace sauce** with ¼ pint (150ml) white wine and 1 chopped shallot. Simmer for 30 minutes, strain, add 1 tbsp (15ml) capers, 4 tbsp (4×15ml) raisins. *Serve with meats*

CHARCUTIERE Cook 1 peeled and finely chopped onion in 1oz (25g) butter. Add 1 tbsp (15ml) wine vinegar and **demi-glace sauce.** Add 2 tbsp (2×15ml) shredded gherkins. *Serve with fried or grilled pork*

CHASSEUR Fry 4oz (125g) chopped mushrooms, 1 shallot in 2oz (50g) butter. Add ¼ pint (150ml) white wine, 3 tbsp (3×15ml) tomato paste. Reduce by half. Add **demi-glace sauce,** 3 tbsp (3×15ml) fresh fines herbes. *Serve with poultry, game*

CHATEAUBRIAND Put 1 chopped shallot in a saucepan with ¼ pint (150ml) white wine and boil till reduced to one-third. Add to **demi-glace sauce** with 2oz (50g) butter, 1 tbsp (15ml) chopped tarragon and a pinch of cayenne. *Serve with steaks*

CHAUD-FROID BRUN Add ½ pint (300ml) jellied meat stock to **demi-glace sauce** and boil till reduced by one-third. Add 2 tbsp (2×15ml) sherry or Madeira.
Serve with cold beef, veal

DIABLE Put ¼ pint (150ml) white wine into a pan with 1 tbsp (15ml) vinegar, 1 chopped shallot, 1 bay leaf, sprig of thyme and plenty of freshly-ground black pepper. Boil till reduced to one-third, add to **demi-glace sauce** and strain. Stir in pinch of cayenne and 1 teasp (5ml) parsley.
Serve with poultry, lamb, veal

PIQUANTE Add 2 tbsp (2×15ml) each of chopped parsley and gherkins to **diable sauce.** *Serve with chicken, chops, veal*

DUXELLES Add 6 tbsp (6×15ml) white wine and 2 tbsp (2×15ml) duxelles – a mixture of chopped mushrooms fried with diced shallots – to **demi-glaze sauce** with 2 tbsp (2×15ml) tomato paste and 1 tbsp (15ml) parsley. *Serve with eggs, fish, veal*

ITALIENNE Add 2 tbsp (2×15ml) diced lean ham and 1 tbsp (15ml) each of chopped parsley, chervil and tarragon to **duxelles sauce.** *Serve with chops, poultry*

MADEIRA Add 6 tbsp (6×15ml) Madeira to **demi-glace sauce.** *Serve with meats*

FINANCIERE Add 2 tbsp (2×15ml) diced lean ham, 1 tbsp (15ml) each of mushroom and truffle trimmings, 1 teasp (5ml) thyme and 1 bay leaf to **Madeira sauce.** Simmer for 10 minutes, then strain. *Serve with poultry, offal, vol-au-vents*

MOUTARDE BRUNE Cook 1 peeled and finely chopped onion in 1oz (25g) butter. Add ¼ pint (150ml) white wine and the **demi-glace sauce** and boil till reduced by one-third. Add 1 tbsp (15ml) Dijon mustard and 1 teasp (5ml) lemon juice.
Serve with chops, grilled meats, trotters

PERIGOURDINE Add 2 tbsp (2×15ml) Madeira to **demi-glace sauce,** reduce by half. Strain, add 2 sliced fried truffles.
Serve with roast meats, game, steaks

REGENCE Cook 4oz (125g) diced ham and 1 peeled and chopped onion in 2oz (50g) butter without browning. Add ¼ pint (150ml) each of Graves and chicken stock and boil till reduced to one-third. Add to **demi-glace sauce,** sieve.
Serve with poultry, offal

ROBERT Cook 1 peeled and finely chopped onion in 2oz (50g) butter till transparent. Add 6 tbsp (6×15ml) white wine and **demi-glace sauce** and boil till reduced by one-third. Add 2 teasp (2×5ml) prepared mustard. Strain. *Serve with grilled meats*

ROMAINE Dissolve 1 tbsp (15ml) sugar in 1 tbsp (15ml) wine vinegar and boil till golden. Add to **demi-glace sauce** with 6 tbsp (6×15ml) game stock and simmer for 10 minutes. Add 2 tbsp (2×15ml) each of lightly toasted pine nuts and sultanas.
Serve with game, especially venison

ESTRAGON Put ¼ pint (150ml) white wine into a saucepan with 2 tbsp (2×15ml) chopped tarragon and boil till reduced by half. Add to **demi-glace sauce** and strain. Stir in 2 tbsp (2×15ml) chopped tarragon.
Serve with eggs, chops, fish, poultry

Porto

Rich sauce with strong colour for roast game, duck or beef

Add ¼ pint (150ml) port and juice of ½ orange to demi-glace sauce. Simmer

After 10 minutes, strain then stir in 3 tbsp (3×15ml) single cream

Bordelaise

Robust wine sauce for roast and grilled meats, especially steaks

Finely chop 1 shallot, put into pan with 1 sprig of thyme and bay leaf

Add $\frac{1}{2}$ pint (300ml) red wine, then add demi-glace, reduce to one-third

Mash 1 tbsp (15ml) each butter and flour, then whisk into boiling sauce

Strain, add 2 tbsp (2×15ml) each chopped cooked bone marrow, parsley

Lyonnaise brune

A brown onion sauce, good with roast and grilled meats, leftovers

Fry 1 chopped onion in 1oz (25g) butter. Add 1 tbsp (15ml) flour

Cook for 3 minutes. Gradually add 3 tbsp (3×15ml) white wine vinegar

Add 3 tbsp (3×15ml) each of white wine and light stock. Bring to boil

Reduce by one-third. Add demi-glace sauce and simmer for 5 minutes

Zingara

Flavoursome meat sauce for roast veal or pork, pasta, leftovers

Simmer bay leaf, 6 mushrooms in $\frac{1}{4}$ pint (150ml) stock for 10 minutes

Whisk 1 tbsp (15ml) each tomato paste, butter and flour into sauce

Boil sauce, add chopped mushrooms, 2oz (50g) each ham and tongue

Add to demi-glace sauce with $\frac{1}{2}$ teasp (2.5ml) paprika. Simmer 5 minutes

Hot emulsions-Hollandaise

A rich, pale golden sauce that's served warm rather than hot. It is fairly easy to prepare, but the egg yolks must be heated very slowly, and the butter added just a little at a time so each addition is absorbed by the eggs

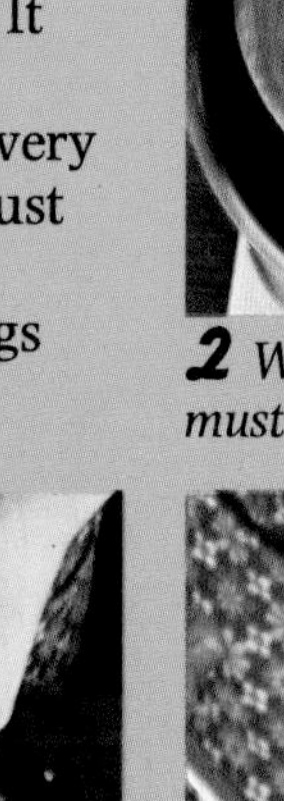

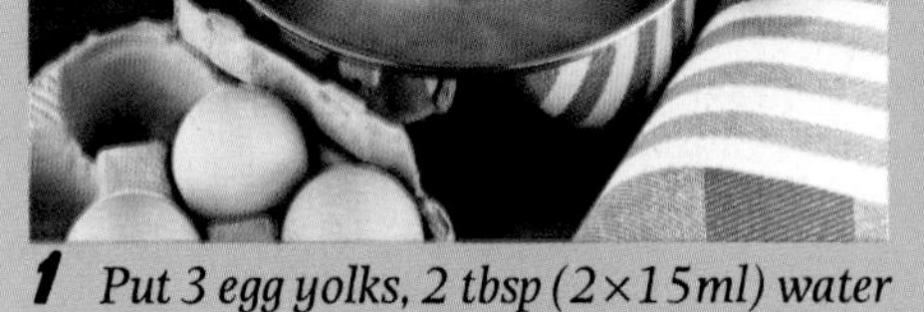

1 Put 3 egg yolks, 2 tbsp (2×15ml) water in bowl over pan of simmering water

2 Whisk over low heat till thick – bowl must not touch water. Remove from heat

3 Gradually whisk in 7oz (200g) melted unsalted butter and little lemon juice

Below: Hollandaise sauce – traditionally served with asparagus and fish (salmon)

Hollandaise-based sauces

All these add flavour to Hollandaise. In noisette and vin blanc, cool butter and wine before using or it will cause the sauce to curdle

The quantities given below are for a three egg yolk amount.

CAPRES Add 2 tbsp (2×15ml) drained capers to **hollandaise sauce.**
Serve with poached or steamed fish

MOUSSELINE Add 2 tbsp (2×15ml) whipped cream to **hollandaise sauce.**
Serve with fish, poultry, vegetables

MOUTARDE Add 2 tbsp (2×15ml) Dijon mustard to **hollandaise sauce.**
Serve with grilled fish, steaks

NOISETTE Heat the butter for **hollandaise sauce** till golden, then cool before whisking gradually into sauce.
Serve with poultry, vegetables

VIN BLANC Boil 6 tbsp (6×15ml) dry white wine till reduced by two-thirds, cool. Add instead of water to **hollandaise sauce.**
Serve with fish, poultry, vegetables

Maltaise

Hollandaise with an orange tang. Serve with steamed vegetables

Wash 1 blood orange and remove rind with potato peeler. Squeeze out the juice, whisk into hollandaise sauce

Shred rind neatly, blanch in boiling water for 5 minutes till tender. Drain well and stir into the sauce

Béarnaise

A rich, slightly piquant sauce to serve with grilled meat or fish

Mix 3 finely chopped shallots, 3 tbsp (3×15ml) fresh chopped tarragon and 4 tbsp (4×15ml) red wine vinegar

Bring to boil and boil till reduced to one-third. Allow to cool slightly. Add 1 tbsp (15ml) water, seasoning

Whisk 3 egg yolks into sauce over low heat (or over simmering water) till thick. Remove from heat

Gradually whisk in 7oz (200g) unsalted butter. Whisk over low heat for 1 minute. Add pinch of cayenne

Paloise Make up béarnaise sauce, replacing tarragon with chopped mint. *Serve with grilled meat, poultry*

Choron Serve with grilled or sautéed meats, especially steaks

Whisk 2 teasp (2×5ml) tomato paste into béarnaise sauce over a low heat

Remove from heat and whisk in 2 tbsp (2×15ml) double cream. Adjust seasoning

Below: Choron sauce – a creamy, tomato flavoured sauce based on béarnaise

Countdown

Traditional porridge
Kedgeree
Brioche

A full leisurely breakfast is only possible for most of us at the weekend when we have more time to prepare and eat it. Start with satisfying porridge, which can be made the traditional way or for speed using rolled oats, taking 10–15 minutes to make. For the kedgeree, the rice, smoked haddock and eggs can be cooked the day before and stored in the fridge until morning. The brioche need to be prepared and baked in advance. When cool, wrap in foil, polythene or place in the bread bin until breakfast time. Brioche freeze well, so any not eaten can be frozen. Squeeze oranges to make fruit juice (see below)

Day before Make brioche and bake. Cool and store. Cook rice for kedgeree and drain. Cook smoked haddock, drain and flake. Hard-boil eggs, then plunge in cold water to prevent dark rings forming around the yolks. Store rice, fish and eggs in covered container in fridge.

40 mins before Start making porridge

30 mins before Prepare and chop onion, capsicum and egg for kedgeree

25 mins before Add salt to porridge and simmer

15 mins before Set oven to 300F (150C) Gas 2. Finish kedgeree, cover and keep warm in oven

5 mins before Warm brioche in oven

Serve the porridge with sugar or syrup and individual bowls of cream or milk. Follow with tasty kedgeree and finish the breakfast with warm brioche served with butter.

Whether to serve refreshing tea, a strong brew of coffee or chilled fruit juice depends on personal taste. You could squeeze your own orange juice. Six average size oranges will provide ample juice for four – 1¼ pints (700ml). Serve unsweetened or add sugar to taste.

Traditional porridge

The Scots usually sprinkle salt on their porridge, but it can be served with brown sugar or golden syrup, hot or cold with cream or milk.

BREAKFAST Serves 4

Overall timing 40 minutes

Equipment Saucepan

Freezing Not recommended

INGREDIENTS

2 pints	Water	1.1 litres
6oz	Medium oatmeal	175g
2 teasp	Salt	2×5ml
½ pint	Creamy milk	300ml

METHOD

1 Put the water into a saucepan and bring to the boil. Sprinkle in the oatmeal, stirring constantly, and bring back to the boil. Simmer for about 10 minutes. Add the salt and simmer for a further 25 minutes.

2 Remove pan from the heat and divide the porridge between individual bowls. Serve with individual bowls of cold creamy milk and crunchy brown sugar to sprinkle on top. Dip each spoonful into the cold milk before eating.

VARIATIONS

To make rolled oats porridge, which is quicker than oatmeal porridge, bring 2 pints (1.1 litres) water to the boil in a large saucepan. Sprinkle in 4oz (125g) rolled oats and boil for about 5 minutes, stirring to break up any lumps, Add a pinch each of salt and sugar, stir and leave to stand, covered, for a further 5 minutes before serving.

To make a fruity porridge, peel, core and finely chop 3 apples and peel and chop 2 bananas. Soak the fruit in lemon juice and stir into the porridge just before serving. Alternatively, add 4oz (125g) dried fruit to the pan with the oatmeal, and stir in the grated rind of 1 orange. Use raisins, dried apples or a mixture of dried fruit. If using dried apricots or prunes, soak overnight before adding to the oatmeal. If using coarse ground or pin head oatmeal, it is best cooked the night before in a double saucepan, as cooking time can be up to 2 hours.

Above: Traditional porridge – a nutritious and hearty breakfast whether made slowly with oatmeal or quickly with rolled oats

Kedgeree

In the days when a huge breakfast was a major event, kedgeree was a common sight on the sideboard. The dish is Anglo-Indian in origin, its name coming from the Indian word *khicharhi*

BREAKFAST OR SUPPER Serves 4

Overall timing 40 minutes

Equipment 2 saucepans, frying pan

Freezing Cool, pack into rigid container, cover, label and freeze. Freezer life: 1 month. To use: reheat slowly from frozen

INGREDIENTS

6oz	Long grain rice	175g
	Salt	
1lb	Smoked haddock fillets	450g
3	Eggs	3
1	Onion	1
1	Green capsicum	1
3oz	Butter	75g
2 tbsp	Chopped parsley	2×15ml
$\frac{1}{4}$ teasp	Cayenne pepper	$\frac{1}{4}$×5ml
	Pepper	

METHOD

1 Cook the rice in boiling salted water for 15–20 minutes until tender. Drain well.

2 Poach the haddock fillets in water in a frying pan for 10 minutes or until tender. Drain and flake, discarding skin.

3 Hard boil the eggs, drain and chop.

4 Peel and chop the onion. Wipe, deseed and chop capsicum. Heat the butter in a large pan and fry onion until just soft. Add capsicum and cook for 5 minutes.

5 Add the rice, flaked fish, chopped eggs, parsley and cayenne. Stir over a moderate heat for 5 minutes, season to taste and pile on to a warmed serving plate. Serve immediately.

VARIATION

For a mildly curried flavour, add 2 teasp (2×5ml) curry paste to the melted butter. Stir in 2 tbsp (2×15ml) each of sultanas, toasted flaked almonds and chopped mango chutney with the rice and omit the cayenne and parsley. Serve at suppertime.

Right: Brioche – large or small breads to serve warm for breakfast with butter

Brioche

The name means little rock but this refers to the shape not the texture of these superb yeast rolls

BREAD Makes 1 large or 12 small

Overall timing $1\frac{1}{4}$ hours plus proving

Equipment 2 bowls, saucepan, 8 inch (20cm) brioche tin or 12×3 inch (7.5cm) brioche tins

Freezing Put dough into oiled polythene bag at end of Step 5, seal, label and freeze. Freezer life: 6 months. To use: thaw in bag at room temperature for about 6 hours. Complete Steps 6–9

INGREDIENTS

2 tbsp	Hot water	2×15ml
2 teasp	Caster sugar	2×5ml
$\frac{1}{2}$oz	Fresh yeast *or*	15g
2 teasp	dried yeast	2×5ml
8oz	Strong flour	225g
	Salt	
2oz	Butter	50g
2	Eggs	2
	Milk for glazing	

METHOD

1 Put the water and $\frac{1}{2}$ teasp (2.5ml) of the sugar into a small bowl and stir till the sugar dissolves. Crumble in the fresh yeast or sprinkle the dried yeast over. Mix well and leave in a warm place for about 15 minutes till frothy.

2 Sift the flour, a pinch of salt and the remaining sugar into a large bowl and leave in a warm place. Melt the butter in a small saucepan, leave to cool.

3 Make a well in the centre of the flour. Pour in the frothy yeast mixture, the butter and eggs and mix with a wooden spoon to a soft but not sticky dough.

4 Knead the dough on a floured surface for about 5 minutes till smooth and glossy. Shape into a ball, return to the bowl and cover with oiled polythene. Leave to prove in a warm place till doubled in size.

5 Turn the dough out and knock back. Knead for 3–4 minutes till smooth.

6 To make 1 large brioche, cut off a quarter of the dough and shape both pieces into balls. Place the large one in the lightly greased tin and push a finger down through the centre to the base. Place the smaller ball in the indentation and press down lightly.

7 To make 12 small brioches, divide the dough into 12 pieces and remove a quarter from each. Shape all pieces into balls. Place each large ball in a small tin, push a finger down through the centre, then top with the small balls, pressing down lightly.

8 Cover with oiled polythene and leave to prove till doubled in size. Meanwhile, preheat the oven to 450F (230C) Gas 8.

9 Brush each brioche with milk and bake in the centre of the oven for 8–10 minutes (small) or 15–20 minutes (large) till well risen and golden. Remove from the tin and place on a wire rack. Serve warm.

Polonaise

The topping is meringue cuite – a mix that's set or "cooked" by heat then baked till golden but not dry (see page 471)

DESSERT Serves 8

Overall timing 1¼ hours plus chilling

Equipment 2 bowls, 2 saucepans, 2½ pint (1.5 litre) Charlotte mould, piping bag with star nozzle, ovenproof plate

Freezing Not recommended

INGREDIENTS

4	Eggs	4
5oz	Caster sugar	150g
3 tbsp	Plain flour	3×15ml
¾ pint	Milk	400ml
1 teasp	Vanilla essence	5ml
2 tbsp	Rum	2×15ml
4oz	Granulated sugar	125g
¼ pint	Water	150ml
1	Large brioche (see page 497)	1
4oz	Chopped glacé fruits	125g
7oz	Icing sugar	200g

METHOD

1 Separate 3 of the eggs, putting the yolks and whites into separate bowls. Add remaining egg to the yolks with the caster sugar and flour and beat together with a wooden spoon.

2 Heat the milk till almost boiling. Gradually pour on to the eggs, stirring constantly. Strain the custard back into the saucepan, add the vanilla essence and rum and bring to the boil, stirring constantly.

3 Cook, stirring, for 2 minutes. Remove from heat and leave to cool, stirring occasionally to prevent a skin forming.

4 Put the granulated sugar and water into a saucepan and stir over a low heat till the sugar dissolves. Stop stirring, bring to the boil and boil for 5 minutes. Remove from the heat.

5 Cut the brioche into 4 horizontal slices. Place the smallest slice in the base of the Charlotte mould. Spoon a little syrup over to moisten the brioche.

6 Reserve a few pieces of glacé fruit to decorate. Add the rest to the custard. Spread some of the custard over the brioche and cover with the next slice of brioche. Moisten with syrup and spread with custard. Repeat layers, finishing with the largest slice of brioche. Press down firmly and chill for at least 2 hours.

7 Preheat the oven to 450F (230C) Gas 8.

8 To make the meringue, sift the icing sugar into the reserved egg whites. Place the bowl over a pan of simmering water and whisk till the meringue is very white and glossy and forms stiff peaks.

9 Remove from the heat. Spread two-thirds of the meringue over the turned-out cake to cover it completely. Smooth the surface. Put the rest of the meringue into a large piping bag and pipe decoratively over the dessert. Bake on an ovenproof plate in the centre of the oven for 5–10 minutes. Decorate with glacé fruit and serve immediately.

VARIATION

Use soft fruit like raspberries or strawberries to replace custard. Lightly mash liqueur or sherry and 4–6 tbsp (4–6× 15ml) icing sugar to taste and leave to macerate for 1 hour. Then layer with brioche slices, first piercing brioche with skewer so juices can soak in. Chill, cover with meringue, bake.

Below: Polonaise – a gâteau that will grace the most elegant of occasions. If you like, you can use Italian meringue (see page 471) which can be made in advance and stored in the fridge until needed

Apple-cider pie

Spices and tart-flavoured apples are layered in a pie dish, then topped with cider and covered with puff pastry

DESSERT Serves 4

Overall timing 1 hour

Equipment Bowl, 2 pint (1.1 litre) pie dish, rolling-pin, pastry brush

Freezing Not recommended

INGREDIENTS

2oz	Softened butter	50g
½ teasp	Ground cinnamon	2.5ml
½ teasp	Ground ginger	2.5ml
2oz	Dark brown sugar	50g
2lb	Sharp-flavoured apples	900g
6 tbsp	Medium-sweet cider	6×15ml
8oz	Packet of frozen puff pastry	227g
1	Egg	1

METHOD

1 Preheat the oven to 425F (220C) Gas 7.

2 In a bowl, mix together the butter, cinnamon, ginger and brown sugar.

3 Grease pie dish. Wash, peel and core the apples. Slice half the apples thickly, and layer in the bottom of the dish, dot the spiced butter mixture over and pour in the cider. Put remaining apples, sliced thickly, on top so they come above level of dish.

4 Roll out thawed pastry on a floured surface to an oval about 1 inch (2.5cm) larger than dish and to ⅛ inch (3mm) thickness. Trim off ¾ inch (2cm) strips, moisten 1 side with water and place round edge of pie dish. Dampen surface of pastry strips with a little cold water.

5 Lift pastry on to rolling-pin and place over dish. Press down firmly to seal pastry edges round dish. Holding dish in palm of one hand, trim off excess pastry with knife in other hand; place knife vertically against lip of dish, and make sharp cuts away from you. Slash edges of pastry at 1 inch (2.5cm) intervals.

6 In a bowl beat the egg and brush over pastry. Make a tiny slit in top of pie to allow steam to escape. Bake near top of oven for 20 minutes, then reduce heat to 350F (180C) Gas 4 and continue baking a further 15–20 minutes until pastry is golden brown and crisp. Serve warm or cold with whipped cream.

Above: Scarlet and black fruit salad – a dish that's spectacular to look at, delightful to eat

Scarlet and black fruit salad

A dramatic partnership of jet black prunes and bright red strawberries to please all the family or make a stunning finale for a dinner party

DESSERT Serves 6

Overall timing 30 minutes plus chilling

Equipment 2 saucepans and steamer or metal sieve

Freezing Not recommended

INGREDIENTS

1lb	Large prunes	450g
2 tbsp	Caster sugar	2×15ml
¼ pint	Water	150ml
6 tbsp	Orange juice	6×15ml
1lb	Strawberries	450g
4 tbsp	Grand Marnier* (optional)	4×15ml

*If preferred replace with 1–2 tbsp of lemon juice and an extra 2–3 tbsp of orange juice.

METHOD

1 Put the prunes into a metal sieve or steamer and place over a saucepan of boiling water. Cover and steam for 15 minutes till plump.

2 Put the sugar and water into a saucepan and stir over a low heat till the sugar dissolves. Bring to the boil and boil without stirring for 5 minutes. Remove from the heat, stir in the orange juice and leave to cool.

3 Wipe and pick over the strawberries and remove the hulls. If large, cut them in half lengthways. Slit prunes and carefully remove stones. Arrange prunes and strawberries in serving dishes.

4 Add the Grand Marnier to the cold syrup and spoon over the fruit. Leave to macerate in a cool place for 3–4 hours before serving with whipped cream or a mixture of equal quantities of double and sour cream. Almond biscuits would also make a good accompaniment to this dessert (see page 416).

Crème de menthe roulade

A melt-in-the-mouth swiss roll, filled with a rich minty cream. Melted chocolate and egg whites replace the customary flour to give a lighter, more airy texture

DESSERT OR TEA-TIME Serves 6–8

Overall timing 45 minutes plus overnight standing time

Equipment Non-stick cooking paper, baking tray, small bowl, saucepan, 2 bowls, greaseproof paper, piping bag

Freezing Open freeze without the decoration. Foil-wrap, label and freeze. Freezer life: 4 months. To use: unwrap, place on serving plate, thaw in a cool place for 4–6 hours, then decorate

INGREDIENTS

4oz	Plain dessert chocolate	125g
4	Large eggs	4
6oz	Caster sugar	175g
½ pint	Carton of double cream	284ml
4 tbsp	Crème de menthe	4×15ml
1oz	Chocolate squares	25g

Below: Crème de menthe roulade

METHOD

1 Preheat oven to 350F (180C) Gas 4.

2 Make a case from a 12 inch (30cm) square of non-stick paper, cutting 1½ inches (4cm) diagonally through each corner. Fold up the edges to make a "case" 1 inch (2.5cm) deep and fasten the corners securely with staples or paper clips. Place case on a greased baking tray.

3 Break up the chocolate and place in a small bowl over a pan of gently simmering water. Stir till melted, then cool.

4 Separate eggs. Place yolks in a large bowl, add 4oz (125g) caster sugar. Place bowl over a pan of simmering water and whisk till mixture is thick and leaves a trail on surface for 20 seconds. Stir in the cooled chocolate.

5 In a large bowl, whisk the egg whites until they form soft peaks, then fold gently into the chocolate mixture. Pour the mixture into the paper case, spreading it into the corners. Smooth the surface. Bake just above centre of oven for about 15 minutes or until firm.

6 Remove from the oven and cover with a damp tea-towel. Leave overnight.

7 Remove cloth and undo paper case. Crush remaining sugar and spread on greaseproof paper. Invert the roulade on to paper. Trim off the crisp edges.

8 Whip the cream till soft peaks form and fold in the crème de menthe. Spread two-thirds of the cream over the roulade and roll up. Place on the serving dish. Pipe the remaining cream on top and decorate with halved chocolate squares. Chill before serving.

Caramel trifle

A different version of a family favourite

DESSERT Serves 6

Overall timing 55 minutes plus chilling

Equipment 2 saucepans, 2 baking trays, bowl

Freezing Not recommended

INGREDIENTS

6oz	Granulated sugar	175g
4 tbsp	Water	4×15ml
1oz	Flaked almonds	25g
	Oil for greasing	
1 pint	Milk	560ml
	Vanilla pod	
4	Eggs	4
2 tbsp	Plain flour	2×15ml
4 tbsp	Caster sugar	4×15ml
1	Jam-filled swiss roll	1
11oz	Can of mandarin oranges	311g
3	Bananas	3
4 tbsp	Sherry	4×15ml
½ pint	Whipping cream	284ml

METHOD

1 Put the granulated sugar and water into a saucepan and stir over a low heat till sugar dissolves. Stop stirring, bring to the boil and boil till golden brown.

2 Toast almonds on baking tray under grill till golden. Quickly stir almonds into the caramel mixture and pour on to an oiled baking tray. Leave to set.

3 Meanwhile, put the milk and vanilla pod into a saucepan and bring almost to the boil. Remove from the heat, cover and leave to infuse for 10 minutes. Beat the eggs, flour and caster sugar together.

4 Reheat the milk till almost boiling. Remove the vanilla pod, and gradually pour the milk on to the egg mixture in a thin stream, stirring constantly.

5 Strain the custard back into the pan and bring to the boil, stirring constantly. Cook for 2 minutes till thick. Remove from heat. Cover custard surface with wet greaseproof paper. Cool.

6 Slice the swiss roll and arrange in a deep glass serving dish. Drain the oranges, reserving the syrup. Peel and slice the bananas, scatter over the sponge with the oranges. Add 4 tbsp (4×15ml) of the syrup to the sherry, spoon over the sponge, add custard and chill.

7 Whip the cream till soft peaks form. Spread it over the custard in swirls.

8 Break caramel in pieces. Scatter over the trifle. Serve immediately.

Above: Swiss-style potatoes served on a creamy mixture of curd cheese and onion

Swiss-style potatoes

More sophisticated than the usual baked potatoes – more substantial too, and a good dish for lunch. Select even-sized waxy potatoes

LUNCH OR SUPPER Serves 4

Overall timing 1 hour

Equipment 2 bowls, shallow ovenproof dish, small saucepan

Freezing Not recommended

INGREDIENTS

2lb	Potatoes	900g
3 tbsp	Caraway seeds	3×15ml
1 tbsp	Sea-salt	15ml
2oz	Butter	50g
8oz	Curd cheese	225g
4fl oz	Milk	120ml
1	Onion	1
2 tbsp	Chopped parsley	2×15ml
2 tbsp	Chopped mustard and cress	2×15ml
	Salt	
	White pepper	
	Garnish	
	Parsley sprigs	
	Mustard and cress	

METHOD

1 Preheat the oven to 350F (180C) Gas 4. Wash and halve potatoes. Mix caraway seeds and salt together in a bowl. Dip the cut sides of potatoes into mixture. Place potatoes in greased ovenproof dish with the caraway seeds facing up.

2 Melt the butter in saucepan and pour a little on each potato half. Place in the oven and bake for 45 minutes.

3 Mix cheese with milk in a bowl. Peel and finely chop onion, add to cheese. Mix chopped parsley and chopped mustard and cress into cheese and season.

TO SERVE

Divide cheese mixture between warmed serving plates and place the potatoes on top. Garnish with parsley and cress, and serve with a salad if liked.

VARIATION

To serve Swiss-style potatoes as an accompaniment (they go particularly well with roast pork), spread the cheese mixture over the top of the potatoes and bake for a further 10–15 minutes.

Bacon and spinach salad

Use really fresh spinach; it does not keep for more than 1–2 days. Wash spinach well in several changes of water, as it can be gritty, then dry. There should be a lovely sizzling sound as you mix the hot bacon fat in with the spinach – eat the salad up quickly before the dressing has time to set

STARTER OR SIDE SALAD Serves 4

Overall timing 20 minutes

Equipment Heavy-based frying pan, salad bowl

Freezing Not recommended

INGREDIENTS

8oz	Streaky rashers	225g
1lb	Fresh spinach	450g
1	Medium-size onion	1
	Rock salt	
	Freshly-ground black pepper	

METHOD

1 Chop bacon including rind into small pieces. Cook in frying pan over gentle heat until fat runs and bacon is crisp.

2 Wash spinach and drain well. Pull off any stem pieces and tear the leaves roughly. Place in salad bowl. Peel onion and slice into fine rings. Add to spinach. Grind in salt and pepper.

3 Pour hot bacon bits, and the fat, into salad bowl and quickly toss so that spinach and onion are coated. Serve immediately.

TO SERVE

This salad complements egg and cheese dishes, baked jacket potatoes, fried or grilled chops, steaks or veal escalopes.

Above: Curried aubergine omelette – cooked till golden on both sides

Curried aubergine omelette

A rather unusual omelette that's flavoured with curry. The aubergines are finely diced to ensure that they cook quickly

LUNCH OR SUPPER Serves 4

Overall timing 30 minutes

Equipment Saucepan, large omelette or frying pan, mixing bowl

Freezing Not recommended

INGREDIENTS

1	Large onion	1
9oz	Aubergines	250g
4fl oz	Oil	120ml
1 teasp	Madras curry powder	5ml
1 teasp	Salt	5ml
	Freshly-ground black pepper	
4	Large eggs	4

METHOD

1 Peel and slice the onion. Wash and dry the aubergines then cut them into small squares.
2 Heat a little of the oil in a saucepan. Cook the onion till golden brown then remove from pan.
3 Put a little more of the oil into the saucepan and heat. Add the diced aubergines and quickly brown on all sides. Season with curry powder, salt and pepper. Return the onions to the pan and continue to cook for a few minutes until aubergines are tender. Remove from heat and plunge pan into cold water to cool aubergines and onion quickly.
4 Lightly beat the eggs and mix them carefully into the cooled aubergine and onion mixture.
5 Heat the remaining oil in a large omelette or frying pan. Pour in the egg and aubergine mixture and cook over a strong heat for about 5 minutes, shaking the pan to prevent the omelette sticking and to distribute the egg mixture evenly.
7 Cut the omelette into sections first and then turn the pieces over one at a time with a spatula, so that both sides become browned.

TO SERVE

Serve the omelette portions immediately with a dressed mixed green salad and some crusty French bread, warmed pitta bread or rolls.

Avocados stuffed with chicken

A good way of using up leftover chicken and avocados that are a little overripe. If they're reduced in price for just this reason, this dish becomes cheap to make. Alternatively, smoked fish or peeled prawns can be used instead of chicken

LUNCH OR SUPPER Serves 6

Overall timing 40 minutes

Equipment Bowl, ovenproof dish, saucepan

Freezing Not recommended

INGREDIENTS

4	Avocados	4
2 tbsp	Lemon juice	2×15ml
1 teasp	Cognac or dry sherry	5ml
2oz	Butter	50g
3 tbsp	Plain flour	3×15ml
$\frac{1}{4}$ pint	Chicken stock	150ml
	Salt	
2 tbsp	Parmesan	2×15ml
4 tbsp	Single cream	4×15ml
8oz	Cooked chicken	225g
	Paprika	

METHOD

1 Cut avocados in half lengthways and lift out stones. Remove flesh with a teaspoon and place in a bowl. Add lemon juice, mash flesh well then sprinkle with Cognac or sherry. Put shells aside for the moment.
2 Preheat the oven to 400F (200C) Gas 6. Grease a shallow ovenproof dish with 1oz (25g) of the butter.
3 To make the white sauce, melt the remaining butter in a saucepan. Stir in the flour then gradually mix in the cold chicken stock. Bring to the boil, stirring constantly until sauce thickens. Add salt to taste. Remove from heat and cool slightly.
4 Add 1 tbsp (15ml) of the Parmesan, the cream and the avocado purée. Beat well with a whisk. Cut the chicken into thin strips and stir into the sauce, mixing well.
5 Fill avocado shells with the mixture. Sprinkle with the remaining Parmesan and a little paprika.
6 Place avocados in prepared dish and cook on the middle shelf of the oven for 15 minutes. Serve immediately with toast.

Bubble and squeak

This traditional English dish is made in minutes. Add chopped cold meat, tomatoes, eggs, anything you like in fact. A great way of using up leftovers

LUNCH OR SUPPER Serves 4–6

Overall timing 15 minutes

Equipment Bowl, frying pan

Freezing Not recommended

INGREDIENTS

1lb	Mashed potatoes	450g
1lb	Cooked cabbage	450g
	Salt	
	Freshly-ground black pepper	
2oz	Butter	50g

METHOD

1 Beat together mashed potatoes and cabbage with a wooden spoon, adding plenty of seasoning.

2 Heat the butter in a heavy frying pan and add the potato and cabbage mixture, spreading it over the base of the pan. Fry, turning the mixture occasionally, until crisp and golden brown. Serve immediately.

Below: Bubble and squeak – its name comes from the sounds of the cooking cabbage

cook's know-how

Kidneys, full of protein, vitamins iron and other minerals essential for health, are today the most highly rated offal because they can be cooked in a wide variety of ways. In fact, they have as much a place at a grand dinner party as at a family meal. While lamb and pig kidneys are the familiar bean shape, beef, calf and veal kidneys are an elongated cluster of lobes joined together with gristle.

Beef kidney, the largest at about 1½lb (700g), has a strong flavour. It's rather coarse in texture and needs slow, moist cooking (such as braising or stewing) to become tender. It is especially good when cooked with stewing steak to make a casserole, pie or pudding, but shouldn't be fried or grilled.

Smaller and more tender, **calf kidneys** are cooked in the same ways as beef kidney, but as the flavour is more delicate, for much shorter time. **Lamb kidneys** are small, well flavoured and can be grilled or fried for 2–3 minutes per side – overcooking causes toughness. **Pig kidneys** are larger and more strongly flavoured than lamb, and not quite so tender. They can be halved and grilled or fried, or chopped and used in stews.

Kidneys in wine and parsley

Use the beef jelly from the base of the dripping pot to give this dish a truly exquisite taste

LUNCH OR SUPPER Serves 4

Overall timing 30 minutes

Equipment Bowl, frying pan

Freezing Not recommended

INGREDIENTS

1lb	Calf or lamb kidneys	450g
1	Onion	1
2oz	Butter	50g
1 tbsp	Chopped parsley	15ml
3 tbsp	Dry white wine	3×15ml
1 teasp	Beef extract	5ml
1 teasp	Lemon juice	5ml
	Salt	
	Freshly-ground black pepper	

METHOD

1 Prepare, wash and thinly slice kidneys. Peel and chop onion.

2 In a bowl, mash together 1oz (25g) of the butter and the chopped parsley. Set aside.

3 Melt remaining butter in frying pan and brown kidneys over a high heat for about 10 minutes, turning them occasionally. Reduce heat and cook for 15 minutes, then remove from pan and keep hot.

4 Add onion to pan and cook for 5 minutes or until golden brown. Add the wine, beef extract and lemon juice and bring to the boil, stirring to release sediment on bottom of pan.

5 Return kidneys to pan and cook for a further 3 minutes. Taste and adjust seasoning, stir in parsley butter and serve immediately with brown rice, mushrooms and peas.

Above: Corn with petits pois

Corn with petits pois

A dish that makes the most of two storecupboard or freezer standbys

VEGETABLE Serves 4

Overall timing 15 minutes

Equipment Saucepan

Freezing Not recommended

INGREDIENTS

12oz	Can of sweetcorn kernels	350g
10oz	Can of petits pois	283g
2oz	Butter	50g
½ pint	Stock	300ml
	Salt	
	Freshly-ground black pepper	
	Sugar	
1 tbsp	Plain flour	15ml
	Nutmeg	

METHOD

1 Drain corn and peas. Heat butter in a saucepan. Add corn and peas, then cover with stock (made with ½ a stock cube if necessary). Cover and cook over a moderate heat for 5 minutes. Season with salt, pepper and a pinch of sugar.

2 Mix flour with a little water in a cup. Stir into corn and peas mixture and cook for 5 minutes. Add a pinch of nutmeg and serve immediately.

Cumin-braised beef

Cumin gives a less-tender cut of beef extra flavour and a delectable aroma during the slow cooking. Larding with pork fat, which is well worth the effort, keeps the meat moist. Serve with a colourful vegetable accompaniment and boiled potatoes tossed in butter and chopped parsley

MAIN MEAL Serves 6

Overall timing 3 hours

Equipment Larding needle, large flameproof casserole, saucepan

Freezing Place overlapping meat slices in foil container and pour sauce over. Cover, label and freeze. Freezer life: 2 months. To use: heat from frozen in a moderate oven

INGREDIENTS

3oz	Pork fat	75g
4lb	Braising beef	1.8kg
4 tbsp	Oil or dripping	4×15ml
	Salt and pepper	
¼ pint	Dry white wine	150ml
2	Onions	2
2	Garlic cloves	2
4	Tomatoes	4
2 teasp	Paprika	2×5ml
1 tbsp	Ground cumin	15ml
½ pint	Beef stock	300ml
4oz	Mushrooms	125g
1oz	Butter	25g

METHOD

1 Cut the pork fat into ½ inch (12.5mm) thick strips. Chill for 20 minutes.

2 Dry beef well with kitchen paper. Insert strips of chilled fat with a larding needle along the grain of the meat (see cook's know-how page 287). If necessary, tie joint with string

3 Heat the oil or dripping in a large casserole and brown the joint on all sides for 10 minutes. Season with salt and pepper, pour in the wine and cook over a high heat for 2 minutes.

4 Peel and finely chop onions and garlic. Blanch, peel and chop tomatoes. Add all to casserole with paprika, cumin and half the stock. Cover tightly and cook gently for 2 hours, turning the joint over from time to time.

5 Wipe and slice mushrooms. Sauté for a few minutes in the butter in a small pan.

6 Remove joint from casserole, place on serving plate and keep warm. Add remaining stock and mushrooms to the casserole and bring to the boil. Cover and simmer for 15 minutes. To serve, slice meat and serve sauce separately. Accompany with boiled potatoes and corn with petits pois (see left).

Below: Cumin-braised beef – a joint made succulent with gentle cooking and larding

Pork chop suey

One of the most famous recipes using bean sprouts. Chop suey is not an authentic Chinese dish, but was invented by a Chinese immigrant in the USA. This recipe can be easily adapted by using finely cut chicken instead of pork

MAIN MEAL Serves 4–6

Overall timing 1½ hours including soaking time

Equipment 2 bowls, large saucepan, large frying pan or wok

Freezing Not recommended

cook's know-how

The garnish on this dish of Chop suey is "cloud ears", in Chinese *wun yee*. A cultivated fungus, it looks unimpressive in the dried state but after soaking opens out luxuriously to the pretty shape you can see in the picture. *Wun yee* are edible and can be bought at Chinese supermarkets.

Above: Pork chop suey, famous the world over, can be quickly and easily made at home

INGREDIENTS

1lb	Pork tenderloin or fillet	450g
2 tbsp	Amontillado sherry	2×15ml
2 tbsp	Soy sauce	2×15ml
	Salt and pepper	
	Ground ginger	
1 tbsp	Chinese dried mushrooms *or*	15ml
7½ oz	can of morel mushrooms	213g
4oz	Noodles	125g
3	Stalks of celery	3
7½oz	Can of bamboo shoots *or*	213g
8oz	fresh green beans	225g
4oz	Fresh mushrooms	125g
2	Onions *or*	2
½ bunch	spring onions	½ bunch
8oz	Fresh bean sprouts	225g
8 tbsp	Vegetable oil	8×15ml
3 tbsp	Soy sauce	3×15ml
1 teasp	Sugar	5ml
	Monosodium glutamate (optional)	
1 tbsp	Cornflour	15ml
4 tbsp	Dry white wine or sherry	4×15ml

METHOD

1 Cut pork into fine strips or slices and put into bowl with sherry, soy sauce, salt, pepper and a pinch of ginger. Mix together well, then cover and leave for 1 hour. If you are using dried mushrooms, put them in another bowl with water and leave to soak.

2 Meanwhile bring a well-filled saucepan of lightly salted water to the boil. In sequence add noodles, sliced celery and thinly sliced fresh green beans if using. Cook each for 5 minutes, then lift out and set aside to drain.

3 Drain dried or canned mushrooms, wipe and slice fresh ones. Peel and slice or chop onions, drain bamboo shoots, (if using), wash and drain bean sprouts.

4 Heat the oil in frying pan or wok till very hot. Add pork and brown all over for 2 minutes. Remove from pan.

5 Put fresh, dried or canned mushrooms, and onions, beans or bamboo shoots, and bean sprouts into frying pan or wok, cook for 3 minutes. Add the pork, celery and noodles with the soy sauce, sugar and a pinch of monosodium glutamate (optional). Using a wooden spoon, turn over mixture as you fry it for 3 minutes.

6 Mix together the cornflour and wine or sherry and stir into mixture in pan. Cook for 4 minutes and then serve immediately with boiled rice.

Chicken and cheese rolls

Delicious combination of Derby cheese and bacon, rolled up in chicken breasts, then cooked in light ale

MAIN MEAL Serves 6

Overall timing 45 minutes

Equipment Kitchen string, heavy-based casserole

Freezing Not recommended

INGREDIENTS

6	Large chicken breasts	6
	Salt and pepper	
2 teasp	Prepared mustard	2×5ml
6	Thin slices of Derby cheese	6
6	Thin rashers of fat or streaky bacon	6
	Plain flour	
2oz	Butter	50g
2 tbsp	Oil	2×15ml
½ pint	Light ale	300ml
12	Pitted green olives	12

METHOD
1 Remove skin and wipe chicken breasts. Season one side of chicken breasts and spread with mustard, then add a slice of cheese to each. Roll up and wrap a rasher of bacon around. Tie rolls firmly with string and coat lightly in flour.
2 Heat butter and oil in casserole. Lightly brown chicken rolls all over.
3 Add beer gradually, taking care that it does not fill more than half the casserole. Add more seasoning if required. Cover and simmer over a low heat for 10 minutes.
4 Meanwhile, scald olives in boiling water. Drain well and add to casserole. Cover and simmer for 10 minutes more.
5 Carefully remove string from chicken rolls and serve with rice or potatoes and celery or celeriac. Tangy celeriac (below) would complement this dish well.

Season underside of chicken breasts, spread with mustard, top each with slice of cheese

Roll up and wrap a rasher of bacon round each. Tie rolls into parcels with string

Above: Chicken and cheese rolls – bacon-wrapped chicken breasts with cheese filling

Tangy celeriac

In a lemony sauce, this dish is a treat with chicken, pork and veal. You can also try this recipe using a head of celery instead

VEGETABLE Serves 4

Overall timing 45 minutes

Equipment Large saucepan, small bowl

Freezing Make up to Step 2. Cool, pack into rigid container, seal, label and freeze. Freezer life: 6 months. To use: thaw overnight in fridge or for 5 hours at room temperature. Turn into pan, reheat gently, then proceed as Step 3

INGREDIENTS

1½lb	Celeriac	700g
2oz	Butter	50g
	Salt and pepper	
¾ pint	Chicken stock	400ml
3	Egg yolks	3
3 tbsp	Lemon juice	3×15ml

METHOD
1 Wash and peel celeriac and cut into chunks. Heat butter in a large saucepan and fry celeriac for 2 minutes on each side. Season with salt and pepper.
2 Pour stock (made up with 1 stock cube if necessary) into pan. Simmer for 20 minutes or until celeriac is tender.
3 Mix egg yolks in a small bowl with lemon juice and 2 tbsp (2×15ml) of stock from the pan. Remove pan from heat and pour in egg mixture. Season with salt and pepper, then transfer to warmed serving dish.

American-style goose

The sweet-spicy sauce is a great favourite in American cooking

MAIN MEAL Serves 8

Overall timing 3 hours

Equipment Roasting tin with wire rack, 2 saucepans

Freezing Not recommended

INGREDIENTS

10lb	Ovenready goose	4.5kg
	Salt and pepper	
3oz	Butter	75g
4 tbsp	Water	4×15ml
1 tbsp	Chopped fresh basil	15ml
1lb	Chestnuts	450g
1 tbsp	Caster sugar	15ml
1 pint	Stock	560ml
1lb	Chipolatas	450g
4oz	Streaky bacon	125g
	Sauce	
6 tbsp	Cranberry jelly	6×15ml
2 tbsp	Red wine	2×15ml
¼ teasp	Ground cinnamon	¼×5ml
½ teasp	Caster sugar	½×5ml

METHOD

1. Preheat the oven to 400F (200C) Gas 6.
2. Wipe the goose. Season with salt and pepper and prick all over with a fork. Coat goose legs and wings with 1oz (25g) of the butter. Place goose on rack in roasting tin and cook for 20 minutes.
3. Add the water and basil to roasting tin and continue cooking for 2 hours, basting frequently. Remove tin from oven and place chipolatas below goose and cover goose legs with bacon rashers. Return tin to oven for a further 30–40 minutes.
4. Meanwhile, score round each chestnut from base to pointed end with a sharp knife. Place in pan of boiling water and cook for 15 minutes. Shell and skin, and leave in water.
5. Melt remaining butter in saucepan, add sugar and chestnuts and cook, stirring, until golden. Add stock and cook for 15 minutes.
6. To make the sauce, put cranberry jelly, wine, cinnamon, sugar, salt and pepper in pan and heat through gently.

TO SERVE

Place goose on warmed serving plate. Arrange bacon and chipolatas on top and surround with the chestnut mixture. Serve with the spicy cranberry sauce.

Bacon and bean hotpot

This is a really hearty one-pot meal for four, which makes the most of a quite small joint of bacon with the addition of vegetables. Simple to prepare, it requires no extra vegetable as potatoes are already in the pot

MAIN MEAL Serves 4

Overall timing 1½ hours

Equipment 10 inch (25cm) heavy-based flameproof casserole with lid

Freezing Not redommended

INGREDIENTS

1oz	Dripping	25g
2	Onions	2
1lb	Tendersweet bacon joint	450g
1 pint	Stock	560ml
12oz	Fresh or frozen green beans	350g
1lb	Potatoes	450g
2	Sprigs of fresh mint *or*	2
½ teasp	dried mint	½×5ml
	Salt and pepper	
½ teasp	Mixed herbs	½×5ml
	Fresh parsley	

METHOD

1. Peel the onions and chop them roughly. Melt dripping in casserole. Add onions to casserole and cook gently for 2–3 minutes. Cut bacon into cubes, add to casserole and brown.
2. Pour in the stock (made up with 2 chicken stock cubes if necessary), cover and cook over a medium heat for 1 hour.
3. In the meantime, if using fresh beans, wash them, top and tail and remove strings. Break or cut into short lengths. Peel and thinly slice potatoes.
4. Add fresh beans, mint, roughly chopped, if fresh, and potatoes to the casserole. Season and add mixed herbs.
5. Cover and cook for about 30 minutes or until potatoes are done. Add frozen beans 10 minutes before end of cooking time.

TO SERVE

Garnish with parsley sprigs and serve with fresh crusty bread.

Grilled cod with bacon

If you haven't tried fish with grilled bacon, you will find this a pleasant surprise. The cod fillets are given extra taste and piquancy with lemon juice. Try chopped or puréed spinach instead of lettuce to serve

MAIN MEAL Serves 4

Overall timing 25 minutes

Equipment Small saucepan

Freezing Not recommended

INGREDIENTS

4	Large cod fillets	4
4 tbsp	Oil	4×15ml
	Salt and pepper	
4oz	Thin streaky bacon rashers	125g
1oz	Butter	25g
2 tbsp	Lemon juice	2×15ml
	Fresh parsley	
1	Lemon	1

METHOD

1 Preheat grill. Brush the cod fillets with oil and season with salt and pepper. Place under a fairly hot grill for about 15 minutes, turning fillets over halfway through cooking time.

2 Remove rind then grill or fry the bacon. Drain on kitchen paper.

3 Just before serving, heat the butter in a small saucepan taking care not to colour it. Arrange the fish and bacon on warm serving plates. Pour the butter over and sprinkle with lemon juice. Garnish with parsley sprigs and lemon, cut into wedges. Serve with boiled potatoes tossed in butter and sprinkled with chopped parsley, and a crisp lettuce salad.

Below: Grilled cod with bacon – an unusual combination of tastes

Poached bass with lemon sauce

Fish cooked to perfection in a deliciously tangy sauce

MAIN MEAL Serves 4

Overall timing 30 minutes

Equipment Shallow flameproof casserole

Freezing Not recommended

INGREDIENTS

$2\frac{1}{4}$lb	Bass	1kg
	Salt and pepper	
2oz	Butter	50g
$\frac{1}{2}$ pint	White wine	300ml
1	Lemon	1
2 tbsp	Chopped parsley	2×15ml
1 tbsp	Olive oil	15ml

METHOD

1 Clean, wash and gut fish. Dry well. Season with salt and pepper.

2 Melt the butter in a casserole. Add the fish and fry on both sides till golden. Add wine and the rind of a lemon cut into strips. Cover and poach gently for 20 minutes. Squeeze lemon and set aside juice.

3 Remove fish and fillet it (see right). Put fillets on warm serving dish and keep warm. Discard lemon rind, then raise the heat to reduce liquid in casserole by half.

4 Stir in lemon juice, parsley and oil, then reheat (do not boil). Taste and adjust seasoning if necessary.

TO SERVE

Stir sauce well and spoon over fish. Serve with boiled potatoes and green beans.

cook's know-how

Bass can be found off the southern and western coasts of England and Ireland, and as far south as the Mediterranean.

It is a round fish with yellowish flanks and a silver belly. Its flesh is white and delicate and needs careful cooking. It is at its best when poached, grilled or baked whole and some people even place it in the same class as salmon. When buying bass allow 8oz (225g) per person – they start small (just under 2lb /900g) and can be as big as 10lb (4.5kg).

filleting a cooked bass

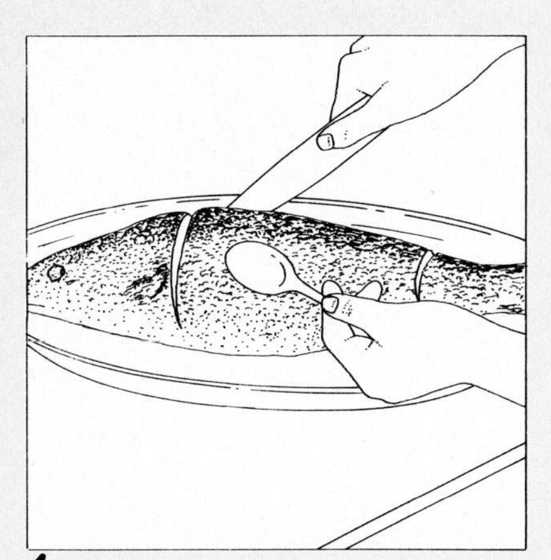

1 *Using a sharp knife, make one cut through to the back-bone behind the gill and another in front of the tail. Gently press down on top of fish with a spoon and then starting at the gill cut along fish just above back-bone*

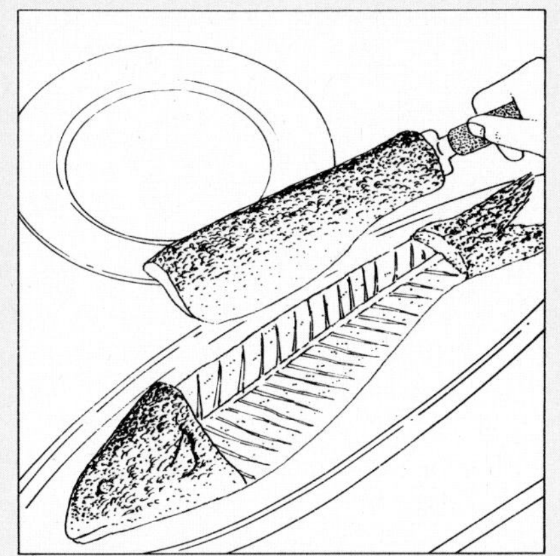

2 *When you've cut all the way along the fish to the tail, slide a metal palette knife, spatula or egg slice under the top fillet. Lift up carefully, then, supporting it evenly, transfer fillet on to warmed serving plate*

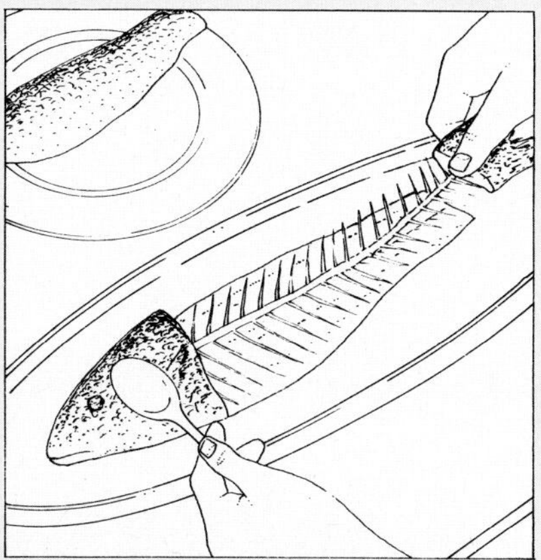

3 *Press down firmly on the head with a spoon. Pick up the tail, lift out the back-bone and discard. Cut through flesh behind gill and in front of the tail. Transfer bottom fillet to plate*

Above: Jewish carp – a traditional method of braising the fish steaks in wine, garnished with chopped parsley and lemon slices and served with a sauce

Jewish carp

This traditional method of braising freshwater carp provides a buttery wine sauce to accompany the fish

MAIN MEAL Serves 4–6

Overall timing 1 hour

Equipment Flameproof dish, small saucepan

Freezing Place slices of cooked, drained carp in foil container. Prepare sauce and pour over. Cool, cover, label and freeze. Freezer life: 2 months. To use: cook from frozen in foil container in hot oven for 30 minutes.

INGREDIENTS

2½lb	Prepared carp	1.1kg
¼ pint	Olive oil	150ml
4oz	Chopped onions	125g
2oz	Chopped shallots	50g
1 tbsp	Plain flour	15ml
8fl oz	Dry white wine	220ml
8fl oz	Water	220ml
	Salt	
	Cayenne pepper	
2	Crushed garlic cloves	2
	Bouquet garni	
2oz	Butter	50g
1 tbsp	Chopped parsley	15ml
6	Slices of lemon	6

METHOD

1 Wash and dry the fish, then cut into 1 inch (2.5cm) slices.
2 Heat the oil in flameproof dish, and lightly fry the onions and shallots but don't let them colour. Sprinkle in the flour, mix well and cook for 2 minutes.
3 Place the slices of carp in the dish and cover with wine and water. Add salt, cayenne pepper, garlic and bouquet garni. Bring to the boil, then cover and simmer for 45 minutes.
4 Lift out carp with draining spoon and arrange on serving dish and keep warm. Strain the sauce and pour into small saucepan. Bring to the boil and cook till reduced by two-thirds. Add butter pieces to sauce. Whisk until it boils.
5 Pour the sauce over the carp, sprinkle with parsley and garnish with lemon slices. Serve immediately.

cook's know-how

Gefilte fish (from the German word *gefüllte* meaning "stuffed") is a traditional Jewish way of enhancing the flavour of freshwater fish like carp. Minced fish, seasonings, raw matso meal or ground almonds and breadcrumbs are shaped into balls, poached in stock, cooled, then eaten cold with a little jellied stock and horseradish sauce. Or the mixture can be used to stuff a whole fish – fill the stomach cavity, or press into 2–3 slits cut in the back. The fish is then usually braised.

Black Forest gâteau

The lusciously indulgent *Schwarzwalder kirschtorte* – the most famous of the specialities of Germany's Black Forest. Layers of crisp biscuit, chocolate sponge and cherry sauce are coated with whipped cream sweetened with Kirsch and sugar. It takes time to make, but well worth it for a really special occasion

TEA-TIME OR DESSERT Cuts into 12

Overall timing $1\frac{3}{4}$ hours plus cooling time

Equipment 9 inch (23cm) loose-bottomed round cake tin, 3 large bowls, electric or rotary whisk, 2 saucepans, pastry brush, palette knife, piping bag with star nozzle

Freezing Open freeze until firm. Wrap carefully, seal and label. Freezer life: 4 months. To use: unwrap, place on serving plate, thaw overnight in fridge

Above: Black Forest gâteau – layers of sponge and cream, black cherries, liqueur and chocolate

INGREDIENTS

	Sponge	
6	Eggs	6
6 tbsp	Hand-hot water	6×15ml
5oz	Caster sugar	150g
	Pinch of salt	
2oz	Plain flour	50g
3oz	Cornflour	75g
2oz	Cocoa	50g
	Biscuit base	
5oz	Plain flour	150g
1	Egg yolk	1
3oz	Caster sugar	75g
	Pinch of salt	
	Grated rind of $\frac{1}{2}$ a lemon	
5oz	Butter	150g
	Filling and topping	
2×15oz	Cans of pitted black cherries*	2×425g
2 teasp	Arrowroot	2×5ml
8 tbsp	Kirsch or Cognac	8×15ml
3 tbsp	Redcurrant jelly	3×15ml
1 tbsp	Caster sugar	15ml
1 pint	Double cream	560ml
$\frac{1}{2}$ pint	Single cream	284ml
2 tbsp	Icing sugar	2×15ml
2oz	Plain dessert chocolate	50g

*Use $1\frac{1}{2}$lb (700g) fresh morellos if available. Remove stones, keep 12 whole but quarter rest. Cook all in sugar syrup till just tender.

METHOD

1 To make the sponge, grease and base-line the tin. Preheat the oven to 350F (180C) Gas 4. Separate eggs. Put yolks in large bowl with water and caster sugar. Whisk at high speed for about 3 minutes till blades leave a trail when lifted which "holds" for 15 seconds. Wash whisk. In another bowl, whisk whites with salt till mixture forms soft peaks. Fold whites into yolks with metal spoon and gentle figure of eight action.

2 Sift flour, cornflour and cocoa into a bowl and resift half at a time into egg mixture. Fold in, then pour mixture into tin. Bake in centre of oven for 1 hour.

3 To make the biscuit base, sift flour into bowl and make a well in the centre. Add egg yolk, sugar, salt and lemon rind. Cut butter into small pieces and rub in to a smooth dough. Chill until cake is cooked. Remove cake from oven and turn out of tin. Wash and dry the tin. Place biscuit dough in centre of the tin base and roll out to fit. Replace base in tin and bake for 30 minutes.

4 Drain cherries, saving juice and set aside 12 cherries for decoration. Roughly chop remaining cherries and put in saucepan with 8 tbsp (8×15ml) of the juice. Blend arrowroot with 2 tbsp (2×15ml) of juice and stir into cherries. Bring to the boil, stirring. Remove from heat and stir in 4 tbsp (4×15ml) Kirsch or Cognac. Cool.

5 Remove biscuit base from oven and place on flat serving plate. Cool. Meanwhile, place redcurrant jelly and caster sugar in a small pan and bring to the boil, stirring till smooth. Remove from heat and add 1 tbsp (15ml) Kirsch or Cognac. Brush biscuit base with glaze, reserving 1 tbsp (15ml).

6 Cut cooled sponge into 3 layers and place top layer, cut side up, on glazed biscuit base. Spread with half the cold cherry sauce.

7 Place double and single creams in a large bowl and whisk until stiff. Whisk in icing sugar and remaining Kirsch or Cognac. Divide cream into five. Spread a fifth of cream over the cherries with a palette knife, and cover with second sponge layer. Spread over rest of cherry sauce and one more fifth of cream. Top with final sponge layer. Smooth two-fifths of cream over top and sides of gâteau.

8 Grate chocolate coarsely. Save some for the top of the gâteau and flick rest on to sides with a palette knife. Mark top of gâteau into 12 slices. Put remaining fifth of cream in piping bag fitted with star nozzle and pipe a whirl on each slice.

9 Top each whirl of cream with a whole black cherry and brush carefully with the 1 tbsp (15ml) reserved redcurrant glaze. Sprinkle the remaining chocolate over centre of gâteau. Chill well.

1 To make sponge, beat yolks, water and sugar till thick enough for blades when lifted to leave a trail for 15 seconds

2 Sift dry ingredients into bowl and resift half at a time into yolk/white mix. Fold in carefully with a metal spoon

3 To make biscuit base, add yolk and butter to dry ingredients, and mix with fingertips to give a smooth dough

4 Place chilled biscuit dough in centre of tin base and roll out to fit. Replace base in tin and bake for 30 minutes

5 To make cherry sauce, combine cherries, arrowroot and juice. Remove from heat and stir in Kirsch. Leave to cool

6 To assemble gâteau, place cooked and cooled biscuit base on serving dish. Brush with prepared redcurrant glaze

7 Cut cooled sponge into 3 layers. Place top layer on glazed biscuit base. Spread with half cold cherry sauce

8 Smooth whipped cream over cherry layer, cover with second sponge, repeat. Coat top and sides with cream

9 Flick coarsely grated chocolate on to sides of gâteau with knife. Pipe on cream whirls, add cherries, rest of chocolate

Sweet almond boats

These attractively-shaped sweet pastries make a change for high tea. The cherry brandy adds even more flavour to the almonds

TEA-TIME Makes 24

Overall timing 1 hour 20 minutes plus 30 minutes refrigeration

Equipment 2 mixing bowls, 24 barquette tins

Freezing Place in rigid container. Cover, label and freeze. Freezer life: 3 months. To use: thaw at room temperature

INGREDIENTS

	Pastry	
8oz	Plain flour	225g
1	Egg	1
4oz	Sugar	125g
	A few drops of vanilla essence	
4oz	Butter	125g
	Filling	
6 tbsp	Apricot jam	6×15ml
4	Egg whites	4
7oz	Sugar	200g
2 tbsp	Cherry brandy	2×15ml
9oz	Ground almonds	250g
	Decoration	
2oz	Flaked almonds	50g
1 tbsp	Icing sugar	15ml

METHOD

1 Preheat the oven to 350F (180C) Gas 4.

2 To make the pastry, put the flour in a large bowl, making a well in the centre. Break in the egg and add the sugar and vanilla essence. Put small knobs of butter round the edge then, working from outside to in, knead well till all ingredients are combined. Put in fridge for 30 minutes.

3 Roll out pastry on a floured board to about ¼ inch (6mm) thickness and line 24 greased barquette tins. Spread on a little apricot jam.

4 Beat the egg whites in a bowl until stiff. Gradually add the sugar and cherry brandy then fold in the almonds.

5 Place a little of the mixture in each barquette. Decorate with flaked almonds and sprinkle lightly with icing sugar.

6 Cook for 30–40 minutes on the middle shelf of the oven. If boats show signs of over-browning, cover with foil.

7 Remove boats and cool on wire rack. Sprinkle with more icing sugar.

Left: Sweet almond boats – delicious

Nut bread

TEA-TIME Cuts into 12 slices

Overall timing 1¾ hours plus cooling

Equipment Bowl, jug, 2lb (900g) loaf tin

Freezing Not recommended

INGREDIENTS

16oz	Plain flour	450g
4oz	Caster sugar	125g
½ teasp	Salt	½×5ml
3 teasp	Baking powder	3×5ml
1 tbsp	Cinnamon	15ml
2oz	Butter	50g
4oz	Chopped mixed nuts	125g
2	Eggs	2
8fl oz	Milk	220ml
3 tbsp	Orange juice	3×15ml

METHOD

1 Preheat oven to 350F (180C) Gas 4. Sieve flour, sugar, salt, baking powder and cinnamon into a bowl. Cut and fold in butter, then add the nuts.

2 Beat the eggs till fluffy in a jug, then beat in the milk. Pour into the flour mixture, add orange juice and knead together quickly.

3 Pour mixture into greased loaf tin and bake in oven for about 1½ hours. It will be cooked when a skewer comes out clean. Remove from oven.

4 Leave for 5 minutes then ease out of tin and place on wire rack. Serve sliced and buttered on the day of making – this sort of bread does not store well.

Cream sponge

TEA-TIME

Overall timing

Equipment Two 8 inch (20cm) sandwich tins, 2 mixing bowls, small saucepan, cake wire

INGREDIENTS

4	Large eggs	4
6oz	Caster sugar	175g
2 tbsp	Warm water	2×15ml
4oz	Plain flour	125g
1 teasp	Baking powder	5ml
2oz	Butter	50g
2 tbsp	Milk	2×15ml
4 tbsp	Apricot jam	4×15ml
2oz	Split or flaked almonds	50g
¼ pint	Carton of double cream	150ml
2 tbsp	Strawberry jam	2×15ml

METHOD

1 Grease and flour sandwich tins. Preheat oven to 375F (190C) Gas 5.
2 Separate eggs. Place yolks in mixing bowl and beat till light and fluffy, then add sugar with warm water and beat well. Sift flour and baking powder and mix in a little at a time, alternating with milk. Melt butter and add.
3 Whip whites till stiff. Use a spatula or metal spoon to fold them carefully into egg/flour mixture.
4 Divide mixture between sandwich tins and cook on middle shelf of oven for 15–20 minutes. When cooked, the sponges will shrink away from the sides of the tins. Turn out on to cake wire.
5 When cold, spread top of one sponge with apricot jam. Place second sponge on top. Whip cream and fold in strawberry jam. Spread cream over top of sponge, then sprinkle almonds over.

Apple scones

TEA-TIME Makes 8

Overall timing 20 minutes

Equipment Mixing bowl, baking tray, scone or biscuit cutter

Freezing Not recommended as they take so little time to prepare

INGREDIENTS

8oz	Plain flour	225g
3 teasp	Baking powder	3×5ml
	Pinch of salt	
2oz	Butter	50g
2 tbsp	Caster sugar	2×15ml
¼ pint	Milk	150ml
1	Apple	1
	Top of the milk *or* egg for glazing	

METHOD

1 Preheat oven to 450F (230C) Gas 8. Sift flour, baking powder and salt into a mixing bowl. Rub in butter. Add sugar and milk. Mix to a soft dough.
2 Roll out quickly to ½ inch (12.5mm) thickness on a lightly floured board.
3 Peel and core apple, then grate it on to the dough. Fold dough in half and press firmly together.
4 Lightly flour scone cutter and cut out scones. Glaze tops with top of the milk or lightly beaten egg. Place on lightly floured baking tray and bake towards the top of the oven for 10 minutes. Wrap in tea-towel till ready to serve.

Canadian fare

a taste of the wide open spaces

It has been said that Canadians consume more bottles of ketchup per capita than any other nation on earth. It is likely that a visitor's first impression of Canadian cuisine is that it almost wholly consists of French fries, hamburgers, hot dogs, fried chicken and milk-shakes, cooked, served and eaten with almost indecent haste in tens of thousands of restaurants, self-service cafeterias and drive-ins. It is difficult to understand why Canadians eat vast quantities of such food, especially as Canada abounds with some of the finest meat, fish, poultry, game, fruit and vegetables to be found anywhere.

You have to look beyond this apparent reliance on pre-packaged convenience foods because strong culinary traditions do exist, and they reflect the heritage of the dozens of ethnic groups that constitute the remarkable mosaic of Canadian culture. The majority of the population – around 75% – are descendants of immigrants from the British Isles and France (with the Anglo-Canadians outnumbering the French Canadians by slightly less than two-to-one). The remainder are either descendants of Dutch, German and Scandinavian settlers who came in the 18th and 19th centuries, or Ukrainians, Poles and Jews from Central Europe who emigrated in great successive waves during the late 1800s and early 1900s. These were followed by large influxes of Italians in the 1940s and 50s, Hungarians in the mid 50s and, most recently, Asian refugees from Africa.

Legacy of the settlers

There is consequently a bewildering *mélange* of dishes prepared daily in Canada. Some are cooked exactly as they were in Europe or Asia while others have either been altered to suit the raw materials found in Canada or to allow for the dietary necessities imposed by the extremes of climate. And the different ethnic groups adopt dishes from each other – French Canadians, for example, enjoy plum pudding at Christmas just as Anglo-Canadians will prepare their own version of *tourtière*, or minced pork pie.

The process of adaptation goes back to the earliest days of Canadian history. The native Indian tribes in what is now Quebec prepared *Pag-wadjawessi* (six-game pâté), a pie made with rabbit, partridge, deer, moose, beaver and wild duck with each layer separated by a crust and seasoned with cloves, cinnamon and wild onions. The first English-speaking settlers substituted fish for game and called their creation "Sea pie". The French in turn adopted the recipe and transliterated the name to *cipaille*. Down through the centuries, *cipaille* has now come to refer to any multi-layered pie whether made from fish, game or fowl.

Marriage of tastes

Similarly, both French and Anglo-Canadians enjoy bannock, an unleavened bread sometimes made with raisins or berries, smoked salmon, fish soups (later called *la chaudière*, or chowder) and barbecues without perhaps realizing that these were eaten by the Indians long before a European ever set foot on the shores of Canada's wilderness.

It is impossible to describe a typical Canadian meal for it depends on where in Canada you happen to be and with whom you are dining. On the Pacific coast of British Columbia a dinner might feature salmon or seafood salad (or a curious hybrid served in many resturants called "Surf and turf", lobster tail and steak!). The people of the prairie provinces – Alberta, Saskatchewan and Manitoba – might prefer chuck-wagon stew, Lake Winnepeg goldeye (a bright red smoked fish), Saskatoon berry pie or blueberry muffins. On the other hand, people from Ontario, especially the southernmost part of the province, would load their ample tables with sour cream salads, smoked meats and sausages, and shoofly pie – a tart made with molasses and raisins that on a hot summer's day lives up to its name by attracting every winged insect in the immediate vicinity.

Quebec is, of course the home of the French Canadian cuisine. In some Montreal restaurants it is possible to order a combined dish of *filet mignon* and frogs legs (which vies with "Surf and turf" as an improbable marriage of tastes) but less jaded palates can choose heartier dishes like *soupe aux pois aux habitants* (the famous pea soup), or *ragoût de pattes et boules* (stewed pigs trotters and meatballs). Canadians from the Maritime provinces on the Atlantic coast – New Brunswick, Prince Edward Island, Nova Scotia and Newfoundland – would enjoy potato salads, fish chowders and seal-flipper pie. But in any given neighbourhood of Canada's major cities, the traditional centres of immigrant settlement, families might just as well be sitting down to a meal of *Bortsch* and *holubtsi* (beet soup and stuffed cabbage rolls, the latter particularly beloved by Ukrainians), Hungarian *gulyàs* (a rich piquant stew flavoured with paprika), *gefilte* fish (a Jewish favourite of fried fish balls), *sauerbraten* (a German dish of pot-roasted beef served in a tangy sauce) or spaghetti and meatballs. And next day they are just as likely to prefer plainly cooked roasts, chops or steaks, corn-on-the-cob with salt and butter, and pumpkin pie.

Today there is a wide range of dishes made from foods that are really native to Canada – berry-based desserts, jellies and preserves, chokecherry wine, crisp apples from the Okanagan and Annapolis valleys, Queen crabs and Malpèque oysters from the Atlantic, Oka cheese made by Trappist monks in Quebec, fiddlehead fern from New Brunswick tasting like a cross between broccoli and asparagus, wild rice from prairie marshlands and bass, pickerel, perch, pike, trout and whitefish from innumerable inland lakes. And no Canadian, regardless of origin, would, if offered the chance, forego one of the essential rites of spring in eastern Canada – tapping maple trees for their syrup and ladling the boiled-down golden liquid concentrate on to pans of clean snow to make unforgettable toffee.

Dishes of Canada, left, clockwise; Canadian bacon and potato salad (recipe page 481); Ham and bean chowder (recipe page 516); Cherry pie (recipe right); Canadian wild rice-stuffed duck (recipe page 517)

CHERRY PIE

Ingredients 8oz (225g) shortcrust pastry; 2lb (900g) fresh cherries or 2×15oz (425g) cans of cherries; 1oz (25g) ground rice; 2oz (50g) caster sugar; rind and juice of 1 lemon; 1 egg white and caster sugar.

Method On a lightly floured board, roll out two-thirds of pastry and line bottom and sides of 7½ inch (19cm) fluted, loose-bottomed flan tin. Stone cherries (drain first if using canned) and place in saucepan with rice, sugar, rind and juice of lemon. Bring gently to the boil, cook for 2 minutes, stirring. Cool, spread evenly over flan. Preheat oven to 450F (230C) Gas 8. Roll out remaining pastry to a circle, moisten edges then place on top of filling. Trim edges, then press top and bottom firmly together. Brush with lightly beaten egg white and dredge with caster sugar. Bake in centre of oven for 10 minutes. Reduce heat to 350F (180C) Gas 4 and bake for 40–45 minutes more till top is golden. **Serves 4–6**

Countdown

Ham and bean chowder
Canadian wild rice-stuffed duck
Potato and onion casserole
Buttered broccoli
Cherry pie

Hearty, wholesome fare for a special family treat

4½ hours before Put haricot beans to soak for 2 hours

3½ hours before Make pastry for cherry pie. Preheat oven to 450F (230C) Gas 8. Prepare cherry filling. Assemble pie and bake. Lower heat after 10 mins

3 hours before Prepare rice stuffing and simmer

2½ hours before Make up chowder and simmer. Put dried mushrooms to soak for 2 hours

2 hours before Stuff duck. Increase oven temperature to 400F (200C) Gas 6 and roast duck

1¾ hours before Prepare potatoes and onions. Assemble casserole. Place in oven below duck

1 hour before Prepare broccoli

30 mins before Purée half the chowder and cube ham. Simmer chowder

20 mins before Put broccoli to cook. Transfer duck to serving dish. Pour chowder into tureen

15 mins before Prepare sauce

5 mins before Reduce oven temperature to 300F (150C) Gas 2. Drain broccoli, toss in butter and transfer to serving dish. Put sauce in sauce boat. Keep both warm

Serve the chowder with warm rolls or toast if liked

Remove casserole from oven and place pie to warm

Carve duck at the table and serve with accompaniments

Serve the cherry pie with cream

To complement this North American meal why not try a Californian wine? The red wines are very fruity and have plenty of flavour and the whites are clean tasting and fresh. Either colour would go well with the chowder and the duck.

Above: Ham and bean chowder – a warming and nutritious soup

Ham and bean chowder

Ideal to serve the family on a cold winter day, this is a filling soup made with haricot beans and flavoured with ham hocks. Serve with warm wholemeal rolls or black bread for lunch

STARTER OR LUNCH Serves 4–6

Overall timing 2½ hours plus soaking

Equipment Large heavy-based saucepan, frying pan, blender or vegetable mill

Freezing Not recommended

INGREDIENTS

4 pints	Chicken stock	2.3 litres
8oz	Haricot beans	225g
4	Onions	4
4	Stalks of celery	4
3 tbsp	Oil	3×15ml
2	Garlic cloves	2
2	Medium-size ham hocks	2
14oz	Can of tomatoes	397g
2	Cloves	2
1	Bay leaf	1
	Freshly-ground black pepper	

METHOD

1 In large saucepan, bring the stock (made with cubes if necessary) and the beans to the boil over high heat, then boil for 2 minutes. Remove from heat, cover. Leave to soak for 2 hours.
2 Peel and chop the onions and chop celery. In a frying pan, heat the oil and add onions and celery. Peel, crush and add the garlic. Cook, stirring frequently, for about 5 minutes, until soft but not brown.
3 Add to saucepan with ham hocks, tomatoes and their juice, cloves and bay leaf. Press tomatoes with a spoon to break them up.
4 Bring to the boil, then reduce heat, cover and simmer for 1½–2 hours, until the ham is tender when pierced with a thin skewer.
5 Transfer ham hocks to a plate and cool slightly. Remove the skin, fat and bones and discard. Cut the meat into cubes and set aside. Discard bay leaf and cloves.
6 Purée half the soup in a blender or vegetable mill. Return to rest of the soup and add the cubed ham.
7 Simmer for 10 minutes, stirring occasionally. Adjust seasoning, then pour into a warmed tureen. Serve.

Canadian wild rice-stuffed duck

Wild rice is a North American speciality, expensive but prized for its nutty taste. Ordinary rice can be used instead but the flavour will be less pronounced. Garnish duck with tomato and watercress

MAIN MEAL Serves 4–6

Overall timing 5¼ hours plus soaking

Equipment Small bowl, heavy 8–10 inch (20–25cm) frying pan, wire rack, roasting tin, small saucepan

Freezing Not recommended

INGREDIENTS

½oz	Dried mushrooms (morels or Chinese)	15g
5lb	Ovenready duck	2.3kg
	Stuffing	
2oz	Butter	50g
2oz	Chopped onion	50g
4oz	Wild rice	125g
½ pint	Chicken stock	300ml
¼ teasp	Salt	¼×5ml
	Freshly-ground black pepper	
	Sauce	
4oz	Chopped onion	125g
2 tbsp	Plain flour	2×15ml
¼ pint	Chicken stock	150ml
2 tbsp	Brandy	2×15ml
¼ teasp	Dried thyme	¼×5ml
2 tbsp	Double cream	2×15ml

METHOD

1 Place the dried mushrooms in a small bowl with 6fl oz (170ml) of water and leave at room temperature for at least 2 hours. Drain, reserve soaking liquor and chop mushrooms coarsely.

2 To make the stuffing, melt the butter in frying pan over moderate heat. When foam begins to subside, add the finely chopped onion and cook for about 5 minutes, until soft and transparent. Rinse the rice thoroughly and add to onion. Stir for 2–3 minutes to coat rice in butter. Pour in 8fl oz (220ml) of the chicken stock (made up with 1 cube if necessary), the salt and a little pepper. Bring back to boil over a high heat. Reduce the heat to low, cover tightly and simmer for about 30–45 minutes. Check from time to time and if the rice is too dry, add more stock.

3 Preheat oven to 400F (200C) Gas 6.

4 Remove pan from heat, taste and adjust seasoning. Place stuffing in cavity, then weigh duck. Stand duck on wire rack in roasting tin. Prick all over and rub skin with salt and pepper. Cook the duck for 1¾ hours or until the juices run clear when the thigh is pierced with a fine skewer.

5 When the duck is cooked, transfer it to a warm dish, cover and keep warm.

6 To make the sauce, pour away all but 2 tbsp (2×15ml) of the pan juices and add the finely chopped onion. Cook over medium heat, stirring frequently, for about 5 minutes, till the onion is transparent. Add flour and mix well. Stirring constantly with wooden spoon, add stock, reserved liquor from mushrooms, brandy and thyme and cook over a high heat till sauce boils and thickens.

7 Reduce the heat to low and simmer for 2–3 minutes to cook the flour. Remove from the heat and stir in the cream, strain sauce through a fine sieve into a small saucepan, pressing down hard on the onions to extract juice before discarding pulp. Add reserved mushrooms and heat through. Taste and adjust seasoning, then pour sauce into sauce boat to accompany the duck. Serve with a green vegetable such as buttered broccoli.

Potato and onion casserole

An ideal vegetable accompaniment to roasts as it can be cooked in the oven at the same time

VEGETABLE Serves 4–6

Overall timing 1¾ hours

Equipment Frying pan, ovenproof casserole

Freezing Not recommended

INGREDIENTS

1lb	Onions	450g
4oz	Butter	125g
2½lb	Waxy potatoes	1.25kg
	Salt and pepper	
	Bouquet garni	
¾ pint	Stock	400ml

METHOD

1 Preheat the oven to 375F (190C) Gas 5.

2 Peel and thinly slice the onions. Heat 2½oz (65g) of the butter in a frying pan and fry the onions till transparent.

3 Peel the potatoes and slice thinly. Grease the casserole and put in a layer of potato, season, and add a layer of onion. Top with bouquet garni, and continue layering, finishing with a layer of potato.

4 Pour the stock (made with a cube if necessary) over and dot with the remaining butter. Bake in the centre of the oven for about 1¼ hours till the potatoes are tender.

Above: Beetroot and apple salad – dressed with wine vinegar or lemon juice and oil

Beetroot and apple salad

Fruit and vegetables mixed together make a highly successful partnership for unusual salads – in winter or summer. In this one, the ingredients are all simple but the result is a sweet-sharp, tangy salad with a colourful, attractive look. It has to be put together more or less when you need it so that the apples won't be coloured by the beetroot. Try it with cold meat for supper – it's delicious

STARTER OR SALAD Serves 4–6

Overall timing 1 hour 40 minutes plus cooking time

Equipment Saucepan, mandolin or fluted slicer

Freezing Not recommended

INGREDIENTS

$1\frac{3}{4}$lb	Uncooked beetroot	750g
$2\frac{1}{2}$ pints	Water	1.5 litres
	Salt	
4 tbsp	Oil	4×15ml
2 tbsp	Wine vinegar or lemon juice	2×15ml
1 teasp	Sugar	5ml
8oz	Dessert apples	225g
1	Onion	1

METHOD

1 Wash beetroot then cut off tops. Take care not to pierce the skin when you are preparing beetroot or the colour will boil out, leaving them a rather washed out pink. Place prepared beetroot in saucepan and cover with water. Add a little salt, cover and cook for $1\frac{1}{4}$ hours over a low heat. Leave to cool.

2 Drain beetroot, cut off root and pull off skin. Slice with a mandolin or fluted grater. Dry slices and put them in layers in a salad bowl.

3 Mix together oil, wine vinegar or lemon juice and sugar then pour over beetroot. Chill for 2 hours.

4 Peel, core and chop apples. Peel and finely chop onion. Mix in to beetroot and serve before the beetroot has time to colour the apple and onion.

Ravioli

For your home-made pasta, use the strong white breadmaking flour, wholewheat flour, or durum wheat flour from Italian specialist shops

STARTER, LUNCH OR SUPPER Serves 4

Overall timing 30 minutes (not including filling)

Equipment Bowl, pastry wheel or small cutter, saucepan

Freezing Make as Steps 1–3. Open freeze, then pack into rigid containers, interleaved with greaseproof paper. Cover and label. Freezer life: 1 month. To use: cook from frozen

INGREDIENTS

12oz	Strong flour	350g
1 teasp	Salt	5ml
3	Eggs	3
	Chosen filling (see right)	

METHOD

1 Sift the flour and salt into a large bowl or on to a working surface. Make a well in the centre and add the eggs. Mix with your fingers to give a firm, not sticky mixture. Knead lightly till smooth and glossy.

2 Roll out on a floured surface to a large rectangle. Dot the filling at regular intervals over half the pasta. Fold remaining pasta over.

3 Press round each little mound of filling, then cut out with a pastry wheel or small cutter.

4 Cook in boiling salted water for 10–15 minutes until pasta is al dente. Drain and serve with tomato sauce (recipe page 121), topped with grated cheese or use as a garnish for soup.

FILLINGS

Meat: peel and chop 1 small onion and 1 garlic clove. Fry for 3 minutes in 1 tbsp (15ml) oil. Add 2 derinded and chopped bacon rashers and 8oz (225g) minced beef. Fry until browned. Add 4 tbsp (4×15ml) red wine and 1 tbsp (15ml) tomato paste. Cover and cook for 15 minutes. Remove from heat and stir in 2oz (50g) grated Parmesan. Leave to cool before using.

Cheese: mash 6oz (175g) Ricotta in a bowl with a fork. Add 2 tbsp (2×15ml) grated Parmesan, 2 eggs, salt and freshly-ground black pepper and mix well.

1 *Sift flour and salt on to a clean working surface or into a bowl. Make a well in the centre and then add the eggs*

2 *Mix the eggs into the flour using your fingertips to give a firm, smooth dough, then knead lightly and shape into a ball*

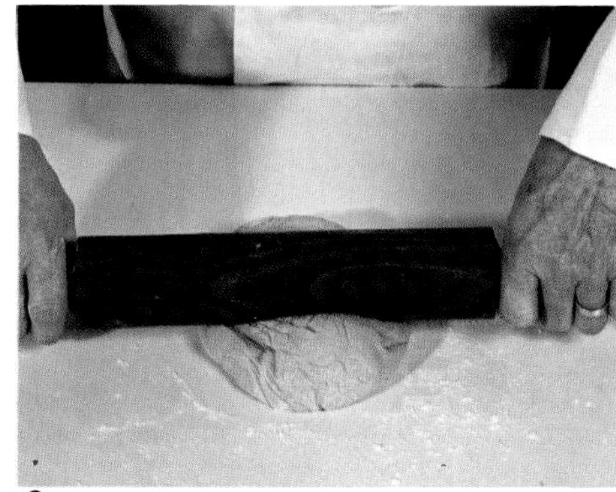

3 *After kneading for a few minutes, roll the dough out on a floured surface to a large rectangle. Prepare the filling*

4 *Dot the filling at regular intervals over half the rolled-out pasta. Using the rolling pin, fold the remaining pasta over*

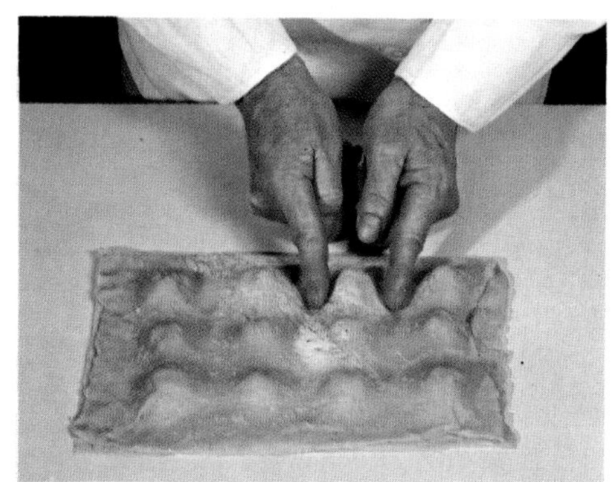

5 *Press round mounds of filling with your fingers to mark out where they are and to encase them in parcels of pasta*

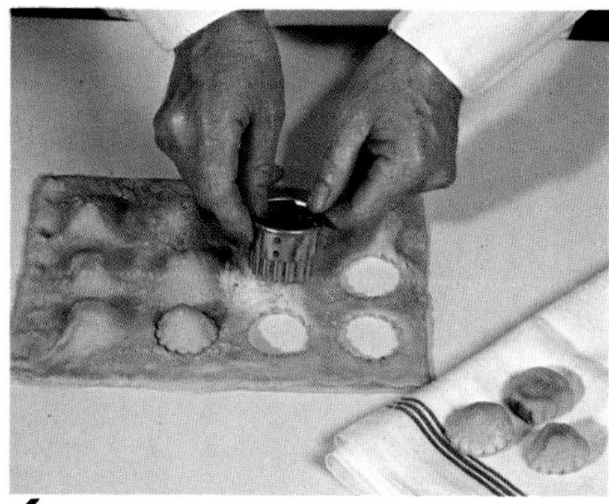

6 *Cut round each mound of filling with a pastry wheel or small cutter. Cut out small pasta shapes from remaining dough*

cook's know-how

In Italy, all the filled pastas are known as *pasta ripiena*. Throughout the country different names are given to the different shapes. These include fluted round or square **ravioli**; straight-edged **cappelletti**, which look like little hats; large and small **tortellini**, which look like folded table napkins; fluted half-moon shaped **tortelloni**; and **agnolotti**, which look like large postage stamps. Every town claims to have the best filling. They are often rich mixtures of pork, ham, veal, poultry, Ricotta and spinach. Basil, borage, thyme and parsley are favourite herbs; nutmeg is the most frequently used spice. Most filled pastas can be home made, or bought fresh, dried or frozen.

Right: Ravioli — stuffed with a creamy mixture of Ricotta and Parmesan, cut into squares and served hot, sprinkled with a generous helping of grated Parmesan

7 *Cook ravioli in boiling salted water, then drain and serve in tomato sauce, topped with grated cheese, or in a soup*

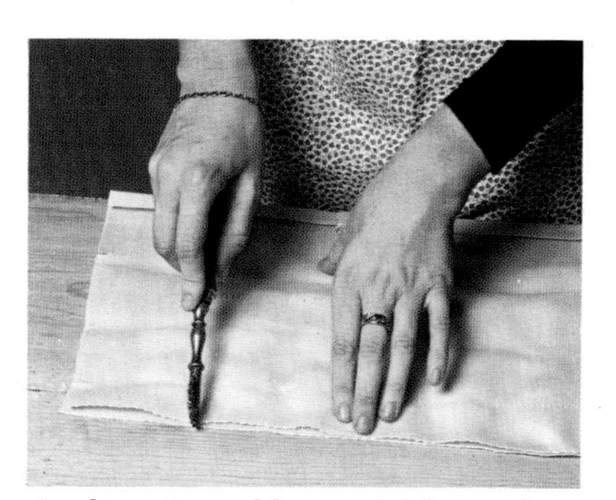

An alternative and less wasteful way of cutting out the ravioli is to make squares by cutting straight lines with pastry wheel

Ham and spinach savouries

Rounds of puff pastry are topped with ham and spinach and covered with a creamy cheese sauce

STARTER Serves 4

Overall timing 35 minutes plus thawing and cooling

Equipment Baking tray, 3½ inch (9cm) pastry cutter, saucepan, ovenproof dish

Freezing Not recommended

INGREDIENTS

7oz	Packet of frozen puff pastry	212g
12oz	Frozen spinach	350g
2oz	Butter	50g
	Salt and pepper	
4	Slices of smoked ham	4
2 tbsp	Chopped onion	2×15ml
¼ pint	Béchamel sauce (see page 451)	150ml
1	Egg yolk	1
2oz	Grated Gruyère	50g
2 tbsp	Single cream	2×15ml

METHOD

1 Allow pastry and spinach to thaw, then preheat oven to 425F (220C) Gas 7. Grease baking tray with half the butter.
2 Roll out pastry to ¼ inch (6mm) thickness. Using pastry cutter, cut 4 circles of pastry. Place them upside down on baking tray. Bake for 10–15 minutes till well risen and golden. Remove and allow to cool.
3 Meanwhile, chop spinach and place in a sieve to drain. Season with salt and pepper. Using pastry cutter, cut 4 circles out of the ham and finely chop the trimmings.
4 In a saucepan, melt the remaining butter and cook the onion until golden brown. Add chopped ham and half the Béchamel sauce. Stir well and add salt and pepper to taste.
5 Divide half the mixture between pastry circles, cover with ham circles, then top with the spinach. Place in ovenproof dish.
6 Stir egg yolk, cheese and cream into remaining sauce and pour over spinach. Bake above centre of oven for 10 minutes until cheese is golden brown and bubbling. Serve immediately.

Below: Ham and spinach savouries – a colourful and appetizing start to a meal

Danish cod loaf

Savoury fish loaf flavoured with bacon and served with a cream sauce

STARTER OR PARTY SNACK Serves 4

Overall timing 1½ hours

Equipment Mincer, 2 bowls, roasting tin, saucepan, 2lb (900g) loaf tin

Freezing Cool thoroughly in tin. Cover and overwrap with foil, label and freeze. Freezer life: 1 month. To use: thaw overnight in fridge. Remove wrappings and lid. Reheat in moderately hot oven 375F (190C) Gas 5 for 45 minutes

INGREDIENTS

1½lb	Fresh or frozen cod fillets	700g
2	Slices of white bread	2
2oz	Softened butter	50g
2	Eggs	2
1oz	Potato flour or cornflour	25g
	Salt and pepper	
8oz	Bacon rashers	225g
¼ pint	Carton of double cream	150ml

METHOD

1 Thaw frozen cod if using. Put cod through a fine mincer with decrusted bread.
2 Beat the butter until creamy in a mixing bowl with a wooden spoon. Gradually add the minced cod, beaten eggs, potato flour or cornflour, and a generous amount of salt and pepper. Preheat the oven to 375F (190C) Gas 5. Grease the loaf tin and line with derinded bacon rashers.
3 Beat double cream in another bowl till it begins to stick to the beaters, then gently mix into cod mixture with a wooden spoon. Spoon mixture into prepared tin, packing it down and smoothing the surface. Cover with foil, place in a roasting tin, half-filled with hot water, and cook just above centre of the oven for 50 minutes.
4 Remove cod loaf from oven, loosen sides from tin with the blade of a knife and turn on to a hot serving plate.

TO SERVE

Make a sauce by frying 2 chopped onions in 2oz (50g) butter till transparent. Stir in 1 tbsp (15ml) plain flour and ½ pint (300ml) milk. Stir till thick. Stir in 2 tbsp (2×15ml) chopped parsley and 4 tbsp (4×15ml) single cream. Season.

Above: Pineapple and chicken salad – a multi-coloured, many flavoured meal in itself

Pineapple and chicken salad

A delectable mixture that's full of contrast. Fresh pineapple can be used when available, as can fresh corn – simply cut kernels off the cob. Extra taste can be added with sliced avocados or artichoke hearts

LUNCH OR SUPPER Serves 4–6

Overall timing 30 minutes plus chilling

Equipment Saucepan, 2 bowls

Freezing Not recommended

INGREDIENTS

4oz	Long grain rice	125g
	Salt	
4oz	Frozen sweetcorn kernels	125g
1	Bunch celery	1
1	Cold roast chicken	1
8oz	Can of pineapple rings	227g
4	Small firm tomatoes	4
2oz	Black olives	50g
3 tbsp	Salad oil	3×15ml
1 tbsp	Lemon juice	15ml
1 tbsp	Chopped chives	15ml
	Freshly-ground black pepper	
1	Round lettuce	1
1	Hard-boiled egg	1

METHOD

1 Cook the rice in boiling salted water, add the sweetcorn for the last 5 minutes of cooking time. Drain and rinse under cold water, then leave to drain thoroughly.

2 Meanwhile, wash and trim celery heart. Cut stalks into 2 inch (5cm) lengths and put into a large bowl with the celery leaves. Carve the chicken into bite-size pieces, discarding the bones. Add to the bowl.

3 Drain the pineapple, cut 3 of the rings into sixths. Wash and quarter the tomatoes. Add both to the bowl with the olives, rice and sweetcorn.

4 Mix together the oil and lemon juice with the chives and seasoning. Pour over the salad and toss lightly. Chill for 30 minutes.

5 Trim the lettuce, wash and dry the leaves and use to line a salad bowl. Pile the salad into the centre and garnish with remaining pineapple ring and the hard-boiled egg cut into 4 lengthways. Serve immediately with crusty bread.

Above: Pork brochettes – chunky pieces of pork and kidney are threaded with bay leaves

Pork brochettes

Pork and kidneys are flavoured with bay leaves in this quick-to-make dish

LUNCH OR SUPPER Serves 4

Overall timing 30 minutes

Equipment 4 skewers

Freezing Not recommended

INGREDIENTS

1lb	Lean pork	450g
4oz	Belly pork rashers	125g
2	Pigs kidneys	2
12	Bay leaves	12
	Oil	
	Salt and pepper	

METHOD

1 Cut lean pork into 1 inch (2.5cm) cubes. Remove rind and chop belly pork rashers. Wash and dry kidneys. Cut them open, remove the fat then cut each into four. Preheat grill.

2 Arrange bay leaves, meat cubes, belly pork and kidney pieces on skewers. Brush with a little oil and season.

3 Grill for about 20 minutes, turning skewers occasionally during cooking. Serve with boiled rice and peas, and a colourful salad.

Sweet-sour carrot salad

Grated carrots add moisture and sweetness to a salad, and make a perfect accompaniment to serve with grilled meats, especially kebabs. This salad has a piquant flavour – try adding sultanas or substituting pine kernels for chopped walnuts

SALAD OR STARTER Serves 4

Overall timing 35 minutes plus marinating

Equipment bowls, grater

Freezing Not recommended

INGREDIENTS

12oz	Carrots	350g
3 tbsp	Lemon juice	3×15ml
3	Dessert apples	3
	Salt and pepper	
2 tbsp	Honey	2×15ml
2 tbsp	Orange juice	2×15ml
4fl oz	Carton of double cream	113ml
	Pinch of ground ginger	
2oz	Chopped walnuts	50g

METHOD

1 Scrape and wash carrots. Grate coarsely into serving bowl. Mix in lemon juice.

2 Peel and core the apples, then grate coarsely and mix into the carrots with salt and pepper.

3 Mix together the honey and orange juice. Whip the cream lightly, then gently stir in juice mixture. Sprinkle carrot and apples with ginger, pour over the cream. Place in fridge for 15 minutes. Sprinkle the nuts on top and serve.

cook's know-how

For a salad using new carrots, trim and scrub a bunch of baby carrots. Place in a pan of cold salted water, bring to the boil, cover and blanch for 3 minutes. Drain, plunge in cold water and drain again. Halve the carrots lengthways. Stir 3 tbsp (3×15ml) cream, 1 teasp (5ml) prepared mustard (English or French), 2 teasp (2×5ml) lemon juice and salt and pepper together. Blend in ¼ pint (150ml) mayonnaise, then the carrots. Transfer to a serving dish and chill before serving.

Broccoli with cheese sauce

Sliced frankfurters are added to the cheese sauce to make a meal of this delicious broccoli dish. Choose mustard instead of nutmeg if you prefer a stronger flavoured sauce

LUNCH OR SUPPER Serves 4

Overall timing 40 minutes

Equipment Large saucepan, measuring jug, small saucepan

Freezing Not recommended

INGREDIENTS

$1\frac{3}{4}$lb	Broccoli	750g
$\frac{1}{4}$ teasp	Salt	$\frac{1}{4}\times$5ml
1oz	Butter	25g
1oz	Plain flour	25g
$\frac{1}{4}$ pint	Milk	150ml
$\frac{1}{4}$ teasp	Nutmeg *or*	$\frac{1}{4}\times$5ml
1 teasp	prepared mustard	5ml
2oz	Cheddar cheese	50g
4oz	Frankfurters	125g
	White pepper	

METHOD

1 Wash and trim broccoli into spears. Cook in a large saucepan of boiling salted water for 10 minutes or till tender. Drain, reserving $\frac{1}{4}$ pint (150ml) of the cooking liquor. Put broccoli in a warm serving dish. Cover and keep warm.

2 Heat butter in a saucepan and stir in flour. Remove pan from heat and stir in cooking liquor and milk. Return pan to the heat, bring to the boil and simmer for 4 minutes. Add nutmeg or mustard, if using, and cheese, grated, and stir till well mixed.

3 Slice the frankfurters. Add to the sauce and cook for a further 4 minutes. Season to taste. Pour sauce over broccoli and serve.

Lamb cutlets with garlic and anchovy

Lamb cutlets with a difference – the garlic brings out the delicate flavour of the meat, while anchovies add a contrasting piquancy

LUNCH OR SUPPER Serves 4

Overall timing 40 minutes

Equipment Large frying pan or flame-proof casserole, mortar and pestle

Freezing Not recommended

INGREDIENTS

2lb	Best end of neck lamb cutlets	900g
5 tbsp	Oil	5×15ml
2	Garlic cloves	2
	Salt and pepper	
	Fresh rosemary	
2	Desalted anchovy fillets	2
3 tbsp	White wine vinegar	3×15ml

Below: Lamb cutlets with garlic and anchovy – sprigs of fresh rosemary give a delightful aroma

METHOD

1 Trim cutlets of all fat. Heat the oil in a large frying pan or casserole. Add 1 peeled and crushed garlic clove and the cutlets. Fry quickly on both sides till golden, then season, reduce heat and cook for 10–15 minutes.

2 Put a few pieces of fresh rosemary, the remaining garlic clove, peeled, and the anchovies in a mortar. Pound with a pestle, gradually mixing in the vinegar.

3 Add garlic mixture to pan and cook till the liquid reduces by half.

TO SERVE

Arrange cutlets on warmed serving dish and spoon cooking juices over. Garnish with remaining rosemary sprigs.

cook's know-how

The Greeks have a delicious way of increasing the flavour of green olives using garlic – good for those who like strong tastes. Place 8oz (225g) drained olives in a glass or pottery dish and add 2–3 peeled and lightly bruised garlic cloves, 1 tbsp (15ml) coriander seeds, the juice of 3 lemons and 1 whole lemon (flesh and rind) chopped. Leave to marinate in fridge for 24 hours, turning mixture over occasionally.

Chicken in beer

If you've tried chicken in wine, try this for something different. A versatile chicken casserole, cooked on top of the stove or in the oven, to serve as an everyday meal or when entertaining. Cooked in light ale, the chicken is finally served with a deliciously rich sauce made by adding cream to the cooking juices

MAIN MEAL Serves 4

Overall timing 1½ hours

Equipment Flameproof casserole

Freezing Cool, pack into a foil-lined rigid container, leaving ¾ inch (2cm) headspace. Cover, label and freeze. Freezer life: 4–6 months. To use: heat gently but thoroughly in a moderate oven (350F/180C/Gas 4)

INGREDIENTS

2¼lb	Chicken, jointed *or*	1kg
8	Chicken legs and wings	8
2 tbsp	Plain flour	2×15ml
	Salt and pepper	
2	Onions	2
4	Carrots	4
4	Stalks of celery	4
3oz	Butter	75g
2 tbsp	Gin	2×15ml
½ pint	Can of light ale	275ml
1	Garlic clove	1
1	Bouquet garni	1
3 tbsp	Single cream	3×15ml

METHOD

1 Place the chicken pieces in a plastic bag with well seasoned flour and toss till well coated.

2 Peel and quarter onions, scrape carrots and cut into thick slices. Slice celery diagonally. Melt butter in casserole, add the vegetables and cook gently for 5 minutes. Lift vegetables out with a draining spoon and set aside.

3 Add the chicken to the casserole and cook until golden brown on all sides adding a little more butter if necessary. Pour on the gin and set alight.

4 When flames have died down, add the vegetables, light ale, salt and pepper, peeled and crushed garlic, and bouquet garni. Cover and simmer for about 55 minutes on a low heat or alternatively cook the dish in the oven at 350F (180C) Gas 4.

TO SERVE

Lift out chicken and vegetables on to warmed serving dish. Boil juices in casserole then remove from heat and stir in cream. Pour over chicken and serve immediately. A dish of plain boiled rice would be a good accompaniment.

Below: Chicken in beer – chicken joints in a rich, creamy sauce

Bean and spinach soup

A good basic soup that is flavoured by the vegetables and "spiced" by the sausage. Choose one that has a strong taste – chorizo, salami, pork ring or garlic sausage are a few to consider. If spinach is not available, use spring greens or brussels tops or, for a different texture, broccoli or courgettes

LIGHT LUNCH OR STARTER Serves 6–8

Overall timing 2½ hours plus overnight soaking

Equipment Bowl, flameproof casserole

Freezing Cool; pack in polythene containers leaving ¾ inch (2cm) headspace. Seal, label, and freeze. Freezer life: 4 months. To use: thaw in fridge then reheat

INGREDIENTS

5oz	Dried butter beans	150g
1	Onion	1
2	Large tomatoes	2
3oz	Lean bacon	75g
1lb	Spinach	450g
1lb	Potatoes	450g
1 tbsp	Tomato paste	15ml
2½ pints	Hot water	1.5 litres
2 teasp	Salt	2×5ml
5oz	Rice	150g
4oz	Spicy sausage	125g

METHOD

1 Put the beans in a bowl, cover with warm water and leave them to soak overnight.

2 The next day, drain the beans and transfer to a casserole. Barely cover with cold water and cook, uncovered, over a low heat for about 1 hour or until they have absorbed most of the water.

3 Peel and chop onion and tomatoes. Dice bacon. Add to the casserole, cover and cook over moderate heat for 10 minutes, stirring from time to time.

4 Wash the spinach and cut or tear into pieces. Peel and chop potatoes. Add both to casserole with tomato paste and hot water. Season with salt and simmer, uncovered, for 25 minutes.

5 Add the rice and diced sausage and continue cooking for a further 20 minutes. Remove casserole from heat, taste and adjust seasoning if necessary. Leave to "rest" for 5 minutes before serving with crusty bread.

Above: *Savoury bean cake – slices beautifully*

Add blanched French beans to fried chopped celery, onion and parsley. Cover, then let the mixture cook very gently in its own steam

Meanwhile, make a Béchamel sauce, season and add Gruyère. When bean mixture is cooked, drain off excess liquid and add sauce

Savoury bean cake

An unusual oven-cooked egg dish delicately flavoured with Gruyère

LIGHT LUNCH OR STARTER Serves 4

Overall timing $1\frac{1}{4}$–$1\frac{1}{2}$ hours

Equipment 2 saucepans, frying pan with lid, 2 pint (1.1 litre) ovenproof dish, roasting tin

Freezing Cook loaf in foil dish. Leave to cool, then wrap, label and freeze. Freezer life: 3 months. To use: thaw at room temperature for about 3 hours then reheat in oven at 300F (150C) Gas 2 for 30 minutes

INGREDIENTS

1lb	French beans	450g
1	Celery stalk	1
3oz	Butter	75g
2 tbsp	Oil	2×15ml
1 tbsp	Chopped onion	15ml
1 tbsp	Chopped parsley	15ml
1oz	Plain flour	25g
9fl oz	Milk	250ml
	Salt and pepper	
4oz	Gruyère cheese	125g
2 tbsp	Crisp breadcrumbs	2×15ml
3	Eggs	3

METHOD

1 Wash beans and remove strings. Blanch for 5 minutes in lightly salted, boiling water. Drain.

2 Chop celery. Heat 2oz (50g) of the butter, and the oil, in a frying pan and brown the onion, celery and chopped parsley. Add beans, cover and cook very gently for 10 minutes. (See step-by-step pictures, right.)

3 In the meantime, make a thick Béchamel sauce: heat remaining butter in a pan, remove from heat and stir in flour, then milk. Return to heat and cook for 2 minutes. Add salt, pepper and grated Gruyère and cook for further 5 minutes. Remove from heat.

4 Preheat the oven to 425F (220C) Gas 7. Grease ovenproof dish and coat bottom and sides with breadcrumbs. Lightly beat eggs.

5 Drain bean mixture and mix it into sauce until well combined, then mix in eggs. Spoon mixture into ovenproof dish. Stand dish in roasting tin of water and cook in oven for 25 minutes. Reduce heat to 400F (200C) Gas 6 and cook for 10 more minutes.

6 Remove dish from oven, leave to stand for 5 minutes then invert on to serving plate. Serve either hot or cold.

Beat the eggs lightly with a balloon whisk and then stir them into the bean and sauce mixture with a wooden spoon

Grease sides and bottom of ovenproof dish and coat with crisp breadcrumbs. Add bean and egg mixture. Cook, set in tin of water

Combine minced pork and bacon with egg, salt, pepper, allspice and juniper berries. Sprinkle with half the chopped parsley

Season flattened-out slices of meat with salt and pepper and put a fifth of the stuffing in the centre of each one

Fold the edges of the meat slices over the stuffing, overlapping them as necessary, and making each a well-wrapped parcel

Using fine string, tie up the beef olives securely – not too loosely or the stuffing will escape. Right: the finished dish

Beef olives

Beef olives are thin slices of meat stuffed and rolled, then cooked in very little liquid. They can make a simple dish – originally they used up leftovers – or quite a grand one, according to the kind of meat, stuffing and cooking liquid used – often wine or some kind of alcohol. This version has a distinctive flavour because of the gin and juniper berries

MAIN MEAL Serves 5

Overall timing 2½ hours

Equipment Mincer, bowl, string, flameproof casserole or frying pan with lid

Freezing Cool rapidly after 1 hour's cooking. Add the onions. Pack into suitable containers, seal, label and freeze. Freezer life: 3 months. To use: thaw over gentle heat, bring to the boil, then simmer for 30 minutes. Or, place in a cold oven, set at 400F (200C) Gas 6, and allow to heat through for 1½ hours.

INGREDIENTS

	Stuffing	
12oz	Lean pork	350g
4oz	Streaky bacon	125g
1	Egg	1
	Salt and pepper	
½ teasp	Allspice	½×5ml
4	Crushed juniper berries *or* pinch of powdered juniper berries	4
2 tbsp	Chopped parsley	2×15ml
	Beef parcels	
5	Thin slices of rump steak	5
	Salt and pepper	
2oz	Butter	50g
12	Small, peeled onions	12
3 tbsp	Gin	3×15ml
1	Garlic clove	1
1 pint	Beer	560ml
1 teasp	Tomato paste	5ml

METHOD

1 To make stuffing, finely mince the pork and bacon. Place in a bowl with the egg, salt, pepper, allspice and crushed or powdered juniper berries. Mix well. Sprinkle with half the chopped parsley.

2 Spread out the slices of meat; salt and pepper them lightly. Put some stuffing on each slice, and roll up (see step by step, far left). Tie securely with string.

3 Melt the butter in casserole or frying pan, add the peeled onions and cook until golden brown. Remove the onions and reserve. Add the rolls and brown over a medium heat, and then spoon over the gin. Allow the alcohol to warm for a moment before setting alight.

4 When flames die down, stir in peeled and crushed garlic, beer and tomato paste. Bring to the boil, reduce heat, cover and simmer for 1 hour.

5 Return the onions to the pan and simmer uncovered for a further 30 minutes.

6 Remove pan from heat and lift the rolls and onions on to a warmed serving dish. Remove string from olives, pour over the sauce and sprinkle with the remaining chopped parsley before serving.

VARIATION

As an inexpensive alternative, use pork sausage meat instead of minced pork for the stuffing. Either of the stuffings could be varied by adding two dill gherkins, chopped – this is something they do in Germany where the combination of pork or sausage and gherkins is common. The gherkins add crunch and texture to the stuffing as well as extra flavour and sharpness. This dish may also be cooked in a moderate oven, 350F (180C) Gas 4, for 45 minutes or longer according to the thickness of the cut of meat.

cook's know-how

When buying meat for beef olives ask your butcher to suggest different cuts and compare prices. Sirloin and rump will often be dearer than "leg of mutton" cut, which is medium grade, or top rump/thick flank, another suitable cut, both of which lend themselves well to cutting in thin slices which can be made even thinner with a meat bat. Beef olives can also be made from lamb, veal or pork slices, which should also be well flattened.

Haddock in white wine

Haddock baked with white wine and topped with crispy breadcrumbs

MAIN MEAL Serves 4

Overall timing 45 minutes

Equipment Ovenproof dish

Freezing Make as Steps 1–3. Open freeze, wrap and label. Freezer life: 3 months. To use: cook from frozen as Step 4, adding 15 minutes to cooking time

INGREDIENTS

2lb	Haddock fillets	900g
2	Lemons	2
3	Onions	3
1 tbsp	Chopped parsley	15ml
1 tbsp	Chopped fresh dill	15ml
	Salt and pepper	
$\frac{1}{4}$ pint	Dry white wine	150ml
6 tbsp	Fresh breadcrumbs	6×15ml
2oz	Butter	50g

METHOD

1 Preheat the oven to 425F (220C) Gas 7. Grease ovenproof dish.
2 Wash haddock and pat dry on kitchen paper. Cut into 2 inch (5cm) pieces and place in bottom of dish.
3 Cut away the peel and pith and thinly slice the lemons. Peel and slice onions. Arrange lemon and onion slices on top of fish. Sprinkle with herbs, salt and pepper. Pour wine over and sprinkle breadcrumbs on top.
4 Dot with butter and bake in the oven for 25–30 minutes. Serve hot with buttered boiled potatoes and salad.

Trout topped with almonds

One of the most popular dishes on a menu – and very easy to prepare restaurant-style at home. The almonds are fried with the trout to add taste as well as texture

MAIN MEAL Serves 2

Overall timing 20 minutes

Equipment Large frying pan, serving dish

Freezing Not recommended

INGREDIENTS

2	Trout, gutted and cleaned	2
1oz	Flour	25g
2oz	Butter	50g
	Freshly-ground salt and pepper	
2 tbsp	Chopped parsley	2×15ml
2oz	Flaked almonds	50g
2	Lemon slices	2

METHOD

1 Wash and dry trout. Dust with flour.
2 Melt butter in frying pan. Add trout and cook gently on one side for 5 minutes.
3 Turn trout over with a fish slice. Add salt, pepper, half the parsley and the almonds.
4 Cook for a further 7–8 minutes until fish is tender and almonds are golden brown (turn them as they cook).

TO SERVE

Place on a warm serving dish and garnish with lemon slices and remaining chopped parsley. Serve with boiled potatoes and a side dish of mixed salad.

Above: Trout topped with almonds – very easy to prepare and to cook

Herring with baby corn cobs

The corn cobs here are miniatures – a special variety pickled in brine to give dishes an unusual look. If you have difficulty in obtaining them, use corn kernels sprinkled round the dish instead

LUNCH OR STARTER Serves 6

Overall timing 30 minutes

Equipment 1 bowl

Freezing Not recommended

INGREDIENTS

6	Matjes herring fillets	6
1	Green capsicum	1
4	Tomatoes	4
6 oz	Jar of corn cobs	180g
½ pint	Carton of whipping cream	284ml
1 teasp	Strong prepared mustard	5ml
1	Dill pickle	1
	Salt and pepper	
1 tbsp	Freshly chopped dill	15ml

METHOD

1 Rinse herrings under cold running water and dry well on kitchen paper. Arrange on serving plate.
2 Wash, deseed and slice capsicum into rings using a sharp knife. Wash and quarter tomatoes; drain corn cobs.
3 Beat cream in a bowl till thick and fluffy. Mix in mustard, finely chopped dill pickle, salt and pepper.
4 Spoon cream in a strip down the middle of the herrings, sprinkle with chopped dill and surround with the capsicum rings, tomato quarters and corn cobs. Serve from the plate with wholemeal bread or hot toast.

Below: Herring with baby corn cobs – Matjes herrings are pickled and raw

Scallop soufflé

An unusual soufflé that helps make a few scallops go a long way. Fold in the egg whites very carefully to ensure a light, airy texture. Always serve hot soufflés immediately

MAIN MEAL Serves 4

Overall timing 1 hour

Equipment 2 saucepans, bowl, 2 pint (1.1 litre) soufflé dish, roasting tin

Freezing Not recommended

INGREDIENTS

8oz	Prepared scallops	225g
1	Slice of onion	1
1	Stalk of celery	1
1	Small carrot	1
1	Bay leaf	1
½ pint	Milk	300ml
2oz	Butter	50g
2oz	Plain flour	50g
	Salt	
	Freshly-ground white pepper	
3	Large eggs	3
1 teasp	Lemon juice	5ml
1 tbsp	Chopped parsley	15ml
	Cayenne pepper	

METHOD

1 Put the scallops into a saucepan with the onion, celery, carrot and bay leaf. Add the milk and bring to the boil. Reduce the heat, cover and simmer gently for 10 minutes.
2 Preheat the oven to 375F (190C) Gas 5.
3 Lift the scallops out of the pan, chop into fairly small pieces and reserve. Strain the cooking liquor into a jug, discard the flavourings.
4 Heat butter in a large saucepan, add flour and cook for 1 minute. Gradually add strained cooking liquor and bring to the boil, stirring constantly. Remove from heat, taste and adjust seasoning, allow to cool slightly.
5 Separate the eggs, put whites into a large bowl, beat yolks into the sauce. Add chopped scallops, lemon juice, parsley and a pinch of cayenne.
6 Whisk the egg whites till stiff but not dry. Stir a large spoonful into the sauce to lighten it, then carefully fold in the rest.
7 Pour mixture into soufflé dish. Place in a roasting tin containing 1 inch (2.5cm) hot water. Cook in centre of oven for 30–35 minutes till well risen and golden. Serve immediately with a green salad.

Short and sweet

Courgettes – or zucchini as the Italians call them – are part of the same family as the cucumber, melon, squash and pumpkin, and are in fact specially-developed, hybrid varieties of marrow, cultivated to be eaten when they are small and succulent. *Courge* is French for marrow – hence, courgettes, little marrows. Courgettes did not become widely available in Britain until the early 1970s, since when they have become very popular. This is not entirely unexpected because they are easy to grow, easy to prepare and easy to cook. Although a summer vegetable, the popularity of courgettes has led to year-round supplies, and home production is supplemented by imports during the winter months. When buying, choose the smallest available – not longer than 6 inches (15cm) – and avoid any that look dull or wilted or feel soft and spongy. You should also be able to nick the skin very easily with your thumbnail – if you can't, the courgettes will be dry and flavourless. If you grow your own, you can have white and butter-yellow ones as well as the common green ones, and this combination of colours can look most attractive in a finished dish. Courgettes are mostly grown from bush varieties, marketed as "zucchini" or "courgettes", and are, therefore, eminently suitable where growing space is limited. As soon as the courgettes are ready, they should be picked straight away as this encourages further growth. Gardeners can also grow the round Little Gem marrows which can be left to trail along the ground or trained up a trellis or stakes. If harvested when they are the size of an apple, they can be cooked in the same way as courgettes.

Courgettes are one of the simplest vegetables to prepare as they need only to be washed and the ends trimmed; they can be cooked whole or sliced but never for longer than a recipe says, otherwise they will collapse and go watery. If they are to be fried, they will be crisper if treated like aubergines – sprinkled with salt to draw out excess moisture and left to drain for 45 minutes before wiping dry and cooking. They can also be boiled, steamed, deep-fried, baked in foil, and used in soups, stews and flans. Combined with aubergines, peppers, onions and tomatoes, they make the famous *ratatouille*, a French vegetable stew served hot or cold. A novel Italian way of treating them is to slice them into tiny chips, the size of a matchstick, coat in flour and deep fry them for 2 or 3 minutes. Very small, very fresh courgettes – especially those straight from the garden – can be eaten raw in salads. They also make a delicious hors d'oeuvre when steamed or boiled and served cold in a vinaigrette, and they blend happily with a variety of stuffings. You can even eat courgette flowers. They can be dipped in thin batter or egg white and deep fried, or stuffed and baked, either as a savoury or a dessert. Frozen courgettes, usually sliced, are on sale at freezer centres, and they can be frozen at home as well. Choose young ones, no more than 4 inches (10cm) long, slice them, then blanch for 1 minute, cool, drain and open freeze or sauté in butter for 1 minute, cool and place in rigid containers or polythene bags. Freezer life is 1 year. Cook blanched, sliced courgettes from frozen in boiling water or thaw and then follow recipe. If sautéed, thaw and continue sautéeing till tender. Stuffed courgettes can also be frozen (recipes, pages 532–533). Courgettes are excellent for slimmers. Like all the marrow family they are about 95 per cent water and low in carbohydrates. Raw, they have only 2 calories per oz (28g).

Below: Courgettes in all their shiny glory. Butter-yellow ones mingle with the more common green ones and courgette flowers, which are tasty dishes in their own right if stuffed and battered and deep-fried. And a round Little Gem marrow (at back), thinly peeled and blanched, cooks and eats like a courgette

Courgette salad

Lightly fried courgettes in a tangy dressing. For a crisper texture, leave the courgettes raw and choose very firm ones, then add a few sliced black olives or matchstick-thin pieces of raw carrot

SALAD Serves 4

Overall timing 35 minutes plus cooling

Equipment Frying pan, large serving bowl

Freezing Not recommended

INGREDIENTS

1¾lb	Courgettes	750g
3 tbsp	Oil	3×15ml
¼ pint	Water	150ml
1 tbsp	Lemon juice	15ml
	Salt	
	Dressing	
4 tbsp	Olive oil	4×15ml
5 tbsp	White wine vinegar	5×15ml
	Mustard powder	
1	Small onion	1
	Salt	
	Freshly-ground black pepper	
	Sugar	
	Garnish	
1 teasp	Chopped fresh parsley	5ml
1 teasp	Chopped fresh chives	5ml

METHOD

1 Wash courgettes and trim ends, then slice. Heat oil in a frying pan, add courgettes and cook gently for a few minutes. Drain off excess oil, then add water, lemon juice and pinch of salt. Cover and cook for 10 minutes.

2 To make dressing, beat together oil, vinegar and a pinch of mustard in a large serving bowl. Peel and finely chop onion and add with salt, pepper and sugar. Beat well.

3 Add courgettes to bowl. Allow to cool completely, then sprinkle with chopped parsley and chives just before serving.

Above: Stuffed courgette flowers – fill them with any kind of meat or vegetable stuffing of your choice before baking

Stuffed courgette flowers

A truly novel dish, well worth the effort if growing your own courgettes and have a glut of them. Certainly this dish would be quite a talking point

STARTER Serves 4–6

Overall timing 45 minutes

Equipment Food mill or fine mincer, bowl, ovenproof dish

Freezing Not recommended

INGREDIENTS

36	Courgette flowers	36
1	Potato	1
1	Courgette	1
2oz	Green beans	50g
1oz	Melted butter	25g
	Salt and pepper	
2oz	Grated Parmesan	50g
1 tbsp	Chopped basil	15ml
1	Garlic clove	1
1	Egg	1
4 tbsp	Oil	4×15ml

METHOD

1 Preheat the oven to 350F (180C) Gas 4. Wash and dry courgette flowers on kitchen paper. Peel and finely chop potato. Trim ends of courgette and green beans and finely chop. Put the potato, courgette and beans through a food mill or fine mincer.

2 Put mixture in a bowl, add melted butter, salt, pepper, cheese, basil and peeled and crushed garlic. Mix well, then add the egg, lightly beaten.

3 Fill courgette flowers with mixture, being careful not to rip or overfill them. Arrange side by side in ovenproof dish. Spoon over the oil and bake in the oven for about 20 minutes.

cook's know-how

For a simple courgette and tomato dish, blanch, peel and chop 1¾lb (750g) tomatoes. Peel and thinly slice 2 large onions. Heat 3 tbsp (3×15ml) oil in a large pan. Add tomatoes and onions. Season and cook gently for 15 minutes, stirring occasionally. Trim 1½lb (700g) small courgettes and add whole to pan. Cover and cook gently for 30 minutes. Sprinkle with chopped fresh basil and serve hot or chilled.

Stuffed courgettes

Yet another way of showing the versatility of courgettes. Stuffed, they make excellent lunch or supper dishes. Here are three fillings to try, two use minced lamb, the third using cooked chicken and ham or canned tuna

Tunisian

LUNCH OR SUPPER Serves 4

Overall timing 1¼ hours

Equipment 2 bowls, large frying pan, blender or sieve

Freezing Place in rigid or foil container, cool, cover, label and freeze. Freezer life: 1 month. To use: bake from frozen, covered, in moderate oven 350F (180C) Gas 4 for about 45 minutes or till bubbling hot

INGREDIENTS

1lb	Courgettes	450g
1	Onion	1
8oz	Minced lamb	225g
1 tbsp	Chopped parsley	15ml
2	Eggs	2
	Salt	
	Freshly-ground black pepper	
	Cayenne	
4 tbsp	Plain flour	4×15ml
4 tbsp	Oil	4×15ml
8oz	Can of tomatoes	227g
	Parsley	

METHOD

1 Wash courgettes and trim ends. Using a long thin knife or melon-baller, slice out centre of each whole courgette, working from both ends if necessary and trying to keep the sides an even thickness. Reserve cut-out flesh.
2 Peel and finely chop onion and put in a bowl with the chopped courgette flesh, minced lamb, parsley, 1 egg, salt, pepper and a pinch of cayenne. Mix with a wooden spoon.
3 Fill courgettes with prepared mixture. Roll any leftover mixture into little meat balls.
4 Beat remaining egg in a bowl and dip stuffed courgettes and meat balls in it. Coat lightly with flour.
5 Heat oil in a large frying pan. Add courgettes and meat balls and cook on all sides (about 20 minutes). Remove from pan and drain on kitchen paper.
6 Put tomatoes and their juice in a blender or push through a sieve. Add tomato purée to pan juices with a pinch of salt and a little black pepper and cook over a moderate heat for about 15 minutes.
7 Return courgettes and meat balls to pan and cook for a further 15 minutes, then turn into a warm serving dish. Pour tomato sauce over and serve hot, sprinkled with chopped parsley.

Below: Tunisian stuffed courgettes

Above: Lamb and rice stuffed courgettes

Lamb and rice

LUNCH OR SUPPER Serves 4

Overall timing 1½ hours

Equipment Sieve, saucepan, frying pan, bowl, ovenproof dish

Freezing Place in rigid or foil container, cool, cover, label and freeze. Freezer life: 1 month. To use: bake from frozen, covered, in moderate oven 350F (180C) Gas 4 for about 45 minutes or till bubbling hot

INGREDIENTS

2oz	Long grain rice	50g
	Salt	
1	Large onion	1
2 tbsp	Oil	2×15ml
6oz	Minced lamb	175g
	Freshly-ground black pepper	
4	Courgettes	4
2	Tomatoes	2
1	Garlic clove	1
2oz	Petits pois	50g
½ pint	Stock	300ml
4oz	Emmenthal cheese	125g
1oz	Butter	25g

METHOD
1 Wash and drain rice in a sieve. Cook in pan of boiling salted water for 10–12 minutes until just tender. Preheat the oven to 350F (180C) Gas 4.
2 Peel and finely chop onion. Heat oil in a frying pan and cook onion for 5 minutes, then add minced lamb and cook till brown, stirring all the time. Season well with salt and pepper.
3 Wash courgettes, trim the ends, then halve them lengthways. Scoop out most of the flesh from courgettes with melon baller or small spoon. Sprinkle courgette shells with a little salt.
4 Chop scooped out flesh and put into a large bowl with the cooked lamb. Blanch, peel and finely chop tomatoes. Peel and crush garlic. Add tomatoes and garlic to meat.
5 Add peas and drained cooked rice to meat and mix well. Season to taste, then fill courgette shells with mixture.
6 Place stuffed courgettes side by side in dish, pour round the stock (made with 1 stock cube if necessary), cover and cook in oven for 25 minutes.
7 Remove from oven, sprinkle generously with grated cheese and dot with butter. Return to oven and cook, uncovered, for a further 10 minutes.

Au gratin

LUNCH OR SUPPER Serves 4

Overall timing 1½ hours

Equipment Bowl, blender or sieve, flameproof casserole

Freezing Place in rigid or foil container, cool, cover, label and freeze. Freezer life: 1 month. To use: bake from frozen, covered, in moderate oven 350F (180C) Gas 4 for about 45 minutes or till hot

INGREDIENTS

5oz	Mixed cooked chicken and ham	150g
	or	
3½oz	can of tuna (optional)	100g
2 tbsp	Chopped parsley	2×15ml
1	Garlic clove	1
4 tbsp	Fresh breadcrumbs	4×15ml
2 tbsp	Grated cheese	2×15ml
1	Egg	1
4	Large courgettes	4
14oz	Can of tomatoes	397g
1 tbsp	Olive oil	15ml
1oz	Butter	25g
2 teasp	Dried basil	2×5ml

METHOD
1 Finely chop chicken and ham or drain tuna, discarding oil, and mash with a fork.
2 In a bowl, mix together the meat, or tuna if using, parsley, peeled and crushed garlic, 2 tbsp (2×15ml) breadcrumbs, cheese and egg.
3 Wash courgettes and trim ends. Halve them lengthways. Scoop out centres with a melon baller or small spoon, chop finely and add to bowl. Fill courgette shells with prepared mixture.
4 Purée drained tomatoes in a blender or push through a sieve. Heat oil and butter in a casserole, add tomato purée and basil and cook for about 10 minutes. Meanwhile heat the oven to 350F (180C) Gas 4.
5 Add stuffed courgettes to casserole, sprinkle with remaining breadcrumbs, baste with tomato sauce, cover and cook in the oven for 50 minutes. Remove lid for last 10 minutes of cooking to help crisp the topping. Serve hot.

Below: Stuffed courgettes au gratin – with either a meat or fish filling, then topped with a sprinkling of fine breadcrumbs before cooking in the oven

Countdown

Onion quiche, Peperonata, Moist date and ginger cake

Wholemeal honey squares

Mutton hot-pot, Green salad, Plum crumb pudding

You can plan to have the weekend free by shopping on Thursday and cooking on Friday. Remember to check the date stamp on perishable goods

Friday morning Prepare hot-pot. Simmer for $1\frac{1}{4}$ hours

Make pastry for quiche and chill

Prepare Peperonata. Simmer for 1 hour

Make quiche filling. Preheat oven to 400F (200C) Gas 6. Line tin with pastry, bake blind for 15 mins. Add filling. Bake for 25 mins

Cool hot-pot and store in fridge in a flameproof casserole

Cool quiche, cover with foil or cling film and store in fridge

Store Peperonata in fridge

Friday afternoon Make plum crumb mix and stand for 15 mins. Prepare plums. Preheat oven to 350F (180C) Gas 4. Finish pudding and bake for 50 mins

Prepare dates for cake, cool. Make cake and bake for 50–60 mins

Make squares. Bake for 30–40 mins

Cool pudding and chill in tin

Cool cake and store in tin

Cool squares, cut into squares and store in airtight tin

When pudding has chilled for 3–4 hours, transfer to serving dish, cover and store in fridge

Prepare green salad and store in polythene container in fridge

Make vinaigrette dressing

For Saturday lunch, heat quiche in a moderate oven for 15 mins, and Peperonata for 10 mins. Serve cake with cream.

For Sunday dinner, heat hot-pot on top of cooker for 15 mins and toss green salad in dressing. Slice pudding and serve with cream.

Onion quiche

Serve with a simple tomato salad or with a flavourful Peperonata

LUNCH Serves 4

Overall timing $1\frac{1}{2}$ hours

Equipment 2 bowls, frying pan, $8\frac{1}{2}$ inch (22cm) flan dish or loose-bottom tin

Freezing Open freeze till firm. Remove from dish, foil-wrap, seal and label. Freezer life: 2 months. To use: replace in dish, cover loosely with foil and reheat from frozen at 350F (180C) Gas 4 for about 20 minutes

INGREDIENTS

	Pastry	
6oz	Plain flour	175g
$\frac{1}{2}$ teasp	Salt	$\frac{1}{2}\times$5ml
3oz	Butter or margarine	75g
1	Egg yolk	1
2–3 tbsp	Water	2–3× 15ml
	Filling	
1lb	Medium-size onions	450g
2oz	Lard	50g
4oz	Smoked streaky bacon	125g
3	Eggs	3
$\frac{1}{4}$ pint	Milk	150ml
$\frac{1}{4}$ pint	Carton of single cream	150ml
	Salt	
	Freshly-ground black pepper	

METHOD

1 Sift the flour and salt into a bowl and rub in the fat till the mixture resembles fine breadcrumbs. Add the egg yolk and water and mix to a soft, but not sticky, dough. Knead lightly till smooth, wrap in foil and chill for 30 minutes.

2 Meanwhile, peel and thinly slice the onions. Heat the lard in a frying pan and fry the onions over a moderate heat till pale golden.

3 Derind and dice the bacon and add to the pan. Fry for a further 4–5 minutes till the onions and bacon are golden brown. Preheat the oven to 400F (200C) Gas 6.

4 Roll out the pastry on a floured surface and use to line the dish or tin. Prick the base and bake blind for 15 minutes.

5 Remove foil and baking beans and spread the onion and bacon mixture over the pastry base. Put the eggs into a bowl and add the milk and cream. Mix well with a fork and season to taste. Pour over the onions.

6 Bake in the centre of the oven for a further 25 minutes till lightly set and golden. Serve hot.

VARIATIONS

You can vary the filling in numerous ways according to your taste. Here are a few ideas for different ingredients: blanched, peeled and thinly sliced tomatoes or courgettes; sliced, fried capsicums or mushrooms; cooked sweetcorn; herbs; soured cream instead of single; grated cheese – try smoked cheese for a change.

Below: Onion quiche – best served hot, but still delicious when cold

Above: Peperonata – an Italian speciality

Peperonata

An Italian vegetable dish that's colourful and full of flavour. It can be served hot or cold as a starter or side salad, or as an accompaniment to grilled or roast meats, or used as a filling for omelettes

For Peperonata, cook onions then capsicums

Tomatoes, garlic and seasonings are added

VEGETABLE OR STARTER Serves 4

Overall timing $1\frac{1}{2}$ hours

Equipment Flameproof casserole

Freezing Cool rapidly. Pack into rigid container, seal, label and freeze. Freezer life: 6 months. To use: bring slowly to the boil over a low heat, then cook for 10 minutes

INGREDIENTS

2	Large red capsicums	2
2	Large green capsicums	2
1	Onion	1
4 tbsp	Olive oil	4×15ml
6	Tomatoes	6
1	Garlic clove	1
	Salt and pepper	
12	Basil leaves	12

METHOD

1 Deseed capsicums and cut into thin strips. Peel and slice the onion, then fry with olive oil in casserole until golden brown. Add capsicums and cook for 15 minutes.

2 Blanch, peel and roughly chop tomatoes. Add to the casserole with peeled whole garlic clove. Season with salt and pepper to taste.

3 Cover and simmer over low heat for about an hour until all vegetables are soft. Remove garlic, garnish with basil leaves and serve hot or cold.

Wholemeal honey squares

Wholemeal flour and honey are used to make a nutritious and healthy dough mixture which is filled with raisins and grated citrus peel flavoured with cinnamon. Remember when sifting wholemeal flour to tip the bits of wheat left in the sieve back into the mixture

TEA-TIME Makes 12

Overall timing 1 hour

Equipment 7 inch (18cm) square tin, mixing bowl, small saucepan

Freezing Not recommended

Storage Airtight tin

INGREDIENTS

6oz	Butter or block margarine	175g
3oz	Clear honey	75g
5oz	Plain flour	150g
5oz	Wholemeal flour	150g
	Filling	
3oz	Raisins	75g
1 teasp	Grated orange peel	5ml
1 teasp	Grated lemon peel	5ml
2 tbsp	Milk	2×15ml
1oz	Unsalted butter	25g
$\frac{1}{4}$ teasp	Cinnamon	$\frac{1}{4}$×5ml

METHOD

1 Preheat the oven to 350F (180C) Gas 4. Grease and base line tin. Cream butter and honey in a bowl till light and fluffy, then mix in the sifted flour.

2 Roll out half the mixture on a floured surface and press into tin.

3 Place all filling ingredients in a saucepan and stir over gentle heat till the butter melts. Spread over dough, then roll out the remaining dough mixture and place on top of filling.

4 Bake in centre of oven for 30–40 minutes till golden. Leave to cool in tin. Cut into squares when cold.

Moist date and ginger cake

True to its name this moist cake simply melts in the mouth and is especially good served hot or warm with whipped cream for dessert. Nevertheless, if left to cool it will still retain both flavour and softness and slice to perfection for a tea-time treat

DESSERT OR TEA-TIME Cuts into 12 slices

Overall timing 1¼ hours

Equipment 9 inch (23cm) round cake tin, 2 bowls, wire rack

Freezing Cool completely and wrap in foil or polythene. Freezer life: 6 months. To use: thaw in wrappings at room temperature for 4–6 hours

Above: Moist date and ginger cake – flavoured with ground ginger and deliciously sweetened with brown sugar, treacle and syrup

INGREDIENTS

8oz	Stoned dates	225g
1 teasp	Bicarbonate of soda	5ml
¼ pint	Boiling water	150ml
4oz	Margarine	125g
4oz	Soft dark brown sugar	125g
2 tbsp	Black treacle	2×15ml
1 tbsp	Golden syrup	15ml
2	Eggs	2
8oz	Self-raising flour	225g
2 teasp	Ground ginger	2×5ml
2 tbsp	Icing sugar	2×15ml

METHOD

1. Preheat the oven to 350F (180C) Gas 4. Grease and base-line the tin.
2. Chop the dates and place in a small bowl. Sprinkle with bicarbonate, then pour on the boiling water. Leave to cool.
3. In a mixing bowl, cream the margarine and sugar until light and fluffy. Beat in the black treacle and syrup, then the eggs, one at a time, beating well.
4. Sift in the flour and ginger, and add the dates and soaking liquid. Stir till well blended.
5. Pour into the prepared tin and bake in the centre of the oven for 50–60 minutes or until the centre of the cake springs back when lightly pressed.
6. Run a knife around the edge of the tin to release the cake and turn on to wire rack to cool. Dredge with icing sugar.

Mutton hot-pot

This economical all-in-one meal of mutton, turnips and potatoes can be made with lamb and cooked for a slightly shorter time

MAIN MEAL Serves 4

Overall timing 1¾ hours

Equipment heavy-based saucepan or flameproof casserole

Freezing Not recommended

INGREDIENTS

4oz	Streaky bacon	125g
2	Onions	2
1oz	Butter	25g
2 tbsp	Oil	2×15ml
2½lb	Neck of mutton chops	1.1kg
1 tbsp	Plain flour	15ml
¾ pint	Light stock	400ml
1lb	Turnips	450g
1lb	Potatoes	450g
2	Garlic cloves	2
1 teasp	Caster sugar	5ml
	Bouquet garni	
	Salt and ground black pepper	
4	Large tomatoes	4

METHOD

1 Derind the bacon and cut into strips. Peel onions and slice into thin rings.
2 Heat the butter and oil in a saucepan and fry the bacon and onions.
3 Meanwhile, wipe and trim the mutton. Add to the pan and fry over a high heat till browned on both sides.
4 Sprinkle in the flour and cook, stirring, till it browns. Gradually add the stock (made with cubes if necessary) and bring to the boil.
5 Peel and wash the turnips and potatoes and cut into quarters. Add to the pan with the peeled and crushed garlic, sugar, bouquet garni and seasoning. Cover and simmer for $1\frac{1}{4}$ hours.
6 Remove bouquet garni, add the tomatoes and cook for a further 15 minutes.
7 Taste and adjust the seasoning. Arrange the meat and vegetables on a warmed serving dish and spoon the cooking liquor over. Serve immediately.

Above: Plum crumb pudding – use red plums as the sponge crumbs absorb the colouring

Below: Mutton hot-pot – serve this meat and vegetable dish with a green salad

Plum crumb pudding

This chilled cut-and-come-again pudding will keep a peckish family happy. You can turn it into a hot dish with a meringue topping by making it up without the egg whites and baking for 40 minutes. Whisk the whites with 4oz (125g) caster sugar. Spoon over the pudding and bake for a further 15 minutes

DESSERT Serves 8

Overall timing $1\frac{1}{2}$ hours plus chilling

Equipment 9 inch (23cm) springform tin, 3 bowls, 1 saucepan

Freezing Not recommended

INGREDIENTS

4oz	Sponge cake	125g
3	Eggs	3
2oz	Caster sugar	50g
1 pint	Milk	560ml
1oz	Butter	25g
	Grated rind of 1 lemon	
$\frac{1}{2}$ teasp	Ground cinnamon	$\frac{1}{2}\times$5ml
1lb	Red plums	450g

METHOD

1 Grease and base-line the tin. Crumble the cake into a bowl. Separate 2 of the eggs, putting the yolks and remaining whole egg into a bowl with the sugar. Put the milk and butter into a saucepan and bring almost to the boil.
2 Beat the yolks and sugar together and pour the milk on to them, stirring constantly. Strain over the cake crumbs. Add the lemon rind and cinnamon, mix well and leave to stand for 15 minutes.
3 Meanwhile, wash and halve the plums, discarding the stones. Dry thoroughly on kitchen paper. Preheat the oven to 350F (180C) Gas 4.
4 Whisk the 2 egg whites in a large bowl till stiff but not dry and fold into the crumb mixture with a metal spoon. Pour the mixture into the tin.
5 Arrange the plums cut side down on the mixture and bake in the centre of the oven for about 50 minutes till set.
6 Remove from the oven, leave to cool in the tin, then chill for 3–4 hours. Remove pudding from tin and place on a serving dish. Serve cut into slices, with pouring cream.

Macaroon pudding

Baked and served hot with a rum cream sauce, this rich pudding consists of layers of macaroons and a spongy mix packed with sultanas

DESSERT Serves 6

Overall timing 1 hour 20 minutes

Equipment 2 saucepans, 3 bowls, 8 inch/20cm ($2\frac{1}{4}$ pint/1.3 litre) brioche or kugelhopf mould

Freezing Open freeze pudding in mould, then wrap and label. Freezer life: 3 months. To use: thaw in wrappings for 4–6 hours at room temperature,

INGREDIENTS

1 pint	Milk	560ml
4oz	Breadcrumbs	125g
4oz	Butter	125g
3	Eggs	3
2oz	Caster sugar	50g
8oz	Sultanas	225g
8oz	Macaroons	225g
	Rum cream	
4	Eggs	4
3oz	Caster sugar	75g
4 tbsp	Rum	4×15ml
	Juice of ½ a lemon	

METHOD

1 Preheat the oven to 400F (200C) Gas 6.

2 Put the milk into a saucepan and bring to the boil. Add the breadcrumbs and simmer gently for 10 minutes.

3 Meanwhile, beat 3oz (75g) of the butter in a bowl till light and creamy. Separate the eggs. Whisk the yolks with the sugar till light and fluffy, then gradually beat into the butter. Add the milk and breadcrumbs and the sultanas, mix well.

4 Whisk the egg whites till stiff and fold into the mixture.

5 Grease the mould with the remaining butter. Arrange the sultana mixture and the macaroons in layers in the mould, beginning and ending with the sultana mixture. Cook for 1 hour in the centre of the oven.

6 To make the rum cream, mix the eggs, sugar, rum, lemon juice and 3fl oz (90ml) water in a bowl. Place the bowl over a pan of simmering water and cook, stirring constantly, till the mixture is thick enough to coat the back of the spoon. Strain into a warmed sauceboat or serving dish.

7 Turn the pudding on to a warmed serving plate and serve hot, cut into thick wedges, with the rum cream.

Above: Baked bananas—quickly cooked dessert

Baked bananas

This simple-to-prepare dessert can be cooked at the same time as the Sunday roast

DESSERT Serves 4

Overall timing 15 minutes

Equipment Ovenproof dish

Freezing Not recommended

INGREDIENTS

4	Large ripe bananas	4
2oz	Butter	50g
2 teasp	Caster sugar	2×5ml
2 tbsp	Water	2×15ml
	Ground cinnamon	

METHOD

1 Preheat oven to 425F (220C) Gas 7.

2 Wipe the bananas and peel them three-quarters of the way down. Fold back the skin to give a petal effect.

3 Place in a greased ovenproof dish and dot each banana with butter. Sprinkle with sugar, water and a little ground cinnamon.

4 Cook at the top of the oven for 10 minutes. Serve immediately with custard or vanilla ice cream

Carob pudding

A substitute for chocolate, carob is available in a bar or powder

DESSERT Serves 4

Overall timing 15 minutes plus setting time

Equipment Cup, saucepan, mixing bowl or electric blender, mould

Freezing Not recommended

INGREDIENTS

2 teasp	Powdered gelatine	2×5ml
8fl oz	Warm water	225ml
3 tbsp	Honey	3×15ml
2 tbsp	Carob powder	2×15ml
4fl oz	Vegetable oil	120ml
1 teasp	Vanilla essence	5ml
2	Eggs	2

METHOD

1 Mix gelatine with 1 tbsp (15ml) of the water in a cup. When firm, place cup in saucepan of water and heat gently until gelatine is dissolved.

2 Place in mixing bowl or blender with rest of water, honey, carob, oil, vanilla and eggs. Blend until smooth and pour into a mould, Chill in fridge for 1 hour.

Apple soufflé

A special-occasion dessert flavoured with Calvados – apple brandy

DESSERT Serves 6

Overall timing $1\frac{3}{4}$ hours

Equipment Deep ovenproof or soufflé dish, 2 saucepans, metal ladle, 2 large mixing bowls

Freezing Not recommended

INGREDIENTS

	Base	
1lb	Dessert apples	450g
1oz	Butter	25g
1 tbsp	Caster sugar	15ml
6 tbsp	Calvados	6×15ml
6	Digestive biscuits	6
	Topping	
½ pint	Milk	300ml
1	Vanilla pod	1
5	Eggs	5
4oz	Caster sugar	125g
1oz	Plain flour	25g
2 tbsp	Calvados	2×15ml
5	Egg whites	5
	Pinch of salt	
	Grated rind of ½ a lemon	
1oz	Icing sugar	25g

METHOD

1 Preheat oven to 350F (180C) Gas 4. Grease ovenproof or soufflé dish.
2 To make base, peel, core and finely slice apples. Melt the butter in saucepan, add the apples and sugar. Cover and cook gently for 5 minutes. Warm 3 tbsp (3×15ml) Calvados in a ladle, pour over apples and flambé.
3 Lift apples out with a draining spoon and place in bottom of prepared dish. Break the biscuits up roughly into pieces and place on top of apples. Pour over 3 tbsp (3×15ml) Calvados.
4 To make the soufflé topping, place the milk and vanilla pod in a saucepan and bring to the boil. Remove from heat, cool quickly, then lift out pod.
5 Separate eggs. Place yolks in bowl with caster sugar and beat till creamy. Beat in the flour, Calvados and cooled milk a little at a time until mixture is smooth.
6 In another bowl, whisk the 10 egg whites and salt till stiff. Add the grated lemon rind, then carefully fold into creamed mixture.
7 Pour into dish over apples and biscuits. Cook in the middle of the oven for 45 minutes. Sprinkle with icing sugar and serve immediately.

Below: Apple soufflé – biscuit and fruit base, liqueur flavoured topping

Apricot parfait

An ice cream dessert made with curd cheese, two fruits and cherry liqueur

DESSERT Serves 6

Overall timing 10 minutes

Equipment Sieve or liquidizer, 6 glass serving dishes

Freezing Not recommended

INGREDIENTS

1lb 13oz	Can of apricots	822g
17fl oz	Block of vanilla ice cream	460ml
2oz	Ground almonds	50g
2 tbsp	Maraschino or Kirsch	2×15ml
8oz	Curd cheese	225g
8oz	Raspberries	225g
1 tbsp	Nibbed almonds	15ml

METHOD

1 Drain apricots. Reserve 4 for decoration. Press rest through a sieve or liquidize.
2 Quickly mix together the apricot purée, ice cream, ground almonds, liqueur and curd cheese.
3 Wash and drain raspberries. Divide between 6 serving dishes and top with apricot cream mixture. Decorate with reserved apricots, sliced, and nibbed almonds. Serve immediately.

Tortellini in tomato and meat sauce

With a crisp salad, this makes a well balanced lunch or supper – the same quantity will be enough for 6 as a starter on its own. The sauce contains red wine and oregano – a herb the Italians love to use with pasta

LUNCH OR SUPPER Serves 4

Overall timing 35 minutes

Equipment 2 saucepans, colander

Freezing Not recommended

INGREDIENTS

1	Large onion	1
2 tbsp	Oil	2×15ml
8oz	Minced beef	225g
1	Garlic clove	1
14oz	Can of tomatoes	397g
1 tbsp	Tomato paste	15ml
$\frac{1}{4}$ pint	Red wine	150ml
$\frac{1}{2}$ teasp	Oregano	$\frac{1}{2}$×5ml
	Salt	
	Freshly-ground black pepper	
12oz	Tortellini	350g
1oz	Butter	25g
2 tbsp	Grated Parmesan	2×15ml

METHOD

1 Peel and finely chop the onion. Heat the oil in a saucepan, add the onion and fry till transparent. Add the minced beef and fry for 5 minutes, stirring frequently to break up the meat.

2 Peel and crush the garlic and add to the pan with the tomatoes and juice, tomato paste and red wine. Bring to the boil, then stir in the oregano and seasoning. Simmer uncovered for 20 minutes, stirring occasionally.

3 Meanwhile, cook the tortellini in a pan of lightly salted boiling water for 12–15 minutes till al dente. Drain in a colander. Melt the butter in the pan, add the tortellini and toss lightly till coated.

4 Add the cheese to the meat sauce, then taste and adjust the seasoning. Stir the sauce gently into the tortellini.

5 Arrange in a warmed serving dish and serve immediately with a crispy mixed salad.

Below: Tortellini in tomato and meat sauce – serve extra Parmesan for a cheesier taste

Crêpes with Camembert

Savoury crêpes filled with Camembert and topped with spicy tomatoes and grated Gruyère or Emmenthal

LIGHT LUNCH OR SUPPER Serves 4

Overall timing 45 minutes

Equipment 1 bowl, small frying pan, blender or sieve, ovenproof dish

Freezing Prepare as Steps 1–4, but assemble dish in foil container. Seal, label and freeze. Freezer life: 2 months. To use: bake from frozen in oven at 400F (200C) Gas 6 for 30–40 minutes

INGREDIENTS

4oz	Plain flour	125g
	Pinch of salt	
2	Eggs	2
$\frac{1}{4}$ pint	Milk	150ml
1 teasp	Brandy (optional)	5ml
4oz	Butter	125g
$\frac{1}{2}$	Ripe Camembert	$\frac{1}{2}$
8oz	Can of tomatoes	227g
	Worcestershire sauce	
4oz	Grated Gruyère or Emmenthal	125g
	Freshly-ground black pepper	

METHOD

1 Put flour, salt, eggs and milk into a bowl and whisk well together. Add the brandy (optional), cover and chill for 2 hours.

2 Make 8 crêpes from the batter in a small frying pan, adding a nut of butter between each so they brown evenly. Preheat the oven to 400F (200C) Gas 6. Grease ovenproof dish.

3 Mash Camembert and remaining butter with a fork until well blended. Spread a little of the cheese mixture over each crêpe. Roll up and arrange in ovenproof dish, seam-side underneath.

4 Blend tomatoes and juice for a few seconds with a dash of Worcestershire sauce or press through a sieve. Pour over crêpes and sprinkle with grated cheese and freshly-ground black pepper.

5 Cook in oven for 20 minutes. Serve immediately with sweetcorn or peas flavoured with mint.

Artichoke salad

Artichoke hearts make an exciting addition to salads, providing a sophisticated touch. The canned kind are as good as fresh ones, with the obvious advantage that you can always keep a tin of them in your storecupboard ready to use at any time of the year. Here, canned hearts are mixed with red and green capsicums which add a nice crunchy texture as well as attractive colour to the salad. It makes a good accompaniment to fried or grilled chops or steaks, and cold meats too

SIDE SALAD OR STARTER Serves 4

Overall timing 20 minutes

Equipment Salad bowl

Freezing Not recommended

INGREDIENTS

	Salad	
14oz	Can of artichoke hearts	397g
3	Large tomatoes	3
1	Green capsicum	1
1	Red capsicum	1
	Freshly-ground black pepper	
	Dressing	
6 tbsp	Olive oil	6x15ml
2 tbsp	Wine vinegar	2x15ml
	Pinch of salt	
	Pinch of sugar	
1	Garlic clove	1
	Fresh parsley	

METHOD

1 Drain and finely slice canned hearts.

2 Put them into a salad bowl with sliced tomatoes and capsicums which have been deseeded and sliced lengthways. Season with pepper.

3 To make dressing, mix together olive oil, vinegar, salt, sugar and crushed garlic. Pour over salad and mix well. Leave to stand in a cool place for 10 minutes then mix in finely chopped parsley and serve.

Below: Artichoke salad with capsicums

Steak au poivre

A coating of crushed peppercorns (white are hotter than black) is put on to steak before it's fried, flamed with brandy and served with a cream sauce. If you prefer, use the less expensive flash-fry steaks. They cook in half the time

LUNCH OR SUPPER Serves 4

Overall timing 15–20 minutes – longer for well-done steaks

Equipment Board and rolling-pin, frying pan, metal ladle

Freezing Not recommended. Steak from freezer should be thawed

Use a heavy wooden rolling-pin to crush the peppercorns coarsely

Dip each steak in a little oil, then press into the crushed pepper to coat

Pat pepper well on both sides of each steak before frying (see finished dish, opposite)

INGREDIENTS

2 tbsp	White or black peppercorns *or* prepared pepper for steak	2×15ml
4	Rump or fillet steaks	4
	Oil	
2oz	Butter	50g
	Salt	
4 tbsp	Brandy	4×15ml
3 tbsp	Single cream	3×15ml
	Garnish	
	Sprigs of watercress	

METHOD

1 If you are using peppercorns, put them on a wooden board and crush them coarsely with a rolling-pin. (See step-by-step pictures, left.) Otherwise, use pepper specially prepared for steak.

2 Brush each side of the steaks with oil, then coat with the crushed peppercorns (or prepared pepper, if used).

3 Heat butter in a frying pan and cook steaks quickly for about $1\frac{1}{2}$ minutes on each side. Reduce heat and cook for about a further 1 minute (for rare steak), 3 minutes (for medium steak) or 7 minutes (for well-done steak).

4 Season with salt. Warm brandy in a ladle. Set it alight and pour over steaks.

5 Remove steaks and arrange on a warm serving dish. Keep hot.

6 Stir cream into the juices in frying pan. Heat gently for a few minutes. Adjust seasoning according to taste.

TO SERVE

Pour gravy over steaks and garnish with sprigs of watercress. Serve with deep-fried potato balls and whole green beans, or choose an unusual salad, such as Artichoke salad, left.

Left: Coq au vin, garnished and ready to be served with boiled potatoes or rice

Coq au vin

Chicken in wine is a classic French dish and the colour and richness of the sauce comes from the wine in which the chicken is first marinated, then cooked. The small measure of brandy adds that special touch to the final taste

MAIN MEAL Serves 6–8

Overall timing 2½ hours plus 8 hours marination

Equipment Large bowl, large flameproof casserole, saucepan, metal ladle

Freezing After cooking, allow dish to cool quickly. *Do not* reduce the sauce. Skim any fat from surface. Pack into a foil container, cover, label and freeze. Freezer life: 3 months. To use: thaw overnight, then thoroughly heat through (about 30 minutes). Carry out Steps 8 and 9, right, and garnish – see To serve

INGREDIENTS

	Marinade	
1	Onion	1
1	Shallot	1
1	Large carrot	1
2	Garlic cloves	2
3 tbsp	Olive oil	3×15ml
18fl oz	Full-bodied red wine	500ml
3	Cloves	3
	Black pepper	
	Bouquet garni	
	Other ingredients	
3–3½lb	Chicken joints	1.5kg
5oz	Streaky bacon	150g
2 tbsp	Plain flour	2×15ml
2 tbsp	Brandy	2×15ml
¼ pint	Water	150ml
2 tbsp	Tomato paste	2×15ml
	Salt	
	Black pepper	
24	Button onions	24
2oz	Butter	50g
8oz	Button mushrooms	225g
2	Slices of white bread	2
	Fresh parsley	

METHOD

1 Peel and coarsely chop onion and shallot; scrape and slice carrot; peel and crush garlic. Place in large polythene bag with oil, wine, cloves, black pepper, bouquet garni and wiped and dried chicken joints. Place the bag in a large bowl for support and tie the end of the bag well. Leave in a cool place (*not* the fridge) for at least 8 hours, turning bag over from time to time.

2 Remove rind and cut bacon into small strips. Put in base of a large flameproof casserole and cook over a gentle heat for about 10 minutes until the fat starts to run.

3 Remove chicken joints from marinade and dry well. Add to casserole and cook until golden brown on all sides. Sprinkle with the flour and cook over a high heat until brown.

4 Remove casserole from heat. In a ladle, heat brandy and set light to it. Pour it flaming over the chicken joints. When the flames have died down, return the casserole to heat.

5 Add marinade, water and tomato paste. Cook for 3 minutes, stirring. Season well. Cover and simmer very gently for 30 minutes.

6 While it's cooking, blanch and peel button onions. If button onions are not available, use the bulbs of spring onions instead. Melt 1 oz (25g) of the butter in a saucepan and cook onions for a few minutes until they are golden brown. Drain well and add to casserole. Continue cooking for 45 minutes more.

7 Wipe the button mushrooms and fry them for 5 minutes in the butter in which the onions were cooked. Add more butter if necessary. Drain well, then add to the casserole. Continue cooking for a further 15 minutes.

8 Remove chicken and vegetables from liquid and arrange in a warm serving dish. Cover and keep warm.

9 Discard bouquet garni. Put liquid from casserole into a saucepan and boil rapidly until reduced by half. Pour the sauce over chicken.

TO SERVE

Toast slices of bread and cut into triangles. Dip ends of triangles first in the sauce then into chopped parsley and arrange on top of the Coq au vin. As this dish is rich, it is best accompanied by small boiled potatoes or rice, and a green vegetable.

Sweet-sour red cabbage

This dish complements game or adds extra taste to bland meat. An exciting, spicy way to use red cabbage, it is also a good supper dish, served with frankfurters or gammon. Delicious with Pot roast pork with apples on page 546

VEGETABLE Serves 4

Overall timing 1 hour 20 minutes

Equipment Large heavy-based casserole with tight-fitting lid

Freezing Pack into containers. Seal, label and freeze. Freezer life: 3 months. To use: reheat slowly from frozen

INGREDIENTS

2lb	Red cabbage	about 1kg
2oz	Streaky bacon	50g
1	Onion	1
1	Cooking apple	1
6	Whole allspice	6
$\frac{1}{2}$ teasp	Salt	$\frac{1}{2}\times$5ml
2 teasp	Honey	2×5ml
3fl oz	Red wine or wine vinegar	90ml

METHOD

1. Discard any damaged outer leaves of cabbage. Quarter and cut away core and thick ribs then shred leaves.
2. Chop bacon. Peel and chop onion. Cook bacon in casserole over a low heat until fat starts to run. Add onion and cook for 5 minutes, stirring.
3. Core and chop apple and add to casserole with cabbage. Crush allspice and add to casserole with salt, honey and wine or vinegar. Turn mixture over with a wooden spoon. Cover and simmer for 1 hour. If there's too much liquid at the end of cooking time, leave lid off, increase heat and reduce liquid by half. Serve hot.

Below: Sweet-sour red cabbage combines the piquancy of allspice and wine vinegar with the smooth sweetness of honey

Creamy spiced lamb and rice

An unusual but delicious dish. The lamb is cooked in milk with onions and spices, then the rice is added. The fruit, grapes and orange, provide contrasting colour, texture and flavour

MAIN MEAL Serves 6

Overall timing $1\frac{1}{4}$ hours

Equipment Large saucepan or flameproof casserole

Freezing Not recommended

INGREDIENTS

3lb	Boned shoulder of lamb	1.4kg
2	Onions	2
3oz	Butter	75g
2	Garlic cloves	2
	Ground cinnamon	
	Ground coriander	
	Chilli powder	
	Ground turmeric	
	Grated nutmeg	
2	Cloves	2
	Salt and pepper	
$1\frac{1}{2}$ pints	Warm milk	850ml
12oz	Long grain rice	350g
2oz	Seedless white grapes	50g
2oz	Ground almonds	50g
1	Orange	1

METHOD

1. Wipe meat and cut into 2 inch (5cm) cubes. Peel and chop onions. Heat butter in saucepan or casserole. Add onions, peeled and crushed garlic, a pinch each of all the spices, the cloves, salt and pepper. Cook, stirring, for 5 minutes over a low heat. Add meat and brown on all sides.
2. Stir milk into pan. Bring to the boil, then reduce heat, cover and cook for 30 minutes.
3. Add rice and cook for a further 15 minutes or until rice is tender (add extra hot milk if necessary to prevent mixture drying out). Stir occasionally to prevent sticking.
4. Stir grapes and ground almonds into pan. Transfer mixture to warmed serving dish and serve garnished with peeled orange slices.

Pot roast pork with apples

Slightly sharp but firm apples add texture and taste to this easy-to-cook dish

MAIN MEAL Serves 4–6

Overall timing 1½ hours

Equipment Heavy-based casserole with lid, saucepan

Freezing Not recommended

INGREDIENTS

2oz	Butter	50g
3¼lb	Rolled pork	1.5kg
	Salt and pepper	
2 tbsp	Cinnamon	2×15ml
8	Granny Smith apples	8

Below: Roast pork with apples and cinnamon

METHOD

1 Preheat oven to 400F (200C) Gas 6.

2 Melt 1oz (25g) butter in heavy-based casserole. Roll joint in a mixture of salt, pepper and half the cinnamon then brown on all sides. Cover dish and cook on the middle shelf of the oven for about 1 hour, turning joint over halfway through.

3 Peel apples and cut into quarters. Put into a saucepan with remaining butter and cinnamon. Cover and cook for about 10 minutes over a low heat, shaking the pan to prevent sticking. Arrange around the roast 15 minutes before the end of cooking time.

TO SERVE

Remove pork from casserole; slice and place on warmed serving plate. Surround with apples. Make gravy. Serve with green or red cabbage.

Lima yogurt salad

A nourishing and healthy salad topped with a cool minted yogurt dressing, which is simple to make. It's well worthwhile experimenting with yogurt in salad dressings – it's less calorie-laden than oil and vinegar mixes and adds a pleasantly smooth texture. If lima beans are unobtainable, use dried haricot or butter beans

LIGHT LUNCH OR SALAD Serves 4–6

Overall timing 1¼ hours plus overnight soaking and chilling

Equipment 2 saucepans, salad bowl, bowl

Freezing Not recommended

INGREDIENTS

4oz	Lima beans (dried)	125g
8oz	Courgettes	225g
4oz	Button mushrooms	125g
4	Large firm tomatoes	4
	Salt	
	Freshly-ground black pepper	
1–2	Garlic cloves	1–2
5oz	Carton of natural yogurt	141g
2 tbsp	Chopped mint	2×15ml

METHOD

1 Put the beans into a saucepan with plenty of cold water and leave to soak overnight.

2 Next day, drain beans, rinse, cover with fresh water and bring to the boil. Cover and simmer for 45 minutes to 1 hour till tender but still whole.

3 Meanwhile, wash courgettes. Top and tail and cut into ¼ inch (6mm) slices. Wipe and quarter the mushrooms.

4 Blanch the courgettes in boiling water for 4 minutes, add mushrooms and boil for 1 more minute. Drain and rinse under cold water. Drain thoroughly.

5 Blanch and peel the tomatoes and cut into wedges.

6 Drain the lima beans and rinse under cold water till cool. Drain thoroughly and place in the salad bowl with the courgettes, mushrooms and tomatoes. Season well and chill for at least 1 hour.

7 Peel and crush the garlic into a small bowl. Add the yogurt and chopped mint and mix well. Season to taste.

8 Pour dressing over salad and toss lightly till evenly coated. Serve with grilled, warm pitta bread.

Wholemeal bread

A delicious bread which can be made into many shapes. To add crunch, crack 2oz (50g) whole wheat grain in liquidizer for 1 minute, and add with the flour. Save some to sprinkle on top after brushing with salted water (Step 6)

BREAD Makes 2–4 loaves

Overall timing 3 hours minimum

Equipment 2 bowls, polythene bags, loaf tins

INGREDIENTS

3lb	Wholemeal flour	1.4kg
2 tbsp	Salt	2×15ml
2 tbsp	Brown sugar	2×15ml
1oz	Lard	25g
2oz	Fresh yeast*	50g
1½ pints	Warm water	850ml

* or 1oz (25g) dried yeast – see Step 2 of method

METHOD

1 To make the dough with fresh yeast, mix the flour, salt and sugar together in a bowl. Rub in the lard. In another bowl, blend the yeast with the water. Add to flour and mix to scone-like dough that leaves the bowl clean.
2 To make the dough with dried yeast, dissolve 1 teasp (5ml) of the sugar in 9fl oz (250ml) of warm water in a bowl. Now sprinkle the dried yeast on top. Leave till frothy, about 10 minutes. In a mixing bowl, mix flour, salt and the remaining sugar. Rub in the lard, then add the yeast liquid and the rest of the water. Mix to scone-like dough.
3 Knead the dough thoroughly till it feels firm and elastic and no longer sticky. This should take 5–10 minutes.
4 Shape the dough into a ball and place in an oiled polythene bag. Leave the dough to rise till it doubles in size.
5 When risen, turn the dough on to a board and knead again till firm. Divide into 2 or 4, flatten each piece firmly with the knuckles to knock out air. Shape and place in loaf tins.
6 Brush the tops with a little salted water and put each tin into an oiled polythene bag. Leave to rise till the dough comes to just over the top of the tin and springs back when pressed with a floured finger – about 1 hour at room temperature. Preheat the oven during this time to 450F (230C) Gas 8.
7 Bake the loaves on the middle shelf of the oven for 30–40 minutes. Turn out and cool on a wire rack.

Lentil and vegetable soup

A thick mix of fresh and dried vegetables served in bread-lined bowls

LUNCH OR STARTER Serves 6

Overall timing 1½ hours

Equipment Large saucepan, sieve or blender, individual soup bowls

Freezing Not recommended

INGREDIENTS

8oz	Continental lentils	225g
3 pints	Water	1.7 litres
4oz	Streaky bacon rashers	125g
1lb	Fresh broad beans	450g
1lb	Fresh peas	450g
1lb	Cabbage	450g
8oz	Fresh spinach	225g
2 teasp	Salt	2×5ml
	Freshly-ground black pepper	
18	Thin slices of wholemeal bread	18

METHOD

1 Wash and pick over the lentils and put into a saucepan with the water. Bring to the boil and simmer for 45 minutes.
2 Meanwhile, derind and dice the bacon. Shell and wash the beans and peas. Wash and shred the cabbage and spinach.
3 Rub the lentils with their cooking liquor through a sieve or purée in a blender. Return to the saucepan and add the salt and plenty of pepper.
4 Stir in the bacon and vegetables and bring to the boil. Simmer uncovered for about 25 minutes till the vegetables are tender.
5 Taste and adjust the seasoning. Arrange 3 slices of bread in each soup bowl and pour the soup over. Serve immediately.

Above: Lentil and vegetable soup, a hearty lunch or starter that should be served piping hot and poured into deep bowls in which thick slices of wholemeal bread have been arranged

Fancy fish loaf in pastry

Delightful combination of textures in this fish loaf cooked in pastry

LUNCH OR SUPPER Serves 8

Overall timing 2 hours plus cooling and overnight chilling

Equipment 5 bowls, 3 pint (1.7 litre) loaf tin

Freezing Not recommended

INGREDIENTS

	Pastry	
14oz	Plain flour	400g
$\frac{1}{2}$ teasp	Salt	$\frac{1}{2}\times$5ml
5oz	Butter	150g
2	Eggs	2
	Filling	
$1\frac{1}{2}$lb	Tail piece of salmon	700g
1	Small onion	1
2 tbsp	Olive oil	2×15ml
1 tbsp	Lemon juice	15ml
	Salt	
	Freshly-ground black pepper	
2oz	Fresh breadcrumbs	50g
$\frac{1}{4}$ pint	Milk	150ml
1lb	Whiting fillets	450g
2	Eggs	2
1 tbsp	Chopped parsley	15ml
2 tbsp	Anchovy essence	2×15ml

METHOD

1 To make pastry, sift flour and salt into a bowl, rub in butter till mixture resembles fine breadcrumbs. Make a well in centre, add eggs and mix to a soft but not sticky dough adding water (2–3 tbsp/2–3×15ml) if necessary. Knead lightly till smooth, shape into a ball, foil-wrap and chill for 30 minutes.

2 Meanwhile, wipe the salmon, place on board with tail towards you and make a cut along the centre through to the back-bone. Scrape flesh on one side of back-bone away from ribs and remove fillet. Remove fillet from other side of back-bone in same way, then turn fish over and repeat to remove the other 2 fillets.

3 Place fillets skin side down on a board. Grasping thin end of one, slip a knife between skin and flesh at 45° angle, and using a sawing motion, work along fillet to remove skin. Repeat with other fillets, place on shallow dish.

Right: Fancy fish loaf in pastry – a fish pie with superior content and taste

4 Peel and finely chop the onion. Add to salmon with oil, lemon juice and seasoning. Marinate for 15 minutes.

5 Soak breadcrumbs in milk for 5 minutes. Skin whiting fillets, wipe and put into a bowl, then pound to a paste with wooden spoon. Separate eggs. Squeeze out breadcrumbs, add to whiting with 1 egg yolk, parsley, anchovy essence and seasoning, mix well. Whisk egg whites till stiff but not dry, fold into whiting mixture.

6 Preheat oven to 375F (190C) Gas 5. Grease and base-line loaf tin. Roll out two-thirds of the pastry.

7 Use pastry to line tin, pressing it into corners and leaving excess hanging.

8 Spread half the whiting mixture into case. Drain salmon fillets and arrange on top, cover with remaining whiting mixture and smooth top.

9 Roll out remaining pastry, use to cover pie. Trim off excess pastry, crimp edges to seal. Roll trimmings and cut into fancy shapes, arrange on pie. Beat remaining egg yolk and brush over top. Bake in centre of oven for 45 minutes till golden. Cool in tin, then chill overnight to set. Remove from tin, bring to room temperature before serving.

Line loaf tin with the pastry, then layer the pounded whiting and marinated salmon

Cover filling, trim pastry, crimp edges to seal. Decorate, then brush on glaze. Bake

Cod with onions and leeks

The cod is first marinated in lemon juice to bring out its full flavour, then gently cooked with sautéed onions, leeks and a little white wine

MAIN MEAL Serves 4–6

Overall timing 35 minutes

Equipment Deep frying pan or sauté pan

Freezing Not recommended

INGREDIENTS

$1\frac{3}{4}$lb	Cod fillets	750g
3 tbsp	Lemon juice	3×15ml
	Salt	
2	Large onions	2
2	Leeks	2
3 tbsp	Oil	3×15ml
$\frac{1}{4}$ pint	White wine	150ml
2 tbsp	Chopped parsley	2×15ml

METHOD

1 Wash and dry cod fillets. Place in a bowl with lemon juice and salt.

2 Peel and chop onions. Trim, wash and chop leeks. Heat oil in pan and cook onions and leeks gently for a few minutes till softened.

3 Add cod fillets, with any juices, and wine to pan and cook for 15 minutes over a moderate heat. Sprinkle with parsley before serving with mashed potatoes and carrots.

Above: Cod with onions and leeks – white wine is used to enhance the flavour

Squid with ginger and vegetable rice

Chinese-style stir-fried squid are served in a spicy, gingery sauce

Above: To prepare squid, wash thoroughly. Grip head and tentacles and pull away bone and entrails. Cut tentacles off head, then discard head, ink sac, entrails and suckers. Pull away skin

MAIN MEAL Serves 4

Overall timing 30 minutes

Equipment Saucepan, bowl, wok or deep frying pan

Freezing Not recommended

INGREDIENTS

12oz	Long grain rice	350g
2	Large carrots	2
4 tbsp	Oil	4×15ml
2 pints	Water	1.1 litres
	Salt and pepper	
$1\frac{1}{2}$lb	Cleaned squid	700g
1	Bunch of spring onions	1
1 inch	Green ginger	2.5cm
2 teasp	Cornflour	2×5ml
5 tbsp	Dry sherry	5×15ml
2 tbsp	Soy sauce	2×15ml
	Mustard and cress	

METHOD

1 Rinse the rice under cold running water, drain and dry thoroughly. Scrape the carrots and cut lengthways into $\frac{1}{4}$ inch (6mm) slices, then into matchsticks.

2 Heat 2 tbsp (2×15ml) oil in a saucepan, add the carrots and fry, stirring, for 2 minutes. Add the water and bring to the boil, then add a little salt and the rice. Bring back to the boil, stirring, cover tightly and simmer for 15 minutes till the liquid is absorbed.

3 Meanwhile, wash and dry the squid and slice into thin rings. Cut the tentacles into 1 inch (2.5cm) pieces. Wash and trim the spring onions and cut into quarters lengthways, then into 3 inch (7.5cm) lengths. Finely grate or chop the peeled ginger. Blend the cornflour with the sherry in a bowl.
the ginger. Blend the cornflour with the sherry in a bowl.

4 Heat the remaining oil in the wok or frying pan. Add the squid and ginger and stir-fry for 3 minutes.

5 Add the spring onions and soy sauce, stir-fry for further 2 minutes. Stir in the blended cornflour and bring to the boil, stirring constantly. Cook for 2 minutes.

6 Fluff the rice with a fork and spread on a warmed serving dish. Season the squid mixture to taste, then arrange on the rice. Scatter with a little mustard and cress and serve immediately.

Pot black

A thick, black and full-flavoured syrup, treacle is obtained during the early stages of sugar cane refining. Golden syrup, first produced by Abram Lyle, is produced at a later stage. Treacle is really molasses (the "sticky, sticky goo . . . it always sticks to you . . ." featured in an American popular song of the 40s) but that word went out of style in Britain in the 17th century. The word treacle is derived from the Greek *theriake* – literally an antidote to the bite of wild beasts – and *triacle*, an old French word for the mixture of drugs, spices and honey made up by apothecaries as a cure-all. Obviously someone decided that the thick syrup was a combination of the two! Interestingly, in the USA molasses describes the black stuff and treacle means golden syrup.

Treacle gives good colour, flavour and moisture to cakes and puddings and is specially prized for its ability to increase the keeping qualities of baked goods like gingerbread. It is also used in confectionery and particularly for making toffee and fudge. It has slightly bitter overtones so it blends well with savoury foods, too. Used with fatty meats, it counteracts any greasiness. Treacle is also good for adding colour to gravies which haven't gone as brown as you'd have liked.

Treacle can be difficult to manage in cooking because it is so sticky. It is easiest to measure it by weight – 1 tbsp (15ml) is about the same as 1oz (25g). Place the can on the scales and remove the treacle with a spoon that's been dipped in boiling water so the syrup will slide off easily. You'll be able to see how much you have taken by the weight reduction shown on the scales.

Keep the top of a treacle can clean and dry, and seal it well after use – this way it will last for years in a cool, dry place. In health terms, you have to remember that treacle is sugar, but it is rich in calcium (added during processing) and iron and is a gentle laxative. An ounce (28g) contains 75 calories.

Treacle and raisin sponge

A raisin-packed sponge that freezes well and will stand you in good stead if visitors arrive unexpectedly – it's a good idea to make several at a time. Replace some of the flour with soya flour for extra protein

TEA-TIME Cuts into 12

Overall timing 1¾ hours

Equipment 8½ inch (22cm) round cake tin, saucepan, bowl

Freezing Wrap the cold cake in foil, seal, label and freeze. Freezer life: 6 months. To use: thaw in wrappings at room temperature, then unwrap and sift icing sugar over the top

INGREDIENTS

4oz	Butter or margarine	125g
6oz	Treacle	175g
2oz	Golden syrup	50g
8oz	Plain flour	225g
1 teasp	Mixed spice	5ml
2oz	Caster sugar	50g
1 teasp	Bicarbonate of soda	5ml
	Grated rind of 1 lemon	
2	Eggs	2
¼ pint	Milk	150ml
4oz	Seeded raisins	125g
2 tbsp	Icing sugar	2×15ml

METHOD

1 Preheat the oven to 325F (170C) Gas 3. Grease and base-line the tin.
2 Put the fat, treacle and syrup into a saucepan and heat gently till the fat melts. Remove from the heat and allow to cool slightly.
3 Sift the flour, spice, sugar and bicarbonate of soda into a large bowl and make a well in the centre.
4 Add the grated lemon rind with the eggs and the treacle mixture and beat well, adding the milk gradually, till smooth. Stir in the raisins.
5 Pour the mixture into the tin and bake in the centre of the oven for 1¼–1½ hours till springy when pressed lightly.
6 Remove from the oven and leave to cool in the tin for 5 minutes. Remove from the tin, discarding the paper, and place on a wire rack. Leave to cool completely. Sift the icing sugar on top and serve.

Below: Treacle and raisin sponge – a luscious, moist cake flavoured with mixed spice

Treacle scones

A mouthwatering tea-time treat that's really quick to make. Add bran if liked or use wholewheat SR flour

TEA-TIME Makes 12

Overall timing 25 minutes

Equipment 2 baking trays, bowl, rolling-pin, 2 inch (5cm) pastry cutter, wire rack

Freezing Cool completely, but do not split. Pack into polythene bag, seal, label and freeze. Freezer life: 6 months. To use: arrange frozen scones on baking trays. Refresh at 400F (200C) Gas 6 for 10 minutes

INGREDIENTS

12oz	Self-raising flour	350g
3oz	Butter or margarine	75g
2 tbsp	Caster sugar	2×15ml
2 tbsp	Treacle	2×15ml
6–8 tbsp	Milk	6–8× 15ml

METHOD

1. Preheat the oven to 425F (220C) Gas 7. Grease the baking trays.
2. Sift the flour into a bowl and rub in the fat till the mixture resembles fine breadcrumbs. Stir in the sugar and make a well in the centre.
3. Add the treacle and enough milk to mix to a soft dough. Knead very lightly, then pat out to ¾ inch (2cm) thickness.
4. Stamp out circles with the pastry cutter and arrange on the baking trays. Brush tops with rest of milk, then bake in centre of the oven for about 10 minutes till well risen and brown.
5. Remove from the oven and transfer to a wire rack. Leave to cool completely. Split and spread with butter or clotted cream before serving.

cook's know-how

In recent years there has been a revival of interest in bran, mainly because our modern diet does not provide us with enough fibre to keep our bowels functioning as they should. To add bran to your diet is therefore an excellent idea. Try sprinkling a little on your breakfast cereal. In baking, add bran to recipes for bread, scones, buns, fruit cakes and even shortcrust pastry.

Above: Battenberg – contrasting sponge squares wrapped in delicious almond paste

Battenberg

Plain and coloured sponge is neatly layered to produce a check design

TEA-TIME Cuts into 10

Overall timing 1½ hours plus cooling

Equipment Greaseproof paper, swiss roll tin, large bowl, saucepan

Freezing Make cake and complete with almond paste. Wrap well, seal, label and freeze. Freezer life: 4 months. To use: thaw for 2 hours at room temperature

INGREDIENTS

8oz	Butter or margarine	225g
8oz	Caster sugar	225g
4	Eggs	4
8oz	Self-raising flour	225g
4 tbsp	Milk	4×15ml
	Red food colouring	
3 tbsp	Apricot jam	3×15ml
	Caster sugar	
8oz	Almond paste	225g

METHOD

1. Preheat the oven to 375F (190C) Gas 5. Cut out a piece of greaseproof paper 2 inches (5cm) wider than the swiss roll tin. Make a 1 inch (2.5cm) pleat down the centre of the paper and place in the centre of the tin so that it divides it in half lengthways. Brush greaseproof lightly with oil.
2. In a large bowl, cream the butter or margarine and the sugar until pale and fluffy. Beat in the eggs one at a time. Sift the flour and gradually fold into creamed mixture with a metal spoon. Add milk and mix to soft consistency.
3. Spread half the mixture into one side of the prepared tin. Add a few drops of food colouring to the remaining mixture and beat well so that colouring is evenly distributed. Spread coloured mixture into other half of the tin.
4. Bake on the centre shelf of the oven for about 45 minutes, or until well risen and firm to the touch. Turn out of tin and leave to cool on wire rack.
5. Trim edges and cut each cake in half lengthways. Warm the jam in a small pan. Spread one strip of plain cake with jam and place one pink strip on top; repeat process with pink strip as base. Stick two halves of cake together with jam.
6. Sprinkle caster sugar over working surface and roll out almond paste to a rectangle large enough to cover cake.
7. Spread remaining jam over the outside of the cake, then wrap in the almond paste, sealing join well. Crimp edges and lightly score top with diamond pattern using a sharp knife, if liked.

Puff pastry

Butter is the vital ingredient for the light layers of crispness used to hold sweet and savoury fillings

PASTRY

Overall timing 3¾ hours including chilling time

Equipment Greaseproof paper, rolling-pin

Freezing Wrap in film or foil, label and freeze. Freezer life: 3 months. To use: thaw for about 8 hours in fridge

INGREDIENTS

9oz	Plain flour	250g
	Salt	
4oz	Softened butter	125g
8 tbsp	Chilled water	8×15ml
4oz	Hard butter	125g

1 *Flour, salt, softened butter and water are mixed together to make a dough*

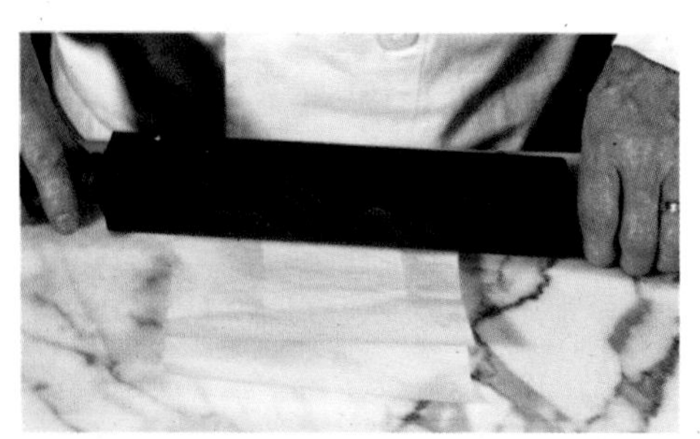

2 *Hard butter is rolled to a rectangle between sheets of greaseproof paper*

3 *Centre rolled butter on rectangle of dough. Fold top third down, bottom third up*

METHOD

1 Place flour, salt and half the softened butter, cut into pieces, on clean work surface. Work the ingredients with your fingers till mixture is like crumbs.

2 Make a well in centre of crumbs and add rest of softened butter. Pour in water and mix quickly to a dough. Cover and place in fridge for 1 hour.

3 At the end of this period, place hard butter between 2 sheets of greaseproof paper. Roll out to a rectangle about 5×3 inches (13×8cm).

4 On a lightly floured surface, roll out dough to a rectangular shape about 10×8 inches (25×20cm). Remove greaseproof and place butter in the middle of the dough. Fold in the top and bottom thirds of the dough to enclose butter in a parcel (see step-by-step pictures below).

5 Give the dough a half turn so that side seam is on your left. Roll out to a rectangle about 5×14 inches (13×36cm). Fold in top and bottom thirds of dough as before. Wrap and chill for 15 minutes.

6 Repeat rolling, turning and folding 4 more times, chilling between rolling.

7 Roll out dough to rectangle for a last time. Bring the 2 small sides to the centre, then fold in half like a book. Cover and chill for 1 hour.

TO USE

After final chilling, roll out dough to ¼ inch (6mm) thickness then cut out as required. Glaze with beaten egg or milk for savoury dishes. Puff pastry should be cooked in a very hot oven (450F, 230C, Gas 8) for about 15 minutes.

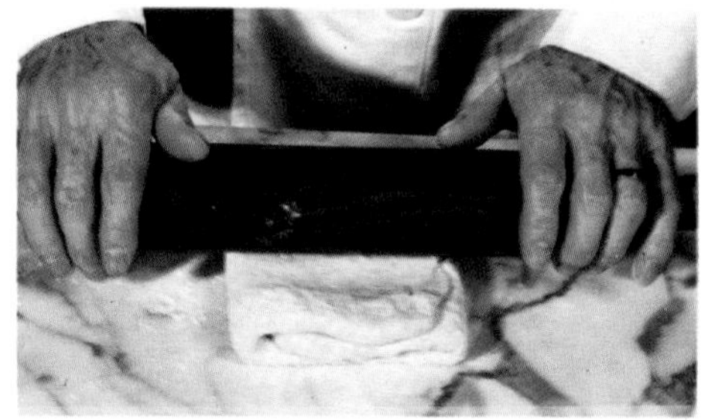

4 *Half turn dough so folds are at sides, roll (forward only), then fold again as Step 3*

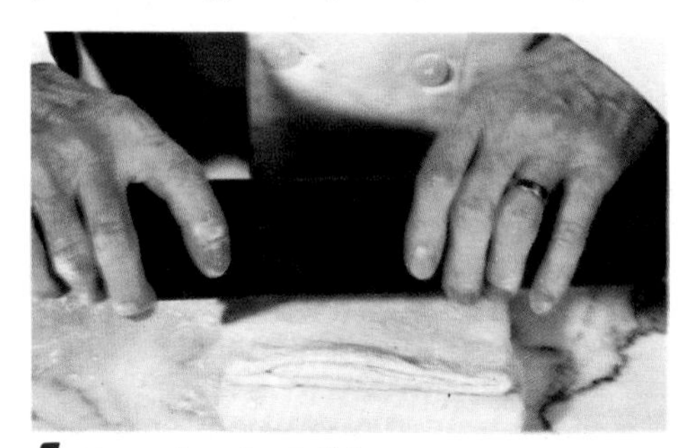

5 *Wrap dough, chill for 15 minutes. Repeat rolling, folding, chilling 4 times more*

Twelfth Night cake

There's a bean or almond hidden in this Epiphany cake. It's delicious to serve at any time of the year

TEA-TIME OR DESSERT Serves 6–8

Overall timing 1 hour plus pastry preparation time

Equipment 10 inch (25cm) plate, brush, baking tray

Freezing Freeze before cooking but do not brush with egg white. Open freeze, wrap and label. Freezer life: 3 months. To use: thaw in fridge for 8 hours, brush with egg white, then proceed as Step 7

INGREDIENTS

	Pastry	
9oz	Puff pastry	250g
	Frangipane filling	
2oz	Caster sugar	50g
1oz	Soft butter	25g
1	Egg	1
2oz	Ground almonds	50g
	Almond essence	
1 tbsp	Rum or lemon juice	15ml
2 tbsp	Icing sugar	2×15ml
1	Bean or almond	1

METHOD

1 Prepare pastry as recipe, this page.
2 Remove pastry from fridge. Cut it into two halves. Roll out each half in a circular shape 1 inch (2.5cm) thick. Use the plate as a guide to make two circles. Cover, chill for 30 minutes.
3 Meanwhile, prepare the frangipane by kneading sugar, butter, egg yolk, ground almonds, few drops almond essence and rum or lemon juice.
4 Preheat oven to 450F (230C) Gas 8.
5 Wet the baking tray and place one round of pastry on it. Brush the edge with egg white.
6 Spread the frangipane on the pastry to within 1 inch (2.5cm) of the edge. Place a bean or an almond on filling and cover with the second pastry round. Press the edges together, then crimp the edges with a knife. Brush the top of the pastry with egg white, then mark a swirl pattern with a sharp knife.
7 Place the cake in oven and leave to cook for 15 minutes. Remove and dust the top with icing sugar, then return to the top shelf of the oven for 3–4 minutes to glaze the top.

Left: Twelfth Night cake

A satisfying spread

Finland is a land of coniferous forests, great lakes and islands with long, indented coastlines. The fifth largest country in Europe, one third of its area lies above the Arctic circle. Although snow blankets parts of the country for eight to nine months of the year, the summers are usually very warm and the climate more temperate than that of Alaska, which is at roughly the same latitude. Surprisingly, Finland is almost self-sufficient in food.

Although geographically Finland is part of Scandinavia, the Finns themselves are of a different ethnic origin to the Swedes, Norwegians and Danes. This is reflected in their language, customs and, to a large extent, in their cookery which has been influenced by neighbouring Sweden who ruled Finland from the 11th until the 19th century (Swedish is still an official language); Russia who annexed Finland's eastern province of Karelia in 1944; and Lapland.

Filling foods

In a climate as cold as Finland's, the emphasis is on nourishing, filling foods made with ingredients that will store well in the winter. Bread and porridge are the staple items of diet, rye flour and whole grains being most commonly used for the purpose. Porridge, historically the forerunner of bread, is made from whole rye, wheat or barley grains, and there are many different varieties and ways of preparing them. One barley porridge is called *talkkuna*. Another, *pito-ja-joulupuuro*, is simmered like a stew in milk for five hours or more, which has the effect of turning it pink. A traditional Easter porridge pudding is called *mämmi*. It is made with rye flour, treacle, orange peel and malt, and is prepared in an unusual way, being first boiled, then whipped and finally baked. *Mämmi* used to be baked in birch baskets, but this is now frowned upon by conservationists, and cardboard baskets are used instead.

Finnish bread is famous throughout Scandinavia for its delicious flavour. It is most often made from rye flour, and the most popular one has a slightly sour taste. Sour dough is made by mixing fermented dough with unleavened dough – the bacteria in the fermented dough makes the dough rise as though yeast had been used. In more isolated areas, a hole is punched in the dough before baking, and the circular loaves are afterwards hung on horizontal poles to dry – a good standby in the winter. Finns also eat a lot of rye crispbread.

In winter, soup is made with meat offal and blood, cooked with potatoes, and with a large chunk of buttered rye bread or dumplings floating in it. Salmon soup is a delicious dish when in season. In high summer, a colourful soup called *kesäkeitto* is made from whatever young fresh vegetables are available, but usually contains carrots, potatoes and spinach.

Importance of fish

Fish has an important place in the Finnish diet. Although the Baltic herring is enjoyed fresh, pickled and preserved in various ways, freshwater fish are just as popular. Pike, trout and, of course, salmon are commonly eaten. A substitute for caviare is the roe of an otherwise tasteless fish, the burbot, which lives in the icy lakes above the Arctic Circle. Crayfish, which also live in these lakes, come into season near the end of the Finnish summer, in July, and are fished until winter sets in. Early in the season, the Finns hold crayfish parties – crayfish are caught and consumed by the light of paper lanterns to the accompaniment of large quantities of ice-cold Finnish or Russian vodka. All fish, including crayfish, are cooked with dill, which is the favourite herb in Finland.

The most famous Finnish institution is, of course, the sauna, which is basically a small wooden hut with a huge stove in it and this plays its part in Finnish cookery. Large pork-and-mutton sausages are grilled or boiled in a pot on the sauna stove and eaten after the sauna with Finnish beer. Many meats are smoked in the sauna. Finns like the strong gamey flavour of smoked meat, and even prepare chicken with juniper berries, so that it tastes like game. Reindeer meat is popular – the flesh is tough and stringy but full of flavour, and the tongue is considered a great delicacy.

Mutton, pork and veal are the most popular meats, beef cattle being difficult and expensive to rear in the cold climate. The most unusual meat dish is *kalakukko*, typically Finnish because it combines fish and meat. It consists of a thick paste of rye dough spread with a mixture of tiny freshwater fish and strips of lean and fat pork. The dough is rolled into a ball and slowly baked for a long time (5 or 6 hours).

Russian influence is marked in the cooking of Karelia. The Karelians make pasties which they call *piirakka*, their version of the *pirogen* or *pirozki* of the Russians. The rye-flour pasty is stuffed with rice, potatoes, carrot or cheese, then deep-fried. The Karelians also eat beef stroganoff, *bortsch* and *blinis*, buckwheat pancakes made with a yeast dough. *Kiisseli* (Russian: *kissel*), another dish common to Russians and Finns, is a berry pudding in which the berries are stewed and the juice thickened with potato flour.

Wild berries

A wonderful variety of wild autumn berries grow in Finland, including some that are unique to Scandinavia, such as the cloudberry, whortleberry and honeyberry. All these are made into liqueurs and splendid puddings, such as *vatkattu marjapuuro*, in which berry juice is whipped with semolina, potato flour or sugar into a thick, pink foam. Another popular Finnish sweet is *pappilan hätävara* "parsonage standby", which is similar to English trifle. Bread or small biscuits are soaked in fruit juice or liqueur and layered with cranberries (see recipe below). Pancakes are popular, eaten with berry jam. So are *tippaleivät*, a liquid doughnut from yeast dough, that is so similar to the *zelebies* eaten all over Asia, it might be one of the dishes the Finns brought with them when they migrated from Central Asia during the dark ages.

The strong, fresh flavours and unusual combination in Finnish food make it distinctive, yet surprisingly light and digestible – as exhilarating as the climate and as attractive as the tableware for which the country is famous.

CRANBERRY LAYER DESSERT

Ingredients 1¼lb (600g) fresh cranberries; 6 tbsp (6×15ml) lemon juice; 6oz (175g) caster sugar; 6oz (175g) rye bread; ¾ pint (400ml) double or whipping cream.

Method Wash cranberries and remove stalks. Cook cranberries and lemon juice in an open pan for 12–14 minutes. Remove from heat, add sugar and cool. Crumble rye bread or place in blender. Whip cream till it holds soft peaks. Mix all but 3 tbsp (3×15ml) crumbs with three-quarters of cranberry sauce. Put a layer of cranberry mixture into six tall serving glasses, cover with layer of cream. Repeat layers, finishing with reserved cranberry sauce. Decorate with a swirl of cream and sprinkle with remaining crumbs. Chill.

Serves 6

Right: Back – Hernekeitto (recipe page 556); centre – Karjalan paisti (recipe page 557) served with Potato and onion purée (recipe page 557); far right – Cranberry layer dessert (recipe above), a Finnish trifle called Pappilan hätävara

Countdown

Hernekeitto
Karjalan paisti
Potato and onion purée
Cranberry layer dessert

The people of Finland need nourishing and filling foods that store well in winter to keep out the cold, such as pulses like dried peas.
The casserole here combines three meats to give a really delectable flavour. In the dessert, the Finns often add a few drops of their own liqueur to add a final touch

Night before Soak peas overnight for soup

4 hours before Prepare meat and onions. Preheat oven to 325F (170C) Gas 3. Assemble casserole and cook for about 3 hours

2½ hours before Simmer bacon knuckle and soaked peas for 1½–2 hours

2 hours before Cook cranberries and cool. Make up dessert and chill

1 hour before Peel potatoes and place in cold salted water. Prepare onions

30 mins before Cook potatoes and fry onions. Remove bacon from pea mixture and cut into cubes. Purée two-thirds of peas. Return all peas to pan. Check meat in casserole for tenderness

10 mins before Mash potatoes, make up recipe, place in serving dish and keep warm. (If browning in oven, start preparation 45 mins before meal.) Bring soup to boil and add bacon. Transfer to warm tureen

Serve soup with crispbread. Place gherkins in dish to accompany casserole. Serve casserole with potato dish. Remove dessert from fridge before starting main course. Serve dessert.

The Finns would probably drink beer with this menu; selecting one of the own liqueurs, made from berries, to round off the meal. However, a full-flavoured red wine would also fit the bill, such as a Côtes-du-Rhône or a Barbera. Try a Vouvray with the dessert.

Hernekeitto

This nourishing pea and bacon soup is a speciality of Finland. Be sure to taste the soup before seasoning as smoked bacon tends to be salty even with overnight soaking

STARTER OR LUNCH Serves 6

Overall timing 2¾ hours plus overnight soaking

Equipment Large saucepan, blender

Freezing As Split pea soup. Freezer life: 1 month

Freezing Pour into a rigid container, leaving 1 inch (2.5cm) headspace. Seal, label and freeze. Freezer life: 1 month. To use: place block in a saucepan, heat gently till thawed. Bring to the boil and adjust seasoning.

INGREDIENTS

12oz	Dried whole green peas	350g
4 pints	Water	2.3 litres
2lb	Knuckle of smoked bacon	900g
	Salt and pepper	

METHOD

1 Wash and pick over peas. Place in the saucepan and cover with the cold water. Leave to soak overnight.
2 Add the washed bacon knuckle to the pan and bring to the boil. Skim off any scum. Cover and simmer for 1½–2 hours, till the bacon and peas are tender.
3 Remove and drain the bacon joint. Discard the skin and bone and cut the meat into small cubes.
4 Reserve a third of the peas. Purée the remaining peas in a blender or by pressing through a sieve. Return the puréed and whole peas to saucepan. Bring to the boil, stirring occasionally.
5 Add the diced bacon, and season. taste. Pour into warmed tureen and serve with Finnish rye crispbread.

TO SERVE

Pour into a warmed tureen and serve with Finnish rye crispbread or a crispbread of your choice. There is an exciting selection of crispbreads on sale these days, including wheat, bran, and bran with sesame seeds. Some are very light and are specifically for slimmers, while others are more satisfying. Crispbread is a useful storecupboard item, and a good standby if your supply of bread runs out. Remember, once opened, store them in an airtight container,

Below: Hernekeitto – serve in small helpings as a starter or in larger ones for lunch

Karjalan paisti

From the Karelian region of Finland, gherkins are an essential accompaniment to this rich one-pot meal. It includes three sorts of meat, which are cooked very slowly in the oven to ensure maximum tenderness

MAIN MEAL Serves 6

Overall timing 3½ hours

Equipment Ovenproof casserole

Freezing Cool, pack into rigid container, cover, label and freeze. Freezer life: 2 months. To use: thaw for 4 hours, then heat through slowly but thoroughly

INGREDIENTS

1lb	Stewing beef	450g
1lb	Lean pork	450g
1lb	Boned shoulder of lamb	450g
1lb	Onions	450g
1 teasp	Ground allspice	5ml
	Salt	
	Freshly-ground black pepper	
¾ pint	Beef stock	400ml
6	Large gherkins	6

METHOD

1 Preheat oven to 325F (170C) Gas 3.
2 Trim the meats but don't remove all lamb fat. Cut meats into 1 inch (2.5cm) cubes, but keep them separate. Peel and slice onions.
3 Spread half the beef over base of casserole and sprinkle with ¼ teasp (¼×5ml) allspice, salt and pepper. Cover with a quarter of the onions and half the pork, ¼ teasp (¼×5ml) allspice, salt and pepper.
4 Repeat layering, then top with lamb. Pour over the stock (made with 1 cube if necessary). Cook on the centre shelf of the oven, uncovered, for about 3 hours until the meat is tender and some of the liquid has evaporated. Serve immediately with large gherkins and Potato and onion purée or creamy mashed potatoes.

Above: Karjalan paisti, a nourishing meat casserole served with side dishes of potatoes and gherkins (kurkku).

Potato and onion purée

This soft, creamy mixture can be served as is or baked till golden

VEGETABLE Serves 6

Overall timing 30 minutes

Equipment Saucepan, frying pan, ovenproof dish

Freezing Not recommended

INGREDIENTS

3lb	Floury potatoes	1.4kg
	Salt	
3	Large onions	3
4½oz	Butter	115g
	Freshly-ground white pepper	
6 tbsp	Milk	6×15ml
½ teasp	Freshly-grated nutmeg	½×5ml

METHOD

1 Peel and quarter the potatoes. Cover with cold salted water, bring to boil and cook for about 20 minutes.
2 If using, preheat the oven to 450F (230C) Gas 8. Peel and finely chop the onions. Heat 1½oz (40g) of the butter in a frying pan and fry the onions till soft and transparent – not browned. Sprinkle with salt and pepper.
3 Drain the potatoes and mash. Melt remaining butter in saucepan with milk, then add the onions, nutmeg and potatoes. Stir over gentle heat till light and fluffy. Serve immediately.

VARIATION

Spread mixture in an ovenproof dish and smooth the surface. Dot with 1oz (25g) butter and cook in the centre of the oven for about 15 minutes till golden.

cook's know-how

Gherkins are a variety of cucumber pickled in flavoured brine or vinegar. They are very popular all over Europe, being one of the few vegetables to prosper outdoors in summer (they are grown like ridge cucumbers), and because they are ideal for preserving they can be enjoyed in winter too. They can be combined with fennel and dill to make a tasty pickle. Gherkins can range from 2–5 inches (5–13cm) in length.

Salami rolls

You could serve these at a party or to start off a light summer meal. The jellied stock, which is a tasty and attractive finishing touch, should be made the night before so that it sets well

STARTER Makes 12

Overall timing 45 minutes not including jellied stock

Equipment Saucepan, muslin or fine sieve, 2 bowls, cake tin, cocktail sticks

Freezing Not recommended

Below: Salami rolls, an appetizing starter

INGREDIENTS

$1\frac{1}{4}$ pints	Light stock	700ml
2 teasp	Wine vinegar	2×5ml
1 tbsp	White wine	15ml
	Pinch of sugar	
2 tbsp	Powdered gelatine	2×15ml
8oz	Cream cheese	225g
1 tbsp	Soured cream	15ml
2 tbsp	Parmesan	2×15ml
4oz	Bottle of cocktail onions	110g
12	Large salami slices	12
	Thick mayonnaise	
	Fresh parsley	

METHOD

1 Put the stock, vinegar, wine and sugar into a saucepan and bring to the boil. Remove from heat and strain through muslin or a very fine sieve. Leave to cool.

2 Put gelatine and a little of the stock into a bowl over a saucepan of boiling water. Stir until gelatine has dissolved. Add to the cooled stock.

3 Lightly grease a cake tin or other suitable container. Pour in stock and leave to set in fridge.

4 Put the cream cheese and soured cream into a bowl and mix well together. Stir in the grated Parmesan. Drain and finely chop the onions and stir into the cheese mixture.

5 Put a little of the mixture on to each salami slice. Pull the slice together and secure with half a cocktail stick.

6 Remove jelly from its container and chop it roughly with a wetted knife.

7 Spoon the chopped jelly over a serving dish. Arrange the salami rolls on top. Garnish with thick mayonnaise, some chopped parsley and parsley sprigs.

Giblet and vegetable soup

Tapioca adds substance to a basic chicken giblet/vegetable soup

SOUP Serves 4

Overall timing 1¾ hours

Equipment Large saucepan, muslin, sieve

Freezing Not recommended

INGREDIENTS

1	Carrot	1
2	Leeks	2
1	Stalk of celery	1
1lb	Chicken giblets	450g
1	Onion	1
1	Clove	1
2½ pints	Cold water	1.5 litres
	Bouquet garni	
	Salt	
	Freshly-ground black pepper	
2 tbsp	Seed pearl tapioca	2×15ml

METHOD

1 Scrape and roughly chop the carrot. Wash, trim and chop the leeks and celery. Wash the giblets. Peel the onion and spike with the clove. Put into a large saucepan with the water, bouquet garni and salt and pepper. Bring to the boil, then skim off any scum. Cover the pan, then reduce the heat and simmer for at least 1 hour.

2 Strain the stock through a muslin-lined sieve, then return to the pan. Bring back to the boil and sprinkle in the tapioca, stirring constantly. Simmer for 30 minutes till thickened.

3 Taste and adjust seasoning and serve immediately with hot buttered toast.

cook's know-how

The giblets of a chicken contain the heart, liver, gizzard and neck. They should be removed from the bird and stored separately in the refrigerator for up to 2 days only, or frozen for 3 months. Always check the giblets are inside the chicken. Chicken livers, rich in iron, have a delicate flavour and can be used in various ways. They can be made into a pâté, skewered and grilled, sautéed in butter, or added to stuffing. Always remove any bitter green gall first.

Above: Rich bean soup – served with fried croûtons for a perfect finish

Rich bean soup

Rich, brown and well textured, this soup may be sprinkled with chopped crisply fried bacon as well as croûtons

SOUP Serves 4

Overall timing 1¾ hours plus overnight soaking

Equipment Bowl, saucepan, frying pan, blender

Freezing Not recommended

INGREDIENTS

7oz	Dried kidney beans	200g
2	Sprigs of parsley and	2
2	Bay leaves *or*	2
1	bouquet garni	1
2	Onions	2
1	Clove	1
1	Garlic clove	1
1 teasp	Salt	5ml
2 tbsp	Dripping	2×15ml
3	Tomatoes *or*	3
1 tbsp	tomato paste	15ml
	Black pepper	
	Caster sugar	
1	Beef stock cube	1

METHOD

1 Place the beans in a bowl and cover with water. Leave to soak overnight.

2 Drain beans and place in saucepan. Cover with fresh water, add the parsley and bay leaves tied together or a bouquet garni, 1 of the onions (spiked with the clove) and garlic, peeled.

3 Bring to the boil over a medium heat and cook for about 35 minutes. Add salt and continue cooking for a further 35 minutes.

4 Melt the dripping in frying pan. Peel and chop remaining onion and cook for a few minutes. Remove from heat, lift out onion with a draining spoon and place in blender.

5 Drain beans and strain cooking liquor into a measuring jug. Discard onion and clove. Put beans into blender with tomatoes or 1 tbsp (15ml) paste, pepper, caster sugar and 1¾ pints/1 litre of stock (made up of cooking liquor and water plus a beef cube). Blend for a few seconds then pour into saucepan.

6 Bring gently to the boil, then simmer for 15 minutes stirring frequently. Taste and adjust seasoning if necessary.

TO SERVE

Pour into tureen and serve with croûtons.

Aubergine salad

Bring some holiday sun to your table with this delicious salad – it can be served either as a starter or as an accompaniment to cold meat. If you haven't any fresh herbs, use half a teaspoon ($\frac{1}{2}\times$5ml) each of the same kinds, dried instead. You'll find they add just as much flavour

STARTER Serves 4–6

Overall timing 1 hour 20 minutes including refrigeration

Equipment Saucepan

Freezing Not recommended

INGREDIENTS

2	Aubergines	2
$\frac{1}{4}$ pint	Water	150ml
$\frac{1}{4}$ pint	Olive oil	150ml
1 teasp	Salt	5ml
1	Garlic clove	1
2	Onions	2
2	Sprigs of fresh chervil	2
2	Sprigs of fresh tarragon	2
2	Sprigs of fresh parsley	2
1	Green capsicum	1
1	Red capsicum	1
4	Tomatoes	4
3 tbsp	Lemon juice	3×15ml
2 tbsp	Tomato paste	2×15ml
	Salt	
	Freshly-ground black pepper	

METHOD

1 Remove stalks from the aubergines, then wash and dry them. Cut into $\frac{1}{4}$ inch (6mm) slices.

2 Bring the water to the boil in a saucepan and add the aubergines, olive oil, salt and the garlic, peeled and crushed. Cook for 10 minutes or until just tender. Lift slices out with a draining spoon and place in a serving dish. Set cooking liquor aside.

3 Finely chop one onion and cut the other into rings; finely chop the herbs; deseed and slice the capsicums; quarter the tomatoes. Place all these in the serving bowl with the aubergines.

4 Add the lemon juice, tomato paste, salt and pepper to the cooking liquor and mix well. Check seasoning and adjust if necessary.

5 Pour dressing over vegetables in serving dish and mix in well. Chill for 1 hour before serving.

Marinated anchovies

When fresh anchovies are about, try this unusual dish (it should be eaten within 24 hours as it will not keep longer) This recipe is equally delicious if you use fresh sardines, whiting or sprats instead of anchovies

STARTER Serves 4

Overall timing 45 minutes plus chilling

Equipment Frying pan, deep dish, saucepan

Freezing Not recommended

INGREDIENTS

1lb	Fresh anchovies	450g
2oz	Flour	50g
	Oil	
	Salt	
2	Bay leaves	2
1	Onion	1
1	Garlic clove	1
$\frac{1}{4}$ pint	Wine vinegar	150ml
$\frac{1}{4}$ pint	Water	150ml
	Few pinches of dried marjoram	
6	Black peppercorns	6

METHOD

1 Cut anchovies along the underside and open out. Cut off the heads and remove back-bones. Leave the tails on.

2 Flour fish lightly. Heat oil in frying pan and fry fish quickly on both sides until cooked. Drain on kitchen paper.

3 Arrange anchovies in layers in a deep dish. Sprinkle lightly with salt. Put the bay leaves, sliced onion, crushed garlic, vinegar, water, marjoram and peppercorns into a saucepan. Bring to the boil and simmer, uncovered, for about 15 minutes.

4 Pour marinade over the anchovies. They should be completely covered, so add extra water if necessary. Cover and chill for a few hours or overnight.

Below: Anchovy back-bones are easily removed

Below: Marinated anchovies – to serve chilled as a starter or fish course

Above: Savoury apple rice — crisp and crunchy lunch or supper dish

Savoury apple rice

A simply prepared sweet-and-sour dish that makes a colourful light meal or accompaniment to grilled meat. If you want to make it more substantial, add leftover chopped lamb or shelled prawns

LUNCH OR SUPPER — Serves 4

Overall timing 20 minutes

Equipment 2 saucepans

Freezing Not recommended

INGREDIENTS

9oz	Rice	250g
	Salt	
2 tbsp	Oil	2×15ml
2	Apples	2
1	Onion	1
3 tbsp	Sultanas	3×15ml
2 tbsp	Flaked almonds	2×15ml
2oz	Mushrooms	50g
2oz	Black olives	50g
2oz	Stuffed green olives	50g
2 teasp	Brown sugar	2×5ml
1 tbsp	Curry powder	15ml

METHOD

1 Put the rice in a large saucepan of boiling, salted water and cook for 15 minutes or until done.

2 Meanwhile, heat oil in another saucepan. Add chopped apples – reserving a few slices for decoration – and finely chopped onion and cook through, stirring occasionally to prevent sticking.

3 Stir in the sultanas, almonds, wiped and sliced mushrooms and olives and cook for a few minutes. Add a pinch of salt, sugar and curry powder. Mix well and cook for 3–4 minutes. (If preferred, use gherkins instead of olives.)

4 Remove rice from heat and drain well. Combine with the curried mixture, garnish with slices of apple and serve alone or as an accompaniment to grilled lamb or pork chops.

cook's know-how

Dried apples are a good standby in a storecupboard as they keep well. If the weather's constantly warm with very little rain about you can dry them yourself by the natural method. Peel and core the apples, cut into thick rings then thread on to strings. Protect the lengths with a loose sleeve of muslin and hang from a ceiling that has a constant flow of warm, dry air. Leave till well dried.

You can also dry apples in the oven. Peel and core them, cut into rings $\frac{1}{4}$ inch (6mm) thick. Place immediately in salt/water solution, 1 teasp/5ml per pint/560ml, to prevent discoloration. After a few minutes, lift rings out and dry well. Arrange rings in single layers, not touching, on baking trays. Put into cool oven (not more than 275F, 140C, Gas 1) with the door slightly ajar. Drying will take about 6 hours – the rings should feel spongy, not wet when pressed with the fingertips. Leave for a further 12 hours in a dry place, then wrap in greaseproof.

Potato ham salad

A filling and creamy meal-in-itself salad containing smoked ham and vegetables

LUNCH OR SUPPER Serves 4

Overall timing 40 minutes

Equipment Saucepan, 2 bowls

Freezing Not recommended

INGREDIENTS

2lb	Waxy potatoes	900g
	Salt	
6	Stalks of celery	6
8oz	Smoked ham	225g
3	Spring onions	3
¼ pint	Carton of single cream	150ml
	Freshly-ground black pepper	
2 tbsp	Cider vinegar	2×15ml

METHOD

1 Scrub the potatoes but do not peel. Cover with cold salted water and bring to the boil. Simmer for about 30 minutes till tender. Meanwhile, trim, wash and slice the celery and shred the ham.

2 Wash, trim and chop the onions and stir into the cream with salt and pepper.

3 Drain the potatoes, rinse, then peel and slice thickly into a bowl. Add the celery, shredded ham and vinegar.

4 Pour the cream mixture over the salad and toss carefully. Arrange in serving dish and serve immediately.

VARIATIONS

Soured cream, a specially cultured single cream, is an excellent alternative to single cream as it gives a slight bite to the dressing. If you are watching your calorie intake, use half soured cream and half natural yogurt.

Small new potatoes are delicious in this salad, left with their skins on and halved. Other cold cooked meats could be used instead of smoked ham.

Below: Wiener schnitzel – one of the best-known Viennese dishes

Wiener schnitzel

Crisply crumbed escalopes of veal make a simple, attractive meal. Serve with lemon for added flavour

LUNCH OR SUPPER Serves 4

Overall timing 25 minutes plus chilling time

Equipment 3 shallow bowls, large flat dish, large frying pan

Freezing Prepare and freeze raw. Wrap in polythene with foil separating slices. Exclude air, seal, label and freeze. Freezer life: 3 months. To use: leave to thaw and cook for 2–3 minutes on each side

INGREDIENTS

4×5oz	Slices of veal	4×150g
	Salt	
2 tbsp	Plain flour	2×15ml
1	Egg	1
2oz	Breadcrumbs	50g
1oz	Butter	25g
2oz	Pork dripping	50g
2	Lemons	2
	Sprigs of parsley	

METHOD

1 Rinse veal slices and dry well on kitchen paper. Mix salt and flour together in a bowl. Beat egg in another bowl. Place breadcrumbs in a third bowl.

2 Dip veal slices into flour, then into the egg and finally coat both sides with breadcrumbs. If possible, chill for 30 minutes on a large flat dish to help the egg and crumb layer adhere.

Cherval omelette

An omelette flavoured with chervil and parsley. Serve with a salad and French bread, if liked

LIGHT LUNCH OR SUPPER Serves 4

Overall timing 15 minutes

Equipment Measuring jug, omelette pan

Freezing Not recommended

INGREDIENTS

8	Eggs	8
	Salt and pepper	
3 tbsp	Chopped chervil *or*	3x15ml
1 tbsp	dried chervil	15ml
1 tbsp	Chopped parsley	15ml
2oz	Butter	50g

METHOD

1 Break the eggs into the measuring jug. Season with salt and pepper, add chopped herbs and lightly beat.

2 Melt a quarter of the butter in an omelette pan over a high heat. When the butter begins to froth, pour in a quarter of the egg mixture. As the omelette starts to set, run a spatula round the edge to loosen it and tilt pan to let uncooked egg run underneath.

3 When firm at the edges but still runny in the centre, fold omelette over and slide on to serving plate. Keep it warm while you make three more omelettes similarly. Serve with a tomato salad.

cook's know-how

Chervil is a good plant for growing indoors. It likes semi-shade in summer and full sun in winter – just the sort of problem that gives gardeners grey hairs. However, a plant grown in a pot on a sunny windowsill will prosper. Once it's flourishing, place it on the table and let your guests help themselves to the leaves to add to salads or egg dishes. But do provide scissors to snip off the leaves – it's a delicate plant and will come up by the roots if tugged. Chervil can be bought dried. It holds its colour well but not everyone considers that it keeps its taste. If you want to store chervil and have a freezer, you could try open freezing washed fresh sprigs, or pack the leaves into ice cube trays, cover them with water and freeze. The cubes can be transferred into a plastic bag and sealed. Simply remove the number of cubes you want to add to the dish you're cooking.

Below: Chervil omelette – delicate flavourful combination of eggs and herbs

3 Heat butter and pork dripping in a large frying pan. Add slices two at a time and cook for 2–3 minutes on each side. Place on a warmed serving plate and garnish with lemon slices and parsley. Serve wedges of lemon separately. Anchovy fillets and capers are other suitable garnishes for this dish.

cook's know-how

The veal slices must be less than ¼ inch (6mm) thick for this dish. If you have bought thicker ones they can be beaten thinner; to do this, place each veal slice between two pieces of waxed or non-stick paper. Beat evenly and firmly with a rolling pin or meat bat.

Above: Braised beef with pumpkin – cut the meat into thick, chunky slices to serve

Braised beef with pumpkin

The unusual addition of pumpkin gives a slight sweetness to this dish. Pumpkins are no more difficult to grow than marrows: British pumpkins weigh from 10–15lb (4.5–6kg)

MAIN MEAL Serves 6

Overall timing $2\frac{1}{2}$ hours

Equipment Fine string, flameproof casserole

Freezing Not recommended

INGREDIENTS

2lb	Top rump of beef	900g
1	Onion	1
2 tbsp	Oil	2×15ml
$\frac{1}{4}$ pint	Beef stock	150ml
	Salt	
	Freshly-ground black pepper	
$1\frac{1}{4}$lb	Pumpkin	600g
3fl oz	Dry white wine	90ml

METHOD

1 Preheat the oven to 325F (170C) Gas 3.

2 Wipe and trim the meat and tie into a neat shape with fine string. Peel and thinly slice the onion. Heat the oil in the casserole, add onion and fry till transparent. Add the meat and fry over a high heat till browned all over.

3 Add the stock (made with a cube if necessary) and seasoning, cover and cook in the centre of the oven for 1 hour.

4 Meanwhile, to prepare the pumpkin, scrape out the seeds and fibrous centre. Remove the skin and cut the flesh into chunks. Add to the casserole with the wine. Cover and cook for 1 hour till the meat is tender. Taste and adjust seasoning.

5 Remove the string, slice the meat thickly and arrange in a warmed serving dish. Arrange the pumpkin around meat and spoon juices over.

6 Serve immediately with creamed potatoes and a green vegetable.

VARIATION

This is an excellent dish to prepare in a pressure cooker. Fry the onion in the cooker, add the meat and fry, then add stock and seasoning. Put on the lid and bring to High pressure. Cook for 30 minutes. Reduce pressure quickly, add pumpkin, bring back to High pressure and cook for 10 minutes. Reduce pressure at room temperature and complete Steps 5 and 6.

Bacon and cabbage bake

A warming and substantial family meal, spiced with caraway

MAIN MEAL Serves 4

Overall timing $1\frac{1}{4}$ hours

Equipment 1 large and 2 small saucepans, ovenproof dish

Freezing Not recommended

INGREDIENTS

1	Medium-size white cabbage	1
2	Onions	2
1oz	Lard	25g
8oz	Back bacon	225g
1lb	Minced beef	450g
1 teasp	Caraway seeds	5ml
1	Beef stock cube	1
$\frac{1}{4}$ pint	White wine or light stock	150ml
	Salt and pepper	
2oz	Butter	50g
8oz	Streaky rashers	225g

METHOD

1 Preheat the oven to 375F (190C) Gas 5.

2 Discard any marked outer leaves of the cabbage. Save 2 or 3 good ones. Cut the remaining cabbage in half. Cut out the stalk, then coarsely shred the rest. Put with reserved leaves into a saucepan of cold water. Bring to the boil and then drain. Set aside.

3 Peel and chop the onions. Melt the lard in a large saucepan, add the onions and cook gently for 3–4 minutes. Remove the rind and cut the back bacon into small pieces. Add to the saucepan. Cook for 2–3 minutes.

4 Add the minced beef to the saucepan and cook, stirring, until brown. Add the caraway seeds, crumbled stock cube, wine or stock and seasonings. Simmer for 10 minutes.

5 Melt the butter in a small saucepan. Put half of the shredded cabbage in the bottom of an ovenproof dish and pour the melted butter over.

6 Spread the mince evenly over the cabbage. Cover with remaining shredded cabbage and top with whole leaves.

7 Arrange the streaky bacon rashers over the top of the cabbage. Cook in the middle of the oven for 45 minutes. Serve hot with dumplings, or with jacket potatoes which can cook in the oven at the same time as the cabbage bake.

Flaky-topped pie

Buttery layers of flaky pastry are used to good effect in this unusual pie which has an egg-enriched but delicate-flavoured cheese filling

LUNCH OR SUPPER Serves 6

Overall timing $2\frac{1}{4}$ hours plus chilling pastry

Equipment Large bowl, rolling-pin, frying pan, deep 10 inch (25cm) foil pie dish

Freezing Prepare to end of Step 8. Cover, wrap in polythene, seal, label and freeze. Freezer life: 1 month. To use: thaw overnight in fridge, uncover and complete Step 9

When the flaky pastry's made, roll to a long strip, halve, then coil each piece

Gently roll each coil (cut side up). Be careful not to squash the layers

Put larger circle in dish, add filling, top with other circle. Open up layers

INGREDIENTS

9oz	Plain flour	250g
	Salt	
8oz	Butter	225g
	Cold water	
1	Large onion	1
8oz	Button mushrooms	225g
3 tbsp	Oil	3×15ml
1	Garlic clove	1
8oz	Cream cheese	225g
2	Eggs	2
1 tbsp	Snipped chives	15ml
	Freshly-ground black pepper	

METHOD

1 Sift flour and salt into a large bowl. Cut the butter into two, chill one half, mash other with a fork to soften it. Rub softened butter into the flour till the mixture resembles fine breadcrumbs. Gradually add enough water to mix to a soft but not sticky dough. Knead lightly till smooth, shape into ball, chill for 1 hour.

2 Place the block of chilled butter between sheets of greaseproof paper and roll out to a rectangle about 5×3 inches (13×7.5cm). Roll out dough on a lightly floured surface to a 10×8 inch (25×20cm) rectangle.

3 Place rolled butter on centre of dough. Fold ends of dough in over the fat to enclose it (see page 572). Press rolling-pin on to edges to seal fat in.

4 Give the dough a half turn so the folds are at the sides, roll out to a rectangle again. Fold and seal pastry in the same way, foil wrap and chill for 15 minutes. Repeat rolling, folding and sealing process 4 more times chilling between each. Chill dough till required.

5 Meanwhile, peel and chop the onion, wipe and thickly slice the mushrooms. Heat the oil in a frying pan and fry the onion till just golden. Add the mushrooms and peeled and crushed garlic and fry stirring for 5 minutes. Cool.

6 Preheat the oven to 425F (220C) Gas 7.

7 Roll pastry out to a long strip about 3 inches (7.5cm) wide and 1 inch (2.5cm) thick. Cut in half lengthways with a very sharp knife, then coil each strip loosely. Place the coils cut side up and roll out – 1 to a 12 inch (30cm) circle, the other to a 10 inch (25cm) circle. Trim circles with sharp knife.

8 Line foil dish with larger circle. Beat together cream cheese, eggs, chives, mushroom mixture, lots of seasoning. Spread into pastry case and smooth top. Cover with other circle, seal edges. With tip of sharp knife, open up layers in the round on pie top.

9 Bake in centre of the oven for 20 minutes. Reduce the temperature to 350F (180C) Gas 4 and cook for 20–30 minutes till well risen and golden.

Above: Flaky-topped pie – a surprisingly different dish to store in a freezer

Potato cake

Serve with roast meats – it can be cooked at the same time

VEGETABLE OR LUNCH Serves 5

Overall timing 50 minutes

Equipment Bowl, ovenproof dish

Freezing Not recommended

INGREDIENTS

2lb	Potatoes	900g
3	Eggs	3
½ pint	Milk	300ml
6oz	Grated cheese	175g
	Salt and pepper	

METHOD

1 Preheat the oven to 375F (190C) Gas 5.

2 Peel and wash potatoes. Grate into bowl. Beat in eggs, milk, cheese and seasoning. Pour into dish and bake for 40 minutes till top is golden. Serve.

Below: Potato cake – the inside is tender and the outside golden and crispy-textured

Above: Pork with thyme and olives – choose garden thyme for a strong, aromatic flavour

Pork with thyme and olives

A succulent roast leg of pork enhanced with a rich tomato sauce. Any leftover pork is delicious served cold the next day with a potato salad

MAIN MEAL Serves 10

Overall timing 2½ hours

Equipment Fine string, roasting tin, saucepan

Freezing Not recommended

INGREDIENTS

3lb	Boned leg of pork	1.4kg
	Sprigs of thyme	
4oz	Small pitted black olives	125g
2oz	Butter	50g
1 tbsp	Oil	15ml
	Salt	
	Black pepper	
1	Large onion	1
1	Garlic clove	1
12oz	Ripe tomatoes	350g
1 pint	Light stock	560ml
1	Bay leaf	1
	Parsley stalks	
½ teasp	Caster sugar	½×5ml
4 tbsp	Dry white wine	4×15ml
4oz	Pitted green olives	125g

METHOD

1 Preheat the oven to 375F (190C) Gas 5.

2 Wipe the pork and remove the skin, leaving a thin layer of fat over the meat. Tie into a neat rectangular shape with fine string, then make several deep incisions through the fat into the meat. Push a small piece of thyme and a black olive into each incision.

3 Heat the butter and half the oil in a roasting tin and fry the meat till browned all over. Season and roast in the centre of the oven for about 2 hours, basting occasionally, till the juices run clear when the meat is pierced with a skewer.

4 Meanwhile, peel and finely chop the onion, peel the garlic. Blanch, peel and chop the tomatoes. Heat the remaining oil in a saucepan, add the onion and fry gently till transparent.

5 Add the tomatoes and garlic to the pan with the stock, and bring to the boil, stirring to break up the tomatoes.

6 Tie the remaining thyme, the bay leaf and parsley stalks together with thread. Add to the pan with the sugar and seasoning and simmer uncovered for 30 minutes till thick.

7 Lift the meat out of the roasting tin and remove the string. Cut into thick slices and arrange on a warmed serving dish. Pour off the excess fat from the tin, add the wine and stir over a low heat to dissolve the sediment.

8 Remove the herbs from the sauce. Add the wine and juices from the roasting tin and the green olives and heat through, stirring. Adjust the seasoning to taste, pour the sauce round the meat and serve immediately with a potato dish, such as oven baked Potato cake, left (make double the quantity).

Grilled trout with cucumber

A dish to delight trout lovers. Because the bone is removed, the trout is easy to eat – and there's more space for the delicate stuffing

MAIN MEAL Serves 2

Overall timing 45 minutes

Equipment Kitchen scissors, saucepan, brush

Freezing Not recommended

INGREDIENTS

2×12oz	Whole rainbow trout	2×350g
6	Spring onions	6
2	Stalks of celery	2
8 inch	Piece of cucumber	20cm
4oz	Butter	125g
2 teasp	Fresh dill weed *or*	2×5ml
1 teasp	dried dill	5ml
4 tbsp	Fresh white breadcrumbs	4×15ml
	Salt and black pepper	
	Lemon wedges	

Below: Grilled trout with cucumber – serve garnished with lemon wedges and dill

METHOD

1 Wash the trout and dry on kitchen paper. Insert a sharp knife on one side of the fin on the trouts back-bone. Slit the fish open along the back-bone from just behind the head to just in front of the tail.

2 Using short knife strokes, cut the flesh away from the bones. Make another slit along the length of the fish on the other side of the fin and scrape the flesh away from the bone. Snip the bone at both ends and remove.

3 Cut a little further into the flesh till the entrails are visible. Remove carefully and discard. Pull the head sharply to one side to open one gill, then snip it out with kitchen scissors. Repeat on the other side.

4 Prepare the second trout in the same way so each has a large pocket to hold the stuffing. Remove grill rack and brush with oil. Preheat the grill.

5 Wash and trim the spring onions and cut into ½ inch (12.5mm) lengths. Wash, trim and thinly slice the celery. Peel the cucumber, cut in half lengthways and scrape out the seeds with a teaspoon. Cut into ¼ inch (6mm) thick slices.

6 Melt the butter in a saucepan. Place the trout with the skin side up on the grill rack so the pocket is held open underneath. Brush a little butter over and grill about 2 inches (5cm) away from the heat for 2–3 minutes.

7 Meanwhile add the onions and celery to the remaining butter and fry, stirring, over a high heat for 2–3 minutes till golden. Remove from the heat and stir in the cucumber, dill (chopped if fresh), breadcrumbs and seasoning.

8 Turn trout over carefully and brush with juices from the grill pan. Arrange the stuffing in the pockets of the fish and grill for a further 4–5 minutes till the trout is tender and the breadcrumbs are crisp. Garnish with lemon wedges and fresh dill if available.

Slit trout along the back-bone from just behind head to just in front of tail. Cut flesh from bones, snip out back-bone

Place pocket side down on rack, brush with melted butter, then grill for 2–3 minutes about 2 inches (5cm) from heat

Turn trout over, brush with pan juices, arrange stuffing in pockets and grill for 4–5 minutes till crisp, golden

Tarragon fish vol-au-vent

An excellent dish to serve at a dinner party. Choose firm, white fish like turbot, cod or monkfish, or you can use a mixture if you like

MAIN MEAL Serves 6

Overall timing 40 minutes plus thawing

Equipment Baking tray, saucepan

Freezing Not recommended

INGREDIENTS

13oz	Packet of frozen puff pastry	375g
1	Beaten egg	1
$1\frac{1}{2}$lb	Firm white fish	700g
4oz	Button mushrooms	125g
4oz	Butter	125g
5 tbsp	Plain flour	5×15ml
$\frac{3}{4}$ pint	Milk	400ml
$\frac{1}{4}$ pint	Carton of single cream	150ml
1 teasp	Lemon juice	5ml
4oz	Shelled prawns	125g
1 tbsp	Chopped tarragon	15ml
	Salt	
	Freshly-ground white pepper	

METHOD

1 Thaw the pastry. Preheat the oven to 425F (220C) Gas 7.
2 Roll out pastry to a rectangle 10×7 inches (25×18cm). Place on wetted baking tray. Trim, knock up and crimp the edges, then make a shallow cut, $\frac{3}{4}$ inch (2cm) in from edge, all the way round. Brush with egg, then bake just above centre of oven for 20–25 minutes till crisp and golden.
3 Wipe and trim fish, discarding skin and bones, and cut into 1 inch (2.5cm) cubes. Wipe and trim mushrooms. Heat half the butter in pan, add the fish and mushrooms and fry for 5 minutes. Remove from the pan and reserve.
4 Heat remaining butter in the pan. Add flour and cook for 1 minute. Gradually add milk, bring to the boil, stirring, and simmer for 2 minutes. Remove from heat.
5 Stir in cream, lemon juice, fish, prawns and tarragon and cook gently for 5 minutes without boiling. Season to taste.
6 Remove pastry case from oven and place on warmed serving dish. Cut round "lid" and remove. Arrange fish mixture in case and replace lid. Serve immediately with broccoli spears.

Above: Bream with mushrooms – the fish is cooked whole with mushrooms and thyme

Bream with mushrooms

Whole bream baked in butter with vegetables and herbs

MAIN MEAL Serves 4

Overall timing 1 hour

Equipment Large ovenproof dish

Freezing Not recommended

INGREDIENTS

$3\frac{1}{4}$lb	Bream	1.5kg
5oz	Button mushrooms	150g
3	Shallots	3
	Salt and pepper	
7fl oz	Water	200ml
1 tbsp	Chopped parsley	15ml
2	Sprigs of fresh thyme *or*	2
$\frac{1}{4}$ teasp	dried thyme	$\frac{1}{4}$×5ml
2oz	Butter	50g
1	Lemon	1

METHOD

1 Preheat oven to 450F (230C) Gas 8. Gut fish, but don't remove head. Trim tail and fins, and wash well. Dry on kitchen paper.
2 Wipe and thinly slice button mushrooms. Peel and finely chop shallots.
3 Cover base of ovenproof dish with most of mushrooms and shallots, and place the fish on top. Season with salt and pepper, and pour in the water. Sprinkle fish with parsley, thyme and remaining mushrooms and shallots. Melt butter and pour over fish. Cover dish with foil or a lid.
4 Cook in oven for 40 minutes, basting frequently. Turn fish over halfway through cooking time and remove foil for last 10 minutes. The fish is cooked when the flesh becomes opaque.

TO SERVE

Garnish with lemon and serve with boiled new potatoes.

The steamier side of the kitchen

Foods that are steamed range from the delicate (fish, whole or in fillets, veal escalopes), through the sturdy (root vegetables, whole cauliflowers) to the hard (couscous, which are bits of broken wheat with a coating of moistened flour). The denser and harder the foods the longer the steaming time, of course, but in all cases the food should be light and tender, moist and succulent when served.

If using a steamer rather than a basket, the water boiling in the bottom can be cooking potatoes or rice – but in the top part put foods which will steam in the time it takes for the potatoes or rice to be tender. Make sure there's enough water in the bottom pan to last out the times suggested in the charts. If you have to remove the lid and top up, it will take some minutes for the steaming level to be re-established, so take that into account. And remember to top up with boiling water always.

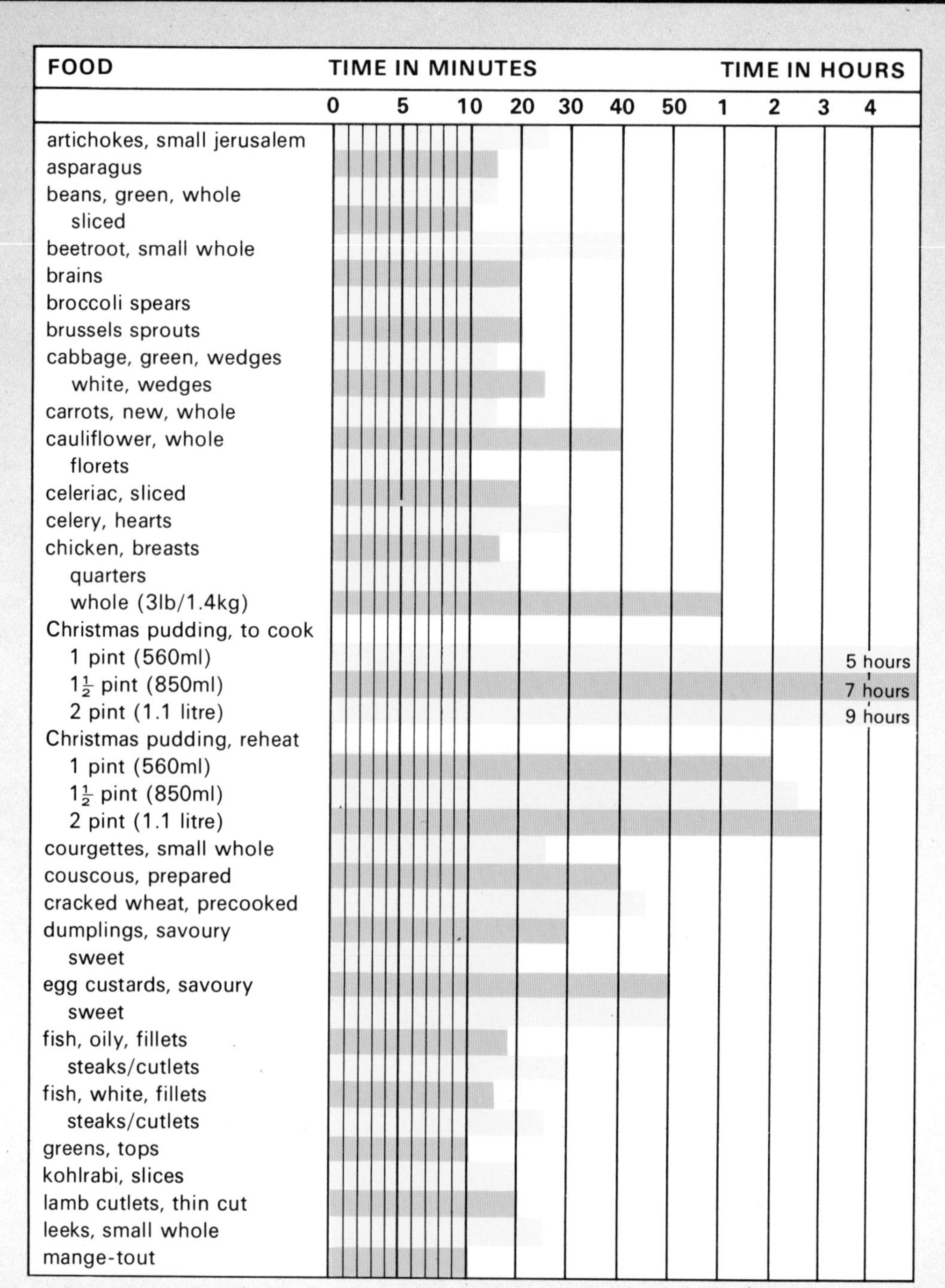

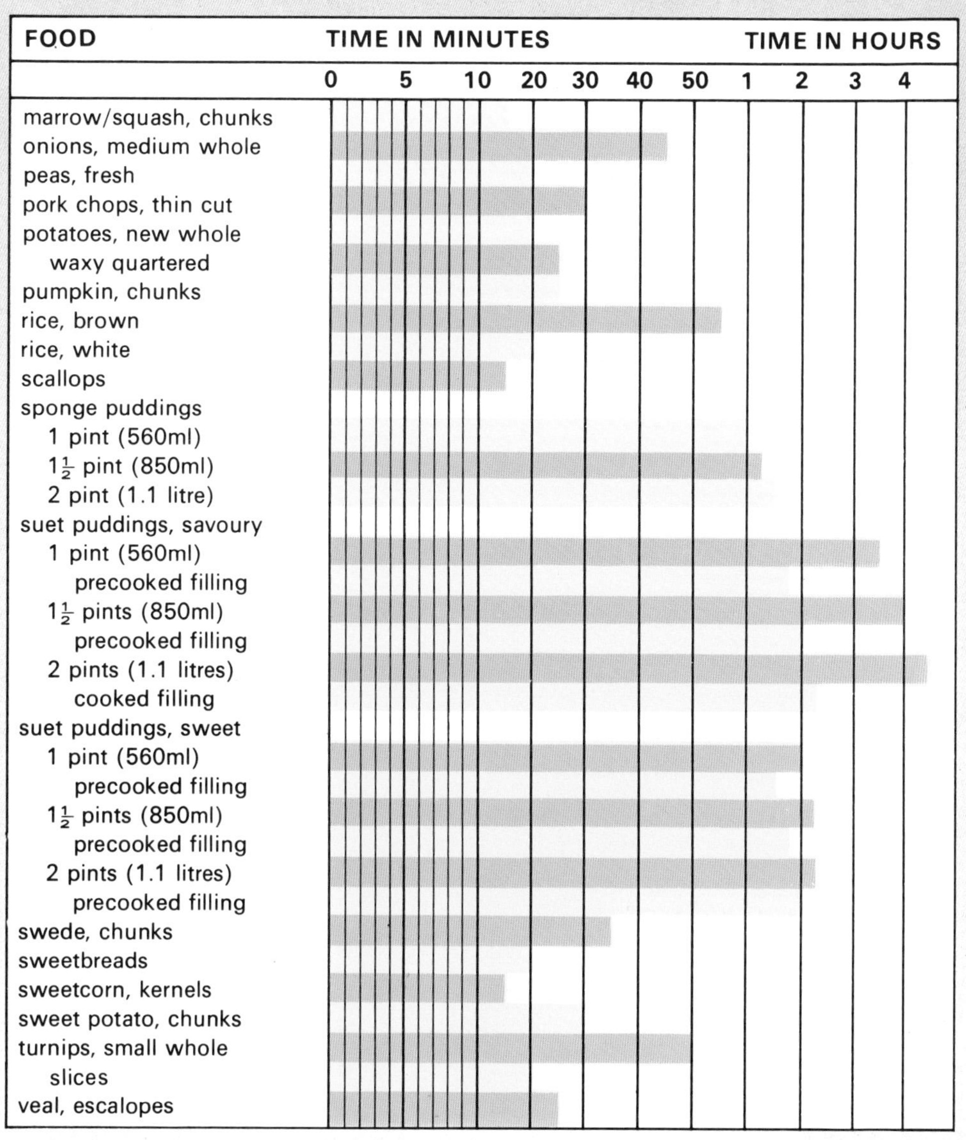

flavourings know-how

As steaming is used to cook foods so that natural flavours are kept in, salt should not be added as it will draw out the juices. It is much better to add after cooking. Spices like mace can be sprinkled over parsnips for extra flavour; herbs like savory over green beans; caraway seeds over cabbage. It is however usual to serve steamed foods with sauces made from some of the water into which some nutrients will have been drawn. Cereals can be steamed over stews or soups so that their flavour will enhance the cereal's.

Under pressure

A pressure cooker is perfect for anyone with a lot of cooking to do, and with little time to do it in. It also provides a good-sized, heavy pan for jam making or cooking pasta or rice for large numbers

In a pressure cooker, the steam is sealed in and, being increased in temperature by pressure, makes food tender in one-third or less of the usual cooking time. The two major points in cooking this way are: it saves fuel, and foods retain more flavour and nutritive value. By cutting down on time so dramatically it also means that meals can be prepared and served up much more quickly.

Pressure cookers are a sort of "cinderella" of cooking. They were very popular in the 50s and 60s but gradually were put aside in favour of the vast numbers of pots and pans arriving on the scene. They have emerged again and their new streamlined shapes are taking their place alongside cookware designed with fuel and time saving qualities in mind. They can only go from strength to strength with clearer instructions and more imaginative suggestions for exploiting their versatility.

Completely automatic cookers are available which make the whole process easier, and also in most others the weight is put on *before* the cooker's placed over the heat so that all you have to do is reduce the heat so the hiss of steam is steady and gentle sounding. The exception to this is when cooking steamed puddings (see right).

Pressure cookers can be used on gas (both mains and bottled), electricity (rings and flat surface) and solid fuel stoves. The open cooker (that is, without the lid) can be used to brown meat and sweat vegetables before pressure cooking, and also provides a large heavy-based pan for cooking a lot of rice or pasta, or for making jam. Large amounts cannot be cooked under pressure for there would not be sufficient space left for the steam to circulate. Soups or stews must never come higher than halfway up the cooker; with vegetables the pan should be no more than two-thirds full.

Liquid, which forms the steam, is the essence of pressure cooking. It should be water, stock, wine or milk, but not melted fat or oil. The minimum quantity required is ½ pint (300ml) for the first 15 minutes of cooking plus ¼ pint (150ml) for each further 15 minutes of cooking time, or part thereof. Thickening agents aren't added till the end of cooking time as they will retard the steam and can cause the food to burn.

Timing is established by the size and density of the foods. Because the trapped steam is forced through the food under pressure it cooks 1lb (450g) or 3lb (1.4kg) of cut-up potatoes in the same time, 4–6 minutes. Similarly 8oz (225g) of stewing steak cut in chunks will take the same time as 1½lb (700g) – 20 minutes.

A joint of meat on the other hand is denser and is cooked by weight – 1lb (450g) will take 15 minutes, 3lb (1.4kg) will take 45. When foods containing raising agents are cooked in containers (eg, puddings in basins), a short steaming time is necessary before pressure cooking (without it the pudding would be heavy). Usually 1½ pints (850ml) of boiling water is placed in the cooker with the trivet and covered pudding, the lid is placed on top, then the pudding is steamed gently for 15 minutes with little steam coming from the vent. After this the weight is added and the cooker brought to pressure.

Plastic boilable basins can be used and they give quicker results (5 minutes less), but the lids can buckle and prevent steam from penetrating the mixture so cover with greased pleated greaseproof and cloth. Some manufacturers recommend adding a few minutes to the cooking time if foil is used to cover.

In long steaming such as with puddings, vinegar or a slice of lemon should be added to the water to prevent the cooker from discolouring.

When cooking custards don't use metal containers which hold the strong heat and spoil the texture of the custard.

After cooking the pressure must be reduced before the lid can be removed. Risen mixtures or those contained in a breakable container are reduced slowly: left off the heat for 10–15 minutes. Other foods: stand cooker in bowl of cold water or place under cold running water. Pressure has been reduced if, when you gently tip the weight, no hissing occurs. Always follow the manufacturer's advice about caring for your cooker.

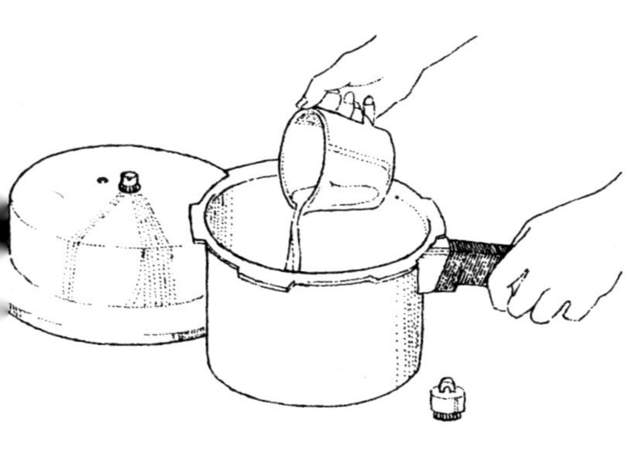

The amount of liquid is based on the time needed for cooking – the formula is ½ pint (300ml) water, stock, wine or milk plus ¼ pint (150ml) for every further 15 minutes

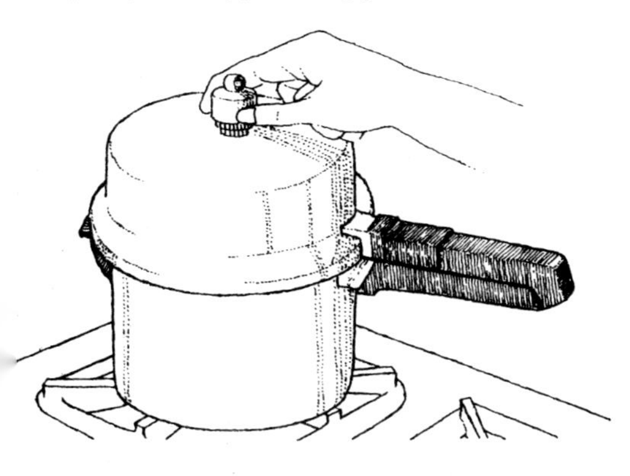

After the food goes in, the top's put on with arrows on cover and base lining up. The correct weight is placed on the centre vent and pressed down till a click is heard. The cooker is then put on high heat

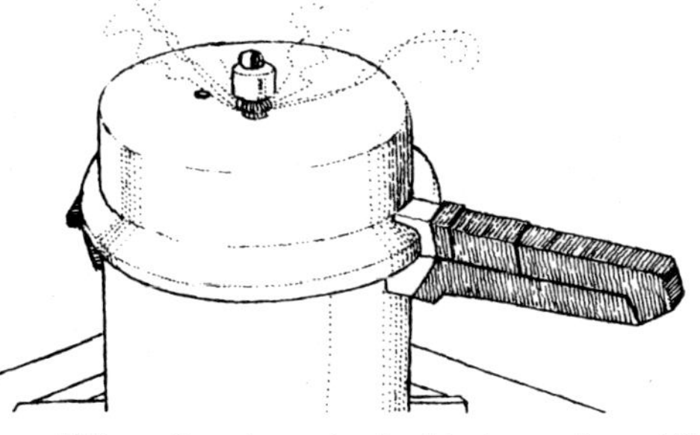

When there's a steady hissing noise with a flow of steam from around weight, reduce heat till a gentle hissing sound is heard. Start the timing from this point

At the end of cooking pressure must be reduced before the cover can be removed. Quickly: run cold water over sides, not top. Slowly: leave at room temperature

FOOD	TIME IN MINUTES (0 5 10 15 20 25 30 35 40)
artichokes, globe	H CW
artichokes, jerusalem	H CW
beans, broad	H CW
runner	H CW
beef, rolled brisket	per lb (450g) H CW
stewing steak, cubes	H CW
beetroot	H CW
broccoli	H CW
brussels sprouts	H CW
butter beans, soaked	H RT
cabbage, wedges	H CW
carrots, old quarters	H CW
new whole	H CW
cauliflower, whole	H CW
florets	H CW
celery, hearts	H CW
chicken, whole	per lb (450g) H CW
quarters	H CW
chickpeas, soaked	H RT
corn on the cob	H CW
custards, 1½ pint (850ml)	H WT RT
individual	H WT RT
fish, oily, fillets	H CW
medium whole	H CW
fish, white, fillets (3½ mins)	H CW
steaks/cutlets (4½ mins)	H CW
fruits, to stew	H RT
gammon/bacon	per lb (450g) H CW
haricot beans, small soaked	H RT
lamb, boned, rolled breast	per lb (450g) H CW
lambs hearts	H CW
leeks, small whole	H CW
lentils, soaked	H RT
onions, medium whole	H CW
button	H CW
oxtail	H CW
parsnips, quartered	H CW
peas, fresh	H CW
dried split	H RT
dried whole	H RT
pheasant, browned	H CW
pork, boned and rolled	per lb (450g) H CW
potatoes, maincrop halves	H CW
new whole	H CW
puddings, 1½ pint (850ml)	
sponge	
steam 15 mins, then	L WT RT
sponge with fruit	
steam 15 mins, then	L WT RT
suet crust with filling	
steam 15 mins, then	L WT RT
Christmas	
steam 15 mins, then	H WT RT per lb (450g) 1¾ hours
rabbit portions	H CW
soya beans, soaked	H RT
stocks, brown	H CW
fish	H CW
poultry	H CW
swedes, quartered	H CW
tripe, blanched	H CW
turnips, small whole	H CW

Pressure cooking abbreviations: H high, M medium, L low pressure; WT with trivet; RT reduce pressure at room temperature; CW reduce pressure under cold water

Countdown

Roe and egg canapés
Ham diamonds
Basic bouchées
Mushroom sauce
Cheese platter
Christening cake

A christening buffet is always a pleasure to plan. This spread caters for about 30 people. As a general guide, allow about 2 pastries and 2–3 items from the cheese platter per person. (You may like to serve a fresh fruit salad or trifle too.)

Advance preparation Make sponges a few days in advance if liked and store in foil in airtight containers, or make well in advance and freeze

Day before Prepare roe sauce; chop egg white; slice smoked cod roe. Cover all and store in fridge. Prepare ham diamonds. Bake, cool and store in foil in an airtight container. For cheese platter: cube cheese; stone dates; halve tomatoes and remove centres; hard-boil eggs; cut gherkin fans. Cover all and store in fridge. Prepare bouchées. Bake, cool and store, unfilled, in an airtight container

Night before make crème au beurre. Assemble cake, wrap in foil and store in fridge. Make mushroom sauce for bouchées, store in fridge.

Morning of christening Make icing. Ice cake and decorate. Assemble cheese platter items and cover with cling film or foil. Toast bread for canapés. Make up and heat in oven

10 mins before Grill canapés. Place all food on table

When the guests arrive from the church after the christening, it is fairly traditional to offer a choice of dry, medium or sweet sherry. Ideally, this is followed by champagne, or a sparkling white wine, to toast the baby.

Roe and egg canapés

Tasty toasts with a soft roe, egg and anchovy topping are decorated with slices of smoked cods roe

APPETIZER/
PARTY SNACK — Makes 12–14

Overall timing 45 minutes

Equipment 2 saucepans, bowl

Freezing Not recommended

INGREDIENTS

$1\frac{1}{2}$lb	Soft roes	700g
	Salt	
6oz	Butter	175g
4 tbsp	Plain flour	4×15ml
1 pint	Milk	560ml
4	Anchovy fillets	4
6	Hard-boiled eggs	6
2 tbsp	Lemon juice	2×15ml
	Freshly-ground black pepper	
12	Slices of bread	12
12oz	Smoked cods roe	350g

METHOD

1 Wash the soft roes then poach in lightly salted boiling water for 5–8 minutes. Drain well, chop finely and reserve.
2 Melt 4oz (125g) of the butter in a pan, stir in the flour and cook for 1 minute. Gradually add the milk and bring to the boil, stirring constantly.
3 Pound the anchovy fillets in a bowl. Shell the eggs and cut in half. Sieve the yolks and stir into the sauce with the anchovies and soft roes. Heat through, add lemon juice and seasoning.
4 Preheat the grill. Toast the bread, spread with remaining butter and arrange on the grill pan. Spread the soft roe mixture over. Finely chop the egg whites and use to decorate the toast. Cut the smoked cods roe into 24 fine slices and place 2 on each piece of toast.
5 Grill for 2–3 minutes till bubbling and golden. Arrange on a warmed serving dish, garnish with tomatoes and parsley and serve immediately.

Ham diamonds

Golden, light-as-air puff pastry with a cheese and ham filling

APPETIZER/
PARTY SNACK — Makes 12–14

Overall timing 40 minutes plus thawing

Equipment Rolling-pin, baking tray, pastry brush

Freezing Not recommended

INGREDIENTS

13oz	Packet of frozen puff pastry	375g
4oz	Ham	125g
2oz	Grated cheese	50g
	Salt and pepper	
1	Egg	1
1oz	Melted butter	25g

METHOD

1 Allow pastry to thaw, then roll out to a large rectangle, about $\frac{1}{8}$ inch (3mm) thick. Cut in half. Preheat oven to 400F (200C) Gas 6. Grease baking tray.
2 Finely chop the ham and mix with the cheese. Add salt and pepper to taste.
3 Place small spoonfuls of the mixture on one of the pastry halves as for ravioli (see page 518).
4 Lightly beat the egg. Brush pastry between the piles of filling with egg. Lift the remaining pastry half on a rolling pin and cover base pastry. Press lightly between piles of filling to seal. Using a sharp knife, cut through the sealed pastry to make diamond shapes. Press edges to seal.
5 Arrange diamond shapes on baking tray and brush with the butter. Bake in centre of oven for 20 minutes until risen and golden. Serve hot.

Below: Roe and egg canapés – good party or buffet food best served hot

Mushroom sauce

A creamy sauce to serve as a filling for bouchées or vol-au-vents, or as a sauce. The mushrooms can be finely chopped if preferred and this recipe can be adapted very easily to make a superb cream of mushroom soup (see Variation below)

SAUCE Makes 1 pint (560ml)

Overall timing 25 minutes

Equipment 2 saucepans

Freezing Pour into rigid container leaving 1 inch (2.5cm) headspace. Seal, label and freeze. Freezer life: 6 months. To use: place block of sauce in pan and heat gently till thawed. Bring to the boil, stirring. Taste and adjust seasoning

INGREDIENTS

½	Small onion	½
½	Small carrot	½
½	Stalk of celery	½
½ pint	Milk	300ml
1	Bay leaf	1
4oz	Button mushrooms	125g
2oz	Butter	50g
2oz	Plain flour	50g
½ pint	Light stock	300ml
4 tbsp	Single cream	4×15ml
1 teasp	Chopped chervil	5ml
	Salt	
	Freshly-ground black pepper	

METHOD

1 Peel the onion, scrape the carrot, wash and trim the celery. Chop the vegetables and place in a saucepan with the milk and bay leaf. Bring slowly to the boil and remove from the heat. Cover and leave to infuse for 15 minutes.

2 Meanwhile, wipe and trim the mushrooms and slice thinly. Heat the butter in a saucepan and fry the mushrooms for 5 minutes till golden.

3 Add the flour and cook, stirring, for 1 minute. Gradually add the stock (made with a cube if necessary) and the strained milk. Bring to the boil, stirring constantly, and cook for 3 minutes.

4 Remove from the heat and stir in the cream, chervil and seasoning to taste.

VARIATION

To make cream of mushroom soup, double the quantities of mushrooms, milk and stock and prepare as above. Stir in ¼ pint (150ml) single cream just before serving, and reheat gently. Serves 4.

Basic bouchées

Mini vol-au-vents – but not made in the same way. Use an apple corer if you haven't got a small cutter to make the centres of the bouchées

APPETIZER/ PARTY SNACK Makes about 30

Overall timing 40 minutes

Equipment Rolling-pin, 2 inch (5cm) and 1 inch (2.5cm) pastry cutters, shallow roasting tin, wire rack

Freezing Pack cooked bouchées in rigid containers, cover, label and freeze. Freezer life: 3 months. To use: arrange on baking trays, reheat at 425F (220C) Gas 7 for 3–5 minutes

INGREDIENTS

9oz	Puff pastry (recipe page 572) *or*	250g
1¼lb	bought puff pastry	600g
1	Egg	1

Above: Bouchées filled with mushroom sauce (right) and served hot

METHOD

1 Preheat the oven to 425F (220C) Gas 7. Roll out the chilled puff pastry on a floured surface till just over ¼ inch (6mm) thick.

2 Stamp out rounds with the larger pastry cutter and arrange in the wetted roasting tin.

3 Press the smaller cutter into the centre of each round to cut only about halfway through the pastry.

4 Beat the egg and brush over the tops, avoiding outside edges. Place the wire rack upside down over the roasting tin to prevent the bouchées overturning as they rise.

5 Bake in the centre of the oven for about 15 minutes till crisp and golden. Remove from the oven and cut out and discard the pastry middles.

6 Place cases upside down on wire rack and return to the oven for 2–3 minutes to dry the insides before filling with hot or cold saucy mixtures, such as Mushroom sauce, right.

Cheese platter

A tasty assortment of eye-catching appetizers. They need only a little preparation and can be put together in a matter of minutes

CRISPY CHEESE BITES
Beat cream cheese until smooth. Lightly shape into small balls and roll in oven-crisped breadcrumbs mixed with sweet paprika or finely chopped walnuts or peanuts. Spear on to a cracker with a cocktail stick.

SMOKED SALMON AND CHEESE
Butter small squares of white bread. Roll up a bite-sized piece of Brie in a slice of smoked salmon or Parma ham and place on top. Garnish with a finely cut, half slice of lemon and secure with a cocktail stick.

CHEESE DATES
Split the dates lengthways and remove stones. Beat together equal quantities of Roquefort or Dolcelatte and unsalted butter until creamy. Pipe into the cavity of the dates and pierce with a cocktail stick.

GHERKIN AND CHEESE
Butter small rounds (cut with a biscuit cutter) of white bread, or small biscuits. Cover with a wedge of Camembert and a gherkin fan. Garnish with fresh cress.

PUMPERNICKEL AND CHEESE
Butter small round of Pumpernickel bread and cover with chunks of Emmenthal and a cocktail onion. Roll up a gherkin in a strip of ham and place on top. Add a strip of red or green capsicum and hold everything together by piercing with a cocktail stick. Garnish with parsley.

ANCHOVIES AND CHEESE
Spread herb cheese on small rounds of Pumpernickel bread. Cover with a slice of tomato and a slice of hard-boiled egg. Top with a rolled anchovy fillet stuffed with caviare, lump fish roe or an olive. Garnish with parsley.

CHEESE CUBES
Cut Emmenthal into 1 inch (2.5cm) cubes. Top with 2 stuffed olives, held together one above the other with a cocktail stick.

STUFFED TOMATOES
Beat together equal quantities of cream cheese and double cream. Add finely chopped pickled gherkins. Cut the tomatoes in half and remove centres. Fill with the cheese mixture. Garnish with parsley and a very fine slice of radish. Sprinkle with a little paprika.

Above: Cheese plattér. Clockwise, from top right: Crispy cheese bites; Smoked salmon and cheese; Cheese dates; Gherkin and cheese; Pumpernickel and cheese; Anchovies and cheese; Stuffed tomatoes; Cheese cubes (centre)

Christening cake

For an occasion as special as a christening, you need a cake that old and young appreciate. This one is deliciously rich with butter featuring in the sponge as well as the crème au beurre filling

CHRISTENING CAKE Serves 30

Overall timing 3 hours plus overnight chilling

Equipment 4 sandwich tins sizes 10 inch (25cm), 9 inch (23cm), 7 inch (18cm), 6 inch (15cm), greaseproof, mixing bowl, bowl, saucepan

Freezing Cook sponges but don't halve them. Wrap, label and freeze. Freeze filling in a separate container. Freezer life: cake, 4 months; filling, 3 months. To use: cake, allow to thaw for 1 hour before icing; filling, allow to thaw for 2 hours (remove 1 hour before cake)

INGREDIENTS

12	Eggs	12
12oz	Caster sugar	350g
14oz	Plain flour	400g
4oz	Ground almonds	125g
2oz	Butter	50g
	Curaçao, maraschino or apricot brandy (optional)	
	Filling	
5	Egg yolks	5
9oz	Granulated sugar	250g
5 tbsp	Water	5×15ml
12oz	Softened unsalted butter	350g
	Icing	
1lb	Icing sugar	450g
2	Egg whites	2
	Hot water	
	Decoration	
1lb	Sugared almonds	450g
	Silver balls	

METHOD

1 Preheat the oven to 375F (190C) Gas 5. Grease and flour cake tins. Line bases with greaseproof or non-stick paper.
2 Make the cake mixture in two separate amounts. First, put 6 eggs and half the sugar into a bowl and beat with an electric mixer or whisk until the mixture is thick and pale yellow.
3 Melt the butter in a saucepan. Sieve half the flour into the egg and sugar mixture and sprinkle with half the almonds. Add half the melted butter and fold in gently, using a metal spoon. Put mixture into largest and smallest of the tins.
4 Cook just above the centre of the oven for about 15–20 minutes for the small cake and about 30 minutes for the large cake.
5 Using the remaining ingredients, make up the sponge mixture as above and put in the two middle-sized tins. Bake for about 30–35 minutes.
6 Allow to cool slightly in tins, then turn out on to a cake wire.
7 When completely cold, cut cakes horizontally and sprinkle the cut sides with a little liqueur.

To make the Crème au beurre filling

1 Put egg yolks into a bowl and whisk them well.
2 Put sugar and water into a saucepan. Heat slowly till sugar melts. Bring to the boil and boil for 2–3 minutes, without allowing it to colour.
3 Pour hot syrup on to the egg yolks, beating continuously. Allow to cool.
4 Gradually work the softened butter into the egg yolk mixture, till a smooth cream is obtained. If liked, stir in liqueur to taste.
5 Spread filling over cut sponge cakes and sandwich them together again. Place cakes one on top of the other, starting with the largest at the bottom and ending with the smallest. Use any remaining filling to secure the cakes in position.
6 Wrap the cake in foil or polythene and leave in fridge overnight.

To make the icing

1 Sieve the icing sugar into a large bowl, add the egg whites and beat well together. Add 1–2 tbsp (1–2×15ml) hot water to give a coating consistency.
2 Coat the entire cake with icing. Place on a serving dish. Decorate with sugared almonds and silver balls.

Left: Christening cake – a rich concoction for children of all ages to appreciate

Lemon meringue pie

Complementing the richness of the condensed milk is the tangy flavour of fresh lemon which combines with the milk and thickens it so little cooking is needed. A little desiccated coconut sprinkled over the meringue is a simple finishing touch

DESSERT Serves 4–6

Overall timing 1¼ hours plus cooling time

Equipment 8 inch (20cm) flan tin, 2 mixing bowls

Freezing Not recommended

INGREDIENTS

	Pastry	
5oz	Plain flour	150g
3oz	Margarine	75g
2–3 tbsp	Water	2–3×15ml
	Filling	
1	Can of sweetened condensed milk	1
2	Egg yolks	2
	Grated rind of 1 lemon	
6 tbsp	Lemon juice	6×15ml
	Topping	
2	Egg whites	2
3oz	Caster sugar	75g
1 tbsp	Desiccated coconut	15ml

METHOD

1 Preheat oven to 400F (200C) Gas 6.
2 To make pastry, in a bowl mix flour, margarine and water together. Roll out and line flan tin. Prick base, then bake blind for about 20 minutes till golden.
3 Meanwhile, place condensed milk, egg yolks, rind and juice in bowl and beat till well combined. Set aside.
4 Remove pastry from oven. Reduce temperature to 375F (190C) Gas 5. Pour filling into pastry case and smooth top.
5 Whisk egg whites till soft peaks form, then add sugar and whisk till mixture is stiff and glossy. Spread over filling, leaving no gap between pastry and egg white. "Peak" the top and sprinkle with coconut. Bake for about 20 minutes till meringue is golden. Remove from oven and leave to cool.

TO SERVE

Serve pie when cold with unsweetened pouring cream.

Apple layer pudding

A warming dish well suited to a large family and a cold wintry day. It is a type of charlotte with the dough arranged in layers and the fruity filling in between

DESSERT Serves 8–10

Overall timing 2¼ hours

Equipment Mixing bowl, deep cast-iron casserole or ovenproof dish

Freezing Not recommended

INGREDIENTS

1lb	Plain flour	450g
8oz	Beef or goose dripping	225g
4oz	Sugar	125g
1	Whole egg	1
1	Egg yolk	1
1	Lemon	1
3lb	Golden Delicious apples	1.4kg
6oz	Caster sugar	175g
4oz	Currants	125g
1oz	Chopped almonds	25g
½ teasp	Powdered cinnamon	½×5ml
1	Lemon	1

METHOD

1 Mix together the flour, grated dripping, sugar, whole egg, egg yolk and grated rind of 1 lemon and knead till well combined and smooth. Squeeze lemon and reserve juice.
2 Grease casserole with butter and preheat oven to 375F (190C) Gas 5.
3 Roll out a third of the pastry and line casserole, leaving an edge all the way round the top rim.
4 Peel and thickly slice apples. Put half the apples in the bottom of the casserole and cover with half the sugar, currants, almonds, cinnamon, 2 tbsp (2×15ml) lemon juice and the grated rind of half the second lemon. Roll out second third of pastry and place over apples. Cover with remaining apples, sugar, currants, almonds, cinnamon, lemon juice and grated rind. Finish with a layer of pastry. Pinch pastry edges together to prevent steam escaping during cooking.
5 Cook for 1½ hours. If pastry top is browning too quickly, cover with foil during cooking.

TO SERVE

This needs to be served while it's hot and moist and should be eaten up at one meal as the fruit filling will make the dough layers soggy. Serve with custard or vanilla ice cream.

cook's know-how

The superb Bramley is the apple mainly used in cooking as it has a good sharp flavour, is juicy and cooks down easily. However, if your recipe calls for apple slices to soften during cooking but remain whole, you will need to choose a different type of apple. Suitable varieties are: Golden Delicious, Granny Smith, Dunn's Seedling, Winter Pearmain, Sturmer and Cox's Orange Pippin. To store apples, keep them in a cool place at an even temperature. Apples can be frozen whole (peeled and cored) or sliced (blanched), and stored for up to a year in a freezer.

Below: Apple layer pudding – a deliciously filling dessert

Hot orange liqueur soufflé

A delicious, soft-in-the-centre dessert that can be flavoured with either Grand Marnier or Curaçao. To taste it at its best, it must be served straight from the oven

DESSERT Serves 4

Overall timing 50 minutes

Equipment Heavy-based pan, 2 pint (1.1 litre) ovenproof or soufflé dish or 6 ramekins

Freezing Not recommended

INGREDIENTS

$1\frac{1}{2}$oz	Butter	40g
1oz	Plain flour	25g
$\frac{1}{2}$ pint	Milk	300ml
$3\frac{1}{2}$oz	Caster sugar	100g
4	Large eggs	4
4 tbsp	Liqueur	4×15ml
	Pinch of salt	

METHOD

1 Preheat oven to 375F (190C) Gas 5.
2 Melt the butter in a heavy-based pan. Stir in the flour and cook for a minute. Remove from heat. From your $\frac{1}{2}$ pint (300ml) milk, measure out 4 tbsp (4×15ml) – this is not required if using liqueur. Gradually add milk to roux then return to heat, bring to the boil and cook gently for a minute, stirring continuously.
3 Remove pan from heat and leave for 5 minutes. Stir in sugar, separated egg yolks and liqueur of choice (see step-by step pictures, left).
4 Add a pinch of salt to the egg whites, whisk until mixture stands in firm peaks.
5 Fold whisked egg whites gently into the liqueur mixture using a metal spoon.
6 Lightly butter ovenproof dish. Turn mixture into dish and smooth surface with a round-bladed knife. If you are using individual ramekins, three-quarters fill with the mixture.
7 Put soufflé dish on a baking tray and cook just above the middle of the oven for 25–30 minutes. If you are using ramekins the cooking will take about 15 minutes.

TO SERVE

Take the hot soulfé immediately to the table and serve with pouring cream (single), or a dish of whipped cream.

1 Caster sugar is stirred into the roux

2 Separated egg yolks are then added

3 Liqueur of your choice is poured in

4 Stiffly-whipped whites are folded in

1 Holding the cake firmly with one hand, cut in half lengthways, with a sharp knife

2 Place one cake half on a baking tray and spoon glacé fruit and liqueur over

3 Trim ice cream to same shape as cake if necessary and place on top of fruit

4 When the ice cream is in position, quickly cover with the other piece of sponge cake

5 Working quickly, spread stiffly whisked egg white over sides of cake and ice cream

6 Pipe or spread more of the egg white on top of the cake to cover it completely

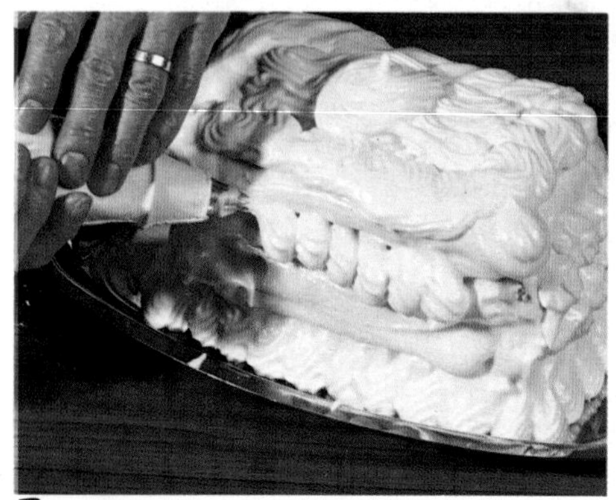

7 To use up any remaining egg white, pipe decorative shapes round sides

8 Dredge with a little icing sugar before baking in a very hot oven for 5 minutes

Baked Alaska

An impressive quickly baked ice cream dessert that is amazingly simple to make. A perfect baked Alaska needs last-minute assembly for the meringue to be a light golden colour and the ice cream inside to be firm so it doesn't melt and make the cake soggy. To avoid this, have the ice cream as hard as possible before putting the dessert together. Although stale sponge cake can be used, freshly baked sponge gives a better result

DESSERT Serves 6

Overall timing 30 minutes plus 1 hour marination

Equipment 2 bowls, saucepan, baking tray, palette knife or piping bag and star nozzle

Freezing Not recommended

INGREDIENTS

4oz	Glacé fruit	125g
4 tbsp	Kirsch or other liqueur	4×15ml
6	Egg whites	6
12oz	Icing sugar	350g
	Pinch of cream of tartar	
	Pinch of salt	
1 tbsp	Lemon juice	15ml
1	Sponge cake	1
1 pint	Block of vanilla ice cream	560ml

METHOD

1 Put glacé fruit and liqueur in a bowl and chill for 1 hour.
2 Preheat the oven to 475F (240C) Gas 9. Put egg whites, sifted icing sugar, cream of tartar, salt and lemon juice in a bowl placed over a pan of hot water. Whisk over a very gentle heat till stiff and dry.
3 Cut sponge cake in half lengthways. Place 1 layer on baking tray. Spoon fruit and liqueur over, then put ice cream on top. Cover with the other sponge layer.
4 Working quickly, pipe or spread whisked white all over cake, making sure all the ice cream is covered.
5 Dredge with a little icing sugar and bake in hot oven for 5 minutes or until meringue is golden. Serve immediately.

Avocado soufflé

The creamy flesh of the avocado responds well to this method of cooking. The fruit may be used when really ripe as it will be blended well into the egg mixture. For even more taste, you can add cinnamon or lemon rind to the sauce. To serve as a starter, see variation, right

LIGHT LUNCH OR SUPPER Serves 4

Overall timing 45 minutes

Equipment 2 pint (1.1 litre) soufflé dish, small saucepan, 2 bowls, baking tray

Freezing Not recommended

Below: *Avocado soufflé – a classic egg dish enriched with delicious avocado flesh*

INGREDIENTS

2oz	Butter	50g
1oz	Plain flour	25g
¼ pint	Milk	150ml
2	Ripe avocados	2
1 teasp	Lemon juice	5ml
	Salt and pepper	
	Pinch of grated nutmeg	
	Pinch of ground cinnamon *or*	
1 teasp	grated lemon rind (optional)	5ml
3	Large eggs	3

METHOD

1 Preheat oven to 400F (200C) Gas 6. Grease a soufflé dish with 1oz (25g) of the butter.
2 Put the remaining butter and the flour into a saucepan and mix together over a low heat. Add the milk all at one go and whisk constantly till sauce thickens and becomes smooth. (If you find it easier, remove the pan from the heat and stir the milk into the roux gradually. Return pan to heat and stir till thick.) Remove saucepan from heat and set aside.
3 Cut the avocados in half lengthways and lift out the stones. Cut out 4 very thin slices, sprinkle with lemon juice and reserve for the garnish. Remove remaining flesh with a teaspoon, place it in a bowl and mash well. Add to the sauce and beat vigorously so that the avocado is well blended.
4 Add salt, pepper and nutmeg. If you like, you can also add either ground cinnamon or lemon rind.
5 Separate the eggs. Add the yolks one by one to the saucepan, beating with a wooden spoon after each addition.
6 Whisk egg whites with a pinch of salt till very stiff then gently fold into the sauce with a spatula or metal spoon, a little at a time. Pour mixture into the soufflé dish. Place on a baking tray and cook on the middle shelf of the oven for about 30 minutes until well risen. Remove from oven, garnish with reserved avocado slices and serve immediately.

VARIATION

To make small soufflés to serve as starters, divide mixture between 6 greased ramekins. Place on baking tray and cook for 15–20 minutes. Serve immediately.

Fried spinach with ham

The perfect dish for spinach enthusiasts – and it's packed with vitamins and protein. Crusty bread with lots of butter is the only accompaniment it needs

LUNCH OR SUPPER Serves 4

Overall timing 30 minutes

Equipment Saucepan, frying pan

Freezing Not recommended

INGREDIENTS

2lb	Spinach	900g
	Salt	
6oz	Slice of ham	175g
1	Garlic clove	1
3 tbsp	Oil	3×15ml
	Freshly-ground black pepper	
2	Hard-boiled eggs	2
2 tbsp	Pine nuts	2×15ml

Below: Fried spinach with ham – don't cook the spinach too long as this impairs flavour

METHOD

1 Wash and pick over the spinach, discarding any withered leaves or coarse stalks. Drain thoroughly and blanch in lightly salted boiling water for 1 minute. Remove from heat, rinse under cold water and drain thoroughly. Chop coarsely.

2 Dice the ham and peel the garlic. Heat the oil in a large frying pan, add ham and garlic and fry for 2–3 minutes. Stir in the spinach, add plenty of pepper and fry gently for 5 minutes, stirring occasionally.

3 Meanwhile, shell and finely chop the eggs. Add to the pan with the pine nuts and cook for 2 minutes.

4 Discard garlic clove. Adjust seasoning to taste and arrange on a warmed serving dish. Serve immediately with thick slices of crusty bread.

VARIATIONS

Diced bacon, fried till crispy, can be used instead of ham, and the pine nuts can be replaced with slivers of almonds.

For a creamy egg sauce, omit the chopped hard-boiled eggs. Instead, beat 4 eggs together in a bowl with plenty of salt and freshly-ground black pepper and pour into the spinach in the frying pan just before serving. Remove from the heat almost at once and turn the mixture over with a wooden spoon so the spinach is coated with the moist egg sauce. The sauce should be smooth, not dry or lumpy like scrambled egg; don't leave the pan on the heat for more than half a minute, and serve immediately or the egg will continue to cook in the heat of the spinach. For a richer sauce, omit the eggs altogether. Just before serving, mix 2 tbsp (2×15ml) port with $\frac{1}{4}$ pint (150ml) single cream and pour into the spinach. Heat through, stirring constantly, over a low heat, but do not allow to boil. Serve when the spinach is well coated. For a sharper flavour, you can replace the fresh cream with soured cream.

Lamb and vermicelli

A delectable dish of lamb, cooked in a wok with vegetables, topped with very crisp deep-fried vermicelli

LUNCH OR SUPPER Serves 4

Overall timing 25 minutes

Equipment Wok or frying pan, deep-fryer

Freezing Not recommended

INGREDIENTS

1lb	Boned lean lamb	450g
2	Small onions	2
2	Carrots	2
1	Large green capsicum	1
2 tbsp	Oil	2x15ml
½ pint	Chicken stock	300ml
	Salt and pepper	
	Oil for deep frying	
2 teasp	Cornflour	2x5ml
2 tbsp	Soy sauce	2x15ml
2oz	Chinese vermicelli	50g

METHOD

1 Wipe and trim the lamb. Cut into fine slices across the grain, then into strips. Peel the onions and cut each through the root into 8 wedges. Scrape and diagonally slice the carrots. Halve and deseed the capsicum, then slice.

2 Heat the oil in the wok or frying pan and stir-fry the lamb till browned all over. Add the onion and carrot and stir-fry for 2 minutes. Add the stock (made with a cube if necessary) and seasoning, bring to the boil and simmer for 5 minutes.

3 Heat the oil in the deep-fryer to 340F (170C).

4 Blend the cornflour to a paste with the soy sauce, add to the wok with the capsicum and bring to the boil, stirring constantly. Simmer for 2 minutes, taste and adjust the seasoning. Loosen the bundle of vermicelli slightly and fry in deep-fryer for about 20 seconds till puffed up and crisp.

5 Arrange lamb mixture on a warmed serving dish and place the vermicelli on top. Serve immediately with boiled or fried rice.

Pork rib chop casserole

Pork chops from the fore loin are sometimes called rib chops. In this quick-to-cook casserole, sour cream adds piquancy to the final flavour

LUNCH OR SUPPER Serves 4

Overall timing 30 minutes

Equipment Flameproof casserole

Freezing Not recommended

INGREDIENTS

1lb	Potatoes	450g
2 tbsp	Oil	2x15ml
4	Pork rib chops	4
	Salt and pepper	
3 tbsp	Water	3x15ml
4oz	Button mushrooms	125g
1 teasp	Garlic salt	5ml
¼ pint	Carton of soured cream	150ml
2 tbsp	Chopped parsley	2x15ml

METHOD

1 Peel potatoes and cut them into very small, thin pieces. Melt the oil in the casserole and fry the potatoes for 5 minutes. Remove from pan with draining spoon.

2 Season chops with salt and pepper, add to casserole and cook for 1 minute on each side. Drain excess fat. Add water, cover and cook for 10 minutes.

3 Wipe and slice mushrooms. Add to casserole with fried potatoes and garlic salt and cook for a further 10 minutes.

4 Stir in soured cream and 1 tbsp (15ml) of the chopped parsley. Heat through. Sprinkle with remaining parsley just before serving. Serve with a green vegetable, such as broccoli, or a crisp green salad for a good contrast.

Right: Pork rib chop casserole – pork chops, potatoes, mushrooms and sour cream

Marrow and potato mornay

The delicate flavour of marrow combines well with other ingredients. Here, it is cooked in a layered baked dish with potatoes and a cheese sauce. Crisply fried or grilled bacon pieces add a tasty finishing touch to the bubbling, golden topping

LUNCH OR SUPPER Serves 4

Overall timing 1 hour

Equipment 3 saucepans, ovenproof dish, frying pan (optional)

Freezing Not recommended

INGREDIENTS

$1\frac{1}{2}$lb	Marrow	700g
1lb	Potatoes	450g
	Salt	
1oz	Butter	25g
3 tbsp	Plain flour	3×15ml
1 teasp	Prepared mustard	5ml
$\frac{1}{4}$ pint	Milk	150ml
4oz	Mature Cheddar	125g
	Freshly-ground black pepper	
4oz	Bacon	125g
2 tbsp	Fresh breadcrumbs	2×15ml

METHOD

1 Peel the marrow and cut off the ends. Cut in half lengthways and scoop out the seeds. Cut flesh into $\frac{1}{2}$ inch (12.5mm) slices. Peel and slice the potatoes.

2 Cook the potatoes in a saucepan of salted water for about 10 minutes till tender. Blanch the marrow slices in another pan of boiling salted water, then drain and reserve $\frac{1}{4}$ pint (150ml) of the liquor.

3 Heat the butter in a third saucepan, stir in the flour and cook for 1 minute, then add the mustard and gradually stir in the milk and the reserved marrow liquor. Mix well and bring to the boil, stirring.

4 Remove pan from heat and grate in the cheese, reserving a little for garnish. Taste and adjust seasoning.

5 Make alternate layers of marrow and potato in the ovenproof dish and keep hot. Preheat the grill.

6 Derind and chop bacon and fry or grill till crisp. Pour the cheese sauce over the vegetables and top with the reserved cheese and the breadcrumbs. Place under grill till golden and bubbling on top. Top with crisp bacon and serve with a fresh green salad or Corn with petits pois (recipe page 504).

Chickpea and lentil curry

To shorten the cooking time of the pulses, boil them in a pressure cooker (instructions on pages 572–573)

MAIN MEAL Serves 6

Overall timing $2\frac{1}{4}$ hours plus overnight soaking

Equipment 2 bowls, large saucepan

Freezing Cool, put into rigid container, leaving $\frac{3}{4}$ inch (2cm) headspace, cover, label and freeze. Freezer life: 3 months. To use: reheat slowly from frozen

INGREDIENTS

6oz	Chickpeas	175g
6oz	Egyptian lentils	175g
2	Onions	2
2 tbsp	Oil	2×15ml
1 teasp	Ground ginger	5ml
$\frac{1}{4}$ teasp	Cayenne pepper	$\frac{1}{4}$×5ml
$\frac{1}{4}$ teasp	Ground cloves	$\frac{1}{4}$×5ml
$\frac{1}{2}$ teasp	Ground cinnamon	$\frac{1}{2}$×5ml
3 teasp	Ground cumin	3×5ml
1 teasp	Ground turmeric	5ml
	Salt	
3 tbsp	Lemon juice	3×15ml
1 tbsp	Chopped parsley	15ml

METHOD

1 Wash and pick over chickpeas and lentils, then soak separately in cold water overnight. Drain pulses. Place chickpeas in a saucepan, cover with water and simmer, covered, for 1–2 hours or until tender. Cook lentils in the same way for 15–20 minutes.

2 Drain chickpeas and lentils and reserve liquid. Peel and chop onions.

3 Heat oil in a large saucepan and fry onions with the spices for about 5 minutes. Add pulses and $\frac{1}{4}$ pint (150ml) of reserved liquid. Season and stir in lemon juice and chopped parsley. Serve with boiled rice and lime pickle, or as part of an Indian meal together with another curry of meat or poultry, such as Lamb curry (page 407) or Chicken biriani (page 88).

Aubergine boxes

In this unusual dish, the basil brings out the flavour of the tomato sauce in which the "boxes" are cooked

MAIN MEAL Serves 4

Overall timing $1\frac{1}{2}$ hours

Equipment Saucepan, mixing bowl, flameproof dish

Freezing Not recommended

Above: *Aubergine boxes, a very different way to serve the vegetable. The stuffing is flavoured with anchovies, capers and basil to complement the tomato sauce in which the aubergines are cooked*

INGREDIENTS

1lb	Aubergines	450g
3	Anchovy fillets	3
2 tbsp	Chopped fresh basil	2×15ml
	or	
2 teasp	dried basil	2× 5ml
2oz	Mozzarella	50g
2 teasp	Capers	2×5ml
1 teasp	Salt	5ml
	Pepper	
2 tbsp	Oil	2×15ml
1	Large onion	1
2	Garlic cloves	2
14oz	Can of tomatoes	397g
1 tbsp	Worcestershire sauce	15ml
	Salt and pepper	
4–5	Fresh tomatoes (optional)	4–5

METHOD

1 Wipe aubergines and cook for 5 minutes in lightly salted, boiling water. Drain and leave to cool.
2 Using a sharp knife, cut off stalks and make a lengthways cut through the aubergines leaving the halves still attached at one side (see first step-by-step picture, below). Ease open and remove most of the flesh with a teaspoon.
3 Chop or mash the flesh so it's very fine and put into a bowl. Drain and chop the anchovies, finely chop the fresh basil, if using, and dice Mozzarella.
4 Mix together aubergine flesh, anchovies, basil, Mozzarella, capers, salt and pepper. Stuff the hollowed-out aubergine shells with mixture (see second step-by-step picture, below).
5 Preheat oven to 350F (180C) Gas 4. In a flameproof dish, heat the oil then brown the chopped onion. Add the peeled and crushed garlic, canned tomatoes, Worcestershire sauce, salt and pepper. Stirring occasionally, simmer the mixture gently for about 10 minutes or until the sauce has become quite "mushy".
6 Arrange the stuffed aubergines on top of the sauce and bake in the oven for 45 minutes. You can add 4–5 fresh tomatoes about 15 minutes before the end of the cooking time – they add attractive colour as well as taste.

TO SERVE

Serve hot with crusty French bread to mop up the sauce and lightly steamed new green beans.

Far left: the vegetables are cut lengthways, but not completely through
Left: the hollowed-out aubergines are filled with the stuffing

Poached chicken

One of the simplest ways of cooking a chicken. The poaching liquid need be nothing more than water, the flavour coming mostly from the chicken itself and the vegetables

MAIN MEAL Serves 4

Overall timing 2 hours

Equipment 2 large saucepans

Freezing Not recommended

INGREDIENTS

8	Chicken legs and wings	8
12oz	Carrots	350g
8oz	Button onions	225g
2	Stalks of celery	2
	Sea-salt	
1lb	Potatoes	450g

METHOD

1 Put chicken joints in a large saucepan and cover with cold water. Scrape and chop carrots, peel onions and chop celery.

2 Add a few pieces of carrot, 4 onions, all the celery and 2 teasp (2×5ml) sea-salt to chicken. Bring slowly to the boil, then reduce the heat until just simmering, cover and cook for about $1\frac{1}{2}$ hours over a low heat.

3 Meanwhile, cook remaining carrots and onions in boiling salted water for 5 minutes, then add the peeled and chopped potatoes. Simmer for a further 20 minutes. Drain.

TO SERVE

Drain chicken (keep the cooking liquor and vegetables for soup) and serve on a warmed plate with the remaining carrots, onions and potatoes. Put sea-salt on the table to be used according to taste.

Below: Poached chicken, served with carrots, onions and potato chunks

Saucy meatloaf

A meatloaf with its own inbuilt sauce which is spooned into the base of the tin before the meat mixture is added. This gives an exquisitely moist result. Serve sliced with green vegetables or a mixed salad

MAIN MEAL Serves 4

Overall timing $1\frac{1}{2}$ hours

Equipment 2lb (900g) loaf tin, saucepan, bowl

Freezing Not recommended

INGREDIENTS

4oz	Button mushrooms	125g
1oz	Butter	25g
8oz	Can of tomatoes	227g
1 tbsp	Chopped fresh marjoram *or*	15ml
2 teasp	dried marjoram	2×5ml
	Salt	
	Freshly-ground black pepper	
1	Large onion	1
12oz	Minced beef	350g
4oz	Pork sausagemeat	125g
1oz	Fresh breadcrumbs	25g
1	Egg	1
1 tbsp	Tomato paste	15ml
2 teasp	Worcestershire sauce	2×5ml

METHOD

1 Preheat the oven to 350F (180C) Gas 4. Grease the loaf tin.

2 Wipe and slice the mushrooms. Heat the butter in a small saucepan and fry the mushrooms for 3 minutes, shaking pan frequently.

3 Add the tomatoes and their juice, a third of the marjoram and salt and pepper to taste. Mix well to break up the tomatoes, then spread mixture in the base of the tin.

4 Peel and finely chop the onion and put into a large bowl. Add the mince and sausagemeat and mix with a fork till evenly blended. Beat in the egg, remaining marjoram, tomato paste and Worcestershire sauce and plenty of seasoning. Mix well.

5 Spoon the mixture into the tin and smooth the surface. Cover with foil and bake on the centre shelf of the oven for $1\frac{1}{4}$ hours till there is no blood in the juices when the loaf is tested with a fine skewer.

6 Turn out carefully on to a warmed serving dish and serve hot with green vegetables or a dressed mixed salad.

Lettuce wedges and cucumber salad

The lettuce is cut into wedges to give this salad a substantial base.

SALAD Serves 4–6

Overall timing 15 minutes plus chilling

Equipment Plate, salad bowl, small bowl

Freezing Not recommended

INGREDIENTS

1	Small cucumber	1
	Salt	
1	Iceberg lettuce	1
2	Hard-boiled eggs	2
3 tbsp	Single cream	3×15ml
1 tbsp	Vinegar	15ml
	Salt	
	Freshly-ground black pepper	
	Fennel fronds or parsley sprigs	

METHOD

1 Peel and slice cucumber. Arrange slices on a plate, sprinkle with salt and leave to stand for 30 minutes.

2 Trim lettuce and cut into wedges. Wash and drain thoroughly, then place in salad bowl and leave in fridge for 15 minutes to crisp.

3 To make the dressing, cut the hard-boiled eggs in half. Remove yolks and press through a sieve into a small bowl. Gradually stir in the cream and vinegar and beat till smooth and creamy. Season to taste.

4 Drain cucumber slices and add to lettuce. Just before serving, pour dressing over salad and toss.

5 Finely chop hard-boiled egg whites and sprinkle over. Garnish and serve with hot or cold meat dishes.

Remove the skin from the cooked tongue by slicing along the length and pulling away

Hold skinned tongue firmly and cut into thick but even slices with a sharp knife

Piquant tongue

Tongue slices in a piquant tomato and gherkin sauce that's enriched with fragrant thyme and oregano

MAIN MEAL Serves 4–6

Overall timing 2½ hours

Equipment Saucepan, flameproof casserole, blender

Freezing Not recommended

INGREDIENTS

2lb	Calves tongue	900g
	Salt	
3	Medium-size carrots	3
2	Medium-size onions	2
3oz	Butter	75g
¼ pint	Dry white wine	150ml
14oz	Can of tomatoes	397g
2 tbsp	Tomato paste	2×15ml
4	Sprigs of thyme	4
	Freshly-ground black pepper	
4	Large gherkins	4
2 teasp	Oregano	2×5ml

METHOD

1 Trim and rinse the tongue and put into a large saucepan. Cover with lightly salted cold water and bring to the boil. Cover and simmer for 20 minutes. Drain the tongue and plunge it into cold water. Drain, then remove the skin, and any bones from the root.

2 Scrape and chop the carrots, peel and finely chop the onions. Heat the butter in the casserole, add the carrots and onions and fry gently for 5 minutes.

3 Place the tongue on top of the vegetables and add the wine, ¼ pint (150ml) water, the canned tomatoes and juice, tomato paste, thyme and seasoning. Bring to the boil, cover tightly and simmer for 1–1½ hours till the tongue is tender.

4 Lift out the tongue and slice thickly. Arrange on a serving dish and keep hot.

5 Discard the thyme, pour the sauce into a blender. Add the roughly chopped gherkins and the oregano and blend thoroughly till smooth.

6 Reheat the sauce and adjust the seasoning to taste. Pour round the tongue and serve immediately with creamed potatoes and a green salad, such as Lettuce wedges and cucumber salad, left. Any leftover tongue is still delicious served cold.

Macaroni with cockles

An attractive dish of elbow macaroni garnished with cockle shells. If your fishmonger sells cockles by the jug measure, you'll need 4 pints (2 litres)

MAIN MEAL Serves 4

Overall timing 45 minutes

Equipment 3 saucepans, fine sieve

Freezing Not recommended

INGREDIENTS

2lb	Fresh cockles	900g
1	Shallot	1
	Bouquet garni	
	Salt	
2oz	Butter	50g
2oz	Plain flour	50g
¼ pint	Dry white wine	150ml
1 tbsp	Tomato paste	15ml
	Cayenne pepper	
8oz	Elbow macaroni	225g
2oz	Grated Gruyère cheese	50g
	Freshly-ground black pepper	

METHOD

1 Wash and scrub the cockles well. Place in a large saucepan. Peel and chop the shallot and add to pan with the bouquet garni and enough salted water just to cover. Bring to the boil and cook for 5 minutes till the shells open. Remove from heat. Discard any cockles that are still closed.

2 Reserve a few cockles in their shells to use for garnish. Remove the rest from the shells. Strain the cooking liquor through a fine sieve and reserve.

3 To make the sauce, heat the butter in a saucepan, stir in the flour and cook for 1 minute. Gradually stir in ¾ pint (400ml) of the reserved cooking liquor and the wine. Stir in the tomato paste and a pinch of cayenne. Bring to the boil, stirring constantly, then reduce the heat and simmer for 10 minutes.

4 Cook the macaroni in a large saucepan of boiling salted water till al dente, then drain well. Place macaroni in warmed serving dish, add the sauce, cockles and half the cheese. Mix well and season to taste. Garnish with the reserved cockles in their shells and remaining grated cheese. Serve immediately with slices of fresh crusty bread.

Cod with tamarind

The fish in this traditional Indian dish is deliciously aromatic

MAIN MEAL Serves 4

Overall timing 1¼ hours plus marination

Equipment 3 bowls, flameproof casserole

Freezing Not recommended

INGREDIENTS

4	Fresh cod steaks	4
6 tbsp	Plain flour	6×15ml
3	Garlic cloves	3
½ teasp	Ground turmeric	½×5ml
	Salt	
2 tbsp	Natural yogurt	2×15ml
1	Large onion	1
1 tbsp	Ground coriander	15ml
¼ teasp	Freshly-ground black pepper	¼×5ml
4 tbsp	Oil	4×15ml
12oz	Ripe tomatoes	350g
1 tbsp	Vinegar	15ml
½ pint	Tamarind water	300ml
3	Cardamom pods	3
	Freshly-grated nutmeg	
1 tbsp	Chopped parsley	15ml

METHOD

1 Trim the cod steaks and prick several times with a fork. Rinse and drain, then coat with the flour. Leave to stand for 10 minutes.

2 Meanwhile, peel and crush the garlic into a bowl. Add the turmeric and a little salt and pound to a paste. Stir in the yogurt.

3 Rinse the fish steaks a second time and spread with the yogurt mixture. Leave to marinate for 30 minutes.

4 Peel and finely chop the onion. Place in a bowl with the coriander, pepper and 1 tbsp (15ml) of the oil and pound to a paste. Blanch, peel and quarter the tomatoes.

5 Put the vinegar into a bowl with ½ pint (300ml) water. Dip the fish steaks into the water to wash away the yogurt. Pat dry with kitchen paper, then rub with the onion paste.

6 Heat remaining oil in the casserole, add the fish steaks and fry for 3 minutes each side.

7 Add the tamarind water, tomatoes, cardamom pods, a pinch of nutmeg and a little salt. Cover and simmer gently for 15 minutes till the fish is tender.

8 Remove and discard the cardamom pods, taste and adjust seasoning. Sprinkle with parsley and serve immediately with boiled rice.

Coat mackerel steaks with flour seasoned with salt, pepper and mild curry powder

Add cooking apple to melted butter, cover and sweat over low heat till pulpy

To make sauce, sieve apple, cook with sugar, cream and egg yolks till thick

Fried mackerel with creamy apple sauce

A splendid combination of textures and tastes lifts mackerel into the gourmet class. The apple in the accompanying sauce is fried in butter

MAIN MEAL Serves 4

Overall timing 45 minutes

Equipment Polythene bag, 2 saucepans, large frying pan

Freezing Not recommended

INGREDIENTS

$2\times1\frac{1}{2}$lb	Mackerel	2×700g
6 tbsp	Plain flour	6×15ml
1 teasp	Mild curry powder	5ml
	Salt	
	Freshly-ground white pepper	
1	Large cooking apple	1
4oz	Butter	125g
3 tbsp	Oil	3×15ml
1 teasp	Caster sugar	5ml
$\frac{1}{4}$ pint	Carton of double cream	150ml
2	Egg yolks	2

METHOD

1 Wash mackerel and pat dry on kitchen paper. Cut into 2 inch (5cm) thick steaks, discarding the heads and tails.

2 Mix the flour, curry powder, salt and pepper together in a polythene bag. Add the fish and toss lightly till evenly coated.

3 Peel, core and chop the cooking apple. Heat 2oz (50g) of the butter in the saucepan, add the apple and stir till coated. Cover and sweat over a low heat for 5–10 minutes till pulpy.

4 Heat the remaining butter and the oil in the frying pan. Add the mackerel steaks and fry over a moderate heat for about 15 minutes, turning frequently, till the flesh is tender and the skin is crisp and golden.

5 Meanwhile, rub the apple through a sieve into a clean pan. Add the sugar and stir till melted. Gradually beat the cream into the egg yolks, then add to the apple purée.

6 Stir constantly over a low heat for 3 minutes without boiling till the mixture is smooth and thick. Add salt and pepper to taste.

7 Pour the sauce into a warmed sauceboat and serve immediately with the fried fish, new potatoes and buttered carrots or Minted peas (page 16).

Right: Fried mackerel with creamy apple sauce – steaks with flavourful coating

Panettone

This is the Genoese version of a rich, fruity yeast cake which is traditionally eaten all over Italy on festive occasions, such as Christmas and Easter

TEA-TIME Cuts into 8

Overall timing 1½ hours plus proving

Equipment 2 small saucepans, 2 bowls, oiled polythene, baking tray

Freezing Cool completely, pack in a polythene bag, seal, label and freeze. Freezer life: 1 month. To use: thaw in wrapping overnight, refresh at 350F (180C) Gas 4 for 10 minutes

INGREDIENTS

¼ pint	Milk	150ml
12oz	Strong flour	350g
1oz	Fresh yeast *or*	25g
4 teasp	dried yeast	4×5ml
2oz	Caster sugar	50g
¼ teasp	Salt	¼×5ml
2oz	Butter	50g
2oz	Pine nuts	50g
2oz	Candied peel	50g
2oz	Raisins	50g
1	Egg	1
1 tbsp	Marsala	15ml

Below: Panettone – to taste it at its best, eat this cake when really fresh, even warm

METHOD

1 Warm the milk. Sift 4oz (125g) of the flour into a small bowl. Stir in the yeast and 1 teasp (5ml) of the sugar. Mix well and gradually stir in the warm milk to give a smooth batter. Leave in a warm place for 20–30 minutes till frothy.

2 Meanwhile, sift the remaining flour and the salt into a large bowl and leave in a warm place till the yeast is ready. Melt the butter in a saucepan and leave to cool.

3 Stir the remaining sugar, the pine nuts, candied peel and raisins into the flour and make a well in the centre. Stir the melted butter, beaten egg and Marsala into the frothy batter, then pour into the well in the flour.

4 With a wooden spoon, gradually draw the flour into the liquid till it binds together to form a soft dough. Turn out on to a lightly floured surface. Knead till smooth and glossy and shape into a ball. Place in the bowl, cover with oiled polythene and leave to prove in a warm place till doubled in size.

5 Turn the dough out of the bowl, knock back to break down uneven air bubbles and knead till smooth. Shape into a smooth ball and place on the greased baking tray. Cover with oiled polythene and leave to prove till doubled in size.

6 Preheat the oven to 400F (200C) Gas 6.

7 Score a cross on top of the Panettone and bake in the centre of the oven for 10 minutes. Reduce the heat to 350F (180C) Gas 4 and cook for a further 25 minutes. Cool on a wire rack.

Spicy fruit rolls

A sweet and spicy fruit and nut bread. Cut into slices and spread with butter for a tea-time treat

TEA-TIME Makes 2

Overall timing 2 hours plus overnight soaking and proving

Equipment 3 bowls, saucepan, mincer, baking tray

Freezing Cool completely, foil-wrap, seal, label and freeze. Freezer life: 1 month. To use: reheat foil-wrapped loaf from frozen at 350F (180C) Gas 4 for about 40 minutes

INGREDIENTS

1lb	Dried pears	450g
6oz	Raisins	175g
2oz	Chopped walnuts	50g
1oz	Chopped candied peel	25g
5oz	Caster sugar	150g
2 teasp	Rose-water	2×5ml
1 tbsp	Kirsch	15ml
2 teasp	Ground cinnamon	2×5ml
¼ teasp	Ground cloves	¼×5ml
1lb	Packet of white bread mix	450g
1	Beaten egg	1

METHOD
1 Put the pears into a bowl, cover with cold water and leave to soak overnight.
2 Next day, put the pears and soaking liquor into a saucepan and bring to the boil. Cover and simmer for 20 minutes. Remove pears and chop or push through a mincer twice. Put in bowl with raisins, walnuts, candied peel, 4oz (125g) sugar, rose-water, Kirsch, cinnamon and cloves. Mix well and reserve.
3 Make up the bread mix, adding the remaining sugar. Knead till smooth.
4 Knead the fruit mixture into one-third of the dough and shape it into two sausages about 6 inches (15cm) long.
5 Roll out the remaining dough to a rectangle about 12×9 inches (30×23cm). Cut in half to give 2 strips 6 inches (15cm) wide. Brush with egg.
6 Place one of the sausage-shaped pieces of dough on each strip and roll up.
7 Place rolls join side down on a greased baking tray. Cover with oiled polythene and leave till doubled in size.
8 Preheat the oven to 425F (220C) Gas 7.
9 Brush rolls with egg and bake for 15 minutes. Reduce the oven temperature to 375F (190C) Gas 5 and cook for a further 25 minutes till the base sounds hollow when tapped.

cook's know-how

Rose-water is available from many Greek, Cypriot and Indian shops as well as chemists, and is used to scent puddings, cakes, biscuits and confectionery. It does need to be used sparingly, as its perfume is best appreciated when it doesn't mask the flavour of the other ingredients.
Rose-water is usually distilled (the best still comes from Bulgaria where roses are the principal crop), but a passable imitation can be made at home. Pick the opened roses (they should be well scented) early in the morning as soon as the dew is off them. Pull off the petals carefully so they don't bruise – you'll need enough to fill two coffee mugs. Put the petals in a large jug, add 8oz (225g) caster sugar and 1¾ pints (1 litre) warm water. Leave for 1 hour, then pour the mix from one jug to another until the roses have scented the water. Strain into a screw-topped bottle. Store in a cool, dark place. If the flavour of rose-water doesn't appeal in cooking, you can always add it to finger bowls.

Above: Crunchy nut biscuits – light-as-air and flavoured with cinnamon and vanilla

Crunchy nut biscuits

These biscuits are similar to macaroons but are lighter and more fragile. They can also be made with almonds or unsalted peanuts

TEA-TIME — Makes about 24

Overall timing 1¼ hours

Equipment 2 bowls, heavy-based frying pan, baking trays

Freezing Cool, pack in rigid container, interleaved with greaseproof paper. Cover, label and freeze. Freezer life: 3 months. To use: thaw for 4 hours at room temperature

Storage Airtight container

INGREDIENTS

8oz	Shelled hazelnuts	225g
6oz	Caster sugar	175g
¼ teasp	Ground cinnamon	¼×5ml
4	Egg whites	4
	Pinch of cream of tartar	
¼ teasp	Vanilla essence	¼×5ml
½oz	Butter	15g

METHOD
1 Spread shelled nuts on grill pan and toast till golden brown all over. Preheat oven to 300F (150C) Gas 2. Grease and flour baking trays.
2 Roughly chop nuts and put in a bowl with sugar and cinnamon.

Whisk egg whites, cream of tartar, vanilla

Lightly fold toasted nuts, sugar and cinnamon into the egg whites

3 In another bowl, whisk egg whites with cream of tartar and vanilla essence till very stiff. Gently fold in nut mixture.
4 Scrape the egg/nut mixture into a greased heavy-based frying pan and cook over a very low heat for about 15 minutes, turning mixture constantly with a wooden spoon, until it is pale brown.
5 Put spoonfuls of the mixture on prepared trays, about 1 inch (2.5cm) apart. Cook in oven for about 30 minutes, then reduce temperature to 250F (130C) Gas ½ and cook for a further 10 minutes until the biscuits are crisp.

Above: Raspberry mille-feuilles – classic French pâtisserie to make at home

Raspberry mille-feuilles

Light and crisp layers of puff pastry are spread with a mixture of jam and Kirsch, then topped with glacé icing. Ideal for tea-time or as a dessert served with cream

TEA-TIME OR DESSERT Serves 4

Overall timing 30 minutes plus thawing

Equipment Baking tray

Freezing Not recommended

INGREDIENTS

13oz	Packet of frozen puff pastry	375g
1 tbsp	Kirsch	15ml
6oz	Raspberry jam	175g

METHOD

1 Thaw pastry. Preheat the oven to 425F (220C) Gas 7.
2 Roll out the pastry to a 12 inch (30cm) square. Cut into 3 even sized rectangles, trim edges and knock up.
3 Place on a wetted baking tray, prick several times with a fork. Mark one of the rectangles into six 2 inch (5cm) wide slices with a sharp knife.
4 Bake for about 10 minutes till well risen and golden, then transfer to a wire rack and allow to cool.
5 Place one of the unmarked rectangles on a flat board. Mix together the Kirsch and jam and spread a third of it evenly over the pastry.
6 Cover with the other unmarked rectangle, spread another third of the jam over, then cover with the marked rectangle and top with the remaining jam or white glacé icing.*
7 Cut into slices along marked lines. If liked, serve with whipped cream or pouring cream for dessert.

*To make white glacé icing, blend 4oz (125g) sifted icing sugar with 1–2 tbsp (1–2×15ml) hot water. The icing should be thick enough to coat the back of a spoon. If too thick add more water, if too runny, add more icing sugar.

Brandy snaps

These can be a little tricky till you acquire the knack. It's best to cook them in small batches so that the snaps don't have time to harden before you can roll them. Otherwise, pop them back into the warm oven to soften again

TEA-TIME OR DESSERT Makes about 12

Overall timing 40 minutes

Equipment Baking trays, saucepan, wooden spoon

Freezing Not recommended

Storage Airtight container

INGREDIENTS

2 tbsp	Golden syrup	2×15ml
2oz	Butter	50g
2oz	Dark brown sugar	50g
2oz	Plain flour	50g
½ teasp	Ground ginger	½×5ml
1 teasp	Brandy or lemon juice	5ml

METHOD

1 Preheat the oven to 350F (180C) Gas 4. Grease baking trays.
2 Put the syrup, butter and sugar in a pan and heat gently till sugar dissolves. Remove from heat.
3 Sift flour and ginger together, then gradually stir into pan. Mix in the brandy or lemon juice.
4 Drop 2 separate teaspoonfuls of the mixture on to each tray. Bake just above the centre of the oven for about 8 minutes or until just golden.
5 Remove from oven and leave to cool on baking trays for about a minute. Lift each snap from tray with a palette knife and carefully roll round the oiled handle of a wooden spoon (place smooth side against the wood). Leave on handle until firm, then slip off. If you find that some of the snaps have hardened on the trays, return to the oven for 1–2 minutes before rolling. Use rest of mixture in the same way.

TO SERVE

For tea-time, fill with whipped cream and dredge with icing sugar. To serve as a dessert, fill with brandy or liqueur-flavoured whipped cream or serve empty as an accompaniment to creamy desserts.

VARIATION

Shape snaps over a rolling-pin (see Tuiles, page 280) instead of round a spoon handle.

Northumberland singin' hinnie

This is a popular fruity scone-type cake from the North East of England and gets its name from the noise it makes as it sizzles on the griddle. For extra extravagance serve with jam and clotted cream as well as butter

TEA-TIME Serves 8

Overall timing 35 minutes

Equipment Large mixing bowl, griddle, rolling pin

Freezing Place cooled round in polythene bag, seal, label and freeze. Freezer life: 6 months. To use: thaw at room temperature or cover with foil and refresh in hot oven (400F/200C/Gas 6) for about 10 minutes

INGREDIENTS

12oz	Self-raising flour	350g
½ teasp	Salt	½×5ml
2oz	Butter	50g
2oz	Lard	50g
4oz	Mixed dried fruit	125g
1oz	Caster sugar	25g
6fl oz	Creamy milk *or* single cream and milk mixed together	170ml

METHOD

1. Sift the flour and salt into a large mixing bowl and rub in the butter and lard until the mixture resembles fine breadcrumbs.
2. Add the dried fruit and sugar and mix with the milk or milk mixture to give a soft but not sticky dough.
3. Grease a griddle, preferably with dripping, and place over a very low heat. Roll out the dough on a lightly-floured surface to a circle about ¾ inch (2cm) thick.
4. Cut into 8 wedges and arrange on the griddle. Cook very slowly on a low heat to allow the raising agent in the flour to work before the crust is cooked. This takes about 10–15 minutes on each side during which time it should hiss and sing.
5. To serve, separate the wedges while still hot, then cut in half and butter them. Or add jam and clotted cream.

Chocolate and walnut tart

Wholewheat flour gives a short texture to the pastry which contrasts well with the rich and creamy filling. It can be served warm or chilled

TEA-TIME OR DESSERT Cuts into 8

Overall timing 1 hour plus chilling

Equipment 2 bowls, 8 inch (20cm) fluted loose-bottom flan dish

Freezing Not recommended

INGREDIENTS

	Pastry	
3oz	Wholewheat flour	75g
3oz	Self-raising flour	75g
4oz	Butter or margarine	125g
1 tbsp	Caster sugar	15ml
1	Egg yolk	1
	Water to mix	
	Filling	
½ pint	Carton of whipping cream	284ml
2	Eggs	2
2oz	Caster sugar	50g
2 tbsp	Cocoa	2×15ml
½ teasp	Ground cinnamon	½×5ml
4oz	Chopped walnuts	125g
2 tbsp	Brandy or rum	2×15ml
	Decoration	
1oz	Walnut halves	25g

METHOD

1. Mix the flours in a large bowl. Rub in the butter or margarine until the mixture resembles fine breadcrumbs. Stir in the sugar and make a well in the centre. Add the egg yolk and enough water to mix to a firm dough.
2. Gather mixture into a ball, wrap in polythene bag and chill for 30 minutes.
3. Preheat the oven to 400F (200C) Gas 6. Roll out pastry on a lightly floured surface and use to line flan dish. Prick base and bake blind near the top of the oven for 15 minutes.
4. Meanwhile, whisk cream in a bowl till lightly thickened, then whisk in egg yolks, sugar, cocoa, cinnamon, chopped walnuts and brandy or rum. Whisk egg whites to soft peaks and fold in.
5. Pour filling into pastry case and bake in the centre of the oven for about 25 minutes or until set.
6. Leave to cool in tin, then lift on to a serving plate and decorate with walnut halves. Serve warm or chilled with pouring cream.

Below: Chocolate and walnut tart – the creamy filling is flavoured with brandy or rum

South America: *a tropical treat*

Despite the size of the continent, there is a certain similarity between the various cuisines of the countries of South America, due both to the similar origins of the inhabitants, and the ingredients available. Much of the continent was conquered by the Spanish in the 16th century. The Portuguese captain, Pedro Alvares Cabral, set foot on what was later called Brazil in 1500. The descendants of natives and colonists now live side by side, and they have been joined by large numbers of immigrants from all over the world. In Brazil, there is also a large population of African descent, brought in as slaves.

The native fruits and vegetables of South America are now so universally cultivated that it is not often remembered where chillies, maize, potatoes, tomatoes, avocados, vanilla and sweet potatoes originated. Chillies are eaten in every part of the continent. In Venezuela, chilli and avocados are combined in a spicy relish called *salsa guasacaca*, served with grilled meat. In Peru and Ecuador a beef and chilli stew called *pebre* is popular. In Peru, the chilli, called *aji*, is a main ingredient in *aji de gallina*, a chicken fricassee.

Maize is the staple diet of every country in South America, with the possible exception of Brazil. *Tamales*, maize flour patties stuffed with meat and vegetables, flavoured with chilli and baked in the leaves encasing the corn cob, are popular in Mexico, Ecuador and Peru. A similar dish, cooked in banana leaves, and called *hallaca*, is popular in Venezuela. *Tortillas* are eaten in all parts of the continent, while *arepa*, a flat bread made from maize flour or cornmeal, is popular in Colombia.

The potato originated in the high Andes, and its use is still confined mainly to the cooler, higher parts of the continent. Only in Peru and Bolivia is it a staple part of the diet. Served with a sauce of cheese, cream, chilli and olive oil, it is called *papas a la huancaina* – a mixture of old and new world influences, for the Indians did not make cheese before the Europeans came.

The third staple of South American diet is beans. There are all sorts and colours of native beans, from the delicate pink rosecoco bean to the black bean. The black bean features largely in the cooking of Brazil and Venezuela. In Venezuela, *frijoles negros*, as the beans are called, are served as a side dish with the popular *pabellon* dishes. These consist of grilled meat, rice, plantains and the beans, cooked with chillies, olive oil, garlic and ground cumin. In Brazil the beans are called *feijão* and are the main ingredient in *feijoada completa* which outsiders consider to be the national dish, but which is mostly enjoyed in Brazil, especially in Rio de Janeiro. The dish consists of pieces of pork, including the tail and ears of the pig, beef, smoked ox tongue, spare ribs and spicy sausages in a black bean stew. It is served with a wide variety of side dishes, including slices of fresh orange to cut the greasiness of the stew, and a dish of *farinha de mandioca*, glistening white manioc flour, to sprinkle over each serving. Manioc is a starchy root that is a staple of the Brazilian diet, especially among the African-descended population. The Amazon Indians make cakes from the flour.

The pampas of South America provide an ample supply of beef for the continent. Peru and Venezuela have less grazing ground, and use the meat more sparingly. In Peru, *anticucho*, marinated strips of beef grilled on skewers, is sold by street vendors, and eaten as an appetizer or hors d'oeuvre. In Chile, Uruguay and Argentina the *parilla*, a similar dish, is the gaucho's favourite meal; it consists of large cuts of beef, and sometimes lamb, often a whole animal, grilled over a wood fire on stakes. The Brazilian equivalent of the gaucho, the *churrasco*, eats his meat cooked on a sword. He has given his name to a dish in which a piece of grilled beef is passed among the diners who cut off individual portions. In Argentina, the *matambra* is a delicious portable meal for long journeys across the pampas. It consists of boned and rolled beef stuffed with vegetables and hard-boiled eggs.

The vast array of tropical and semitropical fruits makes it easy for South Americans to assuage their sweet tooth. There are pineapples, breadfruit, citrus fruits, coconuts and sugar cane, mangoes, custard apples (cherimoyas), acerola cherries and granadillas (passionfruit). There are also the unusual canistel ("egg-fruit") and pitanga (Surinam cherry) as well as indigenous brazil nuts and cashews.

South Americans also have a great love of sweet cakes and pastries, the making of which is a speciality of convents. The nuns originally brought the art from Spain and Portugal. For instance, *fios de ovos*, a Brazilian sweetmeat made of egg yolk and sugar, is based on a Portuguese confection.

Coffee is the natural drink of almost the whole continent, with the exception of Chile and Argentina. Brazil's entire economy was once based on the drink, and the instant variety is banned in some regions. Brazilian wines, mainly from the southern provinces, are becoming widely appreciated, as are the wines of Chile and Argentina. In Brazil, *cachaça*, a colourless strong drink is known as "sugar cane brandy". Made from sugar cane it should be called rum but tastes more like brandy.

MANIOC

Peel 4lb (1.8kg) cassava roots under cold running water. Dry on kitchen paper. Coarsely grate cassava or chop and put in an electric grinder, a little at a time, till broken down. Transfer to a bowl, add ½ pint (300ml) cold water and mix well (alternatively, put water and chopped cassava in a liquidizer and blend for a few seconds). Press through a sieve lined with muslin to extract as much liquid as possible. Use the meal to make sweet cassava pan-cooked bread. Mix 1lb (450g) of it with 4oz (125g) brown sugar and 8oz (225g) desiccated coconut to dough consistency (add a little water if necessary). Place in a large, greased, hot frying pan and cook over high heat for 2–3 minutes on both sides till brown. Serve warm with butter.

QUESILLO DE PIÑA

Ingredients 14⅓oz (410g) can of evaporated milk; 15½oz (439g) can of pineapple rings; 2 eggs; 2 egg yolks; 6oz (175g) sugar; 3 tbsp (3×15ml) water

Method Preheat oven to 325F (170C) Gas 3. Pour evaporated milk into a large bowl with juice from canned pineapple. Beat eggs and yolks lightly with a fork and beat into milk. Put sugar and water into a pan and heat gently, stirring, till dissolved. Bring to the boil, boil without stirring till golden. Pour into 1¾ pint (1 litre) mould, turning mould to coat base and sides. Strain egg mixture into mould, cover with foil and place in a bain marie. Cook in the centre of the oven for 2 hours. Cool, then chill for 4 hours. Turn out on to serving dish and decorate with pineapple rings.

Serves 6

The colourful cuisine of Latin America

Clockwise from the top: Sugar cane brandy, drunk as an aperitif in frosted glasses with lime; Chicken and corn soup (page 596); Quesillo de piña (recipe below left): Feijoada and accompaniments (page 597), and a South American fruit bowl

Countdown

Chicken and corn soup
Feijoada
Brazilian rice
Shredded kale
Chilli and lemon sauce
Manioc
Quesillo de piña

This colourful South American menu for 6 will make a delightful change for your guests.

Night before Wash and soak beans overnight for feijoada

7 hours before Make up dessert and cook in oven for 2 hours

4½ hours before Cool and chill dessert for 4 hours

3½ hours before Simmer spare ribs, pork and steak for 1 hour

3 hours before Prepare chilli and lemon sauce. Place in dish.

2½ hours before Remove meat, add soaked beans to cooking liquor and simmer for 1 hour

2 hours before Simmer onions, garlic, tomatoes, beans, liquor and chilli for 30 mins

1 hour before Prepare and cook chicken and onion for soup. Add cooked meats and sausages to remaining beans and liquor, simmer for 30 mins. Shred kale. Prepare cassava roots and sieve

30 mins before Finish making soup. Prepare and simmer rice

15 mins before Cut meat into serving pieces. Mash beans. Prepare garnish. Cook kale. Place all in serving dishes and keep hot

10 mins before Place avocado, cream and capers in tureen and pour in soup

5 mins before Turn out dessert and decorate

For a really authentic touch, start the meal with sugar cane brandy as an aperitif in frosted glasses decorated with lime slices, and offer cassava bread (page 594) with the soup. A mellow Spanish red such as Rioja would be a suitable substitute for a South American wine.
After the dessert, finish the meal with coffee, the natural drink of South America.

Chicken and corn soup

Maize, or sweetcorn, a staple food in South America, is combined with avocado in this thick, flavourful soup

STARTER Serves 6

Overall timing 1½ hours

Equipment Saucepan, potato masher

Freezing Not recommended

INGREDIENTS

2lb	Chicken portions	900g
1	Large onion	1
1oz	Butter	25g
¼ teasp	Ground cumin	¼×5ml
2½ pints	Chicken stock	1.5 litres
1lb	Floury potatoes	450g
	Salt	
	Freshly-ground black pepper	
2	Cobs of sweetcorn	2
1	Ripe avocado	1
¼ pint	Carton of single cream	150ml
1 tbsp	Drained capers	15ml

METHOD

1. Wipe and trim the chicken. Peel and chop the onion. Heat the butter in a large saucepan, add chicken and onion and fry for 5 minutes, turning chicken occasionally.
2. Add cumin and fry for 2 minutes. Add stock and bring to the boil. Cover and simmer for about 35 minutes till chicken is tender. Meanwhile, peel and dice the potatoes.
3. Lift chicken out of the pan. Add the potatoes to the stock, season and simmer for 10 minutes till tender.
4. Meanwhile, remove skin and bones from chicken and cut flesh into strips. Wash the corn, discarding the husks. Cut into 1 inch (2.5cm) thick slices, slicing across the cob.
5. Mash the potatoes in the soup to thicken it. Bring to the boil and add corn slices and chicken flesh. Simmer for 10 minutes.
6. Peel and halve the avocado, removing the stone, and slice the flesh thinly. Place in a tureen with the cream and capers.
7. Taste the soup and adjust seasoning. Pour into the tureen and serve immediately with fresh bread.

Above: Chicken and corn soup – sweet, young corn cobs are best for this dish

Feijoada

This meaty South American dish with its colourful accompaniments is served on festive occasions. Sliced oranges and sips of sugar-cane brandy help to balance the richness

MAIN MEAL Serves 6

Overall timing 3½ hours plus overnight soaking

Equipment Bowl, 2 large saucepans

Freezing Not recommended

INGREDIENTS

8oz	Dried black beans	225g
8oz	Spare ribs	225g
8oz	Belly of pork	225g
8oz	Piece of chuck steak	225g
2 pints	Cold water	1.1 litres
1	Large onion	1
1 oz	Lard	25g
2	Garlic cloves	2
8oz	Can of tomatoes	227g
1	Large fresh chilli	1
	Salt	
	Freshly-ground black pepper	
8oz	Chorizo sausage	225g
8oz	Fresh coarse pork sausages	225g
1	Orange	1

METHOD

1 Wash beans, cover with cold water and leave to soak overnight.

2 Next day, put ribs, pork and steak into large pan. Add cold water and bring to the boil. Skim off any scum, cover and simmer for 1 hour.

3 Remove meat from pan and reserve. Add beans to liquor, bring to the boil and simmer for 1 hour.

4 Peel and chop the onion. Heat the lard in a large pan, add onion and fry till just golden. Add peeled and crushed garlic, canned tomatoes, a quarter of the beans and 6 fl oz (170ml) of the cooking liquor. Deseed and slice the chilli and add to the pan. Season, cover and simmer for 30 minutes.

5 Meanwhile, add the cooked meats, chorizo and fresh pork sausages to the remaining beans and liquor. Cover and simmer for a further 30 minutes.

6 Lift out the meats and cut into neat serving pieces – separate the ribs, slice the belly of pork, slice the beef and the chorizo, and separate and halve the pork sausages. Keep hot.

7 Mash the beans in the tomato and onion mixture till smooth, then add to beans in other pan. Taste and adjust seasoning. Pour into a warmed serving dish and arrange meats on top. Keep hot.

8 Pare rind from the orange with a potato peeler without removing pith. Slice orange and arrange on meats.

ACCOMPANIMENTS FOR FEIJOADA

Arroz Brasileiro (Brazilian rice) Heat 2 tbsp (2×15ml) oil in a saucepan. Add 1 peeled and chopped onion and fry till just golden. Stir in 8oz (225g) long grain rice and fry for 2 minutes. Add 4oz (125g) canned tomatoes, ½ teasp (½×5ml) salt and 1 pint (560ml) water. Bring to the boil, cover and simmer for about 15 minutes till rice is tender and liquid absorbed. Serve garnished with tomato wedges and parsley.

Couve à mineira (shredded kale) Wash, trim and shred 1lb (450g) kale or spring greens and blanch in boiling salted water for 5 minutes. Drain thoroughly and fry in 1oz (25g) lard for 5 minutes. Season to taste and arrange in warmed serving dish.

Môlho de pimenta e limão (chilli and lemon sauce) Peel and finely chop 1 large onion. Drain and chop 6 pickled chillies and add to the onion with 4 tbsp (4×15ml) lemon juice and 1 peeled and crushed garlic clove. Mix well and arrange in a serving dish.

Manioc Serve a side dish of manioc or cassava meal (see page 594) to sprinkle over servings of the Feijoada.

Below: Feijoada – a variety of tender meats with black beans served with (left to right) Brazilian rice, shredded kale, chilli and lemon sauce and Manioc

Put the asparagus on to a board, chop into short lengths then place in a bowl

Dice the cooked ham and pineapple rings. Add to asparagus and mix together well

Cover the bottom of 4 serving dishes with lettuce. Top with the asparagus mixture

Asparagus cocktail

A deliciously refreshing sweet-sour combination with a mildly alcoholic dressing for a summer evening. You can use fresh asparagus – in which case prepare, cook, drain and cool. Otherwise drain a 12oz (340g) can of asparagus spears

STARTER Serves 4

METHOD

1 Chop asparagus and place in a mixing bowl (see step-by-step pictures, right).

Above: Asparagus cocktail – tasty and light

2 Dice 4oz (125g) of cooked ham. Chop 4 pineapple rings. Add both to asparagus and mix together well.

3 Place pieces of washed and dried lettuce in the bottom of individual glasses. Divide asparagus mixture evenly between them.

4 Mix 8 tbsp (8×15ml) mayonnaise with ½ teasp (½×5ml) Cognac or whisky, 2 tbsp (2×15ml) lemon juice and a pinch of cayenne. Divide dressing equally between glasses. Garnish with chopped tomato, sliced hard-boiled egg and chopped parsley. Chill for 10 minutes before serving.

Divide the flavoured mayonnaise between serving dishes then garnish

cook's know-how

Winkles and whelks, both tasty and cheap, have always been one of the most popular street foods in Britain and Eire. The whelk, called buckie in parts of Scotland, is usually about 4 inches (10cm) long. The winkle, or periwinkle, one of the smallest shellfish eaten, is about 1 inch (2.5cm) long.

Whelks live in deep water and are caught in baited pots. They are usually boiled by the fishermen, then shelled and sold to eat fresh with vinegar or lemon juice.

Winkles are found between the high and low water marks of rocky shores all over the world. They need to be soaked in fresh water for about 12 hours before being boiled in salted water for 10 minutes. There is a special technique for eating them. The scale at the mouth of the shell is picked off and the winkle is wound out with a large pin.

Both winkles and whelks are available all the year round and make an excellent cold starter with brown bread and butter. Whelks can also be made into fritters, and they can be bought bottled. These have a storage life of 3 months, but once opened should be kept in the fridge and eaten within a couple of days.

An ounce (25g) of shelled whelks or winkles contains about 25 calories. Both are a good source of protein and winkles have more calcium and iron than whelks.

Another much underrated shellfish is the cockle. Cockles are used in a satisfying main meal on page 588 – Macaroni with cockles.

Below: Winkles ready to be picked out with a pin. The French eat them with cocktails

Winkle soup with wine

A dish that makes the most of one of the smallest of the seafoods. Bottled winkles (not those in vinegar) can be used, in which case omit the first step

STARTER Serves 6

Overall timing 45 minutes plus overnight soaking

Equipment Saucepan, bowl, blender

Freezing Not recommended

INGREDIENTS

2lb	Fresh winkles	900g
1	Large onion	1
2oz	Butter	50g
$\frac{1}{2}$ teasp	Ground cumin	$\frac{1}{2}\times$5ml
1 teasp	Ground coriander	5ml
$2\frac{1}{2}$ pints	Home-made fish stock	1.5 litres
3 tbsp	Plain flour	3×15ml
$\frac{1}{4}$ pint	Dry white wine	150ml
1 tbsp	Chopped parsley	15ml
1 teasp	Lemon juice	5ml
	Salt	
	Freshly-ground black pepper	
	Lemon slices	
	Croûtons	

METHOD

1. Wash the winkles and soak overnight in plenty of cold water. Drain and put into the saucepan. Cover with fresh cold water and bring to the boil. Simmer for 10 minutes, then drain and rinse the saucepan. Remove winkles from shells.
2. Peel and chop the onion. Heat the butter in the saucepan, add the onion and fry gently till transparent.
3. Stir in the ground cumin and coriander and cook for 1 minute, stirring. Add the winkles and stock and bring to the boil. Cover and simmer for 10 minutes.
4. Blend the flour to a smooth paste with the wine and add to the soup. Bring to the boil, stirring constantly, and simmer for 3 minutes.
5. Purée the soup in the blender, then pour back into the saucepan and reheat. Add the parsley, lemon juice and seasoning to taste.
6. Pour into a warmed tureen and float the lemon slices on top. Sprinkle a few croûtons over and serve the rest in a separate bowl.

Below: Winkle soup with wine – a delightful soup made from an inexpensive delicacy

Pizza turnover

This recipe uses a dough made from packeted white bread mix to make a pizza that's folded in half to enclose a filling. To serve 4 as a starter, roll out dough in 2 small circles, fill, bake, then cut into two

STARTER OR LUNCH Serves 4 or 2

Overall timing 1 hour plus proving

Equipment 3 bowls, baking tray

Freezing Not recommended

INGREDIENTS

10oz	Packet of white bread mix	283g
6oz	Ricotta	175g
1 tbsp	Grated Parmesan	15ml
2	Eggs	2
4oz	Mozzarella	125g
4oz	Piece of Italian salami	125g
	Salt	
	Freshly-ground black pepper	
	Sprigs of parsley	

cook's know-how

Salami is spiced, brined and/or smoked long-keeping sausage. The meat is usually pork or beef; however the bright red Danish salami contains veal and pork. Italian salami varies from region to region. Hungarian and Austrian salami are the least expensive. Slice salami and eat cold or add to hot dishes.

METHOD

1. Make up the bread mix according to the instructions on the packet.
2. Put the Ricotta and Parmesan into a bowl. Beat the eggs and add all but 1 tbsp (15ml) to the bowl. Mix well.
3. Dice the Mozzarella. Slice the salami thickly, removing outer covering, then dice. Add to the bowl with a little salt and plenty of pepper.
4. Roll out the dough to a circle about 12 inches (30cm) in diameter. Spread the filling over half of it, leaving a ½ inch (12.5mm) border. Fold dough over and pinch edges together to seal.
5. Place on a lightly greased baking tray, cover with oiled polythene and leave in a warm place for about 30 minutes.
6. Preheat the oven to 425F (220C) Gas 7.
7. Brush the dough with the remaining beaten egg and bake near the top of the oven for about 30 minutes till well risen and golden.
8. Place on a warmed serving dish and garnish with parsley. Serve immediately with a green or mixed salad.

Above: Pizza turnover – seal the edges well or the melted cheese will ooze out

Iced tomato soup

This refreshing summer starter, served with crisp croûtons, is made in minutes and needs no cooking

STARTER Serves 6

Overall timing 15 minutes plus chilling

Equipment Blender, nylon sieve, bowl, frying pan

Freezing Complete Step 2. Pour into a rigid container, leaving 1 inch (2.5cm) headspace, cover, label and freeze. Freezer life: 3 months. To use: thaw at room temperature for about 4 hours, then complete Steps 3–4

INGREDIENTS

2lb	Ripe tomatoes	900g
2	Stalks of celery	2
1	Small onion	1
1 teasp	Sugar	5ml
¼ pint	Dry white wine	150ml
¼ pint	Water	150ml
2 tbsp	Chopped parsley	2×15ml
1 teasp	Lemon juice	5ml
	Salt	
	Freshly-ground black pepper	
2	Thick slices of bread	2
1	Garlic clove	1
2oz	Butter	50g
3 tbsp	Oil	3×15ml

METHOD

1. Blanch, peel and chop the tomatoes and put into a blender. Wash, trim and chop the celery, peel and chop the onion. Add to the blender with the sugar, wine, water and half the parsley.
2. Blend till smooth, then rub through a nylon sieve into a bowl. Add the lemon juice and season to taste. Cover and chill for 3–4 hours.
3. Meanwhile, cut the bread into ½ inch (12.5mm) cubes, removing the crusts. Heat the butter and oil in a frying pan, add the peeled and crushed garlic and bread cubes and fry till crisp and golden. Drain on kitchen paper, then sprinkle with parsley and salt and leave to cool.
4. Scatter the croûtons into the soup and serve immediately.

Above: Sweet and sour corn salad – corn kernels, diced potatoes, tomatoes, pineapple and bananas on a bed of lettuce

Sweet and sour corn salad

A refreshing alliance of sunshine flavours – sweetcorn, bananas and pineapple. Their sweetness is offset by the tangy dressing made with soured cream

LUNCH OR SUPPER Serves 6

Overall timing 45 minutes including chilling time

Equipment 3 bowls

Freezing Not recommended

INGREDIENTS

8oz	Can of sweetcorn kernels	225g
2 tbsp	White wine vinegar	2×15ml
3 tbsp	Oil	3×15ml
	Salt and pepper	
1lb	Cold boiled potatoes	450g
8oz	Tomatoes	225g
8oz	Can of pineapple chunks	247g
2	Bananas	2
5 tbsp	Lemon juice	5×15ml
	Dressing	
1 tbsp	French mustard	15ml
¼ pint	Carton of soured cream or natural yogurt	150ml
2 tbsp	Milk	2×15ml
	Salt and pepper	
1 teasp	Paprika	5ml
	Garnish	
1	Small lettuce	1

METHOD

1 Drain corn and place kernels in a bowl. Mix together vinegar, oil, salt and pepper and add to corn. Mix well. Cover and place in fridge.

2 Peel and dice potatoes. Slice tomatoes lengthways. Drain pineapple (save 2 tbsp/2×15ml of the juice to add to dressing). Peel and slice bananas. Put all these in a bowl and pour lemon juice over.

3 To make dressing, mix together mustard, soured cream or yogurt and milk. Season well with salt and pepper, add paprika and reserved pineapple juice. Shake or mix well and pour over salad. Place in fridge for 30 minutes.

4 For the garnish, wash lettuce and dry leaves on kitchen paper. Arrange them on serving dish and spoon potato mixture in a ring round the edges. Place the corn in the middle and serve.

cook's know-how

Succotash, an American way of serving corn, is a tasty accompaniment to grilled or fried meats. To make, drain an 11½oz (326g) can of sweetcorn kernels, discarding liquid, and tip into a flameproof casserole with 8oz (225g) chopped frozen green beans or fresh or frozen lima beans, 2oz (50g) butter, ½ teasp (½×5ml) salt, 1 teasp (5ml) of paprika and 2 tbsp (2×15ml) of chopped parsley. Cover with a tight-fitting lid and cook over a moderate heat for 10 minutes.

Shredded omelette with tomato sauce

Herby omelettes rolled and shredded, then added to a rich tomato, bacon and vegetable sauce. In this easy-to-prepare dish, the thin strips of omelette look very much like tagliatelle or ribbon pasta

LUNCH OR SUPPER Serves 4

Overall timing 35 minutes

Equipment Saucepan, bowl, frying pan

Freezing Not recommended

INGREDIENTS

1	Small onion	1
1	Garlic clove	1
1	Stalk of celery	1
1	Carrot	1
2oz	Streaky bacon rashers	50g
1 tbsp	Oil	15ml
14oz	Can of tomatoes	397g
	Salt	
	Freshly-ground black pepper	
9	Eggs	9
1 teasp	Chopped mint	5ml
3 tbsp	Chopped parsley	3×15ml
2oz	Butter	50g

METHOD

1 Peel and finely chop the onion, peel the garlic. Wash, trim and chop the celery, scrape and thinly slice the carrot. Derind and finely chop the bacon.

2 Heat the oil in a saucepan, add the bacon and vegetables and fry gently for 5 minutes. Add the tomatoes and juice, crushed garlic and seasoning, bring to the boil then simmer uncovered for 20 minutes, stirring to break up the tomatoes.

3 Meanwhile, lightly beat the eggs in a bowl with the mint, parsley and seasoning. Heat one-third of the butter in a frying pan. Add one-third of the egg mixture and cook over a moderate heat, drawing the liquid into the centre as the mixture begins to set. When set, slide the omelette on to a board. Use remaining eggs to make 2 more omelettes in the same way. It is important that the omelettes are well set for the next stage of rolling and shredding.

4 Roll the omelettes loosely and cut into strips about ½ inch (12.5mm) wide. Add to the tomato sauce and heat through for 3 minutes. Season to taste.

TO SERVE

Pour into a warmed serving dish. Serve immediately with a side dish of grated Parmesan and a tossed green salad or a mixed salad.

Parmesan, Italy's internationally renowned cooking cheese, can sometimes be bought by the piece and freshly grated when required. This is much nicer than the more commonly available ready-grated Parmesan in packets and drums.

Fry onion, celery, carrot and bacon, add tomatoes and garlic, boil, then simmer

Beat eggs and herbs together and cook, a third at a time, to make 3 omelettes

Roll omelettes loosely, shred, then add to the tomato mixture. Heat through, then season to taste and serve immediately

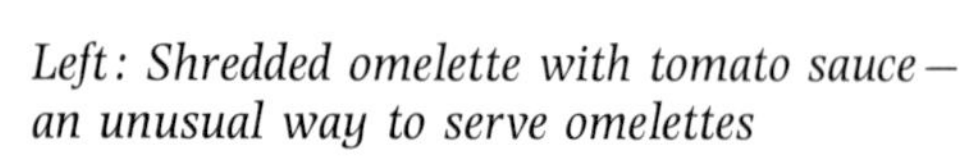

Left: Shredded omelette with tomato sauce — an unusual way to serve omelettes

Pork chops with cranberries

A splendid way to dress up plainly cooked pork chops. The whole berry cranberry sauce, which is used straight from the can, flavours the cooking juices and completes the apple ring garnish

LUNCH OR SUPPER Serves 4

Overall timing 1 hour

Equipment Flameproof casserole, 2 small saucepans

Freezing Not recommended

INGREDIENTS

4	Pork chops	4
2	Onions	2
2 tbsp	Oil	2×15ml
1 tbsp	Plain flour	15ml
8oz	Can of whole berry cranberry sauce	227g
¼ pint	Chicken stock	150ml
2 teasp	Lemon juice	2×5ml
	Salt and pepper	
1	Large cooking apple	1
1oz	Butter	25g

METHOD

1. Trim chops. Peel and slice onions. Heat the oil in a casserole and brown the chops for 10–15 minutes on each side. Remove from pan.
2. Add sliced onions to casserole and fry till golden.
3. Remove casserole from heat and stir in the flour. Return to heat and cook, stirring, till the mixture thickens.
4. Add 4 tbsp (4×15ml) of the cranberry sauce, the stock (made with 1 stock cube if necessary), lemon juice and seasoning. Bring to the boil, then reduce heat and simmer for about 3 minutes.
5. Replace chops in casserole, cover and cook gently for 30 minutes or until tender.
6. Core but do not peel the apple. Cut into 4 slices. Heat the butter in a small pan and fry the apple slices till golden.
7. Put remaining cranberry sauce into another small pan and heat through gently.

TO SERVE

Arrange an apple ring on top of each chop. Fill the centre of each ring with a little of the warmed cranberry sauce. Serve with creamed potatoes and green beans.

Above: Lamb meatballs with herbs – coriander-flavoured fried meatballs

Lamb meatballs with herbs

In the West mint is believed to be the perfect complement to lamb – in the East the same is thought of coriander. Both herbs are used to make these flavoursome meatballs, and any cut of lamb can be minced and used

LUNCH OR SUPPER Serves 4

Overall timing 30 minutes

Equipment Bowl, frying pan

Freezing Shape balls, open freeze till hard, put in polythene bag or rigid container, seal, label and freeze. Freezer life: 2 months. To use: thaw overnight in fridge, then flour and fry

INGREDIENTS

1¼lb	Minced lamb	600g
4	Garlic cloves	4
2 tbsp	Freshly chopped mint	2×15ml
1	Egg	1
	Salt	
	Freshly-ground black pepper	
1 teasp	Ground coriander	5ml
	Plain flour	
2 tbsp	Oil	2×15ml
	Mint or coriander leaves for garnish	

METHOD

1. Place mince in a bowl with the peeled and finely chopped garlic, mint, egg, salt, pepper and coriander and mix with a wooden spoon till well combined.
2. Make little balls of the mixture, flouring your hands so it doesn't stick, and roll in flour to coat.
3. Heat oil in frying pan, add meatballs and cook over a moderate heat for 8–10 minutes on each side till well browned. Drain on kitchen paper, then serve with couscous (recipe page 608) or rice.

Two cheese flan

Two popular Swiss cheeses are combined in this flan

LIGHT LUNCH Serves 4–6

Overall timing 1½ hours

Equipment Saucepan, mixing bowl, 2 bowls, 9 inch (23cm) flan tin

Freezing Cook flan in foil dish. Cool, open freeze, then wrap in polythene, seal and label. Freezer life: 3 months. To use: thaw for 4 hours, then refresh in a hot oven for 10–15 minutes

INGREDIENTS

4oz	Margarine	125g
3 tbsp	Water	3×15ml
¼ teasp	Salt	¼×5ml
8oz	Self-raising flour	225g
2	Medium-size onions	2
1oz	Margarine	25g
1 tbsp	Plain flour	15ml
4fl oz	Milk	120ml
4fl oz	Water	120ml
3	Eggs	3
	Salt and pepper	
¼ teasp	Grated nutmeg	¼×5ml
	Cayenne pepper	
4oz	Emmenthal	125g
4oz	Gruyère	125g

METHOD

1. To make pastry, melt the margarine in a saucepan over a gentle heat. Allow to cool slightly, then stir in water and salt. Put flour into a bowl. Slowly add contents of saucepan and mix until smooth. Cover and place in the fridge for 30 minutes. Grease flan tin. Preheat the oven to 350F (180C) Gas 4.
2. To make filling, peel and chop onions. Melt margarine in a saucepan and fry onions for 10 minutes until soft, but not coloured. Leave to cool.
3. Mix flour and a little of the milk in a bowl, then add the rest of the milk and the water. Separate the eggs. Mix the yolks into the flour and milk mixture. Season with salt, pepper, nutmeg and a pinch of cayenne. Beat egg whites in another bowl till stiff, then fold into yolk mixture.
4. Remove dough from fridge. Roll it out on a lightly-floured surface and line the tin.
5. Spread onions over bottom of flan, then grate both sorts of cheese on top. Cover with egg and milk mixture. Bake just below centre of the oven for 15 minutes. Reduce heat to 325F (170C) Gas 3 and cook for a further 45 minutes. Serve hot with a colourful salad.

Below: Two cheese flan – Emmenthal and Gruyère are both excellent for cooking

Radicchio and lettuce salad

Radicchio, or red chicory, has a similar flavour and texture to the more usual type, with the added bonus of providing attractive colour contrast in all sorts of salads. Equally delicious served with light meals such as savoury flans and omelettes or with grilled steaks and chops

Overall timing 30 minutes

Equipment Small bowl, salad bowl

Freezing Not recommended

INGREDIENTS

	Salad	
1	Webb's lettuce	1
2	Heads of radicchio	2
1	Small onion	1
	Dressing	
2	Garlic cloves	2
1 teasp	Prepared mustard	5ml
2 tbsp	Olive oil	2×15ml
1 tbsp	White wine vinegar	1×15ml
1	Gherkin	1
1 tbsp	Capers	15ml
1 tbsp	Chopped parsley	15ml

METHOD

1. Trim, wash and thoroughly dry lettuce and radicchio leaves. Peel onion and cut into rings. Arrange onion in the bottom of a salad bowl and place lettuce and radicchio on top. Put in the fridge and leave to crisp for 15 minutes.
2. To make the dressing, peel garlic and crush into a small bowl. Add mustard, oil and vinegar and mix well together. Finely chop the gherkin and capers and stir into dressing with the parsley.
3. Pour dressing over salad and toss lightly at the table.

This salad is featured on the front cover.

cook's know-how

Radicchio is a member of the chicory family. First cultivated in Italy, its leaves are red and not so tightly packed as in the white chicory heads. Radicchio is best eaten raw in salads as, although the flavour remains unimpaired, the leaves turn a dull brown when cooked. Radicchio can be rather expensive, so why not try growing your own.

Marinated pot roast of beef

This succulent beef dish can be made well ahead of time as it reheats extremely well. The sauce can be made two ways – but if you intend freezing it, it's best not to add the cream and brandy

Above: Marinated pot roast of beef – served with button onions and sliced carrots

MAIN MEAL Serves 8–10

Overall timing 3 hours plus marinating

Equipment String, large bowl, large heavy-based flameproof casserole

Freezing Cool joint, wrap well. Put sauce in rigid container and cover. Freezer life: 2 months. To use: thaw for 24 hours in fridge, place meat and sauce in casserole. Cook for 1 hour in oven 400F (200C) Gas 6

INGREDIENTS

4lb	Braising beef	1.8kg
6oz	Pork fat with rind	175g
1	Large onion	1
$\frac{1}{2}$ pint	Red or white wine	300ml
3	Stalks of celery	3
3	Carrots	3
1	Garlic clove	1
	Fresh parsley	
2	Bay leaves	2
	Fresh thyme	
	Freshly-ground white pepper	
	Salt	
1oz	Butter	25g
2 tbsp	Oil	2×15ml
1	Pigs trotter	1
4fl oz	Water	120ml
1 tbsp	Tomato paste	15ml
2 tbsp	Cream (optional)	2×15ml
1 tbsp	Brandy (optional)	15ml
$\frac{3}{4}$lb	Button onions	350g
1lb	Carrots	450g

1 Assemble all ingredients. A bouquet garni can be used instead of the fresh herbs

2 Rub beef with pepper and salt. Slice pork fat, secure around beef with string

3 Cover beef with chopped onion, celery, carrots, crushed garlic, herbs, wine

4 After marinating overnight, dry meat. Brown in casserole in hot butter/oil mixture

5 Add marinade, halved pigs trotter, water, paste. Cover and cook gently for 2½ hours

6 Remove beef from casserole. Discard trotter. Strain cooking juices, cool and skim

7 To thicken, either reduce juices, or whisk in beurre manié (recipe page 309)

8 Cream and brandy can be added to sauce with sautéed onions and boiled carrots

Roast veal with bacon

A stuffing of smoked bacon flavours the rolled veal and keeps the meat moist during cooking – very important as veal has a tendency to dry out

MAIN MEAL Serves 8

Overall timing 2¼ hours

Equipment Fine string, flameproof casserole

Freezing Not recommended

INGREDIENTS

8oz	Piece of smoked streaky bacon	225g
3lb	Boned chump end loin of veal	1.4kg
	Salt	
	Freshly-ground black pepper	
1 tbsp	Oil	15ml
2oz	Butter	50g
2 tbsp	Plain flour	2×15ml
½ pint	Light stock	300ml
¼ pint	Dry white wine	150ml

If preferred, cut deep slits in veal and fill with moist stuffing of your choice

METHOD

1 Preheat the oven to 325F (170C) Gas 3. Derind the bacon, remove the bones and cut into 1 inch (2.5cm) wide strips.
2 Place the veal on a board and season. Arrange the strips of bacon lengthways along the veal, then roll the meat round the bacon and tie into a neat shape with fine string.
3 Heat the oil and butter in the casserole, add the meat and fry over a moderate heat for about 10 minutes, turning, till browned on all sides.
4 Season, cover and cook in the centre of the oven for about 1½ hours till the meat juices run clear.*
5 Lift the meat out of the casserole and place on a warmed serving dish. Discard the string and keep the veal hot.
6 Heat the juices in the casserole, add the flour and cook for 1 minute, stirring. Gradually add the stock (made with a cube if necessary) and wine and bring to the boil, stirring constantly. Simmer for 2 minutes. Taste and adjust seasoning, pour into warmed gravy boat.
7 Carve the meat into thick slices and serve with the gravy, new potatoes and sliced green beans. *Or, if preferred, surround joint with peeled and halved parsnips, scraped whole carrots and peeled button onions to make a complete meal in one pot.

Below: Roast veal with bacon – tenderness is ensured by pot roasting in the oven

Cannelloni with spinach

A traditional filling for cannelloni – a mix of spinach, beef and ham

MAIN MEAL Serves 2–3

Overall timing 2 hours

Equipment Saucepan, frying pan, ovenproof dish

Freezing Cook in rigid foil container. Cool, seal, label and freeze. Freezer life: 3 months. To use: cook from frozen at 350F (180C) Gas 4 for 1 hour until heated through

INGREDIENTS

6	Sheets of lasagne	6
1 tbsp	Oil	15ml
8oz	Minced beef	225g
1lb	Fresh spinach	450g
1oz	Butter	25g
	Salt and pepper	
4oz	Ham	125g
1	Egg	1
2oz	Grated Parmesan	50g
½ teasp	Grated nutmeg	½×5ml
½ pint	Béchamel sauce (recipe page 77)	300ml
	Parsley	

METHOD

1 Place the lasagne in a saucepan of boiling, salted water and cook for 10–15 minutes or until al dente. Drain carefully and spread out on a damp cloth to cool.
2 Heat the oil in a frying pan, add the minced beef and cook for 15 minutes, stirring frequently. Remove from heat.
3 Meanwhile, wash spinach and remove coarse stalks. Place in a saucepan with butter and seasoning and cook, uncovered, for 10 minutes over low heat.
4 Finely chop spinach and ham. Stir into the minced beef with the egg, half the Parmesan, nutmeg, salt and pepper.
5 Preheat oven to 400F (200C) Gas 6. Grease ovenproof dish.
6 Place some of the meat mixture on each sheet of lasagne. Roll pasta around the filling and arrange, joins down, in the dish.
7 Make Béchamel sauce. Pour over cannelloni and sprinkle with remaining Parmesan. Cook in centre of oven for 25 minutes or until golden brown. Garnish with parsley. Serve immediately with tomato and onion salad.

Pork, rice and banana stew

To add contrasting texture to this stew with a difference, choose bananas that are on the green side as they will go mushy if too ripe

MAIN MEAL Serves 4

Overall timing $1\frac{3}{4}$ hours

Equipment Large heavy-based saucepan or casserole with lid, measuring jug, frying pan

Freezing Not recommended

INGREDIENTS

12oz	Onions	350g
4 tbsp	Oil	4×15ml
2	Garlic cloves	2
2lb	Pork (top of belly)	900g
3oz	Rice	75g
14oz	Can of tomatoes	397g
1	Chicken stock cube	1
$\frac{1}{4}$ teasp	Paprika	$\frac{1}{4}$×5ml
$\frac{1}{4}$ teasp	Cinnamon	$\frac{1}{4}$×5ml
1 teasp	Saffron (optional)	5ml
8oz	Potatoes	225g
2	Bananas	2
2oz	Salted peanuts	50g
	Salt	

METHOD
1 Peel and chop onions. Heat 2 tbsp (2×15ml) of the oil in saucepan or casserole. Add onions, peeled and crushed garlic, and brown over a moderate heat for about 12 minutes. Stir occasionally to prevent burning.
2 Cut the pork into cubes and add to the pan or casserole. Stir in the rice. Cook till rice has absorbed oil, stirring frequently to prevent sticking. Add a little water if necessary to prevent burning. Remove from heat.
3 Pour juice from canned tomatoes into jug. Sprinkle in stock cube and top up with boiling water to $\frac{3}{4}$ pint (400ml). Chop tomatoes and add to pan or casserole with stock, paprika, cinnamon and saffron, if used. Cover and simmer gently for 20 minutes.
4 Meanwhile, peel and cube potatoes. Heat remaining oil in a frying pan and cook potatoes over a low heat for about 10 minutes then add them to the pan or casserole. Peel and slice bananas and stir into the pan or casserole with the peanuts. Cook for 10 minutes. Taste and add salt if necessary. Serve immediately.

Chicken with almonds

Uncooked chicken is cut into small strips so that it absorbs all the flavours of soy sauce and almonds in this unusual Chinese-style dish

MAIN MEAL Serves 4–5

Overall timing 1 hour

Equipment Mixing bowl, large heavy-based saucepan or casserole

Freezing Not recommended. If using frozen chicken, make sure it is well thawed

INGREDIENTS

$2\frac{1}{2}$–3lb	Chicken	about 1.3kg
1 tbsp	Potato flour or cornflour	15ml
3 tbsp	Soy sauce	3×15ml
	Salt and pepper	
1 teasp	Caster sugar	5ml
2 tbsp	Oil	2×15ml
4oz	Split almonds	125g
2 tbsp	Water or chicken stock	2×15ml

Above: Chicken with almonds

METHOD
1 Remove skin from chicken. With a sharp knife, cut all flesh from carcass then slice it into small strips.
2 In a bowl mix together potato flour or cornflour, soy sauce, salt, pepper and caster sugar. Add chicken pieces and coat well.
3 Heat 1 tbsp (15ml) oil in a heavy-based saucepan and gently brown almonds, turning them occasionally. Drain and remove.
4 Pour remaining oil into the saucepan. Add chicken pieces and cook over a fairly high heat for 15 minutes, continually turning the chicken over.
5 When chicken is golden brown, return almonds to pan and add water or chicken stock.
6 Adjust seasoning, cover and cook for a further 5 minutes.

TO SERVE
Place in hot serving dish and serve plain boiled rice separately.

cook's know-how

The almonds used in this dish are split – which means whole blanched almonds cut through the middle. As this can be quite difficult to do smoothly yourself (you usually end up with nibs rather than halves), it's easier to buy them ready-prepared or to use whole ones, which you have blanched.

Fish with couscous

Although commonly served with meat, couscous goes just as well with seafood. It can be bought ready to steam, or prepared for cooking (right). The type of fish used can be varied, but it should have a firm texture

MAIN MEAL Serves 8

Overall timing 1 hour 20 minutes

Equipment Large saucepan, steamer

Freezing Not recommended

INGREDIENTS

2	Onions	2
2	Stalks of celery	2
2	Large carrots	2
3 pints	Water	1.7 litres
3lb	Mixed fish (conger eel, grey mullet, monkfish, mussels)	1.4kg
1lb	Prepared couscous	450g
	Salt	
8	Saffron strands	8
	Freshly-ground black pepper	
14oz	Can of artichoke hearts	397g
2oz	Butter	50g

METHOD

1 Peel and quarter onions, wash, trim and slice celery and carrots. Put into pan with water. Clean fish, removing heads, and cut into pieces. Add fish trimmings to pan and bring to boil.

2 Put couscous into steamer, place over pan and steam for 30 minutes, stirring occasionally. Meanwhile, scrub mussels.

3 Pour couscous on to a tea-towel, sprinkle with cold salted water and fluff with a fork. Return couscous to steamer and cover with a dry cloth.

4 Strain stock, return to pan. Bring to boil, add saffron, conger eel, mullet and seasoning. Replace steamer and cook for 10 minutes. Add monkfish and mussels to pan, cook for 10 minutes.

5 Remove steamer. Drain and quarter artichoke hearts and add to pan with butter. Cook for 3 minutes, season.

6 Arrange couscous on warmed serving dish with fish and vegetables on top. Serve hot stock separately.

preparing couscous

Buy couscous ready to steam, or prepare semolina as steps below

To prepare couscous at home, put 1lb (450g) coarse semolina in bowl with little salt, pepper. Sprinkle in ½ pint (300ml) cold water, drop by drop

Lift semolina and rub with fingers against palm of hand. Lift and rub for 15 minutes till grains increase in size. Add 4 teasp (4×5ml) olive oil drop by drop. Continue to rub grains till they double in size – about another 15–20 minutes

*Pour rubbed grains into couscousier, steamer or small-meshed metal sieve. Suspend over water, stock or stew, bring to boil, steam for 40 minutes**

**After 30 minutes, the couscous can be turned on to cloth, sprinkled with water and left till stew is cooked. Turn back into steamer, cover with dry cloth, steam for 10 minutes more*

Grouper with orange sauce

Individual grouper steaks covered with a sharp orange sauce

MAIN MEAL Serves 6

Overall timing 20 minutes

Equipment Frying pan, saucepan

Freezing Not recommended

INGREDIENTS

6	Grouper steaks	6
	Salt and pepper	
1oz	Butter	25g
2	Oranges	2
2oz	Butter	50g
2oz	Plain flour	50g
¼ pint	Meat stock	150ml
¼ pint	Dry vermouth	150ml
	Salt	

METHOD

1 Wipe steaks and season on both sides. In a frying pan, melt butter and fry fish for 5 minutes each side till tender and golden. Remove from heat, place on serving dish and keep hot.

2 Pare the zest of ½ orange and shred finely. Blanch in boiling water for 5 minutes, rinse under cold water and drain well. Squeeze juice from oranges.

3 In a saucepan, melt butter and stir in flour until smooth. Gradually stir in stock, vermouth and a pinch of salt. Add orange juice and zest and simmer for 3 minutes, stirring.

4 Pour sauce over fish. Garnish with orange slices and serve immediately with plain boiled rice.

VARIATION

If you prefer a sharper sauce, replace some of the orange juice with lemon or grapefruit juice or the juice of bitter oranges such as Sevilles.

cook's know-how

The grouper is a firm, round white fish that comes from the same family as the sea bass, and is found in warm and tropical waters. Weighing between 1½–50lb (700g–23kg), grouper is sold either whole, or as steaks or fillets. Cod, hake or sea bass may be substituted for grouper.

Huss soup

Generous portions of huss and potato combined with tomato and onion make this a soup that is really a meal in itself. The firm flesh of huss makes it an ideal fish to use in soups, as it does not disintegrate in the cooking

LUNCH OR SUPPER Serves 4

Overall timing 40 minutes

Equipment Large saucepan, frying pan

Freezing Not recommended

INGREDIENTS

1	Large onion	1
1	Garlic clove	1
4 tbsp	Oil	4×15ml
1lb	Tomatoes	450g
2½ pints	Hot fish or chicken stock	1.5 litres
1lb	Boiled potatoes	450g
1lb	Huss fillets	450g
	Salt and pepper	
2 tbsp	Chopped parsley	2×15ml

METHOD

1. Peel and finely chop onion and garlic. Heat 3 tbsp (3×15ml) of the oil in a large saucepan. Cook onion and garlic until transparent.
2. Blanch, peel and chop tomatoes, add to pan and cook for a few minutes, then add fish or chicken stock and potatoes, cut into large chunks.
3. Wipe fish and cut into large pieces. Heat remaining oil in a frying pan and cook fish for 5 minutes, turning mixture constantly.
4. Add fish pieces to the saucepan and cover and cook for 15 minutes, then taste and adjust seasoning. Pour into a warm tureen and sprinkle with parsley. Serve with crusty bread.

VARIATION

To make this soup into an even more substantial meal, add extra fish – conger eel goes well in a soup – and shellfish, such as mussels.

In any mixed fish soup, the different fish will be added to the bouillon at different times, depending on their texture. In this case, the conger eel should cook about 10 minutes longer than the huss, and the mussels for the same length of time as the huss, until they have opened (discard any that don't open).

While the soup is cooking, prepare garlic croûtons by frying bread cubes in mixture of butter and oil and garlic salt.

Sardine bake

To remove backbones, place cleaned fish, skin side up, on board. Press thumb along backbones to loosen. Turn fish over and pull backbones out

LUNCH OR SUPPER Serves 4–6

Overall timing 1 hour

Equipment Bowl, ovenproof dish

Freezing Not recommended

INGREDIENTS

12	Fresh sardines	12
4oz	Grated cheese	125g
4oz	Fresh breadcrumbs	125g
2 tbsp	Chopped parsley	2×15ml
1	Garlic clove	1
	Salt and pepper	
2oz	Melted butter	50g
2	Eggs	2

METHOD

1. Remove the heads from the sardines, slit along bellies and remove insides, including back-bones, under cold running water. Pat dry on kitchen paper.
2. Put the cheese, breadcrumbs and parsley into a bowl. Peel and chop the garlic and add to bowl with seasoning.
3. Preheat the oven to 350F (180C) Gas 4.
4. Pour 1oz (25g) melted butter into an ovenproof dish and arrange 6 sardines on top. Cover with half the cheese mixture, top with remaining sardines and half the remaining butter.
5. Lightly beat the eggs and mix into the remaining cheese mixture. Pour over the sardines and top with melted butter.
6. Bake in centre of oven for about 30 minutes till golden. Serve immediately with Hot potato salad, right.

Hot potato salad

Choose even-sized potatoes. Mix with the dressing while still warm

SALAD Serves 4–6

Overall timing 30 minutes

Equipment Saucepan, blender

Freezing Not recommended

INGREDIENTS

1½lb	Waxy potatoes	700g
	Salt and pepper	
1	Stalk of celery	1
1	Pickled red capsicum	1
4	Anchovy fillets	4
3	Pickled onions	3
2	Gherkins	2
1 tbsp	Capers	15ml
1	Hard-boiled egg	1
3	Basil leaves	3
¼ teasp	Oregano	¼×5ml
2	Sprigs of parsley	2
¼ pint	Olive or salad oil	150ml

METHOD

1. Scrub potatoes. Place in pan, cover with cold salted water, bring to boil. Cook for about 20 minutes till just tender.
2. Meanwhile, wash and dice celery. Halve capsicum and chop one half, reserve rest for garnish. Put celery, chopped capsicum, anchovies, onions, gherkins, half the capers, shelled egg, herbs, oil, salt and pepper in blender. Blend till dressing is fairly runny.
3. Drain potatoes. Spear each one on a fork and peel, then cut into thick slices. Place in serving dish, add dressing. Garnish with reserved capers and capsicum. Serve immediately.

Perhaps because of its claims as a digestive, coffee is considered by a great many people to be an indispensable part of a meal – from the milky *café au lait* drunk at breakfast, to the tiny cup of strong, black after-dinner coffee. A special occasion demands a somewhat out-of-the-ordinary post-prandial drink and, as coffee combines beautifully with alcohol, it is possible to concoct any number of "coffee cocktails" like those pictured right (recipes below). In general, make the coffee in the usual way, then pour into cups or heat-resistant glasses, filling them only two-thirds. Then sweeten the coffee – checking first with your guests whether or not they take sugar – and if you are going to add a sweet liqueur, reduce the amount of sugar by about a half. Now add the rest of the ingredients, except for the cream which is usually poured on at the very end. When this is the case, do not stir, as the sensation of dipping through cold cream to hot, alcohol-laced coffee is highly pleasurable. In any case, stirring in the cream also cools the drink. The recipes below all contain spirits, with the exception of Café anglais which is a kind of coffee milk-shake, to be drunk at any time of day. Café orange, as its name suggests, combines the flavours of coffee and orange. Café noisette achieves its nutty flavour from the addition of kirsch. Caffè capucchino is frothy white coffee, and Café d'amour and Café au rhum both have cinnamon added. Café royal is made with brandy

Café orange

Three-quarters fill 4 small cups with hot black coffee. Add a twist of orange peel and 2 tbsp (2×15ml) brandy or Curaçao to each. Add sugar to taste and float whipped cream on top. Trail a piece of orange peel from each cup, if liked, to decorate. **Serves 4**

Café anglais

In a bowl, mix together ½ pint (300ml) cold strong black coffee, 4 teasp (4×5ml) caster sugar and 4 tbsp (4×15ml) cocoa powder. Chill in fridge, then add 4 tbsp (4×15ml) vanilla ice cream and ½ pint (300ml) cold milk. Stir well and serve in tall glasses with straws. **Serves 4**

Café noisette

Three-quarters fill 4 small cups with hot black coffee. Stir in about 1 tbsp (15ml) single cream to each and the same amount of kirsch. Pass around a bowl of sugar to taste. **Serves 4**

Caffè capucchino

Three-quarters fill 4 small cups with hot black coffee and add sugar to taste. Whisk ¼ pint (150ml) single cream in a bowl till frothy. Float cream on top of each cup of coffee and sprinkle with a little cocoa or ground cinnamon. **Serves 4**

Café d'amour

Three-quarters fill 4 small cups with hot black coffee. Add a pinch of cocoa powder and a pinch of ground cinnamon to each and top up with about 2 tbsp (2×15ml) orange-flavoured liqueur. Mix well and pour into cups. Serve with 1–2 cinnamon sticks in each cup. **Serves 4**

Café royal

Half-fill 4 heat-resistant glasses with hot black coffee, pouring it in over a metal spoon. Add sugar to taste, stir well, then add 4 teasp (4×5ml) brandy to each. Remember that brandy adds sweetness to coffee, so be sparing with the sugar. If liked, float whipped cream on top. **Serves 4**

Café au rhum

Pour 1 pint (560ml) freshly-made black coffee into a saucepan. Add a twist of orange peel, 4 sticks of cinnamon, 4 cloves and sugar to taste. Heat through but do not boil. Strain into small cups. **Serves 4**

Coffee cocktails, reading clockwise from bottom left: Café au rhum, a mulled coffee drink, Café orange, with brandy or Curaçao, Café anglais, with ice cream and milk, Café noisette, with kirsch and cream stirred in, Caffè capucchino, Italian coffee with whisked cream and cocoa or cinnamon sprinkled on top, Café d'amour, with cinnamon and orange, and Café royal, with brandy

Coffee cocktails

Coffees of the world

A selection of the best known ways of preparing coffee, prized for its taste throughout the world

Turkish

DRINK Serves 4

Overall timing 25 minutes

Equipment Saucepan or ibrik (Turkish coffee pot)

Freezing Not recommended

For Turkish coffee, the beans are very finely ground to extract most flavour

Stir coffee into boiled water and sugar in ibrik or saucepan, then return to the heat

Pour coffee into cups so froth rises to the surface. Add cold water to settle grounds

INGREDIENTS

$\frac{3}{4}$ pint	Water	400ml
8 tbsp	Caster sugar or to taste	8×15ml
8 tbsp	Very finely-ground coffee	8×15ml

METHOD

1 Put water and sugar in a saucepan or ibrik and bring slowly to the boil. Remove from heat, stir in coffee and return pan to heat.

2 When a frothy scum forms on top, take pan or ibrik off heat and allow froth to subside. Repeat this process 3 times.

TO SERVE

As soon as grounds have settled on top, while still hot, pour a little of the froth into the cups. Pour in the coffee so the froth rises to the surface. Add a drop of cold water to each cup to settle the grounds at the bottom.

Irish

DRINK Serves 4

Overall timing 5 minutes

Equipment Small metal spoon, 4 heat-resistant glasses

Freezing Not recommended

INGREDIENTS

8 teasp	Brown sugar crystals	8×15ml
1 pint	Freshly-made black coffee	560ml
8 tbsp	Irish whiskey or whisky	8×15ml
4 tbsp	Lightly whipped double cream	4×15ml

METHOD

1 Put 2 teasp (2×5ml) sugar in each glass. Pour in a little of the hot coffee, over the back of a metal spoon. Stir in 2 tbsp (2×15ml) Irish whiskey or whisky into each glass.

2 Top up glasses with coffee to within 1 inch (2.5cm) of rim. Place 1 tbsp (15ml) cream on top and serve at once.

VARIATION

Instead of placing whipped cream on top, pour double cream gently over the back of a dessert spoon on to the hot coffee. The cream then floats on top. Do not stir.

One way to make Irish coffee – put sugar crystals in the bottom of each glass

Pour a little of the hot coffee into each glass, then stir in Irish whiskey or whisky

Top up each glass with freshly-made black coffee to within 1 inch (2.5cm) of the rim

Spoon the whipped cream on top of each gla

Austrian

Fill 4 tall, heat-resistant glasses with h black coffee, pouring it in over a met spoon. Add sugar to taste, top with stiff whipped cream and sprinkle over each little instant coffee powder. **Serves 4**

Latin-American

RINK Serves 4

verall timing 10 minutes

quipment Saucepan

reezing Not recommended

IGREDIENTS

oz	Plain chocolate	50g
l oz	Milk	170ml
½ pints	Freshly-made strong black coffee	850ml
	Sugar	
	Whipped cream	

IETHOD

Put the chocolate, broken into pieces, and milk into a small pan and heat gently until the chocolate has melted. Whisk until frothy.

Mix the chocolate milk into the hot coffee. Serve at once with sugar to taste and whipped cream floating on top of each glass.

bove: Austrian coffee, topped with cream - an excellent way of rounding off a meal

Almond and coffee meringue gâteau

An eye-catching meringue dessert that doubles up as a special tea-time cake. If you have no flan rings, instead mark out circles on non-stick cooking paper on baking trays and spread meringue evenly within circles

DESSERT OR TEA-TIME Serves 6–8

Overall timing 1½ hours plus cooling

Equipment 2 bowls, three 10 inch (25cm) flan rings, 3 baking trays, non-stick cooking paper, spatula or flat-bladed knife

Freezing Pack cooled meringues in rigid container, with sheet of greaseproof paper between each one. Cover, label and freeze. Freezer life: 3 months. To use: remove from container and thaw at room temperature for 1 hour. Complete as recipe

INGREDIENTS

2oz	Chopped almonds	50g
4	Egg whites	4
3oz	Ground almonds	75g
5oz	Icing sugar	150g
	Butter cream	
4	Egg yolks	4
4oz	Icing sugar	125g
2 tbsp	Coffee essence	2×15ml
4oz	Softened butter	125g

To make butter cream, whisk the yolks, icing sugar and coffee essence over hot water

When thickened, leave to cool, then beat in butter. Sandwich meringues with cream

METHOD

1. Preheat the oven to 250F (130C) Gas ½. Place chopped almonds under the grill and toast for 7–10 minutes. Set aside.
2. In a bowl, whisk egg whites till they hold stiff peaks. Using a metal spoon, lightly fold in the ground almonds and icing sugar, sifted.
3. Well grease and flour flan rings and place each on a baking tray, covered with non-stick cooking paper. Using a spatula or flat-bladed knife, spread one third of meringue mixture into each ring. Place baking trays in oven and cook for about 1 hour until meringues are crisp and dry. Change round baking positions twice so all meringues cook at same temperature. Cool before lifting off flan rings.
4. To make butter cream: put yolks and icing sugar in a bowl, place over a pan of hot water and whisk until light and fluffy.
5. Stir in coffee essence and continue whisking until the mixture is thick and foamy, then remove from heat. Leave to cool completely, then beat in softened butter a little at a time.
6. Place 1 meringue round on serving plate, then sandwich all 3 meringues together with two-thirds of the butter cream. Spread remaining cream on top and sprinkle with reserved almonds.

Above: Almond and coffee meringue gâteau – topped with butter cream and chopped almonds

Countdown

Fennel à la grecque
Duck with oranges
Fried potatoes with bacon and button onions
Braised peas with lettuce
Floating islands

If you have something to celebrate, this delectable special occasion menu will help you do just that.

Day before Prepare fennel starter. Cover and chill in fridge

2½ hours before Prepare duck and cook in oven for 45 mins

2 hours before Make egg custard for dessert and chill

1½ hours before Add stock to duck and cook for about 30 mins or until juices run clear

1 hour before Peel, cut potatoes into pieces and place in pan of cold water. Dice bacon and peel button onions. Shell peas, prepare spring onions and lettuce

45 mins before Cut orange and lemon rind into matchsticks. Squeeze juice. Prepare segments for garnish. Heat sugar for orange sauce until it caramelizes, add vinegar. Add duck juices; place duck in low oven. Finish sauce

30 mins before Boil potatoes for 5 mins. Fry onions and bacon for 5 mins. Add potatoes and cook for 15 mins, turning

20 mins before Make up meringue and poach 'islands'. Drain and dry. Place on custard

10 mins before Fry spring onions for 2 mins. Add peas and remaining ingredients. Cover and simmer for 20 mins (during first course). Cut up duck, place on dish. Spoon over sauce. Keep hot

5 mins before Add herbs and seasoning to fried potatoes. Place in serving dish and keep hot

Serve chilled fennel with bread. Serve garnished duck, peas and sauce. Boil sugar and water until caramelized. Pour over dessert and serve.

Try a Rhône with the duck and a Sauternes with the dessert.

Fennel à la grecque

The name *à la grecque* is given to vegetables simmered in wine, oil and herbs, then served cold in their cooking liquor. Bulbs of fennel are particularly well suited to this method of cooking

STARTER Serves 4

Overall timing 45 minutes plus cooling

Equipment Saucepan

Freezing Not recommended

INGREDIENTS

2	Bulbs of fennel	2
4	Large spring onions	4
6	Coriander seeds	6
1	Bay leaf	1
	Salt	
3	Black peppercorns	3
4 tbsp	Oil	4×15ml
4 tbsp	White wine	4×15ml
4 tbsp	Water	4×15ml
2 tbsp	Chopped parsley	2×15ml
1 tbsp	Lemon juice	15ml

METHOD

1. Remove any leaves and set them aside, then wash and trim fennel. Cut into wedges. Trim spring onions.
2. Put fennel leaves, onions, coriander, bay leaf, salt, peppercorns, oil, wine and water in a saucepan. Bring to the boil and simmer for 12–15 minutes.
3. Add fennel wedges and cook for a further 15 minutes until tender.
4. Remove fennel from pan with a draining spoon and place in shallow serving dish. Reduce cooking liquor by boiling fast, uncovered for several minutes. Stir in parsley and lemon juice.
5. Pour over fennel in dish and leave to cool before serving. This dish is best made a day ahead and left, covered, in the fridge for 24 hours before serving. Serve some of the marinade with the fennel, and fresh bread to mop it up.

Below: Fennel à la grecque — a delicious cold starter with the flavour of aniseed

Duck with oranges

One of the best known roast duck dishes. The sauce can be improved by adding a little port or Madeira

MAIN MEAL Serves 4

Overall timing 2 hours

Equipment Roasting tin with rack, saucepan, game or kitchen scissors

Freezing Not recommended

INGREDIENTS

4lb	Ovenready duck	1.8kg
	Salt and pepper	
½ pint	Hot chicken stock	300ml
2 teasp	Caster sugar	2×5ml
2 tbsp	White wine vinegar	2×15ml
4	Oranges	4
1	Lemon (optional)	1

Above: Duck with oranges – garnished with fresh orange segments and strips of rind

Add strips of orange and lemon rind with juice of 2 oranges to pan of cooking juices. Cook gently till rind is tender

After completing the sauce, remove the cooked duck from the oven and cut into serving portions with game scissors

Arrange portions of duck on hot serving plate, pour over a little sauce and garnish with rind. Serve rest of sauce separately

METHOD

1 Preheat the oven to 400F (200C) Gas 6. Prick duck all over with a fork. Season well with salt and pepper and place on rack in roasting tin. Cook for 45 minutes until it is brown and crisp. Remove all but 1 tbsp (15ml) of the fat from the tin.

2 Pour hot stock (made with 1 stock cube if necessary) over duck. Cover and cook for a further 30 minutes or until the juices run clear when duck is pierced with a skewer.

3 Heat sugar gently in a pan until it caramelizes, then remove from heat and add vinegar.

4 Remove duck and strain juices into pan of sugar and vinegar. Replace duck in tin and keep warm in a low oven.

5 Cut the rind of 1 orange and of the lemon if using into thin matchsticks and add with the squeezed juice of 2 oranges and the lemon to the pan. Cook gently for 5 minutes or until the rind has softened.

6 Remove duck from oven and cut into portions with poultry shears or game scissors. Arrange on warmed serving dish and spoon a little of the orange sauce, with the strips of rind, over.

7 Slice top and bottom off remaining oranges. Cut away the peel and white pith, then cut between membranes with a sharp knife and divide into segments. Use to garnish duck. Serve with vegetables (page 616) and the rest of the sauce in a sauce or gravy boat.

cook's know-how

If you can't obtain fresh or frozen duck portions, you can cut them yourself. You'll need game scissors or sharp kitchen scissors. Split the duck in half along the breast bone, then cut out and discard the backbone. Divide each side of the duck into three pieces – a leg joint, wing joint and a portion of breast. Trim off the fat, wing pinions and leg ends. Remove skin, using a sharp knife, if the recipe requires. Cutting a cooked duck into portions is best done in the kitchen so it can be kept hot and served at the same temperature as the accompaniments.

Above: Fried potatoes with bacon and button onions – crisp potatoes sprinkled with fines herbes

Fried potatoes with bacon and button onions

Par-boiled potatoes are fried with button onions and diced bacon before being enhanced by fines herbes. If the quantity is too large to be fried in one go it can be done in two batches; the first kept hot in a warm oven

VEGETABLE Serves 4

Overall timing 45 minutes

Equipment Saucepan, large frying pan

Freezing Not recommended

INGREDIENTS

4oz	Streaky bacon	125g
2lb	Potatoes	900g
4oz	Button onions	125g
2oz	Butter	50g
	Salt and pepper	
2 tbsp	Fresh fines herbes	2×15ml

METHOD

1 Dice the bacon. Peel potatoes and cut into bite-size pieces. Put potatoes into a pan of cold water, bring to the boil and cook for 5 minutes. Drain well and set aside.
2 Peel the onions. Melt the butter in a frying pan, add onions and diced bacon and fry for about 5 minutes until fat begins to run.
3 Add potatoes and cook for a further 15 minutes or until potatoes are tender and crisp, turning them occasionally to cook them evenly.
4 Season with salt and pepper. Stir in fines herbes and serve immediately.

Braised peas with lettuce

An out-of-the-ordinary vegetable accompaniment that's just right for a dinner party – you can prepare the onions, fresh peas and lettuce quarters in advance, then let them gently simmer during the first course

VEGETABLE Serves 4

Overall timing 35 minutes

Equipment Large saucepan

Freezing Not recommended

INGREDIENTS

6	Spring onions	6
1	Cos lettuce	1
2oz	Butter	50g
1lb	Shelled fresh peas	450g
1 teasp	Sugar	5ml
¼ pint	Chicken stock	150ml
	Salt	
	Freshly-ground black pepper	

METHOD

1 Wash, trim and slice the spring onions. Trim and wash the lettuce, discarding outer leaves if necessary. Cut into 4 lengthways.
2 Heat the butter in a large saucepan. Add the onions and fry for 2 minutes. Add the peas, lettuce quarters, sugar, and stock (made with a cube if necessary) and season well.
3 Bring to the boil, cover and simmer gently for 20 minutes. Arrange on a warmed serving dish and serve immediately.

cook's know-how

It is essential to cook fresh peas as soon as possible after they are picked, as their natural sugar begins to turn to starch the moment they leave the plant. Look for pods which are crisp, young and well-filled. The pods should pop when gently pressed between the fingers.

Floating islands

Luscious floating islands of poached meringue topped with caramel – but don't make it more than 2 hours ahead of time

DESSERT Serves 4–6

Overall timing 40 minutes plus chilling time

Equipment 2 saucepans, 2 bowls, glass serving bowl, wire rack

Freezing Not recommended

Below: Floating islands – snowy meringue, custard and a light topping of caramel

INGREDIENTS

1 pint	Milk	560ml
1	Vanilla pod	1
5	Eggs	5
	Pinch of salt	
5oz	Caster sugar	150g
2oz	Icing sugar	50g
2 tbsp	Water	2×15ml

METHOD

1 Slowly heat the milk in a saucepan with the vanilla pod. Separate the eggs. Mix egg yolks, salt and 3oz (75g) of the caster sugar in a bowl. Remove pod and mix milk into eggs.

2 Return to pan and, stirring constantly, slowly bring to just below boiling point – the mixture will lightly coat the spoon. Do not boil.

3 Remove custard from heat and allow to cool slightly before pouring into serving bowl. Chill.

4 Heat a saucepan of water. Whisk egg whites till stiff, sprinkle with icing sugar and whisk well again.

5 Using 2 soup spoons, make egg shapes of the egg white. Carefully lower a few at a time on to the simmering water and leave for 15 seconds on one side, 10 seconds on the other.

6 Remove egg shapes from pan with a draining spoon and place on a cake wire. Do not let them touch. When all are cooked and dried, carefully place the egg shapes on the custard.

7 Dissolve remaining sugar in water in a small saucepan and boil till it turns to caramel. Pour over the egg shapes and serve immediately.

Above: Watermelon basket – cool and refreshing dessert to serve with vanilla ice cream

Watermelon basket

A splendid centrepiece for a summer table. After the basket is shaped, the flesh is chopped and macerated in the fridge to allow the flavours of sugar, rum, orange and cinnamon to enhance the watermelon. To make it more stunning add fresh lychees, slices of kiwifruit and peach

DESSERT Serves 4–6

Overall timing 30 minutes plus maceration

Equipment Sharp knife, bowl

Freezing Not recommended

INGREDIENTS

3lb	Whole watermelon	1.4kg
4oz	Caster sugar	125g
2 tbsp	Rum	2×15ml
2 tbsp	Orange juice	2×15ml
$\frac{1}{4}$ teasp	Ground cinnamon	$\frac{1}{4}$×5ml
4	Mint leaves (optional)	4

METHOD

1 Wipe watermelon all over with clean cloth. Cut thin slice from bottom so melon will stand upright.

2 Using sharp knife, carefully slice off top half leaving an inch (2.5cm) strip of rind through the middle to form the handle of basket.

3 Scoop out flesh from top and base, leaving $\frac{1}{2}$ inch (1.25cm) thick shell. Remove seeds and dice flesh. Place flesh in bowl with sugar, rum, orange juice, cinnamon and finely chopped mint leaves if using. Cover bowl and chill with basket for 3 hours.

4 Fill basket with macerated fruit and serve immediately with scoops of vanilla ice cream.

To make refreshing watermelon sorbet, remove rind from 1½lb (700g) pips and coarsely chop flesh. Purée in blender or rub through sieve. Put 8oz (225g) caster sugar in pan with 1 pint (560ml) water and heat slowly, stirring till sugar dissolves. Bring to boil and simmer for 10 minutes – it must not colour. Cool. Mix purée into syrup, pour into freezer tray and freeze till mushy. Remove from freezer, turn into bowl and beat to break down crystals. Whisk 2 egg whites till soft peaks form and fold into mixture. Return to freezer tray and freeze till firm. Place in fridge 15 minutes before serving to soften. Freezer life: 6 months. **Serves 8**

Apple cream cake

Sweet, firm custard tops a layer of cooked but still crisp apples and a base of ready-made sponge, decorated with cream and nuts

DESSERT Cuts into 12 slices

Overall timing 1 hour

Equipment 2 saucepans, baking tray, piping bag

Freezing Not recommended

INGREDIENTS

1lb	Bramley cooking apples	450g
3oz	Caster sugar	75g
9fl oz	White wine	250ml
9fl oz	Water	250ml
4	Egg yolks	4
3oz	Caster sugar	75g
1	Strip of lemon rind	1
3 tbsp	Arrowroot	3×15ml
2oz	Nibbed or flaked almonds	50g
1	Ready-made 11 inch (28cm) sponge flan	1
6fl oz	Carton of double cream	170ml
1 tbsp	Caster sugar	15ml
	Vanilla essence	

METHOD

1 Peel apples and slice fairly thickly. Put into a saucepan with the sugar and wine. Bring to the boil, reduce heat and stew gently for 3 minutes – the apples should still be firm. Lift out with a draining spoon and set aside. Reserve cooking liquid.

2 To make custard, beat together water, egg yolks, sugar, lemon rind and arrowroot in a saucepan. Pour in 9fl oz (250ml) of the reserved cooking liquid and bring to the boil, whisking constantly. Boil for a few seconds only, then remove from heat. Stand pan in bowl of cold water to cool quickly. Stir mixture occasionally to speed up cooling.

3 Spread almonds on baking tray and place under hot grill until evenly coloured.

4 Place apples on top of sponge base and cover with the cooled cream mixture.

5 Beat the cream, sugar and a few drops of vanilla essence till stiff. Pipe round sides and top of cake. Decorate with toasted almonds.

Orange semolina croquettes

A melt-in-the-mouth semolina dessert, crispy outside and soft inside. With a freezer life of 6 months, these are ideal for making in large batches

DESSERT Serves 6

Overall timing 30 minutes plus cooling

Equipment 2 saucepans, bowl, frying pan

Freezing Prepare croquettes to end of Step 3. Open freeze then pack in polythene bags, seal and label. Freezer life: 6 months. To use: deep fry from frozen in oil heated to 340F (170C) for 3–4 minutes

INGREDIENTS

1 pint	Milk	560ml
	Salt	
	Grated rind of 1 orange	
4oz	Semolina	125g
4oz	Caster sugar	125g
2	Eggs	2
2oz	Dried breadcrumbs	50g
2oz	Unsalted butter	50g
2 tbsp	Oil	2×15ml
5 tbsp	Marmalade	5×15ml
2 tbsp	Water or orange liqueur	2×15ml

METHOD

1 Warm the milk in a saucepan with a pinch of salt and the orange rind. Pour in the semolina and bring to the boil, stirring. Stir over a low heat for 5–7 minutes till mixture thickens. Stir in all but 2 tbsp (2×15ml) of the sugar.

2 Remove pan from the heat. Separate eggs and beat yolks into semolina. Pour into a greased bowl, cover and leave to cool.

3 Shape the semolina into croquettes 1 inch (2.5cm) thick and 2 inches (5cm) long. Lightly beat the egg whites and coat the croquettes, then roll them in the breadcrumbs till evenly coated.

4 Heat the butter and oil in the frying pan, add the croquettes and fry till golden on all sides, turning occasionally. Drain on kitchen paper, then sprinkle with remaining sugar.

5 Heat the marmalade in a small saucepan with the water or liqueur. Serve with warm croquettes.

Below: Orange semolina croquettes – allow at least 3 croquettes per person

Date and apricot quiche

Dried fruits are plumped up with brandy, then used as a base for an almond-flavoured custard which is baked in a pastry case

DESSERT Serves 6–8

Overall timing 1½ hours

Equipment Saucepan, 2 bowls, 8 inch (20cm) flan dish

Freezing Cook in foil dish, cool, then open freeze. Wrap in polythene and label. Freezer life: 3 months. To use: thaw for 4 hours, then reheat in hot oven

½ pint	Milk	300ml
	Vanilla pod	
3oz	Dried apricots	75g
3oz	Chopped dates	75g
4 tbsp	Brandy or apricot brandy	4×15ml
7½oz	Packet of frozen shortcrust pastry	212g
3	Eggs	3
4oz	Caster sugar	125g
2oz	Ground almonds	50g

METHOD

1 Put milk and vanilla pod in a saucepan and bring to the boil. Remove from heat and leave to infuse for 30 minutes, then remove vanilla pod.

2 Chop apricots and place in bowl with dates and brandy of choice. Leave for 30 minutes.

3 Thaw pastry. Preheat oven to 400F (200C) Gas 6.

4 Beat eggs and sugar in a bowl till pale and frothy. Stir in ground almonds and flavoured milk.

5 Roll out pastry on a lightly-floured surface and line flan dish. Cover base with fruit mixture, then pour in egg/milk mix.

6 Bake in the oven for 15 minutes. Reduce temperature to 325F (170C) Gas 3 and cook for a further 25–30 minutes. Serve hot with pouring cream.

Above: *Baked coffee caramel ring – superb tasting dessert to serve with cream*

The milk is heated till almost boiling, then the black coffee is stirred in well

The milk/coffee is whisked into beaten eggs/sugar, placed in caramel-lined mould

After baking and overnight chilling, the set custard and runny caramel is unmoulded

Baked coffee caramel ring

A variation on the theme of the much appreciated crème caramel. The added coffee and liqueur or brandy gives the custard a slightly darker colour and delicious flavour. The custard is baked in a bain-marie to slow down the cooking and prevent bubbles forming in the mixture

DESSERT Serves 6

Overall timing 2 hours plus cooling and overnight chilling

Equipment 2 saucepans, pastry brush, 3 pint (1.7 litre) mould with funnel, bowl, sieve

Freezing Not recommended

INGREDIENTS

7oz	Caster sugar	200g
$\frac{1}{4}$ pint	Water	150ml
8	Eggs	8
$1\frac{3}{4}$ pints	Milk	1 litre
$\frac{1}{4}$ pint	Strong black coffee	150ml
3 tbsp	Tia Maria or brandy	3×15ml

METHOD

1 Put all but 4 tbsp (4×15ml) of the sugar into a saucepan with the water and stir over a low heat till the sugar dissolves. Wash any sugar crystals on the sides of the pan into the syrup with a pastry brush dipped in cold water.

2 Stop stirring and bring to the boil. Boil steadily till a deep golden brown. Pour into the mould, turning it so the base and sides are coated with caramel.

3 Preheat the oven to 325F (170C) Gas 3. Put the eggs and remaining sugar into a large bowl and whisk together lightly. Put the milk into a pan and heat till almost boiling, then pour in the coffee and stir well.

4 Pour on to the eggs in a thin stream, whisking constantly. Add the Tia Maria or brandy, then strain custard through sieve into the mould.

5 Stand the mould in a roasting tin containing $1\frac{1}{2}$ inches (4cm) hot water. Cover the mould with foil and bake in the centre of the oven for about $1\frac{1}{4}$ hours till custard is set.

6 Remove from the oven and leave to cool completely. Chill overnight.

7 To turn out custard, place mould on the table and put a deepish serving dish over it. Hold the dish and mould together and turn them over. Put the dish on the table and lift off the mould carefully. Serve immediately with whipped cream and crisp biscuits.

VARIATION

To make individual custards, line each mould with caramel, then divide custard between them. Cover each mould with foil and place in roasting tin with $\frac{1}{2}$ inch (12.5mm) hot water. Bake at 350F (180C) Gas 4 for 45 minutes till custards are set. Chill overnight, turn out to serve.